ALSO BY PAUL GRONDAHL

Mayor Corning: Albany Icon, Albany Enigma

Paul Grondahl

★★★★★★★★★★★★★★★★★

I ROSE
LIKE A
ROCKET

★★★★★★★★★★★★★★★★★

The Political Education of
Theodore Roosevelt

Free Press

New York   London   Toronto   Sydney

FREE PRESS

A Divison of Simon & Schuster, Inc.
1230 Avenue of the Americas
New York, NY 10020

For information regarding special discounts for bulk purchases,
please contact Simon & Schuster Special Sales:
1-800-456-6798 or business@simonandschuster.com

Designed by Karolina Harris

Manufactured in the United States of America

10   9   8   7   6   5   4   3   2   1

Library of Congress Cataloging-in-Publication Data

Grondahl, Paul, 1959–
I rose like a rocket : the political education of Theodore Roosevelt / Paul Grondahl.
p. cm.
Includes bibliographical references (p.) and index.
1. Roosevelt, Theodore, 1858–1919. 2. Presidents—United States—Biography.
3. Vice-Presidents—United States—Biography. 4. Legislators—New York (State)—
Biography. 5. Governors—New York (State)—Biography. 6. New York (State)—
Politics and government—1865–1950. I. Title.

E757.G76 2004
973.91'1"092—dc22
{B}
2004043232

ISBN 0-7432-2731-X

for Mary

CONTENTS

★ ★ ★ ★ ★ ★ ★ ★ ★ ★ ★ ★ ★ ★ ★

I ROSE
LIKE A
ROCKET

★ ★ ★ ★ ★ ★ ★ ★ ★ ★ ★ ★ ★ ★ ★

Prelude

★ ★ ★ ★ ★

PRACTICAL
POLITICS

The New York State Legislature, which has convened in Albany since it became the state capital in 1797, epitomizes politics as plate tectonics. It represents an ancient clash of opposing forces: downstate versus upstate, Republican versus Democrat, conservative versus liberal, insurgent versus incumbent, reformer versus party-liner. Each January, for more than two centuries, the legislators have migrated to this modest river city, like the shad that have spawned in the Hudson River from time immemorial. One hundred and fifty miles up the Hudson from Manhattan, the lawmakers convene to renew their seismic political battles. Tremors are commonplace and full-scale quakes are expected. In a city settled by the Dutch, which thrived in the Colonial era because of a bustling beaver trade, the coin of the realm in recent centuries has been the acquiring, spending, and replenishing of political capital. Corruption, from the imperceptible to the spectacular, is as central to the rhythm of Albany across the ages of its political history as the tides on the Hudson River estuary.

The atmosphere in Albany during the legislative session is part carnival, part college fraternity. Some of the city's denizens are just passing through, looking to ride along on the political parade for a little while. Others arrive full of idealism and a burn-

1

ing desire to make meaningful change. A few seem perplexed to be elected public officials in the state's capital, as if they had awoken from a Rip van Winkle–like slumber to find themselves holding a seat in the Assembly or Senate. It's a dream job for some, a nightmare for others. Many build their reputations here. A few sacrifice their respectability on the altar of politics, learning the rules only to abuse them. The Legislature is a closed system, a kind of political union shop. The principles of prep school secret societies guide its old boys' network, clubby familiarity, oaths of loyalty, and rituals of initiation.

Shortly upon arriving at the State Capitol in Albany as a freshman assemblyman from Manhattan in January of 1882, Theodore Roosevelt received his first lesson in the ceremonials of this secretive subculture. The State Legislature was a world removed from Roosevelt's familiar universe of cloistered privilege and enormous inheritances in Manhattan's Gramercy Park neighborhood. Albany, by comparison, was a rawboned, outlaw frontier town.

Roosevelt was a boyish-looking and scrawny twenty-three-year-old who stood just five feet eight inches. His education began in a dim corridor outside the Assembly chamber, where he was ambushed by "Big John" McManus, a massive brute and former heavyweight boxer who played the role of chief thug for the Tammany Hall political machine. McManus was an intimidating presence for Tammany, which had its tentacles wrapped around every stratum of the Legislature and state politics.

McManus had been milling about on the third floor of the Capitol with a crew of his sycophants, who were stirring up a plan to knock Roosevelt down a few notches and to pound some of the Harvard pretension out of this young, cocky newcomer. McManus was rallying coconspirators around a plan to toss Roosevelt in a blanket, an embarrassing gag of that era tantamount to the prep school prank of flushing an underclassman's head in a toilet bowl. Roosevelt had caught wind of the hazing being contemplated against him, however. He confronted the massive McManus. Although Roosevelt was a head shorter and some one hundred pounds lighter, he locked eyes with McManus and spoke through clenched teeth, the veins standing up on his sinewy neck. "By God! McManus, I hear you are going to toss me in a blanket. By God! If you try anything like that, I'll kick you, I'll bite you, I'll kick you in the balls. I'll do anything to you—you'd better leave me alone."[1]

Roosevelt's spirited tirade stopped the brutish McManus in his tracks. Quickly sensing that his coconspirators were losing their nerve, McManus called off the blanket tossing and his entourage of thugs cleared the Assembly corridor. Little Teddy Roosevelt had stood up to the bully of the Legislature. It was an auspicious beginning for the youngest state legislator ever to have been elected.

The New York State Capitol in Albany in the nineteenth century was a den of feral politics. It's fitting, then, that the most powerful and longest-running machine dominating state politics, Tammany Hall, was known as "the Tiger." Thanks to Tammany, some of the most memorable rogues and colorful scoundrels practiced the art of what George Washington Plunkitt called "honest graft" and epitomized his classic description, "I seen my opportunities and I took 'em." Albany gave safe harbor to the outrageously corrupt and extremely corpulent William Marcy Tweed, the first to be called "Boss" and the architect of bossism. Richard Croker, the menacing Tammany enforcer, also feasted on political prey in Albany. It was into this Tiger's lair that the young, puny reformer Roosevelt, with a high, squeaky voice and thick eyeglasses, strode. He did not get eaten alive. On the contrary, he attacked Tammany and brought the political beast to its knees. Theodore Roosevelt proved a quick study who knew no fear. He became the lion who tamed the Tiger.

His stint in Albany represented a defining moment for Roosevelt's life and his development as one of the most beloved and enduring figures in American political history. The first three years he spent in the New York State capital as an assemblyman introduced Roosevelt to politics; a decade later he served two years as governor in Albany's Executive Mansion, where he experimented with the emerging political philosophy he would fully develop during his presidency.

New York State politics taught Roosevelt the realities of campaigning for, winning, and retaining office. Roosevelt was a scholar and an indefatigable researcher with an analytical mind; he had been comfortable within the discipline of analyzing, quantifying, classifying, and cataloging since his boyhood days of compiling bird guidebooks and amassing a natural history collection. And so it was with politics. Roosevelt managed to put the inexplicable process of democracy under a microscope, dissecting it, as it were, in order to understand its deep structure. Roosevelt found a like mind and sensibility in the social critic and writer Jacob Riis, with whom Roosevelt shared the philosophy of "practical politics" that five years in Albany had taught the Manhattan dandy. Roosevelt told Riis,

> I stood out for my own opinion, alone. I took the best mugwump stand: my own conscience, my own judgment, were to decide in all things. I would listen to no argument, no advice. I took the isolated peak on every issue, and my people left me...The things I wanted to do I was powerless to accomplish. What did I do? I looked the ground over and made up my mind that there were excellent people there, with honest opinions of the right, even though they differed from me. I turned in to help them, and they turned to and gave me a hand. And so we were able to get things done. We did not agree in all things, but we did in some, and those we pulled at together. That was my first lesson in real politics. It is this: if you are cast on a desert island with only a screw-driver, a hatchet, and a chisel to make a boat with,

why, go make the best one you can. It would be better if you had a saw, but you haven't. So with men.[2]

Of course, Roosevelt's political education was coupled with a character education, not just in Albany and in Washington (as assistant secretary of the navy) or in Manhattan (as police commissioner), but in the Adirondack Mountains, and in Cuba as well. No book about the making of our twenty-sixth president would be complete if it ignored any phase of his early career. Yet in all the famous, near-mythical stories of the weakling transforming himself into a man of vigor, something has been lost: Roosevelt the political master.

This, then, is the story of Roosevelt's political education.

Chapter 1

★ ★ ★ ★ ★

BEGINNINGS

My father, Theodore Roosevelt, was the best man I ever knew.

Theodore Roosevelt Sr. cradled the thrashing, wailing bundle of energy in his arms and paced across the second-story landing, back and forth, like a clock's pendulum. The wooden floorboards squeaked softly beneath his footfalls as he marked time with a measured, soothing cadence of motion. His deep-set, brooding eyes were etched with fatigue as he arched a weary back. The rest of Manhattan slept, or at least so did this genteel stretch of elegant townhouses along East Twentieth Street, as far as Theodore Sr. could see as he gazed out the window of a front sitting room. The street was dark and deserted at this late hour. It had been past midnight when, awoken by his son's piercing yowls, he came to try to quiet and calm the chronically ill child so that his wife might get a rare night of uninterrupted sleep. Soft lamplight shone from the Roosevelts' brownstone at number 28 onto a narrow, darkened street. Three-year-old Theodore Jr. had been bawling, wheezing, and gasping through an asthmatic attack for what seemed like hours. It was a pitiful sight, a little boy suffering and locked in a struggle to breathe, straining against what must have felt like an enormous and crushing weight pressing down upon his thin chest.

From early childhood, Theodore endured asthmatic fits in which he could not draw air into his lungs. At their worst, these attacks of severe asthma created the frightening sensation of drowning. In extreme instances, such asthmatic attacks could prove fatal, and Theodore suffered an acute, frightening form of the lung ailment. His parents carried their sickly son over the shoals of suffering and calmed his gasping fears. "I was very sick last night and Mama was so kind telling me storys [sic] and rubbing me with her delicate fingers," he wrote in a boyhood diary.[1] The mother and father worried about what would become of their sickly little son. Asthma was not well understood by physicians at the time and medications had not been developed to treat what was in the nineteenth century a more frequently life-threatening ailment than it is today. One thing his father was sure about, though. This boy would not grow up to be a shrinking violet. He was going to make some noise. His childhood lungs might not have been healthy, but they could produce wallpaper-peeling yowls. These middle-of-the-night jags seized the small boy with a frightening intensity. He wheezed in between panicky gulps. In such tense moments, Teedie, as he was called, seemed to hang in the balance between life and death. His father felt powerless, and as a prominent businessman and leading New York City civic leader and philanthropist from a wealthy family, he experienced perhaps for the first time a feeling of being unable to control his circumstances.

Frantic to discover anything that might offer his son relief from the tortured gulps for breath and painful heaves that racked his tiny body like thunderclaps, the father summoned a servant to run to the stable and bring around a horse and carriage as quickly as possible. After long and anxious moments, the carriage arrived and the father hustled his son into the front seat alongside him. With manic energy, the father gave the horse the whip and drove the carriage at a gallop along the cobbled roadways of Manhattan, hoping the rushing air would force itself into

Teedie's lungs. Respiratory ailments were common among the children of New York City during an era in which the urban air was befouled by a grimy stew of coal smoke, ash dumped into gutters from cooking fires, dust and windblown dried horse droppings swirling about filthy streets, and a steady spewing of chemicals and toxic particulate matter from an ever-expanding forest of factory smokestacks. The only treatment advice doctors could come up with was to make sure the boy got plenty of fresh air and exercise. Desperate, his father tried his own remedies, ranging from heated mustard plasters on the boy's chest to strong coffee, cigars, and chest massages so vigorous that Teedie recalled that he once bled.

Teedie's father had grown accustomed to sleepless nights. With a thick beard, fierce and penetrating dark eyes, powerful physique, and firm Victorian resolve, Theodore Roosevelt Sr.— known as Thee among his family to distinguish him from his namesake son—was a rock to which his weak and sickly family clung for strength. "I hardly know any other man in this city or elsewhere that had so much strength, so much heart, so much of all that goes to make true Christian manhood," a friend recalled.[2] Theodore—whose name in Greek means "the gift of God"—gave his support, love, and sacrifice unconditionally to his family and freely to many individuals and groups in need as one of New York's most ardent and generous philanthropists. His charity began at home, starting with the tender devotion and deference he showed his wife, Martha Bulloch, a fragile woman from Georgia. Mittie, as she was known, suffered frequent bouts of illness, particularly debilitating headaches and intestinal ailments she obliquely called "my horror." Mittie was the type of woman for whom the Victorian fainting couch was designed. The couple's four children inherited their mother's weak constitution and missed out on the genes of their father's vigorous good health.

Teedie's asthma wasn't his only chronic condition. The eldest son also suffered recurring headaches, stomach pains, and severe insomnia. It was also later discovered that the boy's eyesight was very poor and he required thick corrective lenses. Roosevelt's parents sent their ten-year-old son to neurologist George M. Beard, a noted specialist in neurasthenia and author of the influential text *American Nervousness*. Beard and his partner, Alphonso D. Rockwell, diagnosed Teedie as having inherited neurasthenia from his wealthy, overly refined, aristocratic father—a condition commonly dubbed "the handicap of riches."[3] Beard and Rockwell prescribed electric charges to reverse the nervous system malfunction and the ill effects of excessive affluence. Electrical equipment was attached to Teedie's head, abdomen, and feet so that an electrical current could surge throughout his small body to restore its "vital force" and cancel out the offending "overcivilization." Electrotherapy sessions, forced rest, water cures, and travel to soak in therapeutic mineral baths and to drink restorative sulfur water did not work to alleviate the boy's chronic asthma. Nevertheless, in his mother's protective grasp, the adolescent boy was whisked to therapeutic spas and health resorts across New York State and New England, including Saratoga Springs, Richfield Springs, New Lebanon, and White Sulphur Springs.

Each of Teedie's siblings succumbed to a laundry list of other ailments, both physical and mental, that caused the family to alter their vacation plans, hire private tutors in lieu of formal schooling, and experiment with various treatments and physicians. Ill health dominated Teedie's formative years, for it surrounded the household like a mysterious mist, but sickness did not manage to dim their father's indefatigable optimism and cheerfulness. Teedie's older sister, Anna, nicknamed Bamie, whom the others designated papa's pet, was diagnosed at a tender age with Pott's disease, a form of tuberculosis of the bone that causes a painful curvature and permanent deformation of the spine. The second son, Elliott, known as Ellie, sometimes succumbed to seizures that frightened his parents as he blacked out or spoke in a strange gibberish. The youngest child, Corinne, whom the others called Conie, suffered from an asthmatic condition, though less debilitating than Teedie's. Teedie also suffered from a nervous condition that manifested itself in hallucinations far more frightening than typical childhood nightmares. As a small boy, Teedie had a recurring hallucination of a werewolf that awoke him from a sound sleep and caused him to cry out to his mother. She'd come to his room and try to soothe the wild-eyed child. "Look!" Teedie would scream. "Don't you see the werewolf? He is sitting on the foot of my bed now."[4] His mother would try to shush her crazed, frantic son and humor him about the phantasm, then read soothing stories to him to divert his troubled mind until he fell asleep again.

Diagnosing the Roosevelt children's maladies was often a challenge and an inexact science. Although some of their conditions appeared to be purely physical and easy to confirm with standard diagnostic equipment, others were conjectured to be psychological manifestations. The Roosevelt children and their mother were, in some regards, a household of hypochondriacs whose endless parade of symptoms might have pushed a less virtuous father into abusive behavior. To the contrary, their father took in stride the sundry aches and pains and changes in travel plans required by long stretches of illness at home. Theodore Roosevelt Sr. exhibited qualities of the ideal and proper Victorian family man, a man devoid of egotism and focused on the needs of his wife and children rather than his own desires. They were a close-knit family whose interactions leaned toward the romantic and sentimental. Their letters are filled with gushing, self-consciously lovey-dovey prose. One of their favorite communal expressions of solidarity was a group hug they dubbed "melts." It didn't take much—an apology after an argument, say, or a health setback—for the Roosevelt clan to "melt."

Teedie's mother, Mittie, required high maintenance from her

husband. Those who knew her invariably remarked on her beauty and gracious demeanor, but when it came to running a household, she seemed incapable of managing domestic matters. She delegated a wife's typical tasks, according to a friend of Corinne. "She was quite impractical . . . with long white gloves and a little cap over her hair, dusting the parlor with a pocket handkerchief. Of course, the parlor had been thoroughly dusted before she began, but she liked to make herself believe that she was doing housework." Instead, the eldest child, Bamie, "ran the house almost from her childhood and mothered the young children. The result was that she was very mature for her age."[5]

Theodore Sr. was a disciplinarian who drew a clear and strict line of ethical and moral behavior for his children and would not countenance his sons' or daughters' crossing that line in regards to cruelty, laziness, lying, selfishness, or cowardice. The rambunctious boy who was his namesake certainly tested the elder Roosevelt's patience, but the son recalled his father's physically punishing him on only one occasion. Teedie was four years old when he bit the arm of his older sister. His father found his son hiding under the kitchen table after their Irish cook informed on him. That transgression and the spanking were recounted humorously, but his dad's unyielding measure of what was right and wrong and insistence on proper punishment generally proved deterrent enough. "He was the only man of whom I was ever really afraid," Roosevelt said of his father.[6] Theodore Sr. became Teedie's primary source of inspiration and motivation. "Get action!" and "Seize the moment!" were two of the father's favorite phrases, spoken in exclamation, of course. Those exhortations became a kind of mantra for the boy as he grew up. Despite his illnesses and the demands of spa visits and trips to recuperate in alpine air, Teedie clearly was his father's favored child and the two developed a special bond.

Theodore Roosevelt Jr. was born on October 27, 1858, as the seven Lincoln-Douglas debates in the Illinois race for the

U.S. Senate had just concluded and the nation hurtled toward the Civil War. The aristocratic politics of the Founding Fathers' generation were long past. Jacksonian democracy, in which patronage and party politics ruled the day, could not stop the coming war, but neither would the war stop partisan government. In New York, thanks to the fresh influx of immigrants fleeing the potato famine, "low-class" Irish thugs had seized the city government with the election of the irrepressible Fernando Wood as mayor in 1854. A former congressman and wily entrepreneur, Wood was dubbed a "brilliant desperado" in newspaper accounts of the day. He rose up through the ranks of Tammany Hall and consolidated power with such rapaciousness that he created a framework for the modern machine boss. In addition to pandering to the city's immigrants and disenfranchised lower classes, Mayor Wood pursued strong-arm tactics including paying for votes, stealing elections, rewarding loyal hacks with patronage jobs, and ordering enforcers to beat up challengers.

Amid this social tumult, Theodore Roosevelt Jr. was born into Manhattan's old-line aristocratic ruling class, the Knickerbockers. Because of his family's wealth and social standing, the boy was shielded from many of the problems of the day faced by the working class in America. Teedie was a beneficiary of several generations of successful Roosevelt farmers, landowners, and merchants. The name Roosevelt means "field of roses" in Dutch, and that flower imagery is the dominant visual feature in the family's coat of arms. *Qua plantavit curabit* is the family motto engraved below the coat of arms. It means, "He who has planted will preserve." The primary accomplishments of the Roosevelts came in the arena of business and the steady accumulation of wealth, although there were hints of the political prominence to come. One of Teedie's ancestors was a New York State senator and was among the elected leaders who joined Alexander Hamilton in ratifying the Constitution. His grandfather, Cornelius van

Schaack Roosevelt, elevated the family's fortunes from a comfortably wealthy level to that of one of the richest families in New York by anticipating demand and transforming the family hardware business into a company that imported plate glass—a critical product in a booming building construction trade. C. v. S. Roosevelt also proved prescient when it came to land speculation: he turned substantial profits through the acquisition and sale of Manhattan real estate. His wealth was such that he gave Theodore Roosevelt Sr. the East Twentieth Street brownstone as a wedding present. In Teedie's youth, the family's plate-glass importing firm, Roosevelt & Son, was located at the corner of Maiden Lane and Gold Street. Teedie's father and an uncle, James Roosevelt, were coproprietors of the firm, which specialized in products imported from England.

A former employee described Theodore Roosevelt Sr. as a "dignified, courteous man, who took a lively interest in the welfare of every employee, and was held in affectionate regard by all, from office boy upward."[7] Roosevelt visited his employees who were seriously ill and attended funerals of those who died to offer condolences to the family. He often regularly gave cash advances to employees who were struggling financially and paid for the medical or burial expenses in hardship cases among his workers. There was no shortage of labor in the wake of the 2.5 million immigrants who streamed into the United States in the 1850s. The majority of these new arrivals, desperate for work, came through New York City, particularly a large influx of European Jews and 1 million immigrants from German territories. In the 1860 census, New York remained the most populous state, with 3.9 million inhabitants out of America's total population of 31.4 million. Roosevelt's son Teedie enjoyed the company of Manhattan's diverse workforce and visited his father's warehouse frequently while living at home and during summer vacations from Harvard. His father welcomed these visits. The same former employee noted "the close companionship and gracious intercourse of father and son [was] delightful to view."

As a young boy, Roosevelt inherited a love of reading, particularly history. He trundled along as a little tyke, hoisting the heavy volume of David Livingstone's *Missionary Travels and Researches in Africa* as it threatened to topple his light body—to the amusement of adults whom he begged to read to him a few pages of the missionary's adventurous tales.[8] Their parents set up a nursery class at home for Teedie and his siblings, and their neighbor, Edith Kermit Carow, was invited to attend. She soon became one of the closest childhood friends of the precocious boy. A neighbor recalled seeing Teedie, a youngster at the time, who was crouched cross-legged with his sister Corinne under a table in his home, oblivious to the visitor, animatedly discussing a child's view of a Dickens novel they both had been reading.[9] Roosevelt was obsessed with tales of heroes, such as the *Saga of King Olaf,* a lengthy narrative poem that he read again and again, while dreaming of one day becoming a knighted hero himself. Roosevelt's hero worship also caused him to return repeatedly to "Paul Revere's Ride" and the courageous, patriotic deed it celebrated. Teedie read widely and freely in his family's library, which included several books that belonged to his great-grandfather James Roosevelt, including *Letters of Junius* and biographies of John Paul Jones and George Washington. Details of his early ancestors were sketchy, and Roosevelt was unsuccessful in attempts to flesh out the family tree. He did manage to research his forebears as far back as the American Revolution and reported with an undercurrent of disappointment that "some of my forefathers, North and South, served respectably, but without distinction, in the army."[10]

Along with young Theodore's general interest in history was his intense and focused interest in military history and natural history. When he turned thirteen, Bamie inscribed to her brother a copy of *The Natural History of Selborne,* by the Reverend Gilbert White, a classic work of natural history published in 1864.[11] Growing up, he loved reading and hearing stories about wars and battles, the bloodier the better, and developed a typical boyish romanticism about the moral imperative of waging war and of good triumphing over evil. "Whew! Did not we have fun," Teedie wrote in a boyhood diary entry. "We cracked torpedos etc. etc. Our Cousin Johnny and Maud Elliott came. We had a fight of soldiers using the great torpedos at them."[12] The uncles on Roosevelt's mother's side, the Bullochs from Georgia, had served with distinction for the Confederate army during the Civil War. Roosevelt grew up hearing the stories of their wartime exploits and their manly, robust, militaristic pursuits. Teedie wasn't shielded from the fact of slavery—there were four million slaves across America in 1860—and he was aware that the Bullochs had owned slaves, but in his *Autobiography* this chapter of the family history was filtered through a sentimental reverie based on a rather naive assumption that the slaves knew nothing but happiness and enjoyable service as property of the Bullochs. Roosevelt notes that his maternal grandfather's house was in the path of Sherman's march to the sea and was raided by "the boys in blue"—including the books in their home library. Nearly one-half century after the Civil War, a former soldier in Sherman's army read about Roosevelt's ancestry and returned a book of poems with his Bulloch grandfather's name in it.

Roosevelt allowed his active, dreamy imagination to range over the rich family narratives of his southern agrarian maternal side and his northern mercantile paternal side. His mother was a lively storyteller whose southern gothic tales were lapped up by the impressionable Teedie. The boy borrowed the best of both parents: a vigorous morality from his father and a lively self-invention from his mother. His personality was a curious melding of his parents' attributes, bringing together the stern reserve of Thee and the fanciful emotionalism of Mittie.

Joined to Theodore's romanticized notion of military service, another deep and lasting element imprinted on the soul of the boy through the example of his father was a love of the natural world. Theodore Roosevelt Sr. was a founding member of the American Museum of Natural History. In fact, at his house on East Twentieth Street, Thee hosted the meeting at which the original charter for that museum was approved in 1869, when Teedie was ten years old. His father also spearheaded the fund-raising efforts and served on the committee for designing and planning the new museum building; he escorted President Rutherford B. Hayes on a preview tour of the facility he helped shape. Long before that, though, a similar sensibility had already taken root in the son as a profound attachment to nature and a desire to measure himself against its immutable laws. The initial manifestation of this sensibility was Teedie's boyhood obsession with observing, capturing, and preserving artifacts of natural history. He traced this early scientific bent to his discovery as a boy of a dead seal laid out on a board on a Manhattan street. Teedie made a thorough inspection, measuring the mammal with a pocket ruler he carried and recording detailed field notes and measurements about the seal in a notebook.

Spurred by the chance encounter with the dead seal, Teedie went on a mission of gathering specimens of all sorts. He and two cousins caught small rodents such as mice and squirrels, carried them home in their pockets, preserved them with self-taught rudimentary taxidermy, and stored them in his room under the grandiose title of the Roosevelt Museum of Natural History. The son's collection had grown to one thousand items by the time he was eleven. Eventually, the most offensive specimens were removed from his bedroom after a maid complained. Teedie was not deterred, although asthma attacks slowed the growth of his collection. He entertained family friends by tipping his hat to reveal a convenient carrying space for several frogs under the chapeau, and he outraged the Roosevelt cook by storing dead rodents in the icebox.

All I can say is that almost as soon as I began to read at all I began to like to read about the natural history of beasts and birds, and the more formidable or interesting reptiles and fishes. I was a very nearsighted small boy, and did not even know that my eyes were not normal until I was fourteen; and so my field studies up to that period were even more worthless than those of the average boy who "collects" natural history specimens much as he collects stamps.[13]

Roosevelt made systematic studies of flora and fauna during the summers of his youth spent in the countryside along the Hudson River north of Manhattan and kept voluminous diaries that included a heavy dose of natural history observations. Rigorous compilations and detailed scientific descriptions may help account for Roosevelt's extraordinary powers of recollection—an almost photographic memory, according to accounts of colleagues. By the age of nine, for instance, Roosevelt had written a seven-page study with impressive depth and detail on the natural history of ants. Yet the passion and scholarly energy that burns in his diary entries describing rambles through the natural world did not always carry over into the rigid environment of the school classroom.

One of Roosevelt's most unorthodox tutors in natural history was his eccentric, brilliant, and controversial uncle, Robert Barnhill Roosevelt, born in 1829, two years before Theodore's father. Uncle Rob, as he was called, lived next door to the Roosevelts on East Twentieth Street and maintained a law practice in which Theodore later served a brief apprenticeship. The household and lifestyle of Uncle Rob contrasted sharply with those of Theodore Roosevelt Sr. Compared to his younger brother's Victorian rigidity and strict adherence to a stern moral code, Uncle Rob was a bohemian ahead of his time. His house was filled with an exotic menagerie of animals from snakes to monkeys, which freely roamed the premises. He also wrote several books on fishing, ornithology, and other aspects of natural history and was one of the most prominent conservationists in the latter part of the nineteenth century. He fought the construction of dams on the Hudson River and other New York streams by arguing that they harmed the populations and interrupted ancient spawning routes of shad and other fish species. Uncle Rob's career as an author made a strong impression on Theodore, as did his uncle's wit. Later in life, after he had published several books, Roosevelt sent one to rival William Randolph Hearst as a peace offering. "This is a violation of the principle laid down to me by my uncle," Roosevelt wrote Hearst. "Many years ago . . . he said he had done a good many mean things in the course of his life, but he had never asked anyone to read one of his books."[14] Theodore's uncle, a prominent Democrat, was elected a congressman and was given a diplomatic appointment to the Netherlands. Uncle Rob was the family standard-bearer in the Democratic Party. Theodore's father was a Democrat too, until after the Civil War, when he switched to the Republican Party.

Despite all of his personal charm and professional achievement, an "unhinged" part of Uncle Rob's character sealed his fate.[15] There are virtually no direct references to Uncle Rob in the Roosevelt family's voluminous correspondence and memoirs after the 1890s, apparently because he became a black sheep who embarrassed the prominent Dutch clan with his philandering. Uncle Rob marked his carnal territory, as it were, with gifts of distinctive green gloves to his mistresses across Manhattan, and such gaudy presents hastened his ostracism. The final outrage for his scandalized clan was the discovery that Uncle Rob had long lived a deceitful and complex double life by maintaining a residence—near his East Twentieth Street home—for a mistress with whom he had fathered children out of wedlock. When that transgression was uncovered in his old age, Uncle Rob disappeared from family archives.

Roosevelt's asthma and generally fragile health served to hold him back from his fullest potential as a boy. Family friend George Gromwell recalled eight-year-old Teedie as an "exceptionally bright, but delicate" student and "a tall, thin lad, with bright eyes and legs like pipe stems."[16] His weakness caused Roosevelt to become an object of derision, and he was picked on by the other boys. Luckily, he could count upon his healthier and stronger little brother, Elliott, to protect him against bullies and to fight in his stead. A former student at the McMullen School, where Roosevelt spent his primary years, recalled him as a fragile adolescent whose health problems isolated him from his classmates and peers.

> His chest needed broadening out. His father was troubled about his health . . . He was not considered strong enough for school work . . . I did not think there was anything great about him . . . He was very much alone for some years, say from ten to thirteen, because he was not with the boys in their schoolwork or with their heavier sports. He was not strong enough to take part in football or baseball . . . He had to be at home when other boys were away, and he had to have his fun in his own way.[17]

Another close friend of his sister Corinne's who spent many happy hours playing in the Roosevelt house, especially long games of hide-and-seek, recalled that Teedie never played rough-and-tumble games with other children because of his weak constitution. While the other kids romped about the house, she would often see Theodore "sitting in a great arm chair, propped up with pillows, absolutely absorbed in a book while the wildest games were raging around him."[18]

In 1870, New York City's population, after tripling in three decades, approached 4.5 million people. Industrialization had caused a decline in air quality, which increased the severity of asthma and other respiratory ailments. Cobbled roads were speckled with horse manure and covered with a soup of muck and mire after heavy rains. Roaming pigs scavenged for scraps of food and garbage tossed into street gutters. A quartet of railroads belched choking coal smoke, which hung over rat-infested tenements. Wealthy residents like the Roosevelts tried to escape the fetid metropolis as often as possible. A regular destination for them was Richfield Springs, a rural spa and resort town near Otsego Lake and Cooperstown that was known for its therapeutic mineral waters and palliative care. It was a two-hour boat ride and ten-hour train trip from their summer home in Oyster Bay, Long Island. As an adolescent, Theodore traveled to Richfield Springs regularly as part of his parents' attempts to build up his weakened lungs.

There was something of the selective exhibition of symptoms in Roosevelt's response to his asthmatic condition. A flare-up of coughing and wheezing and gasps for air could easily be dramatized before a Sunday church service, for instance. Such asthmatic attacks also kept him from having to compete in his father's challenge after church each Sunday to determine which child could remember the sermon most accurately and most quickly memorize Bible verses. On the other hand, when Theodore was free to romp and play in the country during summer vacation, the bothersome health problems that struck on Sunday seemed to recede. Typical were these summertime diary entries when he was eleven years old: "Went in swimming. Chased cow. Built fort," and, "We played hunt the stag all day."[19]

Though Roosevelt's biographers have made much of his asthma and illnesses, Theodore's early years were full of rough-and-tumble play. "He was a reg'lar boy," recalled Daniel Henderson, a Long Island stagecoach driver who transported the Roosevelts. "Always outdoors, climbin' trees and goin' birdnestin'; I remember him particular, because he had queer things alive in his pockets. Sometimes it was even a snake."[20] One day a next-door neighbor of the Roosevelts in Manhattan saw young Theodore balancing himself on the second-story window ledge. The woman raced over to alert Mrs. Roosevelt about her son's dangerous predicament. His mother replied nonchalantly, "If the Lord had not taken care of Theodore, he would have been killed long before."[21]

Theodore grabbed every opportunity to get out of the house at 28 East Twentieth and into the open spaces of the countryside. He later described their house as a rather dark and severe brownstone "furnished in the canonical taste" with very little natural light and "bookcases of gloomy respectability" along the borders of rooms decorated with coarse and scratchy "haircloth furniture" more fitting for an ascetic monk than an exuberant child.[22] An archivist who works at the Roosevelt birthplace, now a museum run by the National Park Service, suggests that children roughhousing on the furniture—which was stuffed with horsehair, a popular padding material of the day—would have released airborne fibers and particles that might have contributed to Theodore's respiratory problems.[23]

At any rate, Roosevelt and his brother and sisters longed for the freedom of summer and a retreat from the haircloth furniture and the rigidity of their East Twentieth Street house—where the formal front parlor was reserved for Sunday evening gatherings that capped a stifling day of suit and tie and marathon church services. The flourish of spring and the promise of summer beckoned the Roosevelt children and spurred joyful expectations, as Theodore recalled.

The summers we spent in the country, now at one place, now at another. We children, of course, loved the country beyond anything. We disliked the city. We were always wildly eager to get to the country when spring came, and very sad when in the late fall the family moved back to town. In the country we of course had all kinds of pets—cats, dogs, rabbits, a coon, and a sorrel Shetland pony named General Grant.[24]

Roosevelt described the country in idyllic terms, tracing the family's succession of summer retreats along the rural and undeveloped lower Hudson River Valley at Barrytown, Spuyten Duyvil, Riverdale, and Dobbs Ferry before the family finally settled at Oyster Bay. There the children didn't have to wear shoes and time passed "in a round of uninterrupted and enthralled pleasures" marked by nature's rhythms such as haying, apple picking, nut gathering, building wigwams in the woods and staining themselves with pokeberry juice in childhood reenactments of cowboys and Indians. His father often joined his children at play. "I never knew anyone who got greater joy out of living than did my father," Theodore later wrote.[25]

Theodore spent so much time with his special friend, Edith Carow, and they played so well together that extended absences from her during Roosevelt family trips and vacations left him melancholy. During a European tour in early adolescence, Roosevelt moaned to his mother how deeply he missed his "little Edie." For her part, Edith kept a lock of Theodore's hair in her jewelry box and saved all his letters. When the Roosevelts returned to New York, Theodore was glad to resume the comfortable routine of inviting Edith frequently to his house and escorting her to parties. On the adolescent social circuit, the two could show off the results of the classes they took together in dancing and deportment at Mr. Dodsworth's finishing school in Manhattan. Edith was a hypersensitive, tentative, and somewhat high-strung girl susceptible to wide mood swings from day to day or even hour to hour. Theodore enjoyed playing the valiant prince alongside Edith and dominating their emerging courtship with his dramatic sensibility. He referred to her, in an affected courtliness, as "her ladyship." Edith was a bright student and avid reader. She formed a literary club with Theodore's sister Corinne, which they called P.O.R.E., or "Party of Renowned Eligibles," and in which they wrote poetry and stories.[26] Edith was a frequent guest at the Roosevelt's summer home in Oyster Bay, which the family called Tranquility. Although he flirted with other girls whom he took on picnics and rowing excursions, it was Edith's name that Theodore painted on the stern of his rowboat.[27]

Theodore Sr. passed a generous spirit on to his namesake son, illustrated in random acts of kindness. The wife of a clipper ship captain remembered an incident when she and her husband were docked in New York City. Roosevelt's father had brought along his young son on a ship's inspection that day. The boy looked around the crew's quarters, observed that the sailors had very few books, and decided he'd like to share some of the volumes in his home library with them. The captain said the boy's offer was a nice gesture and he'd gladly accept a donation of reading material. After Roosevelt and his son left, the captain figured he'd never hear from the visitors again. A day or two later, the father and his son returned in a carriage. They carried aboard the ship armloads of books selected by the boy, enough to create an ample shipboard library.[28]

Stories of the father's civic virtue are legion. "He held himself and all that he had at the service of humanity," recalled Louisa Lee Schuyler, president of the State Charities Aid Association. He had "a great moral courage, which, regardless of public opinion and personal consequences, struck for what was right simply because it was right."[29] In addition to his professional, political, and philanthropic commitments, Roosevelt displayed an abiding devotion to his elderly mother, whom he visited each morning, "brightening her quiet life by his cheery presence."[30] Roosevelt also volunteered many late nights to the work of caring and providing for orphaned children through his position as vice president of the State Charities Aid Association. In 1854, Roosevelt contributed a large part of the original funding for the Newsboys' Lodging House; he was a trustee of the Children's Aid Society from 1867 to 1878 and a key adviser to founder Charles Loring Brace. Roosevelt spent time helping at the Eighteenth Street

Newsboys' Lodging House. He also made a tradition of joining the orphaned children at the lodging house for Thanksgiving and Christmas dinner, occasionally accompanied by Theodore. The visits made a deep impression on his son, particularly when the boy observed the reverence in which the father was held, as Brace recounted.

> His work in the Lodging House was not perfunctory; it was not done as a duty. He seemed to attract and win the sympathies of every boy in the house. He knew them by name, he knew their histories, and, whenever he came there, they would gather round him, and he would question each one as to what he was doing, and give him advice and sympathy and directions . . . Undoubtedly the great impelling power of his life was a sense of duty, essentially implanted by his Christian belief.[31]

Theodore Roosevelt Sr. took on as his life's mission the rescue of children from the Dickensian child welfare programs of the day. Even when the import glass trade collapsed in Roosevelt's later years, his passionate sense of *noblesse oblige* did not dampen. Roosevelt was a leading philanthropist in Manhattan; his financial support helped create Roosevelt Hospital, the Bellevue Training School for Nurses, and the New York Orthopaedic Dispensary for the Deformed and Crippled. He was also a major benefactor of the Young Men's Christian Association. There seemed to be no limit to the social ills that required financial resources in that era. In New York City, poverty and crime exploded in the mid-nineteenth century. Crimes against property rose 50 percent from 1848 through 1852, convictions doubled, aggravated assaults rose threefold, and murders quadrupled. Mass riots were also on the rise. Most troubling to Roosevelt was the fact that minors were charged with more than three-quarters of the more serious felonies in this era. The city's vagrant children were deemed "degrading and disgusting" in an 1850 report by New York Police Chief George Matsell. Mayor Ambrose C. Kingsland called them "apt pupils in the school of vice, licentiousness and theft" and described intoxicated, vagabond boys as young as eight gambling on the streets, picking pockets, and stealing to pay for the demon rum they purchased illegally in one of the city's ubiquitous storefront dramshops.[32]

Roosevelt worked tirelessly with managers of the orphan asylums across New York State to help them find innovative ways to provide education and health care for orphaned children as they grew into adulthood. Roosevelt turned his attention particularly to the House of Refuge on Randall's Island and helped the managers to purchase farmland, where the orphaned boys could be reared in the therapeutic environment of a rural landscape rather than the toxic atmosphere of urban life.

Another major thrust of Roosevelt's work on behalf of social justice was aimed at improving the conditions in pauper mental asylums. He developed new funding and programs for the 2,400 "unhappy lunatics who are packed into our city asylums . . . To those unfortunates his heart went out in pity," a colleague wrote.[33] Roosevelt's efforts included working closely for several years with the commissioners of Public Charities and Correction and the Board of Apportionment in a campaign to build new asylums to ease overcrowding and to improve conditions at existing facilities. Roosevelt took the time to make personal visits to insane asylums on Wards and Blackwell's islands in order to understand the problem better and to gather firsthand information. As part of a lobbying effort to gain public funding to improve the asylums, Roosevelt brought along on his visits New York City's comptroller and the president of the Department of Taxes so that they might see the horrible conditions suffered by patients.

Roosevelt was the foundation upon which his namesake son built his life's work. The father was an organizer of the Union League Club, an influential and elite slice of New York's high society that devoted itself to patriotic and civic-minded good works beginning in the Civil War era. Members of the Union League Club—in which his son would become an active and sustaining member—praised Theodore Roosevelt Sr. as "a rare and signal example of exalted and unselfish public spirit, laboring zealously to bring about a higher order of public service and an era of better politics."[34] The son first learned politics at the knee of the father, for whom politics meant public service in the best sense of the term.

In the fall of 1870, after years of arranging trips to alleviate Teedie's asthma, struggling through untold sleepless nights with his sickly son cradled in his arms, and driving him in a carriage in the dark of night to revive the boy's weakened lungs, the father decided to push a physical rehabilitation regimen. Since the doctors had not been able to find a cure, his father reasoned that the best medicine might be to outmuscle the malady. "You have the mind, but you have not the body," the father told his son, whose twelfth birthday approached, in a moment that would become an epiphany for the boy. "You must *make* your body." In order to assist Teedie on his mission, his father bought him a membership at John Wood's gymnasium, which Teedie dutifully visited daily to lift weights on a machine meant to build up his scrawny chest. His father also added new fitness equipment to an enclosed second-floor back porch on their East Twentieth Street house that had been previously fashioned into a gymnasium as a place of treatment for the deformed back of Teedie's older sister, Bamie. "One day a young boy came running along, exclaiming to our group of half a dozen children," recalled a neighbor of the Roosevelts who was playing in Gramercy Park. (The private park, open to neighborhood residents with a key, was one of the first of its kind in the nation.) Theodore invited the children to see his new gymnasium. "As all the others started, I joined in and we trooped out of the Park, around the corner and into a strange house (to me). We went up the stairs and into the gymnasium where I spent one of the happiest of mornings, being taught by my new friend how to 'chin the bars,' 'skin the cat,' and all the other joys of a real gym."[35]

Other family members fell in line behind Roosevelt's father's directive that Teedie needed to be toughened up, within limits. "No one dared to display any of the signs of a mollycoddle, and no one dared to be unduly rough or to claim any improper advantage," recalled Emlen Roosevelt, a relative who spent time with Teedie at Oyster Bay.[36] When Theodore turned fourteen, his father gave him eyeglasses and his first hunting weapon, a French pin-fire, double-barreled shotgun. He also hired hunting guides for his son and a professional taxidermist to teach Theodore how to preserve the animal species he shot.

In the following several summers spent in New York's Adirondack Mountains, Theodore would hunt, mountain climb, canoe, study birds, gather specimens of flora and fauna, develop lasting friendships with wilderness guides, and develop skills as a naturalist and ornithologist. After the first summer up north, Theodore gave to the American Museum of Natural History one of its earliest donations: twelve mice, one bat, four birds' eggs, one turtle, and one red squirrel skull. While his father supplied cash to establish the museum, the son continued to deposit specimens for many years to come.

Theodore's visits to the untamed forests and remote lakes of the North Country were defining moments in the development of his character. He shot his first deer there, the start of a lifelong fervor for game hunting. His initial taste of wilderness hiking and camping came in the Adirondacks and marked the beginning of Roosevelt's devotion to "the strenuous life." A guide to Adirondack birds was his first published book, the start of a productive and varied literary output. Theodore's diaries from the mountains are filled with romanticized entries that underscore the emotional impact upon the teenager who was allowed to roam through what he described as "scenery so wild and magnificent." Months in the mountains lugging bulky packs, bushwhacking up wilderness peaks, tracking game on hunting expeditions, and portaging heavy canoes served the dual purposes of further strengthening Theodore's body and relieving his asthma. Roosevelt described those Adirondack trips as some of the most meaningful times he spent with his father, who was at those times free of the demands of work and politics and eager to delight his children by telling rollicking stories and reading from *The Last of the Mohicans* around the campfire. Theodore also bonded with Adirondack guides and idolized their rugged independence and exceptional mountaineering skills. These outsized mountain men became mentors and important surrogate father figures for Theodore after the death of his own father and influenced his later efforts as a conservationist.

Family vacations in the Adirondacks were restorative to Theodore's health but also, for his father, a welcome escape from city politics. In July of 1871, Manhattan was rocked by religiously motivated riots that erupted between Protestants and Catholics during a Scotch-Irish parade and left thirty-one civilians and two policemen dead. As the Roosevelts departed for the mountains a few weeks after the riots, the ring of Democratic machine operatives surrounding William "Boss" Tweed was charged with raiding the New York City treasury and embezzling millions of tax dollars.

Of course the greatest political event of Theodore's youth had occurred earlier, beginning when he was only three, with the onset of the Civil War. It was a seminal event for the Roosevelt family, dividing his mother's southern roots from his father's northern allegiances. The southern belle had struggled to reinvent herself as a New York Knickerbocker amid the Roosevelts' social set, but her heart and sympathies remained in the Deep South. Her letters to relatives in Georgia underscore a lingering homesickness. Later in his life, Theodore came to see the value of both sides of his parentage. "It has been my very great good fortune to have the right to claim that my blood is half southern and half northern," he said in a speech in his mother's hometown of Roswell, Georgia. "I have the ancestral right to claim a proud kinship with those who showed their devotion to duty as they saw their duty, whether they wore the gray or the blue."[37]

Though Theodore's uncles, the Bulloch brothers, were Confederate naval heroes, so successful that they were denied amnesty after the Civil War, his father decided not to fight for the Union army. Roosevelt's father was a strong and healthy twenty-nine-year-old man when the conflict began and wanted to enlist on the Union side but yielded to Mittie's entreaties and complaints that his taking up arms against her family would prove too much for her fragile constitution. "Mother was very frail, and felt it would kill her for him to fight against her brothers," recalled Bamie.[38] Roosevelt's father took advantage of a loophole in the Conscription Act that allowed the well-to-do to buy their way out of military service. He paid three hundred dollars apiece to hire two surrogate soldiers to fight in his place, a common practice among the wealthy class that brought rebukes and open hatred from poorer folks who couldn't spend their way around the draft. Simmering resentment over this double standard between poor people and wealthy northern businessmen regarding Civil War military service boiled over into New York's Draft Riots during the summer of 1863. "Rich man's war! Poor man's fight!" was the shrill cry of agitated demonstrators who raged through Manhattan during a week-long reign of terror in mid-July. Angry mobs marched through the streets and hurled their bitter slogans—"Down with the rich men" and "There goes a three-hundred-dollar man"—at men like Roosevelt.[39] It was "a carnival of violence." Hundreds of people were injured and hundreds more were killed, perhaps as many as a thousand, in the sporadic skirmishes. Teedie was an impressionable boy of nearly five during the Draft Riots, and the frightening scene of a crazed mob torching mansions, looting stores, attacking passersby, and firing guns made a powerful, confusing impression on the boy. The riots threatened the serenity of the Roosevelts' Gramercy Park neighborhood before rioters were killed by armed homeowners and five regiments of Union soldiers armed with cannons and Gatling guns called in as reinforcements. The unrest was not just a spontaneous explosion; thuggish political organizations were practiced in the art of mob violence, and New York City democracy was veering toward mobocracy.

The Draft Riots and his father's decision not to fight haunted Teedie, according to Bamie, and left him with a lifelong scar and sense of shame. In retrospect, the son wrote that his father "had done a very wrong thing in not having put every other feeling aside and joined the absolute fighting forces."[40] The closest that Roosevelt's father came to fighting was joining a Home Guard cavalry unit that met for military exercises and was issued swords as defenders of Manhattan in case of Confederate attack.[41]

Perhaps the elder Roosevelt's most important contribution was in helping to put the soldiers and the families they left behind on more firm financial footing. Appointed by President Lincoln, Roosevelt worked without pay as a member of the Allotment Commission with the War Department, where he organized a system in which money not needed in the camps would be sent home by the soldiers to their needy families. Millions of dollars that might otherwise have been wasted or squandered were rerouted to the home front and provided incalculable relief to wives and children struggling to survive. It wasn't hazardous duty that put him in harm's way, but Roosevelt's personal sacrifice was substantial, according to a business colleague.

> For long, weary months, in the depth of a hard winter, he went from camp to camp, urging the men to take advantage of this plan. On the saddle, often six to eight hours a day,

standing in the cold and mud as long, addressing the men and entering their names.[42]

The contribution of Theodore's father was more than organizational. He rolled up his sleeves and pitched in with the least glamorous tasks. Upon witnessing the decimation of Union troops at Fredericksburg, Roosevelt assisted with the removal of wounded soldiers from the battlefield and helped load bloody, mangled men onto hospital wagons.[43] "I would never have felt satisfied with myself after this war is over if I had done nothing, and I do feel now that I am only doing my duty," he wrote his wife from a field hospital.[44]

Meanwhile, Mittie lost her bearings back home in Manhattan. With her husband away working on behalf of the Union cause for the better part of two years, Mittie felt isolated and hated as a supporter of the Confederacy. A fragile and high-strung woman to begin with, Mittie fell into a depression and was unable to give her four children the care and nurturing they needed. Luckily, the Roosevelt children were reared by a cadre of caring surrogates: their nurse Dora; Anna Bulloch Gracie, known as Aunt Annie; and Grandmother Bulloch. At social gatherings and society dinners, when she could pull herself together, Mittie became an embarrassment to Thee with her fond recountings of her life in the South and matter-of-fact anecdotes of the family's slaves as an inferior race. Thee was mortified and ashamed of his wife's lack of tact among his friends, all staunch Union supporters, and carefully kept her out of the circuit of dinners and entertaining during the Civil War. His wife's proslavery stance became a growing liability, socially and politically, and was at harsh odds with Thee's evolving friendship with President Abraham Lincoln and his support of Lincoln's position on emancipation.

Roosevelt preserved a powerful memory from his childhood of watching Lincoln's funeral procession through New York City on April 24, 1865, following two weeks that the body of the assassinated president had lain in state at the White House. Teedie was six and one-half years old at the time. To a boy's eyes, he recalled, it seemed as if all of Manhattan was draped in black bunting and shrouded in a heavy veil of public mourning for the martyred leader who achieved through his death the unity he had struggled to create within a nation divided by the Civil War. The day of the funeral procession, Teedie and his younger brother, five-year-old Elliott, were brought to their grandfather Cornelius van Schaack Roosevelt's mansion on the southwest corner of Union Square. The imposing residence was a four-story colossus that stretched an entire block between Thirteenth and Fourteenth streets, befitting one of the city's wealthiest merchants. The brothers' playmate, Edith Carow, almost four, who lived on Union Square, joined them that solemn day. The children vied for a spot at a second-story window to catch a glimpse of the passing cortege, an image that a photographer on the street happened to preserve. What the lensman couldn't capture was the weeping of Edith, who was reduced to tears by the sight of wounded Invalid Corps soldiers marching with pinned-up sleeves or trousers. The macabre sight knocked Edith into a crying fit. Teedie locked her in a closet to quell her disturbing sounds.

In the decade after the Civil War, Theodore's father managed to stay out of what he and other members of his Knickerbocker class considered the low and dirty business of politics until, in 1877, the civic benefactor and philanthropist was unwittingly drawn into a brutal political battle. The clash began when Roosevelt decided to make a stand on principle against Roscoe Conkling, the Republican political boss and spoilsman who sought to seize the selection process of New York's collector of customs and other jobs at the Port of New York in order to dole them out as political patronage. The two men had a history of animosity. Roosevelt had led a reform delegation to the Republican National Convention in Cincinnati in June 1876 with the express purpose to "fight Conkling at all events."[45] Roosevelt dealt Conkling bruising blows in his speech in Cincinnati, charging the powerful senator from New York with widespread corruption; the blistering attack was carried in newspapers around the country. Roosevelt supported reform candidate Benjamin Bristow for the presidential nomination, thus blocking Conkling's behind-the-scenes power play and paving the way for the candidacy of Rutherford B. Hayes. Hayes had long been openly hostile to Conkling, who reciprocated by referring to Hayes as "His Fraudulency." Roosevelt's jeremiad against Conkling was so persuasive that it proved the spoiler at the convention. Hayes won the nomination and an embittered Conkling held a deep grudge.

After his election, as a reward to Roosevelt for his hard work, President Hayes sent to the Senate his nomination of Roosevelt as collector of customs. Hayes also exploited the political naïveté of Roosevelt by using the highly regarded philanthropist to draw out and attack his powerful foe in the Senate. Conkling took the bait, fought back, and set his sights on vanquishing two political enemies at once. While Theodore followed the controversy at Harvard from newspaper reports and letters from home, the press cast Conkling as a corrupt political boss and Roosevelt as an altruistic public servant. The *Nation* said that Roosevelt had "wealth above the temptations of any office, character, and great business experience" with a broad coalition of New York City merchants supporting his nomination.[46]

Although he was vulnerable stuck between the warring Hayes and Conkling, Roosevelt managed to use the controversy of his nomination as a platform to fight for political reform against patronage and corruption and to press for meritocracy in civil service—a system of employment fairness and transparency that would later become his son's signature cause. The senior Roosevelt wrote about his passionate feelings on the matter in a letter to Joseph H. Choate, a prominent lawyer and Republican leader in New York who was a close friend of Roosevelt's.

I am so satisfied that the actual existence of our Country depends upon a reform in our civil service that I will consent to serve as Collector if by so doing I can aid the administration in its efforts in this direction . . . I could not run the Custom House as a party machine, devote my own time to politics, or ask my subordinates to do so, as this would create much discontent among a certain class.[47]

Fearing that Roosevelt's do-good crusade could shut off the spigot of patronage and graft that Conkling controlled at the Custom House, the Republican power broker addressed an executive session of the U.S. Senate and pressured that legislative body to reject Roosevelt's nomination. Conkling said Hayes's appointments were meant to dishonor him politically. Conkling denied that the New York Custom House was a political machine and dismissed Roosevelt's attack as nothing more than a personal vendetta. Conkling's aggressive lobbying at least bought him time, as Roosevelt's nomination was delayed, allowing Conkling to lean on President Hayes. Congress went into recess and the issue quieted down until a new session of Congress resumed and Hayes resubmitted his nominees, including Roosevelt. Their political combat raged on, while Roosevelt remained lodged uncomfortably as a pawn in the middle. This was Roosevelt's first experience with the strain of rough-and-tumble politics, and the stress exacted a physical cost. Roosevelt grew weak, lost weight, and tried to suffer stoically as stomach problems evolved into a serious intestinal blockage. Eventually, Conkling won the battle as the Senate rejected Roosevelt's nomination by a vote of thirty-one to twenty-five in favor of the incumbent, Chester A. Arthur, a Republican of the Stalwart faction, who built his base of power among members of the conservative wing of the party in the corrupt corridors of the State Capitol in Albany. For young Theodore, the bitter defeat was a defining moment. Although his father eventually recovered from the painful intestinal episode, it set in motion a swift decline in the previously healthy and robust forty-six-year-old man. Theodore directly blamed the suffering of his beloved father on the venality of politics and the fight over his nomination as collector of customs. Conkling, Arthur, and Tammany politicians who held sway in Albany became for the son symbols of evil.

Chapter 2

★ ★ ★ ★ ★

HARVARD

I thoroughly enjoyed Harvard, and I am sure it did me good, but only in the general effect, for there was very little in my actual studies which helped me in after life.

Theodore Roosevelt Jr. entered the world of Harvard as a boy among men. He was seventeen years old and looked young for his age. Try as he might, he couldn't leave the frail and asthmatic boy known as Teedie entirely behind on the train ride from Manhattan to Cambridge, Massachusetts. His voice was still high and thin and his teeth seemed too large for his mouth. An attempt to toughen his homely, boyish, bespectacled face by growing bushy sideburns became a source of ridicule rather than acceptance among his new classmates because mutton-chops were considered out of style among voguish college men of that day. When he shaved them off, before his junior year, he wrote to his sister Corinne, "At least the deed is done and I have shaved off my whiskers! The consequence, I am bound to add, is that I look like a dissolute democrat of the fourth ward." Physically, among the other freshmen, he also stood out as immature, with a puny frame that stood barely five feet eight inches and weighed just 130 pounds, despite the years of vigorous exercise as a teenager. As soon as he settled in at college, he asked his classmates to call him Ted, since it sounded more manly, although the shortened version of his name failed to take hold. Self-conscious about his thick and bookish eyeglasses, Roosevelt made sure to remove his spectacles before posing for pictures. By his own account, he was still "pigeon-chested"[1] when he entered Harvard in the fall of 1876.

Rather than accepting a passive, background role in the crucible of Cambridge, however, Roosevelt swaggered straight to the brutal proving ground of the boxing ring. Although he was hampered by a short reach, small hands, and poor eyesight, his fearlessness created a grudging admiration among his peers.

> His delicate appearance amazed those who saw him make his first ventures with gloves in the gymnasium. He weighed only one hundred and thirty and was a very doubt-ful-looking entry in the light-weight class. Besides, he had to go into combat with a pair of big spectacles lashed to his head, a bad handicap, which put his eyesight in peril every time he boxed. To offset this disadvantage, he aimed to lead swiftly and heavily and thus put his opponent on the defen-sive from the start.[2]

There was a recklessness and animalistic rage inside Roosevelt that the blood sport of boxing released. His training in the gym was an extension of trying to fulfill his father's command to build up his body. His favorite exertion at Harvard was sparring, the bloodier the better. (His second favorite was embellishing tales of his outdoor exploits.) Getting beaten to a pulp gave him a strange rush and a pummeling generally put him in a buoyant mood. He had been relishing bloody noses, black eyes, and bruised chins since boyhood, when he and Elliott had engaged in homegrown boxing bouts at the urging of their forceful father. Maybe the barrage of blows knocked the dour Dutchness out of the elder son. At any rate, Roosevelt joined the Harvard boxing club as a lightweight and advanced to a championship match by his junior year. The match pitted Roosevelt against Richard Trimble, a senior. Both Roosevelt and Trimble were undefeated in seven previous matches. Trimble was five pounds heavier and considerably taller, with a longer reach. Roosevelt overcame these disadvantages by being quicker, more sound in his boxing fundamentals, and driven to seize the offense. He also had a pretty powerful right hand. Roosevelt would not back down or give up in the face of Trimble's physical advantages. "Roosevelt received not only one good tap on the nose, but so many and so fast and hard that it was obvious he was hopelessly outclassed," a classmate recalled. "The exhibition was distinctly gory. His shorter reach and height and lesser weight and defective sight were a factor in his poor defense. He was full of animation and attack to the very end."[3]

Another classmate present recounted the round-by-round action:

> The first round was vigorously contested. Roosevelt closed in at the very outset. Because of his bad eyes he realized that in-fighting gave him his only chance to win. Blows were exchanged with lightning rapidity, and they were both hard blows. Roosevelt drew first blood, but soon his own nose was bleeding. At the call of time, however, he got the decision for the round. The senior had learned his lesson. Thereafter he would not permit Roosevelt to close in on him. With his longer reach, and aided by his antagonist's near sightedness, he succeeded in landing frequent blows. Roosevelt worked hard, but to no avail. The round was awarded to the senior. In the third round the senior endeavored to pursue the same tactics, but with less success. The result of this round was a draw, and an extra round had to be sparred.[4]

Although Trimble gained the decision, Roosevelt was a game challenger until the final bell. The loss did not discourage him. Roosevelt poured out all his pent-up passion and anger inside the Old Gymnasium, a small, circular building resembling a railroad roundhouse that stood in front of Memorial Hall. He had never felt more vital or manly than within the boxing ring. At times, his confidence in his boxing abilities got the best of him. One day Billy Edwards, a premier professional lightweight boxer, visited the gym to put on a sparring exhibition. Roosevelt offered to be a sparring partner and laced up his gloves. Roosevelt boxed recklessly, with an aggressive, charging style. "In about two minutes Edwards had banged him until he was ready to acknowledge there was a vast difference between a college amateur and a professional ringster," a classmate recalled.[5]

During another boxing match, Roosevelt was jabbing and counterpunching in a "hot encounter" when the round ended and time was called. Roosevelt dropped his gloves and moved to his corner, but his opponent charged and walloped the defenseless Roosevelt with "a heavy blow square on the nose."

> There was an instant cry of "Foul! Foul!" from the sympathetic onlookers and a scene of noisy excitement followed. Above the uproar, Roosevelt, his face covered with blood, was heard shouting at the top of his voice as he ran toward the referee. "Stop! Stop! He didn't hear! He didn't hear!" Then he shook the hand of the other youth warmly, and the emotion of the little crowd changed from scorn of his opponent to admiration of him.[6]

His fierce pugilism was largely a pose, though, a mask worn over essential insecurities he'd been struggling to overcome since childhood: fear of losing control during the terror of ongoing asthma attacks; desire to be accepted by his peers even though his interests were generally solitary pursuits; the desperate need to live up to his father's stern expectations and the fear of falling short; eagerness to be viewed as rugged and manly even while frightened and insecure. Letters to his older sister, Bamie, a kind of surrogate parent and his closest confidante, poignantly underscored his emotional frailties. "Yesterday I at first entirely forgot it was my birthday," he wrote her, "and the upshot of it was that for about a quarter of an hour I was regularly homesick."[7]

Roosevelt's emotional anchor and emerging romantic interest as he began the transition to Harvard life was his childhood sweetheart, Edith Carow. She was drawn to his fierce intellect and seriousness as a scholar, which complemented her own disciplined pursuit of knowledge. Edith's academic achievements and literary strengths even fueled something of a competition for Theodore's attention between Edith and his sister Corinne. After one of her visits to Cambridge with Theodore's father, sisters, and brother, he wrote to Corinne: "I don't think I ever saw Edith looking prettier . . . Everyone . . . admired her little Ladyship intensely, and she behaved as sweetly as she looked."[8] Friends thought Theodore and Edith made a fine couple and assumed they would one day marry. Neither of them made any attempt to dispel that notion.

When Roosevelt had left home for Harvard, his father had advised, "Take care of your morals first, your health next, and finally your studies."[9] Even as Roosevelt tried to reinvent himself as a rugged outdoorsman and hearty collegian, he never forgot his father's advice. Theodore regularly went to hear the powerful sermons of Phillips Brooks at Trinity College in Boston; he attended mandatory college chapel on campus and taught catechism on Sunday mornings while his Harvard peers were sleeping off Saturday night debaucheries that included heavy drinking and visits to prostitutes. Early on, Roosevelt's father wrote his son, "As I saw the last of the train bearing you away the other day I realized what a luxury it was to have a boy in whom I would place perfect trust and confidence who was leaving me to take his first independent position in the world."[10] He was correct.

Roosevelt proudly reported to his father something of a moralistic scorecard tracking the eleven classmates at his table during communal meals and noted that "no less than seven do not smoke and four drink nothing stronger than beer."[11] He later confessed in his diary that he had tried alcohol at Harvard and concluded that "wine makes me awfully fighting."[12] One of Theodore's favorite professors, William James—physiologist, psychologist, philosopher, and brother of the novelist Henry James—advocated temperance to the students and described the ill effects of alcohol on human physiology. Purity and wholesomeness were the ideals James held up to his students, a theme that Roosevelt took to heart.

Yet Roosevelt's morals were not perfect. He spent freely to outfit his rented rooms at 16 Winthrop Street in Cambridge, or rather, he allowed his older sister to spend freely on his behalf. "Ever since I came here I have been wondering what I should have done if you had not fitted up my room for me," Theodore wrote to Bamie. "The curtains, carpet, furniture—in short everything is really beautiful . . . I do not think there will be a room in College more handsome or comfortable."[13] Theodore leaned on Bamie for the maturity and organizational skills he lacked. She was his strongest supporter and most sympathetic sounding board. He wrote to Bamie religiously each Sunday night—beginning at Harvard and extending throughout the rest of his life—to reveal his fears and most intimate feelings with a level of openness he shared with nobody else. He once referred to her as "the Driving Wheel of Destiny and the Superintendent-in-Chief of the workings of Providence."[14] Certainly she was the superintendent of much of his life.

Furnishings, entertainment, and club dues cost Theodore more than $2,400 during his junior and senior years at Harvard, equal to an average American family's budget for four years during that era.[15] Concerned about how his father might react when he received the bills from his freshman year, Theodore wrote to Bamie in response to Thee's asking his son for a "short account of how I spend my days." Most weekdays, Theodore's day began with rising at 7:15 A.M., followed by prayers, breakfast, and a half-hour study session before three hours of classwork and another hour of study before lunch at 1 P.M. Lunch was followed by another study session and one hour of afternoon classes. The afternoon was free—Theodore walked, boxed, vaulted, and worked out in the gymnasium for exercise—followed by dinner and early evening study. "I have to work harder than I expected; which is the ordinary complaint among the boys," he said.[16]

Theodore's weeknights and weekends at Harvard were filled with visiting his friends or receiving classmates in his apartment at 16 Winthrop Street. Roosevelt's rooms were on the second story of a house owned by a family named Richardson and situated on the corner of Winthrop and Holyoke streets, a few blocks off Massachusetts Avenue and a short walk from the bank of the Charles River. Its location was on the fringe of the Harvard community and removed from the concentration of apartments closer to Harvard Square rented by the Clubmen, who were members of the college's snobbish private clubs. Roosevelt rented from Mrs. Richardson, along with two other student boarders on her second floor. Roosevelt's apartment was a modest, two-room space. The larger room, in the corner, he filled with books and turned into a study where he read, wrote, and entertained visitors. He made the smaller back room his bedroom. With a roaring fire, whose crackling embers occasionally left burn marks on his rugs, the snug confines could begin to close in upon the active Roosevelt, and the close, smoky air threatened to exacerbate his asthma. The smell of the snakes, specimens, and taxidermy projects he kept didn't help his troublesome lungs either, and no doubt put off some of his visitors. Roosevelt looked forward to the fresh air and adventure of traveling on the weekends to formal dinners with the parents of

Harvard chums, such as William Roscoe Thayer and Henry "Hal" Minot.

Bamie had, of course, arranged for her brother's domestic help. "My arrangements are most satisfactory, including the chimney and washerwoman," he wrote to his sister.[17] "I do not think the lattter always acts squarely on the subject of white cravats however. She is a negress, about as large as Cornelius, and as I am rather afraid of her I have not yet ventured to remonstrate concerning the cravats." His mother's dismissive opinion of blacks had rubbed off on Theodore to a degree. "We have fared very well at the hands of our cook, the dark Virginia Minerva, or whatever you call that elderly mulatto," he wrote.[18]

Theodore had an active social life with many extracurricular activities, such as his organizing a whist club in his freshman year. But as a boy who had been coddled by his parents and had relished the communal family "melts," Theodore struggled to stand on his own. "My short visit made me quite homesick," he wrote his sister after just three months away at college. "I enjoy myself ever so much here, and the fellows are very pleasant, but I thoroughly realize that there's no place like home."[19]

He was an object of amusement and some ridicule at college for his odd personality. "He struck his classmates as unusual because of his concentration, enthusiasm and interest in studies," one recalled.[20] Another student remembered Roosevelt as "a good deal of a joke . . . active and enthusiastic and all that."[21] The main impression he made on Harvard President Charles William Eliot was "that he looked feeble. He had a very large mouth and his shining teeth were noticeable even then."[22] Roosevelt combined a belligerent moralizing tone with a lack of the suavity and social skills possessed by the popular Clubmen. He was an outsider from the outset, a New York Knickerbocker, not a Boston Brahmin. He had never been particularly adept at making new friends and he was at a decided disadvantage at snobbish Harvard. Roosevelt also lacked the experience of getting along with a large group of his peers since asthma had excluded him from attending school for most of his childhood and he had been educated primarily by private tutors. Yet he was not overly shy or afraid to throw himself into new social situations. "As you may see by my letter to Corinne I have been having a pretty gay time during the last week," he wrote Bamie after just four months at Harvard.[23] "Some of the girls are very sweet and bright, and a few are very pretty."

Classmates laughed not only at his muttonchops and boyish physique but also at his patrician affectation of traveling around Cambridge in a dogcart pulled by a pony long before such a conveyance was common among young men. Moreover, Theodore's combative and occasionally obnoxious behavior in the classroom caused a strain with instructors and classmates who were not prepared for the jarring break from Harvard's decorum of student silence at lectures. Roosevelt was conspicuous in his insistent and vocal challenge to this pedagogical tradition. "In our classroom, it was not often that any student broke in upon the smoothly flowing current of the professorial address," a classmate recalled. "But Roosevelt did this again and again, naively, with the evident aim of getting at the more detailed truth of the subject." Roosevelt's "novel action" was especially disruptive in political economy class. The entire class "wooded up with laughter" over Roosevelt's frequent "pushing questions at the instructor, and even debating points with him . . . which made Roosevelt a subject of wonder and comment."[24] He didn't take a hint to halt his hectoring by the knitted brows of his professors or the annoyed stares of his classmates. The only method that worked with him was a direct command, such as the type lecturer Nathaniel Shaler gave one day in class: "Now, look here, Roosevelt, let me talk. I'm running this class."[25] As one classmate recalled, "It became evident very early that Roosevelt was a person *sui generis* and not to be judged by ordinary standards."[26]

When frustration or inadequacy caused Theodore to draw up

short of his father's stern expectations, his famous temper flared. Fellow Harvard student William Hooper recalled Roosevelt's being confronted by a drunken classmate, who taunted Theodore about his large teeth and the way he thrust out his jaw in conversation. The inebriated student would not stop, and Roosevelt became so enraged that Hooper had to step in and physically restrain Roosevelt from attacking the fellow. Another time, Hooper recounted, an argument at a Harvard eating club between Roosevelt and a classmate grew so heated that Roosevelt picked up a pastry and hurled it at the man, who dodged at the last moment. The food smashed into the wall and left a dark stain that remained for months. Another classmate recalled another fight in which Roosevelt slammed a pumpkin down upon the head of his adversary.[27]

Roosevelt took his meals at various Harvard eating clubs within walking distance of Harvard Square and made some of his closest and most lasting friends there, such as Richard Saltonstall, Henry Minot, and Charles Washburn. He ate for his first two years at Mrs. Morgan's, located at the corner of Mount Auburn and Story streets. Mrs. Morgan was best remembered for her missing eye and consequent nickname of "Old One-eye," and for her dire threats of expulsion after food fights.

As a junior and senior, he dined at Mrs. Wilson's at 62 Brattle Street, on the corner of Brattle and Hilliard streets. The "club table," which Roosevelt joined with seven other classmates, was a corner room on the first floor. Fellow club members remembered Roosevelt's ritual of preparing his portions carefully on his plate, then removing his spectacles and diving into the steaming mound in front of his murky, unfocused vision. "He did not seem to enjoy eating very much, but he ate as we might stoke a furnace—because it must be done," a classmate said. "He did not live to eat, but he ate to live."[28]

Roosevelt constantly strove to disprove his classmates' opinion of him as a weakling. One winter afternoon with a biting wind that drove temperatures below zero, Roosevelt invited Richard Welling to go skating with him on Fresh Pond. The two often took long walks and exercised together in the gymnasium. "We had in common the ideal of self-development to be achieved through stern training," Welling said.[29] The pond's ice was rough and the brutal conditions caused their ears and toes to burn from exposure, threatening frostbite. Roosevelt pretended to be impervious to the wintry assault. "Isn't this perfectly bully?" he asked repeatedly. Welling didn't answer and refused to be the first to buckle in the competition to see who was toughest. "I grit my teeth, resolved not to be the first to quit. It took every ounce of grit in me," Welling recalled. "One hour we skated or scuffled about, then a second hour, and not until well on into the third with obvious regret did he suggest home."[30]

Roosevelt pushed himself academically too and sought out the advice of his instructors. Professor J. Laurence Laughlin recalled that Roosevelt asked whether he should pursue a career in natural history. Laughlin replied that the natural sciences were an already crowded field and suggested instead that Roosevelt should consider going into political science because very few academics were working in that discipline at the time. Roosevelt also encountered an instructor of history, Henry Cabot Lodge, who would become his lifelong political mentor. Lodge was a popular professor but was known as one of the most demanding teachers at the college. He assigned more reading than any other instructor and had no qualms about flunking a substantial portion of his class. Roosevelt naturally was drawn to such an uncompromising professional. Classmates recalled how Roosevelt would focus so intensely upon his course work that he entered an almost trancelike state as he read, oblivious to all around him. Such powers of concentration, coupled with an almost photographic memory, made studying a breeze for Roosevelt, who made light of how little he worked on homework his senior year. He devoured books with the same gusto he stuffed buttered bread into his maw: hungrily, automatically, for sustenance. He read widely, discriminately, often for research or a specific purpose, and early on displayed a memory that retained an astonishing level of detail from the flood of books that passed through his hands. Roosevelt attacked literature with the same single-minded intensity with which he competed in sports or tests of endurance in the wilderness. "Even when he was reading—perhaps in a fellow student's room, and the room was full of noisy, rollicking mates, he clutched the book with both hands, generally at the top of the under side, and all his energy, physical as well as mental, seemed to be concentrated on the act," a Harvard classmate recalled.[31] It was said that he was once so engrossed in a book that an ember from his fireplace ignited his shoe and burned for a time before he noticed it. From histories to novels, biographies to philosophy texts, Roosevelt plowed through a book or a few books each day when he got on a reading tear. He became a devotee of poetry too, especially romantic verse that appealed to that strong strain in his personality. At Harvard, he read widely among the poets Horace, Pope, Schiller, Longfellow, Shelley, Tennyson, Emerson, Browning, Poe, Coleridge, and Kipling.

A memorable illustration of his prodigious reading comes from Van Wyck Brooks's memoir, in which he recalled a visit by Roosevelt at his college and Roosevelt's encounter with the English writer W. H. Mallock, best known for his satirical novel *The New Republic,* a send-up of the Victorian intelligentsia. Roosevelt introduced himself to Mallock, firmly grasped the author's hand, "and poured forth a flood of comment on Mallock's views and books, every one of which he seemed to have read and remembered. It was like Niagara falling on a fern, for the little old man was stunned with confusion and pleasure."[32]

A student of political science, in the earliest days of the discipline, had much to study in the world outside Cambridge. In 1870 the Civil War still loomed large, and the contested presidential election of 1876 between Samuel J. Tilden and Rutherford B. Hayes gripped the nation's attention. Hayes was eventually declared the winner following months of legal wrangling; Democratic challenger Tilden, governor of New York, had led in the popular and electoral votes but fell one electoral vote short of the required 185. A commission decided in favor of Hayes, who promptly ordered the last federal troops to withdraw from the ravaged South, ending Reconstruction and paving the way for the reassertion of legalized white supremacy there. Other conflicts rankled elsewhere. In June 1876, Colonel George Custer and all 265 troopers of his Seventh Cavalry Regiment were killed in a battle with Sioux and Cheyenne Indians at the Little Big Horn River in the Dakota Territory. In July 1877, the first national railroad strike, over a cut in wages, shut down the rail network; violent clashes erupted between rail workers and police from coast to coast, resulting in hundreds of injuries and deaths. Laborers were increasingly angry, as the new "robber barons"—epitomized by Cornelius Vanderbilt, whose estate was worth $100 million at the time of his death in 1877—built national corporations that enriched stockholders.

As young men of wealth and privilege, the Cambridge collegians were largely insulated from the country's troubles. Harvard in Roosevelt's era was a provincial place, with about two-thirds of his class coming from within one hundred miles or so of Boston. The entire enrollment of Harvard College in 1876 was 821. President Eliot had relaxed some of the college's strictures, such as morning chapel, which was compulsory only to those who lived on campus. Students also were granted a heretofore-unknown level of academic freedom by the advent of elective courses. Attendance also became a fairly lax requirement, with more emphasis placed on final examinations than on a student's record in attending class during the term. Harvard's culture nurtured star faculty, such as Professor Charles Eliot Norton, who taught fine arts. Norton was a contributor to literary magazines, a translator of Dante, and an intimate among top literary circles. He taught Harvard men to study and appreciate classical art and ancient culture as a civilizing and moralizing influence. Another faculty member, historian Henry Adams, of the famous family of American statesmen, would later prove a valuable acquaintance to Roosevelt.

Initially, as an undergraduate, Theodore showed no signs of following his father's political footsteps. He seemed hardly to have given politics a thought as he pursued his twin passions of ornithology and a life of letters. As a student, Roosevelt was one of the youngest members elected to the Nuttall Ornithological Club, a group devoted to bird study and a catalyst for the formation of the American Ornithologists' Union. He did not simply observe wild animals, however; he continued to hunt on vacations. "Most big game hunters never learn anything about the game except how to kill it; and most naturalists never observe it at all," he later wrote.[33]

The closest he came to politics in college was the study of it. Roosevelt was an active member of the free-trade movement and could discuss economic theory competently because of his close reading of John Stuart Mill. Roosevelt was one of the catalysts behind the Finance Club, which invited renowned economists to campus to speak. He was active in a political discussion group, for which he read a paper titled "The Machine Age in Politics," a critical look at political spoilsmen and a harbinger of Roosevelt's later crusade against Tammany Hall.

He did have one political experience—as a voter. He got a taste of losing; during a mock presidential election the spring of his senior year, Roosevelt voted for Democrat Thomas Bayard rather than the eventual winner, Republican James A. Garfield. Roosevelt was nothing if not contrary. "He used to block the narrow gravel path and soon make sparks from an argument fly," a classmate recalled. "He was so enthusiastic and he had such a startling array of deeply held interests that we all thought he would make a great journalist."[34] Another, however, called him "a freak, a poseur and half crazy."[35]

For his part, Roosevelt found little to admire or emulate around him. Without a hint of irony over his own social standing, he sneered at these "fellows of excellent family and faultless breeding, with a fine old country place, four-in-hands, tandems, a yacht, and so on; but oh the decorous hopelessness of their lives."[36] Closer to home, Roosevelt saw his younger brother, Elliott, dissolving into a dissolute lifestyle that saddened and angered Theodore. Elliott was given a job in a family business as a front for his heavy drinking and idle hours at social clubs, fox hunting, polo, and womanizing. "He drank like a fish and ran after the ladies," Edith Carow wrote years later. Though Theodore was no stranger to drink, he prided himself on his sobriety. On the night he was initiated into Harvard's exclusive Porcellian Club, he recorded being "'higher' with wine than I have ever been before—or will be again. Still, I could wind up my watch."[37] He remained true to the promise he had made his father, steering clear of the frequent drunken binges in which his classmates indulged.

Roosevelt did let some of his classes slip. He managed to earn barely passing grades in forensics, Greek, and French literature. "O, I made a miserable failure in my French examination, three weeks ago, owing to being forced to sit up all the previous night with the asthma," he wrote in his diary.[38] The courses in which he performed the best, by comparison, were German, rhetoric, history, and (not surprisingly) natural history.

Roosevelt's emerging philosophy of life was influenced by one of his Harvard instructors, William James, from whom Roosevelt learned about comparative anatomy and the physiology of vertebrates. "Extremely interesting," Roosevelt said of James's course, which he took in his sophomore year. The course was imbued with the teacher's philosophy of pragmatism, in which the true measure of accomplishment was concreteness and facts, action and power. Of course, headstrong Theodore did not accept all of James's teachings without a challenge. "Many were the *rencontres* between him and Dr. James," recalled a classmate. "Theodore Roosevelt *always* had the last word . . . Those little sparring matches I think threw considerable light on his characteristics. He was a great lime-lighter!"[39] Although the classmate said Roosevelt's arguments were generally far-fetched, James was a shrewd teacher who would let Roosevelt bluster ahead while he leaned back in his chair, a wide grin spread across his face as he waited patiently for Roosevelt to finish. James saw in his impetuous pupil a reflection of himself as a young man, particularly in their shared passion for the natural sciences. Both had been sickly as boys and had forfeited much of their formative years to illness. Some of their ailments, in both cases, were as much emotional and psychological as medical. At the end of the term, James gave Roosevelt a mark of seventy-nine, which was an honor grade.

Roosevelt was not alone among Harvard students in his admiration of James, who was one of the most popular faculty members at the college. James lived near campus on Irving Street and, in his rumpled tweeds and full gray beard, cut a striking figure as he walked briskly across Harvard Yard. Students considered James a friend as well as their teacher, and they were drawn to this "irresistible gust of life coming down the street . . . who moved energetically along in a sensitive, universal awareness," as one of his students said.[40] James's research and writing in the disciplines of psychology and physiology taught him to be suspicious of what he called "the bitch goddess success." He nevertheless believed that "the ultimate test for us of what a truth means is the conduct it dictates or inspires."

On February 9, 1878, during his son's sophomore year, Theodore Roosevelt Sr., forty-six years old, passed away. The cause was intestinal cancer. He had battled courageously through the pain and agonizing debilitation after an abdominal strain lingered and developed into an apparent case of peritonitis, which (to the surprise of his doctors) proved to be inoperable cancer. The children could not help but link their father's sudden health decline—which began a few days after his Senate confirmation defeat by Conkling—with the evils of spoilsmen and machine politicians. The death reinforced the family's belief that politics was a low and brutal business that their class should shun. While Theodore studied and socialized at Harvard, shielded by his sisters from their father's sudden deterioration, Corinne helped nurse their father through his pain and torment. "Oh, Edith," she wrote her friend, "it is the most frightful thing to see the person you love best in the world in terrible pain, and not be able to do a thing to alleviate it."[41] When their father's gradual decline abruptly took a turn for the worse, Theodore rushed home from Harvard to Thee's deathbed but arrived after his father expired. The man they called "Greatheart," the center of gravity and emotional anchor of the family, was gone. Given their mother's flighty and fragile nature, the Roosevelt children, all but Bamie still teenagers, had in essence become orphans.

Theodore received a comforting letter of sympathy after the death of his father from his Harvard classmate and friend Henry Minot, "Old Hal," with whom he had written a book on Adirondack birds. Roosevelt was reflective but also judgmental in his reply.

> As yet it is almost impossible to realize I shall never see Father again; these last few days seem like a hideous dream. Father had always been so much with me that it seems as if part of my life had been taken away; but it is much worse for Mother and my sisters. After all, it is a purely selfish sorrow, for it was best that Father's terrible sufferings should end.[42]

His elder son, the child the father called his favorite, had reached the edge of manhood at age nineteen and realized that he would need to recall his father's example in the years ahead.

I was fortunate enough in having a father whom I have always been able to regard as an ideal man. It sounds a little like cant to say what I am going to say but he really did combine the strength and courage and will and energy of the strongest man with the tenderness, cleanness and purity of a woman.[43]

Roosevelt wrote heartbreaking lamentations in his diary about the grief that was consuming him. "O, father, how bitterly I miss you, mourn for you, and long for you."[44] "I feel that if it were not for the certainty that . . . he isn't dead but gone before, I should almost perish . . . He shared all my joys, and in sharing doubled them, and soothed all the few sorrows I ever had."[45] But he also saw his father's death as a moral challenge. "How I wish I could ever do something to keep up his name," he confided in his diary. Still, politics did not occur to him at that time as the possible means.

Theodore also wrote a heartfelt plea to Bamie, asking his older sister to act as a kind of surrogate parent to him. "You will have to give me a great deal of advice and assistance, now that our dear Father is gone, for in many ways you are more like him than any of the rest of the family," he wrote.[46]

In a pattern that would be repeated in response to other personal tragedies, Theodore sublimated his grief over his father's death by throwing himself full-bore into schoolwork and extracurricular activities. But the sorrow, rootlessness, and depression he felt continued to envelop Theodore. "He was everything to me," he wrote in his diary the spring after his father's death. "I have lost the only human being to whom I told everything. I had been so accustomed to go to him for advice that I hardly know how to decide for myself."[47] Roosevelt joined an exhaustive range of clubs and organizations. He seemed to be in perpetual motion, earning the description by a classmate as "a steam-engine in trousers." He was invited to join the Porcellian Club, one of Harvard's most exclusive. Pork, as it was known, boasted illustrious alumni among its patrician roster, most notably Oliver Wendell Holmes. Roosevelt's selection to Porcellian set in motion a rather unexpected rise in his social stock among the class of 1880. The Pork attracted less welcome attention and recognition as well: Roosevelt described drunken escapades among members of the Porcellian, and he struggled not to let himself be entirely sucked into the club's atmosphere of spoiled extravagance. During his junior year, though, Roosevelt briefly indulged his bacchanalian side and worried about its effect on his health and character.

> I am living a life of most luxurious ease at present. I break-
> fast in the Club about 10; my horse is there before the door,
> and I ride off—generally lunching at some friend's house. It
> is very pleasant—but I do not suppose it would be healthy
> to continue it too long. When I do not stay out to tea or
> dinner, I generally have some kind of spree—a "champagne
> supper" up in the club.[48]

Roosevelt was also appointed to Phi Beta Kappa, and he joined the Finance Club and the Natural History Society, for whom he served as vice president. He found social diversion as president of Alpha Delta Phi and membership in the D.K.E. Society. D.K.E., known as "Dickey," chose its members from the highest-status students, as freshmen were ranked by their sophomore upperclassmen. Roosevelt explored his artistic and literary interests in the Arts Club and was secretary of the drama group, the Hasty Pudding Club. He also became an editor of the Harvard *Advocate,* one of three undergraduate papers, and a member of the O.K. Society, which was considered Harvard's ultraliterary group, comprising a select cluster of sixteen editors of the *Crimson* and *Advocate*. William Randolph Hearst—who would become Roosevelt's Democratic political rival on the state and national scene—experienced an extracurricular career that paralleled Roosevelt's at Harvard. Known as the most prominent Democrat in the college in his day, the newspaper titan, four years younger than Roosevelt, was a member of the Porcellian Club, D.K.E. Society, and the Hasty Pudding Club. In other ways, though, Hearst cut a more jagged swath through Cambridge by keeping a working-girl mistress in town and by hosting raucous booze and cigar parties on his $150 monthly allowance—a profligacy that contributed to his eventual expulsion. Hearst's removal from the college would later fuel his hatred of Roosevelt, whom he despised as a Republican and an early success in the two pursuits Hearst had laid out as his own goals: politics and literature.

Just before his sophomore year ended in the spring of 1878, Roosevelt was saddened to learn that his closest friend, Hal Minot, was quitting Harvard because of mental exhaustion and his father's urgings to study law. Minot was one of the few Harvard men with whom Roosevelt felt completely comfortable. During the following summer break—just a few months past his father's death, which continued to wash over him in waves of grief—Roosevelt's cumulative sadness made him difficult to be around. It rubbed off on his relationship with Edith. Their romance was suddenly over. There was no stated cause for their breakup and the reason for the split was never known. Neither ever spoke or wrote about it. "We both of us had . . . tempers that were far from being of the best," Roosevelt said.[49] Speculation swirled that the split resulted from Edith's turning down Theodore's marriage proposal during an idyll at the Roosevelt camp Tranquility, but it remains speculation. Ache and longing would remain just below the surface for both of them as they moved forward.

At the start of his junior year, a week before his twentieth birthday, Theodore met Alice Hathaway Lee. The day he first laid eyes on Alice was October 18, 1878, while visiting classmate Dick Saltonstall, Alice's cousin and neighbor. That first glimpse of Alice became a date he treated with romanticized sanctity. Theodore's emotions had been pressed so low, he responded with a rebound of irrational exaltation. "I loved her as soon as I saw her sweet, fair young face," he said. He rhapsodized that she was "beautiful in face and form, and lovelier still in spirit."[50] Alice was a tall, willowy, and blond seventeen-year-old beauty. She suffered no shortage of suitors, "who circled, like moths around a candle . . . this very vivacious and attractive creature."[51] These rivals caused Roosevelt at first to grow sullen and depressed. He wandered the woods late at night, consumed by his fear of losing Alice to another fellow. Roosevelt fell into such an emotionally troubled state that concerned friends sent word to New York and asked for a relative to come to try to pull him out of his funk. "I have been pretty nearly crazy," he later wrote in his diary.[52]

Theodore vowed to compete for the love of Alice as if it were a wrestling match and she the trophy. She kept his driving, impetuous courtship at arm's length, which only spurred him on. "See that girl? I am going to marry her. She won't have me, but I'll have her," Theodore promised Martha Cowdin, an old family friend.[53] The more she put him off or appeared uninterested, the more often he drove his dogcart from Cambridge the six miles to her family's substantial Victorian mansion in the outlying Boston neighborhood of Brookline to pledge his love. "She is just the sweetest, prettiest sunniest little darling that ever lived, and with all her laughing, teasing ways, she is as loving and tender as she can be," he wrote to his sister Corinne.[54] Roosevelt was instantly jealous of the other beaux who called upon her. Complicating matters was the fact that Roosevelt's unbridled pursuit of Alice was slightly disingenuous, since he still had feelings for Edith. The romantic maelstrom and his competitiveness against Alice's other suitors nearly pushed Roosevelt over the edge, according to a classmate.

> Roosevelt seemed constantly afraid that one or the other of them was going to run off with her, and threatened duels and everything else. On one occasion he actually sent abroad for a set of French dueling pistols, and after great difficulty got them through the Custom House.[55]

Roosevelt told Henry Minot that he had made everything else in his life "subordinate to winning her" and that his single-minded pursuit of Alice caused him to lose interest in natural history and other academic passions. In the end, he won. She accepted his proposal, having been flattered by his devotion and worn down by his entreaties.

Roosevelt won another major battle in his college years: the battle with his scrawny body. A rigid workout regimen paid off in a bullish neck and powerful chest that belied his small physique. When he underwent a physical exam with his fellow seniors in the spring of 1880, Harvard's physician, Dr. Dudley A. Sargent, who monitored the athletic program and promoted physical fitness, was amazed to discover the power Roosevelt had packed into 136 pounds. "Notwithstanding his rather small frame and mediocre muscular development, his total strength was only surpassed by five percent of those in college at this time. His superior strength was largely due to the mechanical advantage he gained by his short arms," Sargent reported.[56] Sargent nonetheless futilely urged Roosevelt to preserve his weakened lungs and prevent future outbreaks of asthma and potential trouble from a heart condition by maintaining a sedentary lifestyle.

It wasn't until his senior year—and a hotly contested class election in the fall of 1879—that Theodore was drawn into politics at Harvard in any sort of active way. The seniors were split between those who wanted to maintain the status quo and those who felt that the Clubmen possessed too much power and should be voted out. Those who were nominated for senior class officer and wanted to register their disapproval of the club crowd rose and, one after another, withdrew their names from nomination. Roosevelt had been nominated for Class Day Committee; when it came to his turn, he was about to rise and to withdraw his name as well.

"Sit down," whispered a classmate. "You can be elected."

"Do you really think so?" Roosevelt asked.

"Of course you can. Hooper can't, but you can."

"If you think that's so, I'll run."[57]

Sure enough, Roosevelt ran and was elected to his first office, secretary of the Harvard class of 1880.

Roosevelt's senior dissertation was independent, unorthodox, and progressive: "The Practicability of Equalizing Men and Women before the Law." At the time, it was not a popular position, yet Roosevelt graduated magna cum laude with a bachelor of arts degree. He was ranked twenty-first among a class of 177 men who earned bachelor's degrees.

Soon after, on October 27, 1880, at the Unitarian Church in Brookline, he and Alice were married. It was Theodore's twenty-second birthday. His brother, Elliott, was his best man; Edith Carow was among the guests. "My happiness now is almost too great," he wrote in his diary. "I am living in dreamland. I wish it could last forever."[58]

After a quiet honeymoon at Tranquility in Oyster Bay, the couple set up their home with Roosevelt's mother, two sisters, and brother at 6 West Fifty-seventh Street. He had enrolled in classes at Columbia Law School. He turned the daily commute of about six miles round-trip into a vigorous walking workout. He supplemented the course work by observing the law practice of his uncle Robert Barnhill Roosevelt. Theodore took up the study of law with typical gusto, scribbling furiously during courses at

Columbia until he had filled seven volumes and more than 1,100 pages with his handwritten class notes.

Roosevelt had chosen law by default. He seemed to be expecting to go like his uncle into private legal practice after law school. Yet he had difficulty building up much interest or passion for the profession and soon found himself casting about for alternatives. When he wasn't attending lectures in law, Roosevelt holed up in the Astor Library to work on a manuscript begun at Harvard, *The Naval War of 1812.* "Am working fairly, at my law, hard at politics, and hardest of all at my book, which I expect to publish this winter," Roosevelt wrote in his diary on October 6, 1881. It was obvious to his law school professors that Roosevelt's attention was focused elsewhere. "He registered however for all the courses in political history, public law, and political science and appeared to be more interested in these than in the topics of municipal law," wrote Professor John W. Burgess.[59]

Roosevelt also joined the National Guard, searching for a position that would challenge him and ignite his passion. Applying himself as a part-time soldier, he quickly rose to the rank of captain. A confluence of events caused his gradual pulling away from the study of law: Columbia Law School changed its requirements in 1882, when Roosevelt was nearing the end of his course work, adding a third year of study in place of the previous requirement of two years. That same year, the New York State Legislature tightened the so-called "diploma privilege" that Columbia had formerly enjoyed. The new stipulation required Columbia graduates to pass a challenging, state-administered bar examination before entering private practice. For Roosevelt as well, it was time for a change.

Roosevelt wandered into politics out of curiosity as much as any other motivating factor, he later wrote. His Harvard colleagues, and the businessmen and lawyers he knew, considered it below their station—a smarmy con game for lowlifes and undesirables.

Yet it was the perfect station for a self-made man, and Theodore, despite his privileges, was very much self-made. "There is nothing brilliant or outstanding in my record, except perhaps this one thing," he said. "I do the things that I believe ought to be done. And when I make up my mind to do a thing, I act."[60]

Roosevelt's attention was drawn to two quintessential big-city machine politicians, Jake Hess and Joe Murray. Hess, leader of the Twenty-first District Republican Association, had known Roosevelt's father through the City Commission of Charities and Corrections. Hess was a member of the commission that Theodore Sr. frequently interacted with through his various philanthropies. Murray was Hess's trusted lieutenant, who had moved up the Tammany Hall hierarchy, switched party affiliation along the way, and earned his status as a political heavyweight through years of door-to-door slogging and late nights in smoke-filled strategy sessions. Their diverse ethnic backgrounds—Hess was a German Jew and Murray an Irish Catholic—were typical of the melting pot of New York City politics, a milieu that greatly broadened young Theodore's insular world. "I went around there often enough to have the men get accustomed to me and have me get accustomed to them, so that we began to speak the same language," Roosevelt wrote.[61] The universe of the Twenty-first was not vast, but it was dense with opportunity. Dubbed the "silk-stocking" district because of its affluence, it lay between Seventh and Lexington avenues from Fortieth to Fifty-ninth streets and between Eighth and Lexington avenues from Fifty-ninth to Eighty-sixth streets. Murray had to overcome Theodore's initial reluctance to appear too opportunistic. Murray recalled asking Roosevelt if he would take the Republican nomination for assemblyman of the Twenty-first, but Theodore initially declined. "No, I wouldn't dream of such a thing. It would look as though I had selfish motives," Roosevelt replied. Yet Murray had already made up his mind that "it was Theodore Roosevelt or no one."[62]

He had good reason to pursue the energetic man with a famous name. Manhattan was then, as now, a Democratic town. Democrats, who represented generally ignorant new immigrants and the lower classes, had seized power by the mid-nineteenth century away from an ambivalent upper class distracted by its drive to build businesses and accumulate wealth after decades of blithely running municipal affairs out of a sense of noblesse oblige. By the time the old-line Manhattan ruling class and mercantile titans turned their attention back to New York politics, they didn't recognize the venal free-for-all it had become in the wide-open 1840s and 1850s.

The Democratic takeover of city politics was epitomized by the thuggish Five Points neighborhood, a brawling, lawless, and licentious slum a few blocks north of City Hall in lower Manhattan. The Five Points turf was ruled by Irish gangs with names such as Dead Rabbits, Bowery Boys, Roach Guards, and Plug Uglies. Tammany ingratiated itself with the gangs and harnessed the rising political power of Irish immigrants in the Sixth Ward by running for elective office street brawlers, saloon owners, and gambling operators. This Democratic political farm system produced the likes of Fernando Wood, John Morrissey, William Marcy "Boss" Tweed, and others in a colorful rogues' gallery whose ascendancy transformed New York's Common Council into a body nicknamed "Forty Thieves."

Refocusing on the state of affairs in Manhattan following the Civil War and Reconstruction, the Republicans set about reconstructing a New York political system they had neglected. The Roosevelts and their socially elite peers took aim at Democratic corruption and struggled to wrest control of local government from the growing lower classes, who they believed perpetuated the social ills of poverty, illiteracy, alcoholism, and other vices. The Committee on Municipal Reform of the Union League Club—a group of pedigreed Republicans with membership drawn from the city's social and business elite, including Theodore Roosevelt

Sr. and later his son—was launched in 1865 with the goal of cleaning Tammany's "Augean stable of its accumulated corruption." With Democrats and their Irish thugs so deeply entrenched in city politics, Republicans continued to maneuver mostly on the state level by electing state legislators who could override local government and supplant municipal corruption through reform legislation. Roosevelt fit the bill, and his career uncertainty coincided fortuitously with stepped-up efforts of Republican leaders trolling for electable candidates to send to Albany.

Within the Twenty-first District, Roosevelt's apprenticeship began at Morton Hall, a proving ground for political aspirants. Its shabbiness belied the power of the place. Located on East Fifty-ninth Street over a store and saloon, it was a gloomy expanse with all the accoutrements of a warehouse. Aside from crude wooden benches and brass spittoons, the only attempts at adornment were portraits of General Ulysses S. Grant and the hall's namesake, Governor Levi P. Morton. Political meetings were held once or twice a month and drew mostly working-class Irish men from the neighborhood, with a preponderance of saloon keepers. Morton Hall was an awakening for the sheltered Theodore in many respects. Members told coarse stories, the scent of beer and liquor on their breath, and punctuated their anecdotes with expertly delivered streams of frothy brown tobacco juice. The regulars played cards for money in the evenings. The rugged muscularity of the place nonetheless appealed to Theodore, even if the men's vices repulsed him and reminded him of how radically he was departing from his father's advice.

At Morton Hall, Jake Hess ran the meetings from a platform at one end of the room, where he sat at a small table. Hess was in his mid-thirties, almost six feet tall, powerfully built, confident, and secure in his political appointment as commissioner of Charities and Corrections. Hess was known to break ranks with the Republican Party leaders and forge his own political paths. He demanded nothing stronger than ice water for his libation. Some suggested it was what ran in Hess's veins, for he viewed politics with the cold, calculating, and emotion-free eye of a veteran of many campaigns.

Theodore's first visits, in the fall of 1880, had been clandestine ones. When his family caught wind of his secret ventures, they were not amused. As a kind of chaperone to protect the family's good name, Roosevelt's cousin, Emlen Roosevelt, a close friend of Theodore's since boyhood and later an investment banker in Roosevelt & Son, tagged along to the initial political gatherings.

> I went with him into Morton Hall—and joined the ranks of the political workers. I dropped out after a year because I could not give the time to it and I did not relish the personnel of that organization. But Theodore stuck to it. He had the personality and the spirit and he was able to impress these people.[63]

Family members were against his newfound interest, except for Uncle Rob. Robert Barnhill Roosevelt, whom Theodore admired, had served in Congress as a Tammany Democrat. He was known as a reformer who worked to increase the number of jobs for the poor and as a champion of clean government who crusaded to stamp out corruption.

Like Robert, his father's associates, who also happened to be some of the most prominent men in Manhattan, were also supportive. They not only blessed Theodore's unorthodox pursuit as a promising representative of their class, they wholeheartedly provided funds for it. Roosevelt was in an enviable position, enjoying an embarrassment of riches the likes of which any other neophyte political candidate could only dream. His backers included a *Who's Who* of Manhattan's wealthy elite: Joseph H. Choate, J. Pierpont Morgan, William Evarts, Elihu Root, and Morris K. Jessup.

Still, the most important referendum on his assessment of a political run came from within his own household. His sister Corinne recalled in her memoir the raised eyebrows. "Many were the criticisms of his friends and acquaintances," she wrote. "At that time, even more than now, politics was considered something far removed from the life of anyone brought up to other spheres than that of mudslinging and corruptions."[64] Yet they could not stop him. Theodore worked his way up the organization and won appointment to the executive committee of the Young Republicans in the spring of 1881.

Jake Hess had been doing his own reconnoitering, spurred by his reading of a restive constituency in the Twenty-first Assembly District by the fall of 1881. The voters had turned against his handpicked incumbent, William Trimble, a loyal Stalwart of machine politics, and sent strong signals they would not reelect him. Trimble was the sacrificial lamb for the leadership's misreading of public support for a nonpartisan street-cleaning bill in the State Legislature. While it might have cleansed Manhattan's foul avenues, the party machinery opposed it out of a fear that it might undermine their control. Since Trimble was tainted by the street-cleaning disgrace, Hess needed a compromise candidate to send up the river to Albany. He believed he'd found one in Roosevelt. Theodore brought to the campaign his family's socially prominent name, his father's reputation as a man of morals and generous philanthropy, and his amazing energy. Roosevelt ran on a platform of clean streets and clean politics that "astounded old-politicians by the fire he put into the staid residents of the brownstone district, who were little in the habit of bothering about elections," wrote Jacob Riis, the social critic and writer who later became a close ally of Roosevelt's.[65]

Roosevelt worked his own contacts and got out the vote, targeting Harvard University athletes and other acquaintances. He knew his pledge of independence would appeal to young voters. In his speeches Roosevelt stressed that he was "owned by no man" and would take his seat in the Assembly "untrammelled and unpledged." If elected to serve the Twenty-first District, Roosevelt vowed he "would obey no boss and serve no clique." Roosevelt's campaign message echoed the most important and lasting lessons he had taken away from Harvard, which biographer William Harbaugh described as "self-reliance, energy, courage, the power of insisting on his own rights and the sympathy that makes him regardful of the rights of others."[66]

He won easily. Roosevelt received 3,490 votes to 1,989 for Democrat Dr. W. W. Strew—nearly twice the margin of victory for previous Republicans. Strew entered the campaign with baggage, having been dismissed for incompetence as director of the Blackwell's Lunatic Asylum. The election had personal overtones for Roosevelt. Strew and his political hack cronies had been objects of enmity for Roosevelt's late father; reform of the state's asylums for the insane had been a special goal of the senior Roosevelt. Roosevelt also rode the support of the party's leadership in the Republican district. Given those factors, the victory was less stunning than it might have appeared. To Choate, he wrote on November 10, 1881,

> As I feel that I owe both my nomination and election more to you than to any other one man, I wish to tell you how I have appreciated both your kind sympathy and the support you have given me. I have taken a somewhat heavy burden of responsibility upon my shoulders, and I regret that I have, of necessity, had so little experience; but at least I shall endeavour to do my work honestly.[67]

That same day, he wrote to a Harvard friend, Charles Washburn, "Too True! Too True! I have become a 'political hack.' Finding it would not interfere much with my law I accepted the nomination to the assembly and was elected by a 1,500 majority, heading the ticket by 600 votes. But don't think I am going into politics after this year, for I am not."[68]

Roosevelt's election came at a time of upheaval on the national political scene, following the assassination of President James Garfield, who died in September of 1881 after being shot twice by a disgruntled office seeker from New York, Charles J. Guiteau. Garfield was succeeded by Vice President Chester A. Arthur, of New York, a lawyer and leader of the Stalwart faction of the Republican Party—that is, a machine man. As a reform Republican, Roosevelt not only took issue with Arthur's agenda, but he carried the added bitterness of the fact that Arthur had beaten out his father in the tainted appointment for New York's collector of customs to the Port of New York four years earlier.

Roosevelt had beaten one hack, but his party and his country were being run by another.

Chapter 3

★ ★ ★ ★ ★

ASSEMBLY

I intended to be one of the governing class.

The five-hour train ride from Manhattan, north along the Hudson River for one hundred and fifty miles to Albany, was familiar to Theodore Roosevelt from his boyhood vacations in the Adirondacks. In those instances, though, Albany was only a whistle-stop, a brief pause that allowed passengers to stretch their legs on the platform before continuing northward. There weren't many Manhattan patricians who got off the train in Albany in the late nineteenth century.

It was not love at first sight. Roosevelt belittled Albany as that "dear, dull old Dutch city." There was no welcoming ceremony or entourage for him on January 2, 1882, though he was met by the sight of the jagged skeleton of the new State Capitol building, rising like layers of a gaudy wedding cake at the top of State Street Hill far above the riverside railbed.

Roosevelt brought to Albany his father's letters, which he kept nearby and referred to as "talismans against evil." In one, from December 16, 1877, just after Roscoe Conkling's defeat of the collector of port appointment, his father wrote, "The 'Machine politicians' have shown their colors . . . I feel sorry for the country however as it shows the power of partisan politicians who think of nothing higher than their own interests, and I feel for your future. We cannot stand so corrupt a government for any great length of time."

If Roosevelt had come to Albany to take up his father's reformist efforts, he could not avoid his father's old foes. As the new Republican assemblyman from the Twenty-first District, Roosevelt would come under the thumb of Conkling, all-powerful boss of the New York State Republican machine. There was a personal edge to Roosevelt's animosity toward the boss. He blamed Conkling for destroying his father's political career before it got started and, in the process, contributing to his father's early death. Revenge against the Roosevelt family's nemesis would not be easy. Conkling stood six feet three inches tall and was powerfully built, "blond and gigantic as a Viking," according to a correspondent. Alongside Conkling, Roosevelt looked like a pipsqueak and his position as a freshman assemblyman only exaggerated the political mismatch. Conkling had a way of reducing the size of his adversaries even further with what Republican reformer George William Curtis called "the Mephistophelean leer and spit." Conkling's squarish head made his face look as tough as a block of granite and his unruly mop of hair came to a point in a way that resembled a ship's prow splitting waves.

Conkling was born in Albany; politics was the family business. His father was a well-connected congressman, federal judge, and a leader of New York's Whig Party. Conkling's wife, Julia Seymour, was the sister of New York Governor Horatio Seymour. Conkling rose in the U.S. House of Representatives, was elected to the U.S. Senate, and was rewarded for his campaign support of President Ulysses S. Grant by being given the reins of state patronage in New York. Conkling took Grant's bequest and built it into a machine in Albany the old-fashioned way: by dividing the spoils of victory among his handpicked lieutenants, local bosses, and ward heelers, all arranged in a hierarchy lorded over by the blond behemoth.

Conkling was a textbook Republican Stalwart, whose goal was to preserve the status quo and thus retain his grip on power. He was a quarrelsome, surly, and vengeful boss who attacked reformers like the Roosevelts, senior and junior, by derisively labeling them "man-milliners"—men who make and sell women's clothing, a thinly veiled allusion to homosexuals. James Garfield, who in his run for the presidency caught the brunt of the boss's fury, described Conkling as "a great fighter, inspired more by his hates than his loves." Garfield absorbed Conkling's assault after stealing the Republican nomination from Conkling's crony, former President Grant, in the presidential campaign of 1880. The defeat began to erode the fear factor that had made Conkling seem so invincible. The wounding of his reputation deepened when Conkling was caught in a scandalous extramarital affair in 1881 with Mrs. William Sprague, a senator's wife, who happened to be the daughter of Chief Justice Salmon Chase. Later that same year, newly inaugurated President Garfield rejected two of Conkling's top appointees to key posts in his cabinet, thus serving notice that Conkling's days of running the Empire State's spoils system as his own private bank account were numbered.

In a fit of pique, Conkling resigned from the Senate in the spring of 1881 and convinced New York's junior senator, Thomas C. Platt, also to quit in a nose-thumbing act of unanimity against Garfield. A political cartoon of the day showed Platt as a small boy sticking out of Conkling's pocket, with a card labeled "Me, too!" in one of his hands. The phrase resonated and entered the political lexicon as a derogatory label pinned on liberal Republicans for a lack of originality and spine. Roosevelt had no use for "Me, too!" Republicans or any others afraid to voice their independence. That was not the end of it, though. In the small, incestuous world of Albany politics, Platt and Roosevelt would square off in a later era in which reformers, Stalwarts, Half-Breeds, and "Me, too!" Republicans were still very much at war.

When Roosevelt entered the Assembly in 1882, his timing

was fortuitous in terms of taking the fight to Conkling. Throughout that year and the next, Conkling, the ex-senator, was coming to terms with how badly he had miscalculated his clout as boss as he watched his political power leaking away like air from a punctured balloon. Both Conkling and Platt stepped down under the assumption that the New York State Legislature, whose care and feeding they had managed, would show their solidarity for their out-of-work leaders by campaigning hard and contributing generously to ensure the prompt reelection of Conkling and Platt. That scenario never played out.

Roosevelt was the beneficiary. During the new assemblyman's first year in Albany, Conkling's grip on power was gradually disintegrating. The pipsqueak didn't have to fear being obliterated by the blond Viking after all. Conkling grew increasingly embittered, dropped out of politics, and rejected a Supreme Court nomination. He died in 1888.

On the other side of the aisle, Tammany's John Kelly controlled the Democratic machine when Roosevelt arrived in Albany. His mission was to rebuild the organization after the disintegration of the Tweed Ring. Boss Tweed and his larcenous cabal were undone by scandals over kickbacks from extravagant overcharges in construction of the New York County Courthouse (dubbed the Tweed Courthouse), in addition to an extensive and complex web of swindles, payoffs, bribes, and assorted political corruptions. After his arrest and incarceration, Tweed escaped and went on the lam to Cuba and Spain for a year before he was recaptured by U.S. authorities in 1876. Tweed died in prison two years later. Kelly was tapped as Tweed's successor in order to clean up Tammany's tainted reputation. He gained the nickname "Honest" John Kelly in the bargain, and although his means were more efficient and less extravagantly corrupt, his ends of tightening his grip on power were the same as Tweed's. Kelly, breaking into politics in the 1840s, became an effective voice against the nativist movement and battled the anti-Catholic and anti-immigrant rhetoric of the Know-Nothing Party. He was elected to Congress in 1854, the only Roman Catholic at the time, and used religion to political advantage. It was Kelly who first harnessed Irish-Catholic immigrants—New York's largest minority—and transformed the disorganized masses into loyal, faithful supporters. Kelly could claim credit for a new "Irish Tammany," which had more potential for growth and longevity than anything Tweed had imagined. There was a backlash against Kelly, though. Criticism of his Catholicism came from, among others, Sir Lepel Griffin, a British administrator who published his impressions of New York in the 1880s for the *Fortnight Weekly* in Britain.

It is what is known in America as Boss rule and it has cost the people many millions, in waste, peculation, and undisguised and unblushing robbery, which is the price they have had to pay for the pretence of freedom. Matters are now less openly scandalous than of old, but the same system is in full force. Boss Kelly, who sways the destinies of New York, has been able, from his near connection with an Irish cardinal, to defend his position with spiritual as well as temporal weapons, and the whole Irish Catholic population vote solid as he bids them. The result of a generation of this regime has been disastrous.[1]

Kelly was admired for his intelligence and organization, as well as feared for his eruptions of anger and his vindictive streak. Lieutenants in his organization did not dare cross the jowly, intense, and hefty six-footer, because once they were on the boss's bad side, they stayed there. Kelly wasn't afraid to get physical, either. As a young tough who grew up on Manhattan's gritty Lower East Side, he had been a formidable amateur boxer who used his fighting skills on behalf of different gangs he joined. He didn't mind flexing his muscle as sheriff of New York, a position that gave him opportunities to enrich himself by pocketing jail fees for which there was little oversight. As boss, Kelly bought legitimacy by persuading prominent and respected Republican officials to join Tammany and parade their membership. Another Kelly innovation was to codify a previously loose practice of assessing candidates a fee commensurate with their office in exchange for Tammany's support. These pay-to-play funds were collected and passed out the day before the election to pay the party machinery of poll watchers and ward heelers who got out the vote. The practice came to be called "Dough Day." Kelly kept the cash flow steady by widespread, low-key extortion: requiring a money drop from merchants who wanted to stay open extended hours, say, or a fishmonger who wanted to display his catch on a street corner where it was prohibited. In Honest John Kelly's view, such kickbacks to Tammany were merely the cost of doing business: the system did not disrupt the church attendance of the boss, a devout Catholic.

Conkling and Kelly were locked in a close fight for control of the Legislature, with neither Republicans nor Democrats able to build a large or lasting majority in the years leading up to Roosevelt's arrival. In the decade since the days of Boss Tweed, there had only been incremental improvement; Roosevelt's per diem pay in Albany was fifteen dollars, compared to the outlandish three hundred dollars per diem in Tweed's heyday of looting the state.[2] The Conkling and Kelly era still thrived on the spoils system, rewarding the fruits of party victory to loyal partisans. The bosses were the dispensers of the spoils and thus had enormous power. "Each had under his direction a train of smaller local bosses and the machine, first of the one part, and then of the other, managed to divide the spoils to the satisfaction of all the bosses," according to a nineteenth-century political observer. "There were few statesmen then in local politics; nearly every man was a spoilsman."[3]

The Tweed Courthouse was the symbol of Tammany's graft

and the excesses of political corruption, but the State Capitol in Albany was a colossal boondoggle in its own right. Still a work in progress when Roosevelt arrived, the rococo heap of pale gray granite would take three decades to build, longer than the construction of the Great Pyramid of Cheops, and cost twice as much as the national Capitol in Washington, D.C. Three architects, eleven governors, scathing Senate Finance Committee reports, and twenty-two million dollars would not be enough to complete what had been slammed by critics as "a public calamity." As Roosevelt churned up Albany's State Street Hill for the first time as a public servant, his Ivy League idealism slammed into the coarse reality of Conkling, Kelly, and construction crews at the Capitol building—each mired in political corruption.

A freshman assemblyman barely rated a hello from veteran legislators. Roosevelt's challenge was to find his niche amid this obstreperous and fractious bunch, overrun by galloping egos and divided into cliques—none of whom wanted any reformers. One of the most famous subcultures Roosevelt first encountered was the Black Horse Cavalry, a group of politicians with little in common save for their common greed. Greed was hardly a shameful pursuit, since an estimated one third, or about seventy members, of the Legislature made it clear that their votes could be purchased for the right price by a corporation, trust, or special interest group.[4] Many of those who weren't overtly corrupt or on the take were nonetheless acquiescent, fearful of not getting reelected without the boss's support. Still others were plainly over their heads, simple men from rural districts who lacked the formal or legal education to make sense of the nuances and loopholes the wily special interests had written into bills. Roosevelt arrived with far-above-average armature against his fellow members' most common failures of venality, stupidity, and fearfulness. Still, his initial place on the political food chain was somewhere between plankton and sea slug.

At 135 pounds, he had only one leg's worth of the weight of

some of the most entrenched lawmakers, who ballooned to obese proportions on the river of rich foods from wealthy businessmen. Albany was a bottomless feeding trough in literal as well as figurative ways. Champagne, oysters, roasts, chocolate, caviar, and cordials—not to mention wads of cash—were lavished upon assemblymen and senators to sway their votes on important legislation. In 1882, the goodies had never been more abundant, thanks to the even division of power between Conkling's and Kelly's parties. In the Assembly, the larger and lower house, the Democrats held a very slim majority. Roosevelt's first term promised to be a long and bitterly contested one.

Roosevelt himself was not without inner conflict about party affiliation. Among his relatives and close family friends, Democrats were nearly as numerous as Republicans. Robert Roosevelt, his uncle, and George C. Lee, his father-in-law, argued the merits of the Democratic Party with Theodore. He also heard the Democratic perspective from Poultney Bigelow, a good friend, and from those who formed his family's inner circle—including the Saltonstalls, the Delanos, and the Hyde Park Roosevelts. Yet, in his *Autobiography*, Theodore opined that "a young man of my bringing up and convictions could join only the Republican Party." Both parties had machines, and they shared the dishonor of Albany in the wake of the Civil War. In northern cities like New York, the Democrats were still the riffraff, the Republicans the aristocrats. His cousin Nicholas Roosevelt described the young assemblyman as "brash and bumptious and still sharing the nineteenth century concept of a class-conscious society."[5] Although his background was thoroughly patrician, however, Roosevelt purposely, at times radically, broke with the dicta of the privileged class. In speeches he attacked America's "plutocrats" and "beneficiaries of privilege." Roosevelt's political agenda of progressive change was aimed at the newly energized middle class, rather than at the immigrants of the slums or the patricians of the mansions. Roosevelt spent his entire political career at once defending his seemingly traitorous about-face toward his class and articulating the mission of the emerging progressive Republicanism that seized the country in the period leading up to the First World War.

Although he came in as a featherweight amid Albany's political bruisers, Roosevelt carried himself with the bravado of a heavyweight. His blue-gray eyes squinted behind thick pince-nez, and his large, round head made his neck and shoulders seem scrawny. Up from the Hudson River flats to the Capitol atop State Street Hill, he strode in what an Albany newspaper correspondent called "elastic movements." The self-assured, dashing figure—some might say arrogant—was evident to an observer who described Roosevelt as a "blond young man with eyeglasses, English side whiskers, and Dundreary drawl in his speech."[6] (Lord Dundreary was the aristocratic English nitwit in a popular satirical play of the day.)

Just twenty-three years old, not only was Roosevelt the youngest member ever elected to the Assembly at that point, but his reputation preceded him thanks to *The Naval War of 1812,* published shortly before he arrived. It was an ambitious military history favorably reviewed on both sides of the Atlantic. It sold through eight editions and was later reprinted as part of the official British history of the Royal Navy. *Harper's* magazine called Roosevelt's book "the most accurate . . . the most cool and impartial, and in some respects the most intrepid, account that has yet appeared of the naval actions of the war of 1812." The *New York Times* called Roosevelt's history "an excellent one in every respect, and shows in so young an author the best promises for a good historian—fearlessness of statement, caution, endeavor to be impartial, and a brisk and interesting way of telling events." Not every young assemblyman is invited to meet in Boston with the celebrated novelist Henry James, but such was Roosevelt's new fame.

Upon his initial arrival in Albany, he stayed a few days at the home of a family friend, William Bayard Van Rensselaer, a member of one of the capital's prominent Dutch families. Van Rensselaer offered Roosevelt a room in his house at 15 Washington Avenue, across the street from the Capitol. Roosevelt wrote his sister Bamie that he was staying with Van Rensselaer "for a day or two looking up our future rooms, which I do not like to decide on without having Alice see." That first winter in Albany, Roosevelt and Alice would rent lodgings in Albany at the Delavan House but spend their weekends in New York with his mother and siblings or with her family in Boston. Roosevelt's family would gather in their mother's Fifty-seventh Street brownstone to hear Theodore's entertaining recaps of each week's events in Albany. "Many were the long talks, many the humorous accounts given us of his adventures as an Assemblyman," his sister Corinne recalled, "and all the time, we, his family, realized that an influence unusual in that New York State Assembly was beginning to be felt . . . ardent and earnest, who pleaded for right thinking."[7] Staying in Albany for the weekend was a last option for the couple, although they made the best of such occasions. "Adjourned, but as Alice and I are all settled here," Roosevelt wrote in his legislative diary, "with our books and everything, as comfortable as possible, we decided to spend Sunday here in Albany."[8]

The newspaper reporters who stayed at the Delavan House, Albany's prime hotel and once the lair of corruption favored by Boss Tweed, were the first to take notice of Roosevelt as an oddity amid the pols. Even though the temperature in early January when he arrived in Albany struggled to break out of single digits, Roosevelt walked the four city blocks from the Capitol building to the Delavan "wearing a broad smile instead of an overcoat," a correspondent noted.[9] His manners were foppish, his voice shrill and sometimes falsetto, with a Harvard locution. When he appeared in a purple satin waistcoat on his way to the Assembly chamber, he looked as if he were heading for a night at the opera. One of the reporters clustered at the Delavan's cigar stand, smoking and trolling for news, George Spinney of the *New York Times* recounted his first impression of Roosevelt, whose "step across the hotel corridor was quick and vigorous, his whole manner alert." He shook hands with Spinney and gave a "good, honest laugh" that revealed his most prominent physical feature. "His teeth seemed to be all over his face," Spinney observed. "He was genial, emphatic, earnest but green as grass." After Roosevelt left, the consensus was that he was "an uncommon fellow, distinctly different."[10]

Roosevelt's appearance at the New York State Legislature was no less striking. Even on residents of Albany—who took little interest in downstate legislators, or their own assemblyman or senator, for that matter—Roosevelt made an impression. Huybertie Pruyn Hamlin, born in 1873, never forgot seeing Roosevelt for the first time as a young girl.

> Mother and I were walking down Washington Avenue by Lord's corner, at Hawk Street, when a man ran out of the Capitol, his hat in one hand and his right arm waving, we did not know at what. He seemed very excited as he shook hands with Mother. He talked about a bill he was pushing and how he was going to herd the members. He dived off down the street very suddenly, and we went our way along Hawk Street.
>
> "Who is that, Mama, and will he herd sheep?" I asked.
>
> "No," said Mother. "He will try to herd them. He is here to reform the state."[11]

Roosevelt wasted no time in setting himself apart from the other legislators. On the night of January 2, 1882, a few hours after his arrival in Albany, Roosevelt and the other Republican members of the Assembly were summoned to the Capitol for their opening caucus of the session. While his GOP colleagues milled about in the warmth of the Delavan House's lobby, awaiting their carriages, Roosevelt declined to ride the four blocks to the statehouse and stated his intention to walk. It was a bitterly cold night, with a breeze off the ice-choked Hudson River making for a numbing windchill. Roosevelt walked briskly across snowy sidewalks, up the steep grade of State Street and through the wintry gusts. Fellow legislators ensconced in comfortable carriages must have stared in disbelief and amusement. "He's a brilliant madman born a century too soon," was the assessment of Assemblyman Newton M. Curtis.[12]

His face flushed from exertion and the stinging cold still frosting his glasses, Roosevelt blew into the caucus meeting room, strode confidently to the front of the room, and sat down next to the chairman of the Republican conference. He was dressed in high formal fashion: silk top hat, cutaway coat with tails, gold-headed cane, gold watch and fob, hair parted in the center, and thick sideburns. He was every inch the young Knickerbocker dandy; his colleagues quickly dubbed him "Oscar Wilde." Others mocked the poseur as "Punkin-Lily" and "Jane-Dandy." But he was there to be noticed, and to address the caucus on the first order of business that session, electing a new Assembly Speaker.

The choice wouldn't be as matter-of-fact as in past years, since the Republicans had lost their majority in the Legislature's lower house. The 128 members of the Assembly were divided between 67 Democrats and 61 Republicans and it took 64 votes to win the speakership. Eight Tammany Hall–backed Democrats had a large enough voting bloc to wield considerable influence and to hold up the choice of a Speaker until the Tammany machine's conditions—essentially demands for leadership of powerful Assembly committees, which would put them in line for bribes—were met. The eight hacks were fuel for Roosevelt's morally righteous fires. "Not even one of them can string three intelligible sentences together to save his neck," he later wrote.[13] Roosevelt didn't kowtow to Republican unity in the Assembly either. He quickly pegged elder statesman of the Republicans and longtime Speaker Tom Alvord, of Onondaga County, as "corrupt" and "a bad old fellow." Roosevelt instead backed General George H. Sharpe, a former Speaker and Civil War hero. Alvord tried to dismiss Roosevelt as a fringe gadfly: "He is just a damn fool," said the man who had been in the Legislature longer than Roosevelt had been alive. Alvord's math was simple: "There are sixty and one-half [Republican] members in the Assembly. Sixty plus that damned dude," he said after the January 2 caucus.

For a young man of boundless energy and a craving for action, Roosevelt's first week in Albany was a disappointment. The obstructionist Tammany bloc, led by Kelly, refused to support any of the candidates for Speaker. With no leader in place, the house rules were inoperative and the Assembly was paralyzed. The days dragged on, especially long and monotonous for Roosevelt. Behind-the-scenes negotiating and maneuvering were fierce, but Roosevelt was shut out of it. He grew gloomy and depressed as he made the meaningless trek up the hill to the Capitol each day, answered the absurd formality of a shadow roll call in the Assembly chamber, and quickly left again since no other business could be conducted. The roster of the Assembly in Roosevelt's first term hinted at the extent of legislative featherbedding. The chamber employed a janitor and two assistant janitors; a head doorkeeper and four assistant doorkeepers; a sergeant at arms and two assistant sergeants at arms; a postmaster and an assistant postmaster; a supervisor of documents and an assistant supervisor of documents. This policy of full employment extended to the Speaker's Room, which had a clerk, two assistants, and a head messenger. The Clerk's Room employed a financial clerk, a bank messenger, and two clerks' messengers. On and on the list of employees grew throughout the legislative offices.

Roosevelt received his first taste of speaking on the floor of the ornate Assembly chamber two weeks after his arrival. He rose to disagree with discussions among some Republicans who talked about joining the Democratic majority to break Tammany's stranglehold. "While in New York I talked with several gentlemen who have large commercial interests at stake and they do not seem to care whether the deadlock is broken or not," Roosevelt said in a strained whine and rushed delivery confounded by nervousness.[14] Spinney likened Roosevelt's inflection to "a man biting ten-penny nails." Roosevelt was nonetheless heartened by claps of approval from some members and an item in the *New York Evening Post* that praised his remarks and said that the freshman Assemblyman had made "a very favorable impression."

Roosevelt filled the idle winter days during the deadlock with long walks through the icy streets of Albany. Isaac Hunt, who once stayed at the same Albany lodging as Roosevelt, recalled that he could always tell when his friend had returned from a weekend in Manhattan because Theodore threw open the front door and bounded up the stairs; he'd be halfway up the flight before the front door banged shut behind him. Roosevelt also kept in shape and staved off boredom by boxing and wrestling in Albany. He was pleased when a sparring partner came along. "A young fellow turned up who was a second-rate prize-fighter, the son of one of my old boxing teachers," Roosevelt wrote in his *Autobiography.* "For several weeks I had him come round to my rooms in the morning to put on the gloves with me for half an hour. Then he suddenly stopped, and some days later I received a letter of woe from him from the jail. I found that he was by profession a burglar, and merely followed boxing as the amusement of his lighter moments, or when business was slack."[15]

The sparring practice was more than just for exercise, given the political climate of the time. As part of a ritual of initiation known as the "scrimmage," Roosevelt was attacked at the Delavan House. It was an attempt to put the cocky Harvard aristocrat in his place and to intimidate him away from his reformist leanings. Roosevelt's enemies in the Legislature hired "Stubby"

Collins, a slugger who had punched the lights out of many men. His assignment was to intercept the swaggering Roosevelt and to "do him up." As Roosevelt was leaving his room at the Delavan, he passed the door leading to the buffet and was surrounded by a knot of toughs. Collins plowed into Roosevelt and angrily demanded to know why Theodore had run into him. Collins took a swing at Roosevelt. "The blow never reached its mark, but it is recorded that Stubby was, in a few moments, a fit subject for the anxious care of his friends."[16]

On another occasion in the Assembly chamber, as members debated various compromise proposals to break the Speaker deadlock, Roosevelt threatened a fellow member from Brooklyn, John Shanley, far larger and older than Roosevelt and known for his tenacity. Shanley ridiculed Roosevelt for hogging the floor and called his long-winded speeches grandstanding. The freshman assemblyman removed his glasses and addressed Democratic Speaker Charles Patterson: "Mr. Speaker, I appreciate the fact that this is neither the proper place nor the time to make an adequate reply to the remarks of the gentleman from Brooklyn," Roosevelt said, his voice rising and dripping with sarcasm, "but if the gentleman will step outside of the Capitol, I will give him the only kind of reply that his remarks deserve."[17] Shanley grew silent, looked away, and made no reply. Roosevelt savored the moment and remained standing for a long beat before taking his seat.

While the standoff over electing a Speaker was dragging on for several weeks, no committee positions could be appointed or bills sponsored. "Stupid and monotonous" was Roosevelt's description of the holdup. He devoured the newspapers, which criticized the Assembly for its inaction. William Hudson of the *Brooklyn Eagle* described watching Roosevelt's breakfast ritual at the Delavan House. "He threw each paper as he finished it, on the floor unfolded, until at the end there was, on either side of him, a pile of loose papers as high as the table."[18]

It was also during the deadlock that Roosevelt actually did

pummel a fellow assemblyman. Roosevelt was trying to kill another day of inaction by walking around the capital city with two other assemblymen he had befriended, Isaac Hunt and William "Billy" O'Neil. Hunt, whose district was in Jefferson County on Lake Ontario along the Canadian border, had not liked Roosevelt at first. "We almost shouted with laughter to think that the most veritable representative New York dude had come to the Chamber," Hunt said. "After a little our attention was drawn upon what he had to say, because there was force in his remarks."[19] Roosevelt had not helped matters when he first quickly sized up the young Hunt and sneered, "You are from the country." But they became fast friends and allies.

O'Neil was an assemblyman from the Adirondack Mountains, where Roosevelt had spent several summer vacations. He ran a small store in Franklin County. Although Roosevelt was not much of a drinker, he stopped on the walk with Hunt and O'Neil at a tavern near the Capitol that was popular with legislators. There Roosevelt was an easy target. J. J. Costello, a powerful assemblyman and the Tammany members' candidate for Speaker, made disparaging remarks about Roosevelt's dandified outfit. Roosevelt, in no mood to shrug off the insult, promptly decked Costello, who crumpled to the floor. Costello struggled to his feet. "He got up and he hit him again, and when he got up he hit him again," Hunt said later of the incident.[20] Costello didn't fight back after the third knockdown and Roosevelt instructed Costello to wash up. Hunt recalled Roosevelt's words to his foe: "When you are in the presence of gentlemen, conduct yourself like a gentleman," he told Costello, before buying the Tammanyite a beer and making a show of having him drink it.[20]

The Tammany blockade finally broke in early February. Democrat Charles Patterson, a compromise candidate deemed least objectionable by the warring factions, polled enough votes to be named Speaker.

Roosevelt's political agenda and his pugilism quickly

emerged in an incident that made the rounds in Albany and assumed near-mythic proportions. The field of battle was a bill to assist the construction of additional terminal facilities in New York City for Jay Gould's Manhattan Elevated Railway. Roosevelt's corruption radar had already zeroed in on the infamous financier, but as a Manhattanite and representative of the Twenty-first Assembly District, he considered the expansion necessary. The railway bill was reported to the Cities Committee, a choice appointment Roosevelt had received through the intercession of a relative. His uncle, the well-connected Democrat Robert Roosevelt, had asked his friend Michael C. Murphy, a powerful Democratic assemblyman and chairman of the Cities Committee, to appoint Roosevelt and to keep an eye on his quarrelsome nephew. Murphy saw he could use Roosevelt's energy and spirit to reduce his own workload and began grooming the freshman Republican. In short order, Murphy stepped back and allowed his young protégé to fill in as acting chairman of the committee. Roosevelt was acting in this capacity when the railway bill was presented, and he vowed to see the legislation through his committee and to preserve it from the taint of blackmail or scandal. Roosevelt anticipated trouble from a couple of committee members whom he called "pretty rough characters," men susceptible to Gould's financial enticements.

Roosevelt came prepared the day his committee met in a room of the Capitol to take action on the railway bill. The acting chairman took his place at the conference table, concealing the leg of a broken chair on the floor beside him. It was not "big stick" foreign policy, but it was an effective small stick for local politics. Roosevelt wasted no time in moving that the railway bill be reported to the full Assembly for a vote. Gould's forces did not want the light of publicity shed on their backdoor dealings, so Roosevelt's motion was voted down. Those paying off committee members wanted the bill quietly held until it could be slipped unnoticed into the flurry of late-night legislation rammed through at the end of the session. Familiar with the ploy, the acting chairman next moved that the bill be reported out unfavorably. He was shot down once more, while some of his foes "leered at me with sneering insolence," Roosevelt wrote in his *Autobiography*. "I then put the bill in my pocket and announced that I would report it anyhow. This almost precipitated a riot . . . The riot did not come off; partly, I think, because the opportune production of the chair-leg had a sedative effect, and partly owing to wise counsels from one or two of my opponents."[21] Simply reaching under the table and displaying the small stick in a defiant gesture was enough to allow Roosevelt to prevail. The bill went to the Assembly.

Reaction to the railway bill on the floor of the Assembly was anticlimactic. The bill stalled as legislators waited for Gould and company to sweeten the pot. Roosevelt was yanked from his control of the bill and the railway measure was passed off to an older assemblyman with experience in sleight-of-hand payoffs to legislators. The railway bill finally slid quietly through both houses of the Legislature and into law without a public outcry. The system worked as the bosses devised it. Money flowed to the Conkling and Kelly organizations to pay for upcoming campaigns, key lawmakers received envelopes thick with cash, and the unwitting citizenry of New York footed the bill in the form of higher taxes. Roosevelt, the chair leg no longer relevant, watched the river of corruption flow past and fumed. He needed a better weapon.

Roosevelt eventually figured out that he could use the media against the machines of both parties. His quotable nature made him a media darling, and he cultivated the correspondents by making himself readily available for interviews. The press corps covering the Assembly numbered thirty correspondents from across New York State; veteran reporters had seats right in front of the Assembly Speaker's dais, while newer arrivals sat in an overflow section in the back of the chamber.

The Legislative Correspondents Association, in lore handed

down by many generations of reporters covering the Capitol, recalls Roosevelt's ability as a publicity hound. To display his physical fitness, Roosevelt made a habit of dashing up the Capitol's seventy-seven granite steps two at a time. The story goes that Roosevelt had a standing deal with correspondents that he would offer an exclusive interview to any one of the scribes who could beat him in the dash up the steps—and retain enough breath to pose questions. None of the reporters is alleged to have ever beaten him. Of course, he found many other ways to capture their attention as well. The freshman assemblyman had star power, and he received far more coverage than any neophyte politician could have dreamed of or bought. Deep resentment festered among more senior lawmakers, who considered him a shameless self-promoter.

As a writer, he exacted revenge with a legislative diary, the sort of petty, yet wickedly funny journal the boy who gets beat up in the schoolyard might scribble as a secret way of getting back at his tormentors. Never intended for publication or shown to others, the diary was simply a method for private venting of frustrations and an exercise that kept his literary skills sharp. Thomas Jefferson had once kept careful track of all political actions and statements of his fellow politicians, but it was nothing like this:

> A number of Republicans, including most of their leaders, are bad enough but over half the Democrats, including almost all the City Irish, are vicious, stupid looking scoundrels with apparently not a redeeming trait. There are some twenty five Irish Democrats in the house, all either immigrants or the sons of immigrants . . . a stupid, sodden vicious lot, most of them being equally deficient in brains and virtue. The average Catholic Irishman of the first generation as represented in this Assembly, is a low, venal, corrupt and unintelligent brute.[22]

There was much more in that vein, and it got personal. He called Higgins "a vicious little Celtic nonentity from Buffalo." Dimon, a rough-edged rural Democrat, was "either dumb or an idiot—probably both." Even Murphy, his uncle's friend and the man who made him acting chairman of the Cities Committee, was mocked for "a ludicrously dignified manner . . . He adds a great deal of stupidity and a decided looseness of ideas as regards the 8th Commandment."

He cataloged his cohorts as he had once cataloged his specimens, but with far more attitude. They were "farmers, mechanics, a half-dozen liquor dealers, a cooper, a butcher, a tobacconist, a compositor, a typesetter, three newspapermen . . . and a pawnbroker." The Albany entries read like the Adirondack bird book, with short bursts of withering prose that displayed the diarist's sarcasm and arrogance. One enemy, John Rains, was said to have "the same idea of public life and civil service that a vulture has of dead sheep." He described McManus as "a huge, fleshy, unutterably coarse and lawless brute . . . more than suspected of having begun his life as a pickpocket."[23]

Roosevelt used his diary as a moralistic scorecard. He estimated that fully one third of the legislators were openly selling their positions and their votes for the best cash offer. Another tactic was to introduce a so-called strike bill. A legislator would cook up a bill that placed some sort of artificial limit or restriction on a corporation. The lawmaker would then make noise about pushing the bill through the Legislature, thus frightening the businessmen into handing over a bundle of cash through the intermediary of a lobbyist. The enriched legislator would then kill the bill, either by burying it in committee or by making sure it was voted down if it reached the floor of the Assembly. It was a significant form of supplemental income for the lawmakers. "For every one bill introduced corruptly to favor a corporation, there were at least ten introduced blackmailing corporations," Roosevelt wrote in his *Autobiography*. Other times such elaborate decisions were dispensed with and lobbyists brazenly worked their influence, not even bothering to hide cash and other payoffs. "I'm in politics working for my own pocket all the time. Same as you" was how one veteran Albany legislator bluntly put it.[24]

Roosevelt became a sleuth who quietly investigated the motivations and potential collusion behind bills. He was aided in these thorough legislative background checks by Mike Costello, an Irish Tammany Democrat from the Seventeenth District of New York City and unlikely ally of the Republican reformer. Costello broke ranks with the Democratic machine out of disgust with its corruption, much as Roosevelt had done on the Republican side. They became reformers and comrades in arms from opposite sides of the aisle in the Assembly. In the chamber, Roosevelt regularly rose from his seat near the front, looking more like a boy than a man. The other members kept talking over his shrill calls for the floor. "Mist-ah Speak-ah!" he keened in his high squawk of a voice. "Mist-ah Speak-ah!" It might take several minutes of Roosevelt's yelping before he would be recognized; sometimes he simply began his monologue anyway. Hunt and O'Neil looked up to Roosevelt for his boldness but also found his methods at times wildly erratic. Hunt recalled for biographer Hermann Hagedorn that Roosevelt was like "a Jack coming out of the box . . . He yelled and pounded his desk, and when they attacked him, he would fire back with all the venom imaginable. In those days he had no discretion at all . . . He was a perfect nuisance in that House."[25] Roosevelt raised such a ruckus that he was occasionally tossed from the chamber by a sergeant at arms. Roosevelt wore such ejections and rejections as a badge of honor.

Roosevelt did find a few members of the Assembly whom he both liked and respected. He praised Newton M. Curtis as a "capital fellow" and found one or two other colleagues who met his high standards. "On questions of elementary morality, we were heartily at one," Roosevelt said of Peter Kelly, a Brooklyn Democrat. And he applauded, of course, Isaac Hunt, the "thoroughly upright" young lawyer from Watertown, and Billy O'Neil, his trusted and closest friend.

Roosevelt formed strong opinions on issues he studied. "He went to the bottom of everything," recalled George Spinney. "By the end of the first session, he knew more about state politics than ninety percent of the others did."[26] He learned quickly in part by being able to juggle many matters in his mind simultaneously. Assembly colleagues recalled that he would burrow into his seat in the Assembly chamber, hunched over the desk, and read a book while keeping track of the proceedings on the floor and occasionally propelling himself to his feet to assault a fellow assemblyman with pointed questions and scathing interrogations.

Almost single-handedly, Roosevelt injected a spirit of reform into the 1882 session, a spirit that came to a head with a project not of his own making. In March, Roosevelt was tipped off by Hunt that an investigation of several insolvent insurance companies revealed financial fleecing by those in receivership of the failed firms. The irregularities amounted to hundreds of thousands of dollars in bogus fees and inflated expenses. Moreover, State Supreme Court Justice Theodore R. Westbrook, along with the judge's son and one of his cousins, was enriching himself at this trough to the tune of thousands of dollars through legal fees and other irregularities, according to Hunt's probe. Hunt urged Roosevelt to enter the fray and spearhead a campaign to impeach Westbrook. At first Roosevelt deferred, partly out of concern about the health of Alice, who had left Albany for gynecological surgery in New York City as the couple struggled to conceive a child. Furthermore, Roosevelt had expended a lot of political capital in unsuccessful efforts to curb the abuses of tenement cigar manufacturing by trying to raise wages for pieceworkers and force cigar companies to improve the grim working conditions. He also aimed at exposing the corruption of Manhattan Elevated Railway.

The impeachment of Judge Westbrook was "a very serious matter," Roosevelt told Hunt. He would think about it. He left Albany and took the train to Manhattan to be with his wife as she recovered from surgery. As his mind roamed over his legislative agenda, Roosevelt was nagged by a vague recollection of reading an article in the *New York Times* about Westbrook some months earlier. He paid a visit to the editorial offices of the *Times* on Park Row, where he pestered city editor Henry Lowenthal until he was granted access to the newspaper's morgue. He found the article. Three months earlier, on December 27, 1881, the *Times* had published a piece on Jay Gould's controversial acquisition of the lucrative Manhattan Elevated Railway. Critics of the deal alleged that Gould had played down and dirty with state regulations, cultivating insider information and corrupt officials to drive down the stock price 95 percent, to a rock-bottom level, before he bought the company. Gould had cheated Manhattan Elevated's regular shareholders of $15 million or so. The company had gone into bankruptcy, and then Judge Westbrook had declared it solvent and handed it to Gould.

He packed up several files, convinced the editor to come along, and teased apart the Gould-Westbrook web at his home at 6 West Fifty-seventh Street through the night and into the early morning hours. The sordid tale of Manhattan Elevated had begun a year earlier, when State Attorney General Hamilton Ward had sued the railway as an illegal, fraudulent corporation. Gould's operatives had apparently made him an offer he couldn't refuse, and the attorney general dropped his suit in favor of the benign declaration that Manhattan Elevated was guilty of nothing more than being broke. Publicly, Judge Westbrook also made a show of cracking down on Gould's fraud, although he had ruled in Gould's favor. Roosevelt's digging revealed that Westbrook not only presided over the court proceedings of Gould's acquisition of Manhattan Elevated, he actually held court sessions in Gould's office and appointed Gould's functionaries as receivers for the insolvent railway. Westbrook had never been challenged on this cozy arrangement and never answered critics' charges that he assisted Gould in the illegal stock manipulation or that he was rewarded with a kickback. Roosevelt seized upon an unpublished letter from Westbrook to Gould that had been leaked to the *Times* in which the judge wrote to the financier, "I am willing to go to the very verge of judicial discretion to protect your vast interests."[27] Here was the smoking gun that Roosevelt sought. In the early morning hours, he let the *Times* editor go and decided to spearhead an impeachment campaign.

Roosevelt returned to Albany on March 28 and told Hunt of his decision. Roosevelt was planning to deliver a resolution demanding the investigation of both Judge Westbrook and Attorney General Ward. "I'll offer it tomorrow," he told Hunt.

What transpired in the Assembly on March 29 was enough to peel the paint on the red-and-blue rococo scrollwork that punctuated the gilded chamber. When Roosevelt rose and called for the privilege of the floor in his shrill, insistent trumpeting, his colleagues at first ignored what they assumed would be a routine point of parliamentary procedure raised by "that damned dude." Instead, reading for ten minutes from a legally worded resolution that included several clauses beginning *"whereas"* and ending *"be it therefore resolved,"* Roosevelt fired with both barrels. He called upon the Judiciary Committee to investigate Ward and Westbrook "on account of their official conduct in relation to suits brought against the Manhattan Railway" which Roosevelt said had not adequately "been explained nor fairly refuted."

The usual buzz of members speaking in clusters in the back of the chamber and aides conferring with assemblymen at their desks was silenced. In a fist-pounding storm, Roosevelt charged Gould, the industrialist Russell Sage, the influential financier Cyrus W. Field, and their Wall Street cronies with "stock-jobbing" to acquire the elevated railway. He called them "sharks" and "swindlers." "The men who were mainly concerned in this fraud are known throughout New York as men whose financial dishonesty is a matter of common notoriety," the *New York World* reported. Roosevelt likened them to Bowery thugs Reddy the Blacksmith, Owney Geoghegan, and other notorious criminals of the day.

As for Westbrook, he had placed "the whole road in the hands of swindlers," Roosevelt said. He added, "We have a right to demand that our judiciary should be kept beyond reproach and we have a right to demand that if we find men against whom there is not only suspicion, but almost a certainty that they have been in collusion with men whose interests were in conflict with the interests of the public, they shall, at least, be required to bring positive facts with which to prove there has not been collusion; and they ought themselves to have been the first to demand such an investigation."[28]

Writer Jacob Riis was deeply moved. "For sheer moral courage that act is probably supreme in Roosevelt's life thus far," Riis wrote. "He could not be blind to the apparently inevitable consequences. Yet he drew his sword and rushed apparently to destruction—alone, and at the very outset of his career, and in disregard of the pleadings of his closest friends and the plain dictates of political wisdom."[29]

Newspaper correspondents scribbled furiously. Roosevelt was making the best copy they'd had in years. The *New York Sun* praised Roosevelt's "boldness" and "almost scathing" attack. *Harper's Weekly* liked the way Roosevelt had finally stood up to the corrupt powers-that-be on the Assembly floor. The *New York Times* praised Roosevelt for a "most refreshing habit of calling men and things by their right names." In a single, audacious strike, Roosevelt had transformed his reputation from that of the dandified dude to a young reformer and trustbuster to watch. The new nickname the press gave Roosevelt pleased him: "the Scotch Terrier." And he wasn't bashful about accepting accolades for the bold legislative move he called "the hit of the season so far" in a letter to Alice.

Roosevelt's demand for an investigation exploded on the Assembly "like a bursting bombshell . . . powerful, wonderful," Hunt later described it. Of course Gould did not take it lying down. He had plenty of minions to call upon. At the time, he owned fully 10 percent of the nation's railroads, worth an astonishing sum, as well as a controlling interest in the Western Union Telegraph Company (along with it the Associated Press) and the politically powerful *New York World.* Gould's reach was wide-ranging and deep, and he could summon an army of spies, sycophants, and assemblymen. Roosevelt was about to learn a lesson regarding the extent of Gould's extraordinary power.

Roosevelt had just finished his speech on the floor when John Brodsky, a Republican lawyer from Manhattan's East Side and a prominent member of the Black Horse Cavalry, jumped to his feet and called for a debate. Brodsky knew that such a move would force the measure to be laid aside temporarily, under the Assembly's rules. This bought time for a counterattack.

After Brodsky made his motion, the cudgel was taken up by old Tom Alvord, the ex-Speaker and elder statesman of the Assembly, who was still playing the political game at seventy with the aid of a cane. Alvord lectured Theodore as if addressing a petulant pupil, referring to him as "the young man from New York." When he was a green and foolhardy assemblyman himself, Alvord droned, he had considered a similarly rash attack. But his cooler, rational side prevailed and he did not follow Roosevelt's course of search and destroy toward his legislative colleagues. Alvord's own experience ought to give pause to the young and headstrong Roosevelt, the former Speaker suggested, before his sweeping allegations destroyed the reputation and character of public servants—a commodity "too precious" to be disregarded. There was still time for Roosevelt to see upon reflection the error of his youthful ways and to reconsider his call for an investigation.

Alvord's rambling monologue had only one purpose: to beat

the clock. If Gould's allies could stall until the session's closing time at five o'clock, they would be saved by recess. A few minutes before adjournment, realizing he was about to be shut out and his resolution shelved, Roosevelt called for the privilege of the floor and asked if Alvord would give way for a motion to extend the discussion time. "No," Alvord shouted, swatting away Roosevelt's request. "I will not give way! I want this thing over and to give the members time to consider it!" The old man puttered on in his scolding of Roosevelt until the ornate grandfather clock in the back of the chamber chimed the hour of five. The session was gaveled into recess. By the Assembly rules, that meant Roosevelt's resolution was tabled. Alvord leaned on his cane and shuffled out of the chamber, murmuring in disgust, "The damn fool, he would tread on his own balls just as quick as he would on his neighbor's."[30]

Meanwhile, behind the scenes, Gould's forces and Tammany Hall's heelers plotted to defuse the explosive reformer. John Kelly sent a special envoy from Manhattan to allay the fears of assemblymen and urge them to stay the course. Gould used the editorial pages of the *New York World* to discredit and undermine Roosevelt's resolution by a personal attack on the rashness of the freshman lawmaker. He also started lubricating the legislative gears with lobbying loot. Aside from Gould's paper, however, newspaper coverage across New York was unanimously laudatory, making the representative of the Twenty-first District a celebrity. Roosevelt became the lawmaker to watch, for whom great things were predicted. Typical was the *New York Times:* "There is a splendid career open to a young man of position, character and independence like Mr. Roosevelt who can denounce the legalized trickery of Gould and his allies . . . without being restrained by the cowardly caution of the politician."

The Gould faction hoped to continue throwing up obstacles behind the cover of parliamentary procedure. One favorite technique to mask inaction was to hold confusing votes. As the

Assembly was called into session the next day, Roosevelt demanded the Speaker put the resolution up to a vote. But Roosevelt did not specify the type, and so the Speaker asked members to stand and be counted. Up and down they feinted, like a game of musical chairs. The Speaker pretended to count, only to declare Roosevelt's resolution narrowly defeated, fifty-four to fifty. Roosevelt pounded a fist and vowed, "By Godfrey! I'll get them on the record yet!"

The session returned to "current business," a monotonous drone of one-house legislative wallpaper. Roosevelt rose and planted himself like a stubborn weed. They ignored him. The bandsaw voice buzzed insistently, "Mist-ah Speak-ah! Mist-ah Speak-ah!" Finally Roosevelt was given the privilege of the floor. He called for a slow roll call with a vote of ayes or nays. This time Roosevelt's resolution carried a majority, fifty-five to forty-nine in his favor. But he was still short of the necessary two thirds required for passage. It was a moral victory but no more.

He wrote Alice that evening, still puffed up with pride, "I've drawn blood by my speech against the Elevated Railway judges, and have come in for any amount both of praise and abuse from the newspapers . . . I think I have made a success of it . . . But the fight is severe still . . . How it will turn out in the end no one can now tell." He received a stream of congratulatory letters from old Ivy League classmates. One of them, Poultney Bigelow, later summarized their feelings when he wrote, "We hailed him as the dawn of a new era, the man of good family once more in the political arena; the college-bred tribune superior to the temptations which beset meaner men . . . our ideal."[31]

Gould's operatives ratcheted up the pressure. Since he spurned their overt bribery and refused to be co-opted, they resorted to physical intimidation. As he walked home in Manhattan one evening, he assisted a woman who slipped and fell on the sidewalk in front of him. He arranged to get her a ride home, and she tried to lure him to accompany her with pleas and tears.

Something about the scene seemed staged, so he declined her invitation and made a note of the address she gave the cabdriver. He asked a police detective to check it out. The cop described preparations for an ambush with "a whole lot of men waiting to spring" on Roosevelt.[32]

For an entire week, the Gould forces kept Roosevelt's resolution off the floor, stalled in committee. But the public, moved by Roosevelt's passionate appeal, demanded an investigation and would not back off until the Assembly was finally forced to vote. The result was a landslide of 104 to 6 in favor of Roosevelt's resolution.

Even that, however, was no victory. The Judiciary Committee conducted a sham inquiry. After six weeks of bogus hearings, the committee released a majority report that excused Westbrook, with only a few committee members recommending impeachment. The night before the committee's report, those in favor of impeachment had held a slim majority. But three members changed their votes at the last moment, after they were paid off with $2,500 apiece. The majority report's conclusion was that Westbrook had been "indiscreet and unwise" but had committed nothing more grievous than an act of "excessive zeal" in trying to save Manhattan Elevated from ruin. As the report's conclusion was being read, Roosevelt rose to request adoption of the minority report. "I cannot believe that the Judge had any but corrupt motives in acting as he did in this case," he seethed. "He was in corrupt collusion with Jay Gould . . . There cannot be the slightest question that Judge Westbrook ought to be impeached. He stands condemned by his own acts in the eyes of all honest people. All you can do is to shame yourselves and give him a brief extension of his dishonored career. You cannot cleanse the leper. Beware lest you taint yourself with his leprosy."[33]

In later years he would adopt a more "practical politics" and "applied idealism." But at the time, Roosevelt simply tried to yell and fight to get results. "He is a fluent and vigorous speaker and has the courage of his convictions," the *New York Herald* wrote, "but he has little tact and says and does many things that a calmer judgment would disapprove."

He was fighting not only Gould's bribes of the moment but a larger way of doing business. Such tirades swayed none of the hardened pols in Albany. "You could see you could not change one of them," Hunt said of Roosevelt's efforts to change his colleagues' minds. "They were adamant. They had been lined up and they knew exactly how many votes they had."[34] Roosevelt's attacks failed to make a dent, and his motion to impeach West-brook was defeated soundly, seventy-seven to thirty-five. The whitewashed report that exonerated Westbrook was accepted.

Roosevelt took it hard. He had invested his entire first year in the effort. Despite the statewide renown he had won, it was an inauspicious debut. "It is their ignorance, quite as much as actual viciousness, which makes it so difficult to secure the passage of good laws or prevent the passage of bad ones; and it is the most irritating of the many elements with which we have to contend in the fight for good government," Roosevelt wrote. "It will be hard to make any great improvement in the character of the legislators until respectable people become more fully awake to their duties, and until the newspapers become more truthful and less reckless in their statements."[35]

On June 2, two days after the defeat of the resolution, the legislative session that the *New York Times* called "the most corrupt Assembly since the days of Boss Tweed" adjourned. Roosevelt's efforts were applauded by many influential dissenters, including leading reformer Carl Schurz, who praised Roosevelt's courage as having "stemmed the tide of corruption in that fearful legislative gathering." A small group of Roosevelt's close Assembly colleagues were so impressed that they organized a testimonial dinner for him at Delmonico's in Manhattan. His sister Corinne echoed the dinner's themes in her memoir. "The characteristics which marked his whole public life never showed more dominantly than as a young Assemblyman in Albany," she wrote. "Uncompromising courage was combined with common sense."[36] In his own mind, though, Roosevelt wasn't so sure. In his *Autobiography,* Roosevelt underscored the futility of his legislative work: "Big business of the kind that is allied with politics thoroughly appreciated the usefulness of such a Judge, and every effort was strained to protect him."

Shortly after the legislative session ended, Judge Westbrook visited Troy, across the Hudson River from Albany, on legal business. He was found dead in his Troy hotel room. Rumors swirled that he had committed suicide. Those rumors, never confirmed, turned Roosevelt's efforts into a tragic success of sorts, since his reputation swelled, but the lessons of his first session were clear. He could not easily overthrow a party machine. He could woo the press and "go public," but if he was to succeed, he needed to cultivate insider support.

Chapter 4

★ ★ ★ ★ ★

TRAGEDY

Although not a very old man, I have yet lived a great deal in my life, and I have known sorrow too bitter and joy too keen.

As Roosevelt finished his first term (they were one-year terms, requiring annual elections), he had reason to consider making a career change. Alice had not made a smooth transition to the role of legislator's wife. She had little to do in the capital city, did not like the sense of isolation from her New York social circle, and had been miserable during the long, harsh winter of Albany. Her remaining in Manhattan and her husband's commuting on the train, attempted several times during the first term, was hardly a workable solution either, since Theodore's extended weekly absences weighed heavily on the newlyweds. "I felt as if my heart would break when I left my own little pink darling, with a sad look in her sweet blue eyes, and I have just longed for her here in this beastly Hotel," Theodore wrote Alice from Albany during one of their separations.[1]

He also revealed to his sister Anna his ambivalence toward Albany and the choices it represented. "I hardly know what to do about taking a place up here; it would be lovely to have a farm, and fortunately Alice seems enchanted with the country," he wrote. "The only, or at least the chief, drawback, is the distance from New York. Still, if I were perfectly certain that I would go on in politics and literature I should buy the farm without hesitation; but I consider the chances to be strongly favorable to my getting out of both—and if I intend to follow law or business I ought to stay in New York."[2]

Financial considerations also factored into Roosevelt's uncertainty. His Assembly salary was a mere $1,500 for a five-month session, which would not have been enough to support himself and Alice—let alone the family they were trying to start. He did have dividends from a sizable inheritance and writing income in the wake of *The Naval War of 1812,* which had led to more freelance magazine work and book contracts. But fiscal matters did weigh on Roosevelt, since he had assumed debt to build a country home at Oyster Bay in Long Island while living at the brownstone the couple had recently purchased at 55 West Forty-fifth Street, twelve blocks from his mother's house. They also had bills from maintaining a seasonal rental property in Albany. The Long Island estate, named Leeholm for his wife, was an exciting future goal that sustained Alice in her dismal present. Planning the house also provided a connection and common dream between Alice and Theodore, both of whom regularly reviewed the drawings and designs from the architects and envisioned their life together there.

Nonetheless, in the fall of 1882 he decided to run again. Across the state, and throughout much of the country, an earthquake was in progress in politics. The seismic shift was symbolized in a huge inaugural Labor Day march in New York for the first working-class holiday, organized by the Social Democratic Party of North America. In the campaign for a second Assembly term, Roosevelt worked hard against his Democratic opponent, Major Elbert O. Farrar of Onondaga. It was a "spirited contest," Roosevelt later recalled, as the Stalwarts waged a fierce battle against the young reformer. Roosevelt proudly pointed out how as a Republican he had managed to buck the trend toward Democrats in the 1882 New York elections. In his Assembly district, he wrote to political colleagues, he had won by a 2,209 vote majority—4,225 votes to Farrar's 2,016—which gave Roosevelt 67 percent of the total ballot, four points better than the year before. It was a landslide win, all the more impressive because Roosevelt won without the benefit of gubernatorial coattails. Democrat Grover Cleveland carried Roosevelt's district by a margin of 1,800 votes. "The Independents stood firm," Roosevelt wrote in his diary, "and we beat them two to one. My strength lay among the country Republicans, all of them native Americans, and for the most part farmers or storekeepers or small lawyers; they are all shrewd, kindly, honest men, with whom I get on admirably."[3]

Meanwhile, Roosevelt noted that the Republican member of Congress from his district won by just 700 votes and Republican candidates generally took a pounding. "All Hail, fellow survivor of the Democratic Deluge!" Roosevelt wrote to O'Neil, his closest ally among Republican assemblymen. Roosevelt's lighthearted tone belied deep concern among his party. The 1882 election as a whole was a landslide for Democrats, who now controlled all three sides of the triangle of power in Albany—the Assembly, Senate, and governorship—in the nation's most populous and powerful state. A Democratic deluge, indeed, and a harbinger, some observers believed, for a Democratic takeover in two years of the White House, which Republicans had held for the previous four terms.

Roosevelt was under no illusions about his imminent return to the Albany political scene for a second term. "As far as I can judge the next House will contain a rare set of scoundrels," Roosevelt continued in his letter to O'Neil, "and we Republicans will be in such a hopeless minority that I do not see very clearly what we can accomplish, even in checking bad legislation. But at least we will do our best."[4]

Roosevelt was being a bit disingenuous, since he both nurtured and appreciated his growing prominence through extensive and flattering news coverage. He parlayed that recognition into the Republican nomination for Speaker—a mostly symbolic bid because of the dominance of the Democratic majority—and at the age of twenty-four became the youngest leader of his party in the Assembly. Even though he lost on a party-line vote, eighty-four to forty-one, to the Democrat for the speakership, it was an astonishing coup. One year earlier, the machine wouldn't have supported even a seasoned Roosevelt as its leader. But his fearlessness in battling Gould and leading the charge in the Westbrook impeachment could no longer be dismissed and his vitality impressed even his detractors. More importantly, major change was coming from within as Roosevelt matured. He began treating his fellow assemblymen not with the disdain that first filled his legislative diary but with an understanding that he needed them as allies if his reform agenda was to move forward. It helped too that Roscoe Conkling was out as boss after a rash decision to quit the Senate the previous spring backfired on him and he remained on the sidelines. In Conkling's wake, the Republican organization was less monolithic and more open to a young reformer. Theodore was prepared to take advantage of his opening. "I rose like a rocket" was Roosevelt's assessment of his trajectory from freshman to sophomore legislator. He had gone from outcast and object of hazing to the leader of the Republicans in the Assembly, the man they tapped to take on the Democrats' overwhelming majority and to chip away at their advantage. Elsewhere, Roosevelt's name already was being mentioned by political pundits as an up-and-comer whose potential seemed unlimited, even on the national scene.

His allies in the Legislature were now dubbed "Roosevelt Republicans," as opposed to "Cleveland Democrats." Roosevelt's clout earned him an invitation from Governor Grover Cleveland to discuss important pending legislation in the governor's office.

After just two years in politics, as the mayor of Buffalo, Cleveland had swept into the governor's office with a record-winning margin on a platform of fighting corruption and reforming the spoils system. They were natural cross-party allies. Their physical disparity was amusing to political cartoonists, who embellished Cleveland's mammoth, three-hundred-pound bulk and lampooned the manic energy of Roosevelt, who was roughly half the governor's weight. The *Brooklyn Eagle's* William Hudson wonderfully captured the incongruity of the match. "The Governor would sit large, solid, and phlegmatic, listening gravely to the energetic utterances of the mercurial young man, but signifying neither assent nor dissent. Not infrequently taking silence for acquiescence, Roosevelt would go away thinking he had carried everything before him."

Early in the session, Cleveland and Roosevelt discussed civil service reform, the biggest issue in many sessions on both the state and national levels. The proposed demolishment of the spoils system was a political powder keg. It would take away the time-honored methods of patronage and graft and the winner-take-all notion that to the victor of an election went the spoils— the hundreds of jobs, necessary and no-show, that the majority party typically controlled. Cleveland, Roosevelt, Hunt, and other reformers in the Legislature sought to award government jobs to those truly qualified to perform them through a series of competitive, written examinations that assessed fitness for a certain task. One's political connections should no longer remain the be-all and end-all of civil service employment, they argued, a sea change that would ultimately result in more efficient and perhaps less costly government services. Roosevelt was ahead of the curve in reading the prevailing public sentiment on civil service reform. He likened the spoilsmen to snakes in the grass, "hissing to all decent men." In 1882, Roosevelt accepted the position of vice president of the New York Civil Service Reform Association. On this issue Cleveland needed Roosevelt as much as Roosevelt needed him. Cleveland also felt that he was playing catch-up to Washington, D.C. While the Albany machine stalled reform, the U.S. Congress passed the Pendleton Civil Service Act in January 1883, which required competitive, written examinations for 10 percent of all federal jobs.

Cleveland and Roosevelt commiserated over the logjam they faced. Thomas Nast depicted them in *Harper's Weekly* in a cartoon titled "Reform Without Bloodshed" with a young, skinny Roosevelt working over a sheaf of reform measures at the feet of the massive Cleveland. "I think he had more personal friends among the Democrats than among the Republicans," Assemblyman F. S. Drecker, a Democrat, said of Roosevelt. "I was a political enemy, of course, but it made no difference in our cordial relations."[5]

Although he was the Assembly minority leader, Roosevelt began his second term as he had ended his last, carefully cultivating the role of outsider. Even his choice of Albany lodgings attempted to show that he was beyond the sphere of influence of both the Stalwarts and the Black Horse Cavalry. He stayed at the Kenmore Hotel on North Pearl Street, a few blocks from the most popular legislative haunt, Broadway's Delavan House. Since his first term, Roosevelt steered clear of the Delavan because of the beer drinking on the veranda, the women visitors, and other activities he considered symptomatic of low morals. The Delavan was the most notorious of the Albany hostelries that catered to the lawmakers at that time; others included the Windsor Hotel, Globe Hotel, Brunswick Hotel, Dunlop House, Stanwix Hall, and apartments in Albany's Center Square neighborhood near the Capitol. No reporters stayed at the Kenmore Hotel with Roosevelt, despite the fact that he had become a media darling; the newspapermen preferred hotels with crowded bars and an active nightlife. The staid Kenmore was home to Roosevelt and just four other assemblymen.

As minority leader, Roosevelt took his place on the powerful Assembly Rules Committee, whose five members essentially established the ground rules for the session and could effectively block any legislation as they saw fit. Additionally, Roosevelt was placed on the influential Cities Affairs Committee, as well as the Militia Committee and the Privileges and Elections Committee. It was a heavy load and Roosevelt would be busier than ever, especially with the duties of his leadership post. His close friend Hunt believed Roosevelt would rise to any challenge. "I think he grew faster than anybody I ever knew," Hunt said. "He increased in stature, in strength, mentally all the time . . . I thought I knew more than he did, but before we got through he grew right away from me."[6]

Roosevelt had few personal distractions in Albany in his second term, since Alice stayed behind in Manhattan to manage her primary assignment: decorating and organizing the brownstone at 55 West Forty-fifth Street. During the week in Albany, Roosevelt threw himself into his legislative work with abandon, but he also looked forward to Friday afternoons and his return to Alice and the domestic bliss he described in his legislative diary in cooing, romantic tones on January 3, 1883. "Back again in my own lovely little home, with the sweetest and prettiest of all little wives—my own sunny little darling. I can imagine nothing more happy in life."

Meanwhile, the young reformer found himself swimming against the tide even as his party's leader. In the early months of the session a battle broke out over an appropriation for a Catholic organization that served destitute and indigent children. Roosevelt infuriated Irish-Catholic assemblymen by arguing against it, despite the institution's noble work. In a speech on the Assembly floor, Roosevelt revealed he had earlier been lobbied by Protestants seeking a "member item"—more derisively known as pork-barrel funds—for a home for inebriates. Roosevelt said he denied the Protestant request, as he was urging now for the Catholics, on the principle that state funds should not be allocated to any religious sect. The Catholic protectory got its funding on a vote of ninety-nine to seventeen.[7] Two weeks later, Roosevelt was on the losing side again during a debate on amendments to the New York City Charter that the minority leader lambasted as "a piece of spoils-grabbing partisanship." He considered the suggested changes, which would give Tammany more power and subject it to less oversight, as making the potential for corruption worse than what was already on the books. Roosevelt made a motion to recommit the original bill, but his initiative was voted down, fifty-eight to thirty-eight.

Roosevelt's second term, in fact, rather than rising like a rocket, resembled a disabled dirigible. His bill to control liquor traffic and consumption by increasing license fees on alcohol was scotched in committee. Roosevelt also came up empty in his drive to spur the attorney general to file a lawsuit to break up the Manhattan Elevated Railway Company. He had hoped, with this antitrust campaign, to revive some of the legislative fervor of his old impeachment effort against Judge Westbrook, but the resolution was voted down.

Not only was Roosevelt failing to produce victories on individual legislation, but his strident leadership style and youthfulness were beginning to grate on the veteran Republican assemblymen—many of whom were old enough to be his father, or even grandfather. Roosevelt's habit of calling these elder statesmen "my men" left many gritting their teeth. The signs of maturity with which he started the session seemed to have vanished. His egotism and myopia—seeing his position as the only correct one and refusing to negotiate or compromise—was wearing thin among some members. "What's got into Roosevelt?" some asked behind his back. "He won't listen to anybody. He thinks he knows it all."[8]

Despite his thick skin and high opinion of himself, Roosevelt at least privately expressed some insight into his own character. His friend Jacob Riis later recalled him saying, "I suppose that my head was swelled. It would not be strange if it was. I stood out for my own opinion, alone. I took the best mugwump stand; my own conscience, my own judgment, were to decide in all things. I would listen to no argument, no advice. I took the isolated peak on every issue, and my people left me."[9]

Eventually, the press began taking potshots at his sanctimonious cant. "His Lordship" was how Roosevelt was sometimes described in print. "When Mr. Roosevelt had finished his affecting oration, the House was in tears—of uncontrollable laughter." Another correspondent remarked on a joke making the rounds "that Mr. Roosevelt keeps a pulpit concealed on his person." In an editorial, the *Albany Argus* chided Roosevelt for "flippancy, prejudice . . . as well as execrable ignorance . . . Let him content himself with a becoming espousal of his own views and avoid patronizing those who agree with him and abusing those who do not. His limitations make him ridiculous in both roles."

Roosevelt's limitations were exposed to disastrous effect on the most important legislative matter in his second term, a bill to lower the fare on the Manhattan Elevated Railway Company from ten cents to five cents. The fare reduction seemed at face value an elegant solution to dual problems. It would both cut into the profiteering of railway owner Jay Gould and also bring some relief to the masses of working poor in New York City. Known as the Five-Cent Bill, it was popular on both counts and Roosevelt enthusiastically supported it. Such a position represented a significant shift from the laissez-faire economic strategies Roosevelt espoused in his business classes at Harvard. The five-cent fare measure passed both the Senate and Assembly by wide margins and Roosevelt voted, for a change, with the winning majority. He was once again breaking ranks with the Republican organization, but so were a lot of others. The Five-Cent Bill was sent to the governor's desk for Cleveland's signature. Roosevelt was prepared to bask in praise for his stewardship of the measure through the Assembly.

Cleveland's background as a lawyer was evident in his careful scrutiny of bills sent to him for signing into law. The train fare reduction, despite its widespread support, was no different. Cleveland researched the background of the statute and surprised everyone when he declared the bill unconstitutional. Cleveland produced documentation that showed New York State had entered into a contract with Gould allowing his elevated railroad to charge a dime for each ride. In Cleveland's opinion, the state had no choice but to continue to honor that contract, no matter how distasteful Gould's profit taking. The newly elected governor knew he risked the wrath of scores of New York City voters who rode the train and that he was risking enormous political capital he had not yet amassed. Cleveland proved himself an immovable object of principle. "The State must not only be strictly just, but scrupulously fair," Cleveland wrote. It was an unpopular stand and "the Big One," as he was known, expected to be slaughtered in the press the next morning.

Instead, the response was overwhelming praise for Cleveland as a man of principle. The veto was read as a political act of courage and Cleveland's popularity soared to new heights. In the Assembly chamber, members were so moved that they undertook the unusual response of applauding Cleveland's veto. Roosevelt's father's morality, running strongly even yet through the son's conscience, propelled the minority leader to his feet to issue—against the advice of Hunt, O'Neil, and others—a most remarkable *mea culpa*.

A *New York World* correspondent recorded Roosevelt's remarks:

> I have to say with shame that when I voted for this bill I did not act as I think I ought to have acted, and as I generally have acted on the floor of this House . . . I have to confess that I weakly yielded, partly in a vindictive spirit towards the infernal thieves and conscienceless swindlers who have had the elevated railroad in charge and partly to the popular

voice of New York . . . I would rather go out of politics having the feeling that I had done what was right than stay in
with the approval of all men, knowing in my heart that I
had acted as I ought not to.

Roosevelt's speech was stomped upon. New loads of mockery
and scorn were heaped upon the minority leader from near and
far. "We deem it a duty we owe to the public to spot a bogus
reformer when we see one," declared the *Evening Star* of Boston.
Many observers considered the damage fatal; newspapers gleefully wrote the obituary of Roosevelt's political career. Other
attacks were even more personal and hurtful. "It is quite bad
enough that a son of Theodore Roosevelt could have brought this
discredit upon a name made honorable by the private virtues and
public services of his father," the *New York World* wrote. "His
strong point is his bank account, his weak point is his head,"
another pundit wrote. It was unfortunate timing, then, when
Roosevelt coined the term "the wealthy criminal class" in his
speech—a phrase that would come back to haunt him.

Roosevelt took another body shot when his friend and
Republican ally, Assemblyman Henry L. Sprague, lost his seat on
allegations of election irregularities, including a charge that people voted multiple times. "There can be no possibility of a doubt
that Sprague was lawfully elected," Roosevelt said, and he recommended that Sprague be allowed to stay as a member of the Committee on Privileges and Elections. But the Democratic majority
rejected the recommendation. Roosevelt fumed like a grounded
prep school lad and quit his seat on the Committee on Privileges
and Elections in a huff. Roosevelt again embarrassed himself in
front of his Assembly colleagues with an overheated jeremiad. He
inveighed against "the shameless partisanship they have displayed; the avidity they have shown for getting control of even
the smallest offices; the way they have endeavored to legislate
Republicans out of office and put their own members in."[10] His

tirade was greeted with more snickering and overt ridicule from the press. "The gentleman should refrain from parroting another form of flap doodle," the *Albany Argus* said. "Mr. Roosevelt got up and said in effect he couldn't have his own way in that House and he wouldn't stand it, so there!" mocked the *New York Observer.* In the first two years of his political career, Roosevelt had gone from damn dude to rocket-man Republican leader to buffoon.

If the ridicule in the papers and the background static from his Republican Assembly members got under his skin, he showed no signs in his correspondence or diaries. It wasn't until two decades later, in a letter to his son Ted, that Roosevelt revealed some perspective on his clumsy handling of his first political leadership post. "I came an awful cropper and had to pick myself up after learning by bitter experience the lesson that I was not all-important and that I had to take account of many different elements in life," father wrote to son. Even in hindsight, it was a remarkable admission from a man of pure action who rarely grew introspective.

In general, in those early years, Roosevelt was a fledgling progressive. When it came to criminal justice he favored draconian punishment and considered inmates something less than human. "The criminal is simply a wolf who preys on society and who should be killed or imprisoned like the wolf of the forest," Roosevelt said, arguing against any attempt at rehabilitation. The *New York Morning Journal* wondered aloud if Roosevelt sought "the re-establishment of the stocks, the ducking stool and the pillory . . . paving the way for the thumbscrew and the rack."[11]

Despite the negative coverage he received, he resisted a proposal aimed at limiting the freedom of the press. A bill that would make it easier to sue newspaper publishers and editors for libel was introduced. Roosevelt worked vigorously to kill the legislation. "I think that if there is one thing we ought to be careful about it is in regard to interfering with the liberty of the press,"

Roosevelt said. "We have all of us suffered from the liberty of the press, but we have to take the good and the bad."[12]

Of course, the pugilist in Roosevelt couldn't entirely be suppressed in his dealings with newspapers. He didn't mind picking a fight with an enemy who bought ink by the barrel; he publicly blasted Gould's *New York World* as "a local stock-jobbing sheet of limited circulation, owned by the arch-thief of Wall Street and edited by a rancorous kleptomaniac with a penchant for trousers."[13]

Roosevelt would not back down from powerful legislators either. He lashed out at the activities of a member of the Black Horse Cavalry. The target of Roosevelt's criticism walked over to the minority leader, clenched his fists, glared at Roosevelt, and appeared to be preparing for a brawl. The sergeant at arms finally convinced the angry fellow to leave Roosevelt alone and to return to his seat. "I thought that chap was going to hit you today!" a colleague told Roosevelt. "I wish he had! I can lick him, the best day he ever saw," Roosevelt said.[14]

When it came to economic ills, such as the plight of the working poor, Roosevelt's patrician streak showed through: he seemed out of touch with the situation of the times. His position on such social issues was a work in progress—ever shifting and often contradictory—as he sought to balance the demands of laborers and capitalists. Meanwhile, New York State and the country remained mired in an economic depression that had begun in 1882 and lasted several years. New York City was particularly hard hit, with rampant unemployment of between 30 and 50 percent among those of working age. Daily wages for laborers ran from $2 to $4.50, and an average annual income was $720. A typical family's rent in New York City was $200 per year, leaving $520, or just $10 per week, to pay for food, clothing, heat, and other necessities—barely enough to survive. Those who were lucky enough to have a job often labored under horrible conditions. Women and children sewed clothing in squalid tenements for sixteen hours at a stretch, earning pennies for piecework and always fearful of being undercut by even more desperate newly arrived immigrants. Bakery workers toiled eighty hours per week for a measly $5 and did so in fetid, filthy, and bug-riddled cellars. Steelworkers were both poorly paid and terribly endangered. Disfiguring or lethal injuries were common where the daily shift was twelve hours and there were no holidays or days off and no safety regulations. The rapid industrialization of the East Coast, which valued mechanization over manpower, and the rising tide of immigration further squeezed an already tight job market. In 1882 alone, 800,000 immigrants entered the United States and many joined the labor force, willing to work for less than the barely livable wages being offered. Yet the dilemma of how state government might try to improve the lives of the working poor while also assisting new immigrants didn't seem to register with the trust funder. "The worst foe of the poor man is the labor leader who tries to teach him that he is a victim of conspiracy and injustice," Roosevelt said. "In the long run the only way to help people is to make them help themselves . . . Once a man was permitted to tie himself to the apron strings of the state, he would become no more self-reliant than an infant."[15]

Roosevelt's independent streak and a scientific curiosity indulged since boyhood led him, from the outset of his political career, to investigate issues that threatened the dominance of his privileged class. As a member of the City Affairs Subcommittee, he asked to investigate a bill introduced by the Cigarmakers' Union that would outlaw the making of cigars inside tenement domiciles. At that time, a staggering one third of the 670 million cigars assembled, rolled, and packed in New York City each year were produced in tenements by newly arrived immigrants who spoke little English and were easily indentured by unsavory landlords who duped them into a kind of serfdom in exchange for marginal living quarters. This system of at-home cigarmaking piecework had been in practice for generations. For the unfortunate workers, there was no division between work and home, only grinding labor for sixteen to eighteen hours each day in dark, crowded spaces for a barely livable pittance. Children were not spared but were made to toil for long shifts until they collapsed in slumber on piles of tobacco.

The Assembly City Affairs Subcommittee tried to ignore the plea from Samuel Gompers and his union for an investigation and, in usual fashion, attempted instead to stall or evade. Roosevelt was expected to look the other way. Michael C. Murphy, the powerful Democratic legislator, had put Roosevelt on the subcommittee in a minority member's slot as a favor to Roosevelt's uncle, and Murphy expected quid pro quo when it came to the cigar bill. "As a matter of fact, I had supposed I would be against the legislation and I rather think that I was put on the committee with that idea," Roosevelt wrote in his *Autobiography*.[16] "For the respectable people I knew were against it; it was contrary to the principles of political economy of *laissez-faire* kind." This time, though, whether out of boredom or a sincere moral outrage, Roosevelt would not go along with the dubious old paradigm. He set himself in charge of the investigation and planned to make it a full airing of the issue.

Samuel Gompers, a son of a cigarmaker and the forceful leader of the Cigarmakers' Union, urged Roosevelt to make an inspection tour of the tenement houses himself. At first Roosevelt declined, but Gompers was persistent. Something appealed to Roosevelt in the tenacity of the short, gnarled, fast-talking young man who'd risen from oppressed beginnings in a London slum and fought through the discrimination faced by a Jew to become a revered labor leader. Both men were young—Gompers was thirty-two years old, Roosevelt nearly twenty-five—and neither lacked for strongly voiced opinions. It was an attraction of opposing forces. This disparate duo eventually made a round of the tenements on the Lower East Side of Manhattan, a transforming experience for Roosevelt, who went back twice more on his own to absorb the full extent of the disturbing scene. He recalled visiting one tiny and horrible room where two families lived and worked. "There were several children, three men, and two women in this room," Roosevelt wrote in his *Autobiography*.[17] "The tobacco was stowed about everywhere, alongside the foul bedding, and in a corner where there were scraps of food. The men, women, and children in this room worked by day and far on into the evening, and they slept and ate there."

Roosevelt was deeply moved by these wretchedly poor families. They aroused the early stirrings of a social conscience in him. To the consternation of his committee members, Roosevelt abruptly made an about-face from his anticipated opposition to the bill and instead became an ardent supporter. "Whatever the theories might be, as a matter of practical common sense I could not conscientiously vote for the continuation of the conditions which I saw," he wrote. The bill proposed to increase wages, limit the workweek, and improve sanitary conditions.

Roosevelt agreed to take the appeal of Gompers and the Cigarmakers' Union directly to Governor Cleveland. It was a bold move, but Roosevelt had established a rapport with Cleveland. Moreover, Roosevelt was fearless in his newfound role of "acting as spokesman for the battered, undersized foreigners." Roosevelt argued passionately for the bill on the Assembly floor and got it passed in his house, but the lobbyists representing the cigar business owners spread cash and bought time in the Senate, where an operative held up the vote indefinitely by stealing the original of the bill on the third and final reading before passage. Roosevelt was not deterred. The Senate finally passed the purloined bill and sent it to the governor. Roosevelt answered all of Cleveland's initial objections and eventually wore him down. In the end Cleveland signed it. Yet Roosevelt's victory was soon moot. The legislation was overturned by the State Court of Appeals, the state's highest court, which declared the law unconstitutional as an affront to the "hallowed" tradition of "home." Roosevelt regarded the decision with a hard-bitten cynicism. "It was this case which first waked me to a dim and partial understanding of the fact that the courts were not necessarily the best judges of what should be done to better social and industrial conditions," he wrote. "It was one of the most serious setbacks which the cause of industrial and social progress and reform ever received."[18]

Roosevelt was beginning to shift from an idealistic approach to the political process to what he called "practical politics." This newfound insight was contained in an analogy Roosevelt once made to his friend, Jacob Riis, regarding a working definition of how to function in the Legislature. "If you are cast on a desert island with only a screw-driver, a hatchet, and a chisel to make a boat with, why, go make the best one you can. It would be better if you had a saw, but you haven't. So with men."[19]

Still not yet twenty-five years old, Roosevelt was maturing. His newfound pluralism was guaranteed to offend many: his family and friends in the patrician class, the Democratic majority in the Legislature, and both labor and capital, depending on the legislation. Yet the political philosophy Roosevelt was auditioning in Albany would take center stage in Washington during his presidency. Roosevelt's essential tenets included self-reliance, individual freedom coupled with responsibility, help for the underclass to help themselves, and the forestalling of a welfare class created by dependence on government assistance. At the same time, he would become one of American history's greatest trustbusters. It was not always a coherent mix in theory, but it was a grand success in practice.

There was an even more profound maturation process at work within the Harvard snob who "came an awful cropper." Like a wolf who cuts a weak deer out of the pack, Roosevelt used his second term to torture Erastus Brooks—an elderly Democrat, editor of the *Richmond Evening Express,* and former U.S. congressman whose best fights were behind him. Brooks assumed that his seat in the Assembly was safely his and expected, like so many others, to coast easily into a retirement enriched by whatever graft came his way. Roosevelt smelled blood; he attacked Brooks mercilessly throughout the session, as described by Assemblyman F. S. Drecker, who represented Greene County, just to the south of Albany.[20] Brooks kept his head down, quietly absorbed Roosevelt's abuse, and refused to be baited into a public retaliation. Roosevelt kept picking away, demanding that Brooks's vote be recorded on a certain bill to expose his motives and allegiances. Finally Brooks snapped, according to Drecker and a *New York Times* account. The old man whipped around in his seat, with "fire flashing from his eyes," and lunged at Roosevelt. "It's none of your business! That was an impertinent question!" Brooks shouted at Roosevelt, who'd been needling him about his vote. Roosevelt shot back, "You are a confirmed dodger."

The bitter argument charged the air in the Assembly chamber, where the normal business was suspended by a most unusual monologue from Brooks in which he defended his position and denounced the tactics of Roosevelt. His moving lament caused tears to well up in Roosevelt's eyes. To the amazement of his colleagues, Roosevelt stood up, walked to Brooks, extended his hands, and said, "Mr. Brooks, I surrender. I beg your pardon." Drecker called it "one of the finest exhibitions of manly confession and honest emotion" he had ever witnessed.

As part of Roosevelt's emerging breadth of perspective, while attacking big business at home, he embraced the then thoroughly unpopular position of free trade abroad. Toward the end of his second term, in the spring of 1883, he spoke at the New York Free Trade Club in New York City on "The Tariff in Politics." It was as if Roosevelt were indulging a political death wish. "I have been warned that it is political suicide to commit myself to free trade," he said. "Perhaps it is. I am glad that I am not dependent upon public office for my livelihood. Whenever important differences arise between my constituents and myself, I will gladly retire."[21] Of course, tariffs were set by the federal government, and he had no major related issue before him in the Assembly. Still, it was a brave position.

A month before the close of his second term, Roosevelt finally scored the legislative win he'd been seeking. Cleveland brought Roosevelt back to the governor's office after the Civil Service Reform Bill managed to get untangled from the Judiciary Committee. Roosevelt's ally Hunt had finessed it out of committee in the absence of the chairman, and now the governor, seeking to increase his profile nationally, was ready to horse-trade to earn passage of the populist measure. Cleveland cut a deal that he could deliver enough "Cleveland Democrats" to pass the bill in both houses of the Legislature if the "Roosevelt Republicans" would get the ball rolling by clearing the Assembly. On April 9, Roosevelt made the final floor speech in support of the Civil Service Reform Bill, and while not his most inflammatory rhetoric, the remarks were forceful and achieved their desired effect, "to take out of politics the vast band of hired mercenaries whose very existence depends on their success, and who can almost always in the end overcome the efforts of them whose only care is to secure a pure and honest government."[22]

Tammanyites and Stalwarts managed to table the bill for several weeks, but the across-the-aisle coalition of Cleveland and Roosevelt and their additional arm-twisting of legislators managed to overcome the blockade. On May 4, the final day of the session, when a blizzard of legislation was passed, the Civil Service Reform Bill was sent from the Assembly to the Senate and passed. Cleveland immediately signed the bill into law, and Roosevelt could finally legitimately claim to be the catalyst of one of the most sweeping and lasting reform measures of the Legislature in many sessions.

Roosevelt was newly hailed for his toughness and fortitude. An assessment of Roosevelt's start in politics by George William Curtis, editor of *Harper's Weekly* and a prominent Republican elder statesman, was revealing: "He has integrity, courage, fair scholarship, a love for public life, a comfortable amount of money, honorable descent, the good word of the honest, he will not truckle nor cringe, he seems to court opposition to the point of being somewhat pugnacious."

But the heavy lifting had taken its toll on Roosevelt. An Assembly colleague described him as "anemic-looking." The pressure of the 1883 session may have accounted for a flare-up of his asthma and a bout of what was known as *cholera morbus,* an intestinal disorder, that summer. Under doctor's orders, Roosevelt sought the refuge and clear air of the country for himself and Alice. He had complained of stomach cramps, vomiting, bad headaches, and "a general feeling of lassitude." He rented a farmhouse on the northern edge of the Catskill Mountains near Richfield Springs, known for its healing waters and therapeutic baths. But the town was so sleepy and provincial, Roosevelt was "bored out of my life" among "underbred and overdressed girls, fat old female scandal mongers, and a select collection of cripples and consumptives," he wrote to his sister Corinne on July 1, 1883. The same letter described a lack of adventurous spirit in his wife, particularly when it came to her rather snobbish attitude toward country vittles. "Alice mildly but firmly refused to touch the decidedly primitive food of the aborigines, and led a starvling existence on crackers which I toasted for her in the greasy kitchens of the grimy inns."

The remedy for his lassitude, Roosevelt decided, was a reprise of his big-game hunting trip out West three years earlier. "Finding the work in Albany, if conscientiously done, very harassing, I was forced to take up some out-of-doors occupation for the summer," Roosevelt wrote to a legislative colleague.[23] The idea crystallized after Roosevelt met Commander H. H. Gorringe, a retired navy officer, at a New York City political rally. Theirs was a meeting of the minds. The commander and the author of *The Naval War of 1812* lamented the current state of U.S. naval affairs and found common ground in their desire to strengthen the navy. The two also happened to share an interest in big-game hunting, particularly buffalo, which had become a popular prey for wealthy New York City men during posh, private hunting vacations out West. Gorringe had just returned from a trip there and was at that moment working on setting up a buffalo-hunting operation. Gorringe spun manly stories of buffalo, elk, antelope, mountain sheep, and bear kills. It was seductive music to Roosevelt's ears. Gorringe invited Roosevelt out to his property on the banks of the Little Missouri in the Badlands of Dakota Territory in the fall.

"While danger ought never to be endlessly incurred, it is yet true that the keenest zest in sport comes from its presence, and from the consequent exercise of the qualities necessary to overcome it," Roosevelt wrote. Nothing could get in the way of this hunter on the stalk, not even the matter of his wife's pregnancy or a sense of urgency in building Leeholm in Oyster Bay. Roosevelt busied himself in August with preparing for the trip and with spending a chunk of his inheritance, $20,000, to purchase an additional 95 acres at Oyster Bay for a total estate of 155 acres. He wrote to Gorringe, "I am now being forced to make my plans in regard to the political campaign this Autumn, and so I am anxious to fix, as nearly as is convenient to you, what will be about the dates of our departure and return. I am fond of politics, but fonder still of a little big game hunting."

At the last moment, without warning, Gorringe backed out of the planned excursion. Alice suggested canceling, out of concerns over her husband's recent illness and the fact that he would be courting danger in the "Bad Lands" without any support—not even the company of his erratic brother, Elliott, Roosevelt's companion on an earlier western hunting trip. Yet Theodore decided he would go it alone. He took leave of his wife, four months pregnant—beginning to show signs of a difficult pregnancy, feeling lonely and fearful—on September 3, 1883. Five days later, while changing trains in Chicago, he wrote to his mother that he was "feeling like a fighting cock."

Roosevelt wrote to his mother from Bismark in the Dakota Territory on September 7 during another layover between trains, his heart clearly rejoicing at the music of the western landscape and people:

> This is a typical frontier town of the northwest; go-ahead, prosperous, and unfinished; the original log cabins and tents have been almost entirely supplanted by frame houses; and there are a number of pretentious brick buildings going up. The streets are crowded with frontiersmen; rough looking but quiet farmers, American, Scandinavian or German; cowboys on shaggy horses, with gaily decked saddles; saturnine hunters, lounging about with long rifles; and squalid, fierce looking Indians; all combined, make a very picturesque appearance. The town stands in the midst of a limitless, treeless expanse of rolling prairie, broken only to the south west by the forests on the edge of the mighty Missouri, beyond which the bluffs rise in grim nakedness.[24]

A day later, after leaving Bismark at two o'clock in the morning, Roosevelt finally reached his destination of the Little Missouri. Roosevelt told his mother this would be his final chance to write and he didn't disappoint, starting with his lodgings at a rustic rooming house in which he was given a room to share with eight other men, "all of more or less doubtful aspect." His words put the reader in the saddle beside him:

> It is a most desolate place . . . The river flows between steep, barren hills, broken by deep ravines and sheer canyons; the brown grass is sparse and scanty, and only every now and then in some more sheltered valley can be seen a few straggling cotton wood trees. The bitter, alkaline water is almost, if not quite, unfit for drink; it is quite as much a poison as a healthful beverage. It is so cold that there are

hardly any rattlesnakes about. I find that elk are very rare; but there seems to be some chance of my finding buffalo.[25]

Over the next two weeks, Roosevelt was a buffalo hunter possessed. He hired a guide, Joe Ferris, a stocky Canadian also in his mid-twenties, who had done his share of manual labor before managing Gorringe's hunting ranch in the Badlands. After the Sioux slaughtered thousands of bison shortly before Roosevelt arrived, the once-plentiful species were a scarce prey for wealthy hunters from New York. They rode for days without seeing a buffalo. Roosevelt would not be skunked. Ignoring protests from Ferris, Roosevelt rode recklessly and pushed himself and his horse to utter exhaustion. His obsessive pursuit put his life and his guide's in danger. They ran out of water on the parched prairie. Roosevelt was thrown from his horse and got stuck in quicksand. The horses ran off one night, spooked by a wolf. The men got drenched by torrential rains one day and sunburned by a searing sun the next. When he did get off a shot at the rare buffalo sighting, Roosevelt missed. "Bad luck followed us like a yellow dog follows a drunkard," Ferris said.[26] No matter the deprivation or danger, though, Roosevelt pushed on. The day before he was scheduled to leave, September 21, Roosevelt finally bagged a buffalo. "I put the bullet in behind his shoulder . . . The blood [was] pouring from his mouth and nostrils," Roosevelt wrote.[27] The kill triggered an orgiastic outburst. Roosevelt hollered and hopped around the dead beast in a primal dance. He shrieked and bellowed in a crazed celebration of the blood sport. "I never saw anyone so enthused in my life," Ferris said.[28]

After the trip, Roosevelt took aim at a different quarry. He won reelection to a third term in the Assembly in a Republican sweep, the party winning both houses of the Legislature by healthy margins. After being swamped by the Democrats in the state legislature the year before, Republicans rode a Tammany backlash, as well as the strength of the Republicans nationally, to regain control in Albany. The powerful position of Assembly Speaker would be the new majority party's greatest reward. As former minority leader, Roosevelt would have to be considered on the shortlist for his house's top post. It was the leadership position he coveted most. Boosting his chances was the fact that Roosevelt's agenda of reforming government and ending the spoils system of corrupt politics had taken hold across the state and beyond. Governor Cleveland, still firmly broken with Tammany Hall, was entering the second year of his two-year term. President Chester A. Arthur, once Conkling's lieutenant and beholden to the Republican Stalwart machine, had made a profound ideological shift in the wake of the shocking assassination of Garfield that put Arthur in the White House. Arthur used the power of the office to break from bossism and shifted from machine politics to urge a merit system for federal employees and creation of a civil service commission. Alongside President Arthur—the one-time Conkling hack and his father's rival—Roosevelt found himself on the forward edge of a fast-moving wave.

By mid-November 1883, Roosevelt had turned his attention to campaigning for the speakership. He wrote to his colleagues in uncompromising prose. Roosevelt's letter on November 20, 1883, to Jonas S. Van Duzer, an assemblyman from Chemung County, was typical of his independent stance. "I am a Republican, pure and simple, neither a 'half-breed' nor a 'stalwart'; and certainly no man, nor yet any ring or clique, can do my thinking for me . . . I believe in treating all our businesses equitably and alike."

In a rare effort to mingle with the masses and fit in with his colleagues, Roosevelt rented a suite in the Delavan House. Roosevelt was sparing no expense in his quest. Those he couldn't buttonhole in New York City or Albany he sought out by traveling to their districts—no matter how remote or rural. He did not consider himself above tramping to a farmhouse and badgering the assemblyman to listen to his positions. Roosevelt gained confidence in the course of his energetic canvass. Some might have even called him cocky about the outcome, despite broad support for Titus Sheard, an elderly and popular clothing manufacturer from Herkimer County—a safe choice. Roosevelt ran into opposition from would-be machine boss Warner Miller, the powerful U.S. senator from Herkimer County, who promised to deliver the speakership to Sheard—an old friend and someone unlikely to challenge Miller's authority. Roosevelt had also created his share of enemies on the Assembly floor, where his preference to go it alone was a liability. His nature, however, was to rise to meet adversity, and this challenge was no different. "I am much stronger than I had dared to hope, and if I am not mistaken I stand an excellent chance of winning in spite of both the lobby and the politicians," Roosevelt wrote to Van Duzer on December 22, 1883. His opponents worked hard to portray Roosevelt as too young and too volatile for Speaker; it was one member's assessment that "that young fellow Roosevelt might go off like a sky-rocket."[29] In addition, Roosevelt faced a fractured field of three candidates. At the last minute, he suffered an unexpected erosion of his supporters, including the crushing desertion of ally Isaac Hunt, who inexplicably threw his support behind his buddy George Z. Erwin. Roosevelt was wounded by Hunt's betrayal. Following up this sucker punch, the forces backing Sheard also resorted to a typical Albany incentive: they offered bribes. The bait was blatant and heavy. The *New York World* called the back-room dealing "the liveliest scene in the halls of the Delavan that has been witnessed since the contest was opened."

Graft sealed the fate of the speakership. In the course of three hours on New Year's Eve, Roosevelt's political support unraveled. "I made a stout fight for the nomination," Roosevelt wrote in his *Autobiography,* "but the bosses of the two factions, the Stalwarts and the Half-Breeds, combined and I was beaten."[30] He was referring to Miller and Erwin, respectively. His loss came at a time when the Republicans remained divided over perennial presidential candidate James G. Blaine, "the Plumed Knight" of Maine, who was at the center of contentious national conventions in 1876, 1880, and 1884. Stalwarts were party regulars who opposed Blaine; Half-Breeds were more independent-minded Republicans who supported the Maine boss. As a reformer who would not swear his allegiance to either faction, Roosevelt fit with neither group. In the end, the fallen minority leader managed thirty votes compared to forty-two for Sheard. It was a bruising defeat, and he could not hide his disappointment. "I was much chagrined for the moment," Roosevelt later said.[31] A reporter for the *Sun* in the January 1, 1884, edition described Roosevelt after the loss as having "an older and less buoyant look than usual when he dropped wearily into his seat." From the remove of years and experience, though, Roosevelt reassessed the outcome in his *Autobiography,* interpreting it as a kind of victory for his independence and refusal to bend to machine forces. "My defeat in the end materially strengthened my position, and enabled me to accomplish far more than I could have accomplished as Speaker," he claimed.[32] In retrospect, he had a point. The role of independent outsider, a politician who could not be bought, had been the source of Roosevelt's greatest strength and popular appeal.

As he had done in rallying against asthma, Roosevelt pumped himself up with internal pep talks. Speaker Sheard did not seek to punish his rival but rather rewarded his energy by giving Roosevelt his pick of committee assignments. Roosevelt chose Banks, Militia, and Cities because of their importance and his own personal interests. He worked harder than ever on legislative matters, putting in extended hours, and also returned to the rough-and-tumble ways of the boxing ring. "I had my first sparring lesson for five years this morning; I felt much better for it; but am awfully out of training," he wrote Alice on January 22, 1884. "I feel much more at ease in my mind and better able to enjoy things since we have gotten under way; I feel as though I had the reins in my hand." Roosevelt soon introduced a trio of major and controversial bills that sought to cut into the power base of machine politicians in New York City.

The first, a hike in liquor license fees, was a bit of résumé padding because Roosevelt knew it was an extreme long shot. He did not fight with his usual vigor, and it died a predictable death. It was also a kind of trial balloon by which Roosevelt early on drew out and marked his opponents on the Cities Committee. "In all sections drunkenness is if anything increasing," Roosevelt said in defense of the bill. He quickly followed up with a second bill that he drove through the Assembly. It reduced how much debt service the City of New York could carry and strengthened oversight of the borrowing practices of machine-controlled treasuries. With the Republicans in control of both houses of the Legislature, it was not hard to pass bills that punished the Democratic machines of the cities. Roosevelt's third bill in the Cities Committee involved legislation that would elevate the position of New York City mayor, while reducing the power of the twenty-four aldermen—traditionally political hacks who answered to bosses and not the electorate. The bill gave the mayor absolute power of appointment and removal of department heads, while taking away the Board of Aldermen's power of confirming those appointments. The proposal amounted to a radical shift in the balance of power in New York's municipal affairs. Roosevelt delivered what he considered one of his finest speeches as an assemblyman in support of the mayoralty bill. His language was unusually simple, clear, and logical. "At present we have this curious condition of affairs—the Mayor possessing the nominal power and two or three outside men possessing the real power," Roosevelt said. "I propose to put the power in the hands of the men the people elect."[33]

Roosevelt's persuasive rhetoric carried the day. He wrote to Alice on February 6, 1884, with pride over his accomplishment. "In the House we had a most exciting debate on my Reform

Charter bill, and I won a victory, having it ordered to a third reading." Perhaps his aggressiveness in pouncing upon opponents of what came to be known as "the Roosevelt Bill" flowed from the savage stirrings he felt after a successful boxing practice earlier the same day. "Today I sparred as usual," Roosevelt wrote in the same letter. "My teacher is a small man and in the set-to today I bloodied his nose by an upper cut, and knocked him out of time."

The press burnished Roosevelt's reputation as a reformer by heralding his victory on the mayoralty bill and highlighting the other reform bills he had introduced. Assemblymen couldn't buy this kind of publicity, and it was certainly a salve to Roosevelt's wounded ego after losing his bid for Speaker. "Mr. Roosevelt, to whom the credit of the bills already passed or certain to pass is due, has displayed a boldness, directness and energy of which much older and more experienced politicians might well be proud," wrote one correspondent.[34] The coverage was widespread and glowing as evidenced by a sampling of newspaper headlines: "Under Roosevelt's Whip," "Roosevelt's Brilliant Assault on Corruption," "Theodore, the Cyclone Hero of the Assembly."

While the print correspondents were searching for more superlatives to describe Roosevelt's flurry of punches at corruption, political cartoonists developed new heroic imagery that sent his political stock soaring higher. One cartoon depicted Roosevelt trimming the claws of the Tammany tiger with giant scissors. Another showed Roosevelt as a lumberjack chopping down a massive trunk of New York City corruption.

When he wasn't waging legislative wars, Roosevelt was conducting an all-out offensive on the social scene. While his wife was suffering through the arduous final days of her pregnancy, Roosevelt was dining with reform-minded Democrat Thomas Newbold one night and Walter Howe, a Republican assemblyman from New York City, the next. On February 6, 1884, he wrote Alice of his planned dinner engagement with the Rathbones, a prominent Albany family, adding, as if to assuage his guilt, "It was very kind to ask me, but I do not anticipate much fun."

He must have been feeling guilty, if not heartsick, when he wrote a second letter to Alice that same day. "Last evening I took dinner at the same table with the Danforths. I think I made a nice strike in my aldermanic bill yesterday; I did not do as well as I have sometimes done, but still it was one of my best speeches—though I do not know that that is saying much." He had no idea at the time how momentous that second and final letter would become with the unexpected, tragic events in the days ahead.

The dual letters home were squeezed between Roosevelt's hectic legislative schedule. In addition to his three pivotal committee assignments, he had been appointed chairman of a special Assembly committee charged with investigating corruption in New York City's government. The committee's hearings, held at the Metropolitan Hotel in Manhattan, gave Roosevelt little time for a life outside Assembly affairs. The investigation would be a tough battle, much like the famous Seabury investigations forty-five years later, when his cousin, Governor Franklin Roosevelt, took on the Tammany machine of New York's dapper mayor Jimmy Walker. As in the later probe, in 1884 politicos brazenly refused to answer pointed queries regarding corruption. They would not turn over financial records either. Theodore's anger was duly recorded by the press as he played his part with a zeal a correspondent described as "a white heat of passion."[35] Eventually, Roosevelt's stubborn persistence wore down his foes; on February 11 the sheriff of New York finally turned over his financial records to the committee. Members had good reason to suspect the worst of those records, given what they knew already. Taxpayers were being fleeced and prisoners were being held under horrible conditions, as well as blackmailed to upgrade their grim circumstances. One inmate said he couldn't afford the $250 payment to jail guards for a better cell and so had to sleep in the foul discharge of a broken toilet. Prisoners' food was infested with insects. "Revolting," Roosevelt called the condition of New York City's jails as he introduced legislation to improve it. After the records were released, Roosevelt adjourned the hearings for one week to provide time for a review of the sheriff's books.

It all made for national headlines. Roosevelt and the presidency were being whispered in the same breath by some; a Philadelphia paper's editorial captured the glow of goodwill surrounding him: "The career of this young man, who has gone boldly and honorably into public life, ought to shame thousands who complain that politics are so dirty that no decent gentleman can engage in them."[36] A Boston editorial writer similarly praised Roosevelt's "wit to organize practical reforms, the faculty to inspire others with his own faith in his measures, and the tact and persistency to secure their adoption by the requisite majority."

The investigating commmittee's adjournment came just in time to let Roosevelt focus on final passage of his reform legislation and the expected birth of his first child, which seemed something of an afterthought in his correspondence. The demands of shepherding the Roosevelt Bill through the Legislature compelled him to return to Albany on Monday, February 11. He left home even though his wife reported feeling very poorly and his mother was confined to bed with a severe cold. As usual, Roosevelt counted on his ever-loyal big sister, Bamie, to attend to their care.

Shortly after her husband departed for the State Capitol, Alice wrote:

Dear Thee, I hated so to leave you this afternoon. I don't think you need feel worried about my being sick as the Dr. told me this afternoon that I would not need my nurse before Thursday—I am feeling well tonight but am very much worried over [the word *baby* was crossed out] your mother. Her fever is still very high and the Dr. is rather afraid of typhoid, it is not the least catching. I will write again to-morrow and let you know just how she is—don't say any thing about it till then. I do love my dear Thee *so* much, I wish I could have my little new baby soon. Ever your loving wife, Alice.[37]

It turned out to be Alice's last letter to her husband.

She went into labor the next day, February 12, and gave birth to a baby girl who weighed nearly nine pounds. The labor and first-time delivery were difficult for the petite Alice, who briefly held her baby and kissed it before collapsing into an exhausted slumber.

The following morning, a day in which Theodore reported fourteen bills out of his Cities Committee, a telegram with the good news arrived in Albany. The proud, jubilant father was engulfed by his fellow assemblymen. "I shall never forget when the news came and we congratulated him," Isaac Hunt recalled. "He was full of life and happiness."[38] The baby was in fine health, while Alice was still recovering, the telegram said. There was no indication of complications. Roosevelt requested a leave of absence from the Assembly to begin later that day, and he took the time to report several bills out of his Cities Committee. Roosevelt excitedly noted that his baby was born on the birthday of his hero, President Abraham Lincoln, but that happy association was tempered by the fact that February 9 had been the sixth anniversary of the burial of Roosevelt's father. Roosevelt took a moment to dash off a telegram to a family friend, Dora Watkins, in New York City. "Dear Dolly. We have a little daughter. The mother only fairly well."

A few hours after the first telegram from home arrived, another followed. It urged Theodore to return to Manhattan immediately.

Heavy fog had blanketed New York City and much of the lower Hudson Valley for days. The *New York Times* called it "suicidal weather" and noted "something suggestive of death and decay in the dampness that fills the world."[39] River, road, and rail traffic endured delays and shutdowns; Roosevelt's train crawled for long, fog-choked stretches. Six years before, Roosevelt had rushed home from Harvard on the train—only to arrive too late, after his father had already died.

Shortly before midnight on February 13, the delayed train finally reached Grand Central Station and Roosevelt pushed as quickly as possible through the eerie halos of the street lamps. As he approached his mother's house, a light shone in the third-floor bedroom that Alice had been using in the late stages of her pregnancy so that she wouldn't be alone in her own home while her husband was in Albany. At the front door, he met his distraught brother, Elliott, who blurted out, "There is a curse on this house. Mother is dying and Alice is dying, too!"[40]

Roosevelt bounded up the stairs to Alice's bedroom. His wife was semicomatose and barely recognized him. Although not properly diagnosed at the time, Alice was in the late stages of Bright's disease, a kidney ailment with symptoms that included severe nausea and indolence—symptoms also not unusual in pregnancy. Alice's case of Bright's had progressed to an end stage of a disease that was almost always fatal in that era. Roosevelt held his wife in his arms as she drifted in and out of consciousness for the next two hours. His bedside vigil was interrupted by a message that he should hurry to his mother's room on the second floor below if he wanted to see her before she died. He stood with his brother and sisters around his mother's bed. "There *is* a curse on this house," Theodore said, as they watched their mother die. She passed away at about three o'clock in the morning of Valentine's Day. She was forty-nine years old.

Roosevelt left one death scene for another. He walked back upstairs to Alice's room and held his wife in his arms again. This day marked the fourth anniversary of their engagement. Alice was twenty-two years old, three years younger than Theodore.

For the next interminable hours of grief, the awful vigil continued. She died at two o'clock in the afternoon, eleven hours after Theodore's mother passed away.

Roosevelt lost the two most profound loves in his young life on the same day. Both losses were unexpected. "The light has gone out of my life," he wrote in his diary for February 14, 1884. He drew a cross beside the entry.

Two days later, in a "dazed, stunned state," Roosevelt buried both women.[41] The dual funeral was held on Saturday morning in the Fifth Avenue Presbyterian Church, its pews packed with social and political friends. "Jesus, Lover of My Soul," "Rock of Ages," and sobs and muffled cries elicited by the Rev. Dr. John Hall's brief eulogy drifted past sprays of fragrant roses and lilies of the valley placed on a pair of rosewood coffins. Dr. Hall, pastor and friend to the late Mrs. Roosevelt, was visibly moved. As the pair of coffins were slowly borne down the aisle, the funeral march from Beethoven's Third Symphony played softly on the organ. Twin hearses took the procession to Brooklyn's Green-Wood Cemetery.

Roosevelt's early tutor and family friend Arthur Cutler watched his old pupil but was unable to offer comfort for Theodore's profound grief. "He does not know what he does or says," Cutler noted. He added that Theodore moved about listlessly "in a dazed, stunned state."[42]

The day after the funeral was the christening of Alice Lee. Roosevelt cradled his five-day-old baby, whose neck had been draped with a locket holding a lock of her late mother's hair. Her father would pass off to Bamie the job of raising Baby Lee, as Roosevelt referred to his child—her given name, Alice, being apparently too painful to say aloud.

In an unprecedented move, Roosevelt's Assembly colleagues unanimously moved for three days' adjournment in shared sympathy. Roosevelt's political enemy Jim Husted rose and offered a moving, heartfelt speech about the sorrow all the members felt "in this moment of his [Roosevelt's] agony and weakness." Seven assemblymen spoke with unrestrained emotion. Some members cried. "Never in my many years here have I stood in the presence of such a sorrow as this," one said.[43] James Haggerty, a Tammany Democrat, quoted poetry: " 'Tis sorrow builds the shining ladder up, whose golden rounds are our calamities."[44]

Roosevelt broke out of his daze and hours of incessant, robotic pacing about his room long enough to write an entry in his diary a few days after the funeral. He summed up Alice's brief life in a few short sentences and wrote of their marriage, "We spent three years of happiness greater and more unalloyed than I have ever known fall to the lot of others . . . For joy or sorrow, my life has now been lived out."[45]

It was one of the few times Roosevelt would ever mention her again. He consciously, willfully worked to purge the painful memory. In his six-hundred-page *Autobiography,* there is not a single entry for her. Photographs of Alice, scrapbook mementos, and their love letters were destroyed. One week after Alice's funeral, Theodore sold their Manhattan house at 55 West 45th Street and gave away its contents to family members. His siblings also moved out of their mother's mansion on West 57th Street because it was too costly to maintain. They found more modest residences after selling the family home.

His reaction, on top of silence, was to bury himself in work. Back in Albany, he carried the heaviest load of legislative assignments of any member in the Assembly. Roosevelt continued as chairman of the City Investigating Committee and shuttled to the anticorruption hearings in Manhattan held during ten-hour marathons each Friday, Saturday, and Monday. Numerous pieces of legislation he championed passed the Assembly, and he reported out of his committees a total of three dozen new bills. Corinne wrote to Elliott about her concerns about their brother on March 4, "He feels the awful loneliness more and more and I fear he sleeps little, for he walks a great deal in the night, and his eyes have that strained red look."[46]

His only acknowledgment of Alice's death came in written form. He gathered the Assembly speeches in her honor, the funeral tributes, and newspaper clippings about her life and had them published privately by Putnam's. Roosevelt wrote his deepest, most personal, and final public description of Alice Lee in that self-published memorial.

> She was beautiful in face and form, and lovelier still in spirit; as a flower she grew, and as a fair young flower she died. Her life had been always in the sunshine; there had never come to her a single great sorrow; and none ever knew her who did not love and revere her for her bright, sunny temper and her saintly unselfishness. Fair, pure, and joyous as a maiden; loving, tender, and happy as a young wife; when she had just become a mother, when her life seemed to be but just begun, and when the years seemed so bright before her—then, by a strange and terrible fate, death came to her.
>
> And when my heart's dearest died, the light went from my life forever.[47]

Roosevelt's crushing loss preceded a demoralizing political defeat that would drive home a terrible lesson: sometimes one's allies hurt more than one's enemies. Roosevelt threw every effort into the final report of the City Investigating Committee, turning the battle against Tammany into an epic struggle. Considering the initial draft too diluted, he set about to rewrite every page of a document that summarized weeks of hearings and more than a thousand pages of testimony. His deadline was so tight, he rushed each of the final forty-seven pages to the printer upon completion, one at a time. He pushed through two more supplemental reports of several hundred pages each that detailed corrupt practices in New York City's jails, sheriff's department, and municipal affairs.

Tammany's corruption in civil service began with the hiring

phase. A person was hired in the jail or sheriff's department upon the recommendation of a district leader as a reward for loyalty to the machine. The labor market was tight and the job of jailer was a good one, even minus the couple of hundred bucks a new employee was expected to kick back in gratitude to the district leader. Law enforcement had other carrots and sticks as well. Sheriff's deputies took money to smuggle contraband into the jails and could extract extra cash by doing favors for families of inmates or improving a cell's comfort for a prisoner who could afford to pay. The investigation of the city's jails turned up an open market of alcohol, drugs, and sex. There was a verticality to the corruption throughout municipal affairs, from lowly civil servants to high-ranking commissioners. The cop on the beat extorted cash from brothel operators in exchange for looking the other way at their flagrant lawbreaking. Blackmail and bribes put property values at the mercy of Tammany because of the chicanery of the Tax and Assessments Department heads.

His suspicions confirmed by the investigation report, Roosevelt was loaded for bear. He overheard scuttlebutt that Assemblyman Patrick Burns was going to demand an apology from Roosevelt over some perceived affront committed in his headlong rush to nail Tammany with the investigation. Roosevelt rushed at Burns with what one observer described as the frenzy of a wild goose. "Hold on, Mr. Roosevelt. For God's sake, don't strike me," Burns pleaded. "Well, you be careful what you say about me or I'll break every bone in your body," Roosevelt said. Burns apologized and sidled off to a safe distance.[48]

Roosevelt's reform legislation was so severe and far-reaching—immediate removal of tenure of all New York City department heads was just one of the provisions—that it produced a near-riot in the Assembly. Armed with the details of his investigating committee report, he could legislate reform through the usual channel of a standing committee. Roosevelt reported thirty-five bills out of his Cities Committee in just two days, arguing that they could save New York $3 million through streamlining and new efficiencies. One created an office of searcher for liens and sales in the Finance Department of New York. Another bill abolished imprisonment for debt in civil actions. A correspondent with the *Evening Post* described the tumult on the floor of the Assembly as a "scene of uproar and violence to all rules of decency." When Roosevelt pushed to bring the bills to a vote by special order, he was knocked down by his adversaries. "Some of the members have been unkind enough to call me arrogant in pushing my measures so closely," Roosevelt told the *Commercial Advertiser.* "I am not arrogant. I am simply in dead earnest."[49] Tammany continued to raise a tumult around the reformer, who would not cave. One assemblyman described him as "rejoicing like an eagle in the midst of a storm."[50] Assemblyman Walter S. Hubbell described how "a howling mob . . . rushed from their seats and assembled in front of the Clerk's desk . . . with yells, hisses and denunciations."[51] The results of Roosevelt's spirited skirmish were anticlimactic. The Assembly adjourned after the outburst, and backroom negotiations commenced. There were plenty of obstacles ahead for Roosevelt's reform package as the bills inched toward the desk of Governor Cleveland.

Riding the band of self-induced high pressure he'd inhabited for two months, Roosevelt charged one hundred miles west of Albany to Utica, an upstate industrial city and slightly smaller version of the capital, for the New York State Republican Convention in 1884. Roosevelt's primary objective was to undercut the momentum for nominating James G. Blaine—at various times senator from Maine, Speaker of the House, and secretary of state—the sort of professional politico and co-opted insider the young reformer despised. "Decidedly mottled" was Roosevelt's assessment of Blaine's checkered past. Nor would Roosevelt countenance the candidacy of President Arthur for a second term, because of both policy disagreements and personal animus over

Arthur's role in his father's sabotaged federal appointment. Blaine had a way of rising in the Republican Party by pulling others down. He could chop an opponent off at the knees with a wicked turn of phrase. He wasn't afraid to skewer his powerful enemy, Roscoe Conkling, by describing his "haughty disdain, his grandiloquent swell, his majestic, supereminent, overpowering, turkey-gobbler strut."[52] When he was Speaker of the House, Blaine had used his powerful position to siphon money from lobbyists willing to pay substantially to have the Speaker steer their bills out of committee and through Congress.

Roosevelt was used to taking the road less traveled and convincing others to follow. He adopted that strategy at Utica, backing a long shot, George F. Edmunds, a senator from Vermont and supporter of a reform agenda. It would take skilled maneuvering from a relatively green negotiator without much experience in the backroom deal making of political conventions to secure a nomination for Edmunds. Roosevelt's calculations at the convention gave him a slight window of opportunity, since all but about 15 percent of the five hundred convention participants were split between Blaine and Arthur. Roosevelt thought he could build a coalition among those seventy or so independent delegates and fashion it into a wedge between the two front-runners. Such a spoiler tactic, Roosevelt figured, just might create enough of an opening for the long shot to slip through the divided gathering to a surprise victory. More importantly, the move would provide a chance for revenge against Blaine, Miller, and other machine leaders who had knocked Roosevelt out of contention for the Assembly Speaker post.

Checking into Utica's Baggs Hotel on April 22, Roosevelt became the leader of the spoilers' faction. His room was dubbed "Edmunds' headquarters" and a clump of passionate Independents gathered there to plot strategy with their leader. The battle lines were sharply drawn. The boss of New York Republicans, Senator Warner "Wood-Pulp" Miller, backed

Blaine. Miller's colorful nickname came from his investments in
the wood and paper industry of his rural base in Herkimer
County, although some wags suggested it might refer to the
way he ground up political opponents. State Republican Chairman James D. Warren, whose title was more impressive than his
hold on party power, supported President Arthur. Neither one
took Roosevelt and his small band of subversives seriously at
first. At stake were four important delegates-at-large positions
for the national convention in Chicago, though those slots were
a mere handful in comparison to the delegates that were already
pledged to one candidate or another. In their negotiations, Boss
Miller and Chairman Warren acted as if they were playing cards
for the four slots. Though five hundred delegates would each
cast a vote for four names of potential delegates at large, the
bosses assumed they could control their men, but the attendees
turned out to be far less beholden to Miller and Warren than
those men hoped.

Among the candidates running for the four slots were Roosevelt, Miller, and several others who were not pledged to any
particular allegiance. Roosevelt and his animated band of Independents were vocal and self-confident. Time-honored machine
tactics of payoffs and patronage jobs suddenly lacked the corrupt lure they once had. Delegates could afford to snub Miller
and Warren. Roosevelt's triumvirate of rabble-rousers in Utica
were Cornell University President Andrew D. White, New
York State Senator John J. Gilbert, and Brooklyn millionaire
Edwin Packard, a spice importer. Sensing they were outgunned,
the bosses reluctantly began to involve Roosevelt's faction in
the backroom dealings, but Roosevelt would not make a deal.
He refused the offer of one Independent delegate at large, which
soon rose to three delegate slots as the machine men grew desperate. Roosevelt displayed the patience of the seasoned big-
game hunter he was. He warily watched and waited. He would
accept no less than all four. When the ballots were counted,

Roosevelt led all candidates with 472 votes, followed by White with 407, Gilbert with 342, and Packard with 256. Roosevelt and his three Independent allies were elected. Boss Miller ran a pathetic fifth, with 243 votes, barely more than half of Roosevelt's total and eight votes short of a majority. Wood-Pulp Miller, as a *Sun* correspondent put it, had "been pulverized finer than his own pulp." Newspaper correspondents wrote the obituary for Miller's reign as party chieftain. Roosevelt rubbed salt in Miller's wounds by confronting the fallen leader and openly reveling in his demise. Payback was sweet against Miller, who had undercut Roosevelt's candidacy for Assembly Speaker. "There, damn you!" Roosevelt said, shaking his fist at Miller. "We beat you for what you did last year!"[53] In the run-up to the Republican National Convention in Chicago, Roosevelt was saluted by the *New York Times* as "the victor, the wearer of all the laurels" and immediately hailed as a new and major figure on the national Republican political scene.

Roosevelt returned to Albany and was bathed in glowing reviews from his supporters in the Assembly, but he clearly had his sights set higher than the lower house in Albany; he deliberately and rather coldly pulled back from his earliest, albeit provincial supporters: Hunt, O'Neil, and the rest. Roosevelt wrote a heartfelt letter to the editor of the *Utica Morning Herald,* Simon Newton Dexter North, whom Roosevelt had befriended at the Utica convention. Roosevelt at least feigned humility by writing to North from Albany on April 30 to assure the editor "that my head will not be turned by what I well know was a mainly accidental success." But he continued,

> I realize very thoroughly the absolutely ephemeral nature of the hold I have upon the people, and a very real and positive hostility I have excited among the politicians. I will not stay in public life unless I can do so on my own terms; and my ideal, whether lived up to or not is rather a high one.

Roosevelt's win in Utica was tempered by a setback upon his return to Albany on April 24. The package of reform legislation he championed in the Assembly had bogged down. He had misjudged the response of Governor Cleveland, with whom Roosevelt had successfully collaborated in the previous session on civil service reform. The cyclone assemblyman was thrown off course when Cleveland threatened to veto the New York City anticorruption bills. Roosevelt stormed into the executive office and noisily confronted the man that a correspondent had dubbed "the Immovable Object." One observer, Daniel S. Lamont, the governor's secretary, likened Cleveland to "a great mastiff solemnly regarding a small terrier, snapping and barking at him."[54] Cleveland had turned his finely tuned legal mind to the blizzard of bills Roosevelt had driven through the Legislature and found them lacking in regard to technical language. The former Buffalo lawyer pointed out to Roosevelt several inconsistencies and picayune details that rendered the bills, in the governor's mind, technically flawed. They would have to be redrafted and the legislative process would have to begin again, from scratch. Cleveland's corrective was a flash of red in front of a bull. Roosevelt chomped off his words, blurting out that he would not tolerate the vetoing of the bills. Cleveland lifted his massive bulk and slammed a meaty fist down onto his desk for effect. His decision to veto the bills was final; the meeting was over. Stunned, Roosevelt slunk out of the governor's office.

Cleveland would go on to win two terms in the White House, and he stands as the most prominent honest Democrat of his era—coming at the end of a period when that party stood for patronage above all. Yet his flaws were as enormous as his body, and they suggest that public sentiment for reform must have been strong indeed to lift even him. As for Roosevelt, he would go to the National Republican Convention in Chicago, although the betrayal by Cleveland was enough to drive him from politics for a while. Trying unsuccessfully to outrun personal grief, he had discovered that he also could not avoid political disappointment.

Roosevelt slogged through the troubled days of gloom and regret until May 31, when he arrived in Chicago. The high energy and buzz of excitement that emanated from a political convention lifted Roosevelt's spirits, as did his reconnecting with friend and political confidant Henry Cabot Lodge, the esteemed Massachusetts senator and literary man, who had also taught history at Harvard when Roosevelt was there. The men were delegates at large of neighboring states. Their friendship and political allegiance deepened and solidified in marathon planning sessions as the two attempted to galvanize the one hundred or so Edmunds supporters into the same sort of spoiler role Roosevelt had pulled off in Utica. They were particularly annoying for their staunch refusal to have their votes bought with cash bribes of upwards of a thousand dollars known as "boodle." Their efforts popularized a new political term: "mugwump," from the Algonquian word *mugquomp,* meaning chief or person of high rank. Used as shorthand for those who bolted the Republican regulars, known as the Old Guard, the term was put into popular circulation by the *New York Sun* with its coverage of the Chicago convention. Despite Roosevelt and company's earnest labors at mugwumpery, however, lightning would not strike twice. Blaine was nominated on the fourth ballot. The reformers dubbed June 6, the day of the vote, Black Friday.

Roosevelt, Lodge, and their crushed cohorts had managed to divide the Republicans and open up deep fissures in the party's philosophy. To help repair the rift, William McKinley, an Ohio congressman with a rising profile in Chicago, worked his way through the clogged convention floor and personally urged Roosevelt to make a unity speech in favor of Blaine. Roosevelt refused.

A reporter with the *New York World* caught up with an ill-tempered Roosevelt outside the Exposition Hall. The delegate said he'd had enough of politics for the time being and was going cattle-ranching in Dakota. Would he support the Republican nominee for president? Roosevelt darkened and refused to mention Blaine by name. "That question I decline to answer. It is a subject that I do not care to talk about."

The most extreme mugwumps were bolting the Republican Party altogether and supporting Grover Cleveland. Some vague remarks to newspaper correspondents were misinterpreted to suggest that Roosevelt would join the defectors in supporting Cleveland. After an agonizing consideration, Roosevelt and Lodge decided not to break Republican ranks; they would support Blaine. "I am by inheritance and by education a Republican; whatever good I have been able to accomplish in public life has been accomplished through the Republican Party," Roosevelt stated. He campaigned for Blaine and was predictably branded a turncoat by the mugwumps. The result was that he had no friends in the party.

"I do not believe that I shall ever be likely to come back into political life," he wrote to Lodge. He was determined to follow protomugwump Horace Greeley's advice and "go west, young man." He professed to be disgusted with politics. In an article for *Century* magazine he declared,

> Legislative life has temptations enough to make it unadvisable for any weak man, whether young or old, to enter it. A great many men deteriorate very much morally when they go to Albany. It will be hard to make any great improvement in the character of the legislators until respectable people become more fully awake to their duties.

Chapter 5

★ ★ ★ ★ ★

BADLANDS

There are few sensations I prefer to that of galloping over these rolling limitless prairies, rifle in hand, or winding my way among the barren, fantastic and grimly picturesque deserts of the so-called Bad Lands.

Les mauvaises terres a traverser ("Bad lands to travel through") was what French trappers called the little-known and largely unexplored region along the Little Missouri River in the western part of the Dakota Territory. Though the Sioux christened the area with a less ominous-sounding description—"Place where the hills look at each other"—the Badlands are geography with attitude. For the bereft New Yorker Theodore Roosevelt—still despondent over the deaths of his wife and mother, beaten down by the grind of Albany politics, and conflicted about his future both personally and professionally—it was topography as therapy. Roosevelt described the Badlands as "a wild romantic rock garden of the gods."[1] Towering bluffs and stark, barren buttes brooded above a vast wasteland of unnamed and primordial chasms. Locals dubbed the Little Missouri the "Little Misery." For a young man with deep and profound miseries to work through, the Badlands offered an environment for uninterrupted soul-searching and rugged meditation. Roosevelt's earlier adolescent adventures and tentative tests of manhood in the forests of Maine and the wilderness of the Adirondacks were only a warm-up act. In 1864, Brigadier General Alfred Sully, fighting in the region during his campaign against the Sioux, said the Badlands looked like "Hell with the fire gone out."[2] General George A. Custer, passing through the region in 1876 en route to his fatal stand at Little Big Horn, remarked that he and his troops found the Badlands "impassable" and the Little Missouri "crooked." "The bottom is quicksand. Many of the horses went down, frequently tumbling the riders into the water."[3]

Roosevelt was twenty-five years old, morose, gaunt, out of shape, and craving rigorous exercise. Within a week, he was writing his sister Bamie animated letters about his deep love of the place and expressing excitement about his success at hunting antelope and his future ranching plans.

Well, I have been having a glorious time here, and am well hardened now. (I have just come in from spending *thirteen* hours in the saddle.) . . . I have never been in better health than on this trip. I am in the saddle all day long . . . The country is growing on me more and more; it has a curious, fantastic beauty of its own.[4]

Roosevelt wasted no time in leaving personal grief and political failure behind. In fact, repeating a pattern he had established in dealing with tragedies since the death of his father, Roosevelt simply outrode the emotional pain by never stopping long enough to give in to melancholy. "Black care rarely sits behind a rider whose pace is fast enough" was how Roosevelt put it in a memoir about his experiences in the West. His tortured years of battling asthma, trying to live up to his father's example, and confronting fears about his manliness were sublimated by the grueling schedule he set for himself in the Badlands. Of course the comfortable inheritance from his father made it all possible.

Roosevelt could afford to own eight horses; he chose a fresh one each day so that his riding knew no bounds. One day, he boasted, he rode from dawn until darkness and covered seventy-two miles—an astonishing distance considering the harsh and difficult terrain.

Getting away from politics and the culture of the eastern ruling class allowed Roosevelt the time and space not only to recover from his loss but to reinvent himself as one of the rugged heroes from the sagas and adventure stories he thrilled to in books during a bedridden boyhood. He wrote of the Badlands in romantic, lyrical images:

> It was a land of vast silent spaces, of lonely rivers . . . In that land we led a free and hardy life, with horse and with rifle . . . In the winter we rode through blinding blizzards, when the driven snow-dust burnt our faces . . . We knew toil and hardship and hunger and thirst; and we saw men die violent deaths as they worked among the horses and cattle, or fought in evil feuds with one another; but we felt the beat of hardy life in our veins, and ours was the glory of work and the joy of living.[5]

Roosevelt arrived at the Little Missouri for the first time in September 1883, where he met brothers Sylvane and Joe Ferris and their partner, William J.Merrifield, who operated the Chimney Butte Ranch—where they lived in a crude log structure with a dirt roof. Joe Ferris earlier had guided Roosevelt on a buffalo hunt, and the quartet developed an easy camaraderie that later shifted into a business partnership. Although they lacked the refinement of his fellow Harvard graduates, the cattle ranchers taught Roosevelt deep virtues such as "self-reliance, hardihood, and the value of instant decision."[6]

Dipping into his inheritance with an initial $14,000 outlay, Roosevelt made a hefty investment in the region's growing open-range cattle industry with the purchase of four hundred head of beef cattle. He hired Merrifield and Sylvane Ferris to run his spread, Maltese Cross Ranch, after a strong lobbying pitch by the politician to overcome their reservations. With little fanfare and even less planning, Roosevelt had transformed himself from politician into cattle rancher. Of course, he couldn't entirely leave a Manhattanite's dude roots behind; he brought along an ornately carved silver knife from Tiffany & Co., silver spurs, and a custom fringed buckskin outfit by Brooks Brothers.

Although he lost about twenty-five head of cattle over the winter from wolves and extreme cold, Roosevelt was upbeat about the condition of his cattle operation in the summer of 1884. After deciding on the spur of the moment to add a second ranch, Elkhorn, along the Little Missouri, Roosevelt now owned a total herd of about 1,600 cattle. He imported his old Maine hunting guides, Bill Sewall and Wilmot Dow, to manage that operation. Roosevelt blasted ahead with his expanding cattle empire against the recommendations of his financial adviser, who warned Theodore that he was severely draining his inheritance. Roosevelt welcomed the news that one hundred and fifty healthy calves were born into his herd that first spring as justification for his spending spree. He planned to continue adding additional cattle to his ranches in order to "make it my regular business . . . I think it will be a good many years before I get back into politics."[7]

The therapeutic aspect of riding across the prairies and participating in the adrenaline rush of a cattle roundup may have hardened Roosevelt, but it did not mellow him. While he exulted in bagging a trophy antelope ("another good head for the famous hall at Leeholm"),[8] he decried the dearth of big-game animals and shot as a kind of consolation prize jackrabbits, curlews, rattlesnakes, prairie chickens, sage hens, grouse, ducks, and a few large bucks. He complained that the rising number of cattle being raised by greedy cattlemen had crowded out the big-game animals, even though he himself was a cattleman with plans to nearly double his herd. Roosevelt's feelings on hunting in the Badlands had brightened considerably by September, when he bagged three grizzly bear, six elk, a half-dozen deer, and numerous smaller quarry—in all, a total of a dozen trophy heads.

Roosevelt arrived in the Dakota Territory at a time when the heroic image of the cowboy and the mythic version of the Wild West were devolving into caricatures. In 1883, former buffalo hunter and cowboy William Frederick Cody presented a new form of entertainment he touted as Buffalo Bill's Wild West Show. Cody rounded up a herd of tame cattle and buffalo, hired struggling cowboys and desperate Indians, and sold tickets to a popular entertainment featuring mock cattle roundups, buffalo hunts, and stagecoach holdups. Cody's showmanship proved immensely popular, his marketing gimmicks earning him a reputation as "the P. T. Barnum of the American West." In turn, Cody's fictionalized version of the place and its people spurred settlement and development in the West.

Roosevelt's first extended visit to the Badlands had come during his buffalo-hunting expedition in the fall of 1883. The recent arrival of the Northern Pacific Railroad had rendered the isolated Great Plains accessible to large-scale commerce and made cattle ranching possible with a transportation network that could support national distribution for an emerging beef industry. Trains also put the superabundant Plains within easy reach of commercial hunting operations and casual sportsmen. In 1882, a hunter described the Badlands teeming with buffalo and other big-game mammals, a "sportsman's Paradise . . . I never saw so many antelope on the uplands and you ran across deer in every draw."[9]

Within two years, the astonishingly swift wholesale slaughter of the buffalo was nearly complete. The largest land mammal in North America since the Ice Age had thrived for centuries across the Great Plains and throughout the continent. The buffalo's population held steady and even increased under the limited hunting pressure of the Sioux and other nomadic Native American tribes that migrated with the vast herds and took what was needed for that season's survival. Killing a buffalo was hardly sport. Because the animals had no natural predators and no ingrained fear of humans on the open range—even of hunters stalking them with rifles—a man essentially could proceed to within point-blank range of a buffalo herd and blast away. What the hunters didn't accomplish, the cattlemen did, as their grazing cattle took the available pasture and drove out the buffalo from the best rangelands. Buffalo carcasses piled up as if felled by a medieval plague. The buffalo population had been estimated at between 40 and 60 million across North America at the start of the nineteenth century, but now the magnificent species was nearly extinct. Fewer than five thousand buffalo survived by the late 1890s.

The buffalo weren't the only species nearly wiped out in the hunting frenzy across the Plains at the close of the nineteenth century. Of the estimated 24 million white-tailed deer, just 500,000 remained. Fifteen million wild turkeys had been reduced to 400,000. Only 25,000 antelope were left out of 10 million. Vast herds of elk, 10 million strong, had been decimated to just 150,000.[10]

The sight of such widespread and utter destruction of Badlands flora and fauna made a powerful impression on the twenty-five-year-old Roosevelt. A seed was planted that would eventually spur Roosevelt to become one of the greatest conservationists in American history.

Roosevelt was every inch a Tiffany and Brooks Brothers cowboy. Without a hint of self-deprecating humor, Roosevelt proudly described his outlandish getup: "I wear a sombrero, silk neckerchief, fringed buckskin shirt, sealskin chaprajos on riding trousers; alligator hide boots; and with my pearl hilted revolver and beautifully finished Winchester Rifle, I shall feel able to face anything."[11] The Harvard dandy who had been mocked as "that damn dude" upon his arrival at the New York State Legislature in Albany was similarly scorned by the hard-bitten ranch hands and unpretentious Dakotans who scratched a living out of the Badlands. They couldn't get over his extravagant daily habit of shaving and brushing his teeth. Roosevelt's reading habits were out of place among the cowboys too. He lugged along a half-dozen thick volumes, often more, on his railroad journeys and read by the light of campfires during roundups on the range. In the side pocket of his outer coat, whether riding horseback or traveling by train, Roosevelt typically carried a single small, heavily bound, dog-eared copy of Plutarch's *Lives* and made it his literary touchstone—taking a daily half hour of Plutarch as if it were some sort of intellectual constitutional. "I have read this little volume close to a thousand times, but it is ever new," he said.[12] Roosevelt also sought out intellectual compatriots, although it was not done in a snobbish way. One of his bookish friends was the father of James W. Foley, who became the poet laureate of North Dakota. Roosevelt called the elder Foley one of very few men in that region with whom he shared a passion for reading and discussing books. "Now and then, after six or eight weeks on the range with valued friends who were distinctly of a nonliterary type, I would come in to spend an evening with Mr. Foley for the special purpose of again listening to a speech about books."[13]

One anecdote from his Badlands days that has gained currency and has no doubt been embellished in the generations of retelling involves Roosevelt's stay at a frontier hotel that doubled as a bar and gathering place for the ranchers along the Little Missouri. Roosevelt was reading a book when a man who apparently had been drinking excessively staggered up to the bar and ordered a round for the house. The other patrons eagerly sidled up to the bar for their drinks. Only Roosevelt remained seated, his nose still buried in his book, reading with his glasses, which locals dubbed "cheaters."

The fellow buying the round grew belligerent over this ungrateful tenderfoot.

"Hey, you, Mr. Four-eyes!" shouted the man. "I asked this house to drink! D'you hear?"

Roosevelt did not acknowledge him, according to the account. So the man drew his pistol, fired at the barroom's clock, and strode toward Roosevelt. When the man reached him, Roosevelt looked up and asked to be excused.

"That don't go down here," the angry drunk said. "Order your drink."

Roosevelt stood up and began to mutter a vague response when his right fist exploded in a punch that caught the startled man square on the chin. The Harvard boxer followed up with a quick flurry of lefts and rights that dropped the stunned bully to the floor. Roosevelt jumped astride the dazed aggressor, pinned the man's arms to the floor, tossed the pistol aside, and glared through his thick spectacles. Roosevelt spoke with clenched teeth. "And when I intimate that I don't care to drink with you, just understand that I don't care to drink," Roosevelt said in his New York accent.[14] Many years later, Roosevelt confirmed the gist of the encounter by recalling the story as the only time in his life that he was "shot at maliciously . . . My assailant was a broad-hatted ruffian of a cheap type. The fact that I wore glasses, together with my evident desire to avoid a fight, apparently gave him the impression—a mistaken one—that I would not resent an injury."[15]

The local cowboys called him by the nickname Teddy— which Roosevelt had previously despised, although he accepted it in this locale with the warmth in which it was given. Despite his flamboyant attire and conspicuous wealth, Roosevelt worked hard to be treated just like any other rancher. He insisted on putting in the same grinding number of hours in the saddle and tackling the same most loathsome jobs as did other ranchers during the spring and fall roundups. The task of maneuvering in close with a red-hot branding iron against a balky calf or cow, whether in a corral or on the open plain, is a job that tests the grit of a cowboy. Roosevelt volunteered for branding duty, which involves finesse and a coordinated technique. Two men called flankers tackle the animal from opposite sides. One flanker ties up the cow's front legs and pins its head to the ground with his knee. His partner braces a foot against one of the cow's hind legs and stretches out the other to full length. A third member of the team, the brander, presses the sizzling iron home on the under-side of the cow's flesh, while a fourth person, known as the checker, enters a mark corresponding to the design of the ranch's brand into the roundup tally book. It was muscle-straining toil, with the ever-present danger of injury from a head butt or kick. Roosevelt wrote his sister Bamie of his happiness after one spring roundup:

> I have been on the round-up for a fortnight and really enjoy the work greatly; in fact, I am passing a most pleasant sum-mer, though I miss all of you very very much. We breakfast at three every morning and work from sixteen to eighteen hours a day, counting night guard, so I get pretty sleepy; but I feel strong as a bear.[16]

By his own assessment, Roosevelt never developed into more than a mediocre roper and rider compared to the standards of vet-eran cattle ranchers. What he lacked in natural talent, he made up for with dogged determination and an ability to withstand pain. Roosevelt endured a cracked rib and a dislocated shoulder after being bucked from his horse during roundups and kept going. Toiling alongside these ranchers taught him that "a man of ordinary power, who nevertheless does not shirk things merely because they are disagreeable or irksome, soon earns his place."[17]

Roosevelt's ability to fit in and gain the acceptance of the cowboys grew out of his real respect for them and their way of life. He compared the lifestyle of the Badlands men favorably with that of Gramercy Park residents in Manhattan.

> I have found them a most brave, and hospitable set of men. There is no use in trying to be overbearing with them for they won't stand for the least assumption of superiority, yet there are places in our cities where I would feel less safe than I would among the wildest cowboys in the West.[18]

In mid-December, after the roundup and ranch duties had been completed, Roosevelt tramped on a hunting expedition through "the most awful country that can be imagined" in harsh winter conditions. Roosevelt marveled at "a bank of huge ice floes that tumbled over each other in the wildest confusion" stretching for miles along the Little Missouri River, forcing the party to "work like arctic explorers."[19] Just after shooting his first mountain goat, Roosevelt stumbled upon the den of a grizzly bear and startled the nine-foot, half-ton monster, which arose just eight paces away. Here was the epic encounter between man and beast that Roosevelt craved.

> He had been roused from his sleep by our approach; he sat up in his lair, and turned his huge head slowly towards us [with] his two sinister looking eyes; as I pulled the trigger I jumped aside out of the smoke, to be ready if he charged . . . the great brute was struggling in the death agony . . . The bullet hole in his skull was as exactly between his eyes as if I had measured the distance with a carpenters rule . . . I had grand sport with the elk too, and the woods fairly sang with my shouting when I brought down my first lordly bull, with great branching antlers.[20]

Later in the same letter, Roosevelt confided to his sister Bamie—his closest confidante, to whom he revealed his fears and deepest feelings—that his hunting successes had helped counter-act his depression. And yet he was like a drug addict who craved more potent drugs and larger, more frequent doses to continue to achieve an intense high.

"So I have had good sport," he wrote, "and enough excite-ment and fatigue to prevent over much thought; and moreover I have at last been able to sleep well at night. But unless I was bear hunting all the time I am afraid I should soon get as restless with this life as with the life at home."[21] And then, for the first time since leaving Albany and politics behind, he conceded that he regretted that his political career was finished—before quickly changing the subject and trying to outride his conflicted feelings.

Cow Boy magazine treated Roosevelt like a temporary amuse-ment who was not to be taken seriously, a mocking tone adopted by others in the Badlands. "Mr. Roosevelt is still at Ferris & Mer-rifield's Ranch, hunting and playing cowboy. It seems to be more congenial work than reforming New York state politics. He is thoroughly impressed with the profit of raising cattle in the Bad Lands."[22] The magazine and other cowboys also made great sport of Roosevelt's Harvard-inspired formal diction. Roosevelt reput-edly gave the command "Hasten forward quickly there," a usage that busted up the cowboys and soon echoed throughout the canyons on roundups, followed by gales of laughter. Roosevelt was also attempting to write biographies of Gouverneur Morris, a neg-lected notable New Yorker who helped press for American inde-pendence from Britain, and Thomas Hart Benton, a hero in the War of 1812 and later a U.S. senator, during his time in the Bad-lands and found his literary work more demanding and difficult than his ranch labors. "The rest of the time I read or else work at Benton, which is making very slow progress; writing is to me in-tensely irksome work."[23] One month later, Roosevelt—who wrote in bouts of muscular prose akin to his Harvard sparring matches—had finished one chapter of the Benton book and chided himself for an output that modern-day biographers would envy.

Roosevelt could not entirely ride fast enough to put the dark cares of his crushing double loss behind him. During periodic returns to New York, he could not help but be confronted with the unresolved matter of Baby Lee, whose name he still could not utter. Only slowly did he begin to adopt a more mature and realistic approach to the fact that he was a father. He knew he could not simply pawn off his daughter upon Bamie, whom he described as his indispensable support network and "the driving Wheel of Destiny and the Superintendent-in-chief of the workings of Providence."[24] He made a point of spending time with his baby daughter on visits to New York, played with her and, for the first time, expressed a father's pride and genuine love for his offspring. "The baby is in a condition of rampant and vocal good health; very happy . . . with inarticulate affection," he wrote.[25] A month after his visit with his infant daughter, after dozens of letters written to his sister Bamie from the Badlands, Roosevelt for the first time concluded a missive with a message to his daughter: "Give my best love to strong hearted Baby Lee."[26] After that, the floodgates of fatherly emotion opened and Roosevelt positively gushed in his effusive messages for his baby daughter. "I miss both you and darling Baby Lee dreadfully; kiss her many times for me; I am really hungry to see her. She must be just too cunning for anything."[27]

Roosevelt entered cattle ranching at the moment when it was climbing rapidly to an apex of production. By 1880, the Northern Pacific Railroad was carrying trains that stretched a mile or more, with cattle cars loaded with beef headed east to the major meatpacking centers. In the spring of 1883, a mysterious and flamboyant French nobleman, Antoine de Vallombroso—who insisted on being addressed by the title of Marquis de Mores—appeared in the rough-hewn cowboy settlement of Little Missouri like some foppish character from a Molière stage comedy. The marquis was immensely wealthy and enthralled with the faux romanticism of cattle ranching. He decided to invest a small fortune in the expanding industry. Naturally, he was about as welcome in Little Missouri as hoof-and-mouth disease. Roosevelt entered the cattle-ranching operation at the same time as the marquis and, although he worked on a much smaller scale, became a bitter rival of the neighboring Frenchman.

The marquis bought a vast tract and carved out his own town from the arid wasteland. He named it in honor of his wife, Medora von Hoffman, and set to fashioning a palatial dreamland for her. She was an American who had inherited a vast fortune. On a promontory above the river, the marquis spent lavishly to import materials and laborers, who constructed a twenty-eight-room French château. His wife filled the mansion with luxurious furnishings and a full complement of servants: a butler, coachman, gardener, laundress, several chambermaids, and a group of cooks. The couple's entourage added significantly to the population of Medora, which stood at 251 in 1884. The locals viewed the fantasy world she created in the harsh and isolated buttes with endless amusement and nicknamed her "the Queen of the Badlands."

Roosevelt's accommodations at Elkhorn Ranch, about ten miles south of the marquis's château in Medora, were considerably less luxurious. A less ostentatious style insulated Roosevelt somewhat from the open hatred local residents directed toward the marquis's extravagances. During the winter of 1883–84, with the help of the Ferris brothers and Merrifield, Roosevelt built a rustic ranch cabin at the Elkhorn on the edge of a low bluff overlooking the serpentine Little Missouri, which ran low and slow much of the year. The nearest neighbor was about ten miles away. They built the plain structure of ponderosa pine and logs salvaged from the flotsam and jetsam tossed above the banks and onto sandbars along the river after springtime's high water. Roosevelt insisted that the ranch-house design include a veranda, where he could sit in his rocking chair, reading or writing, and listening to the melancholic cooing calls of mourning doves that perched in the row of cottonwood trees flanking the porch. Mortar filled the gaps and chinks to help keep out cold drafts in the simple notched-log construction. The wood-shingled roof was high-pitched to shed snow and to provide room for an extra half story with a low attic space for storage, which doubled as a sleeping loft for ranch hands. Two doors and several glass-paned windows were installed for easy access and natural light in the long, dark winter season. The furnishings were minimal, far less than Roosevelt had been used to in any place he'd ever lived, including his Cambridge apartment during his years at Harvard. There was a plain cupboard in the kitchen area, a writing desk, a small rocking chair, a clothing trunk, a few side chairs at the kitchen table, and very little else. Two of his indulgences were to have enough books shipped in to fill three shelves and a rubber bathtub so that he could regularly enjoy a hot soak. He took his cue from the locals and stayed warm in the frigid wintertime by wrapping himself in buffalo robes and bearskins fashioned from his own kills. Most of the meat in his diet came from the big game he shot himself—primarily deer and antelope, since buffalo and elk had been largely wiped out. He managed to domesticate a few chickens and cows, from which he got milk and eggs.

Roosevelt and his ranch hands lived no better than many and probably worse than some who raised cattle in the Badlands. That egalitarian approach—due in part to Roosevelt's limited finances, not just his personal code—gradually helped to endear him to the ranchers. Roosevelt was also happier than he had been in some time and his infectious enthusiasm for the Badlands and his strenuous life there rubbed off on others. "I enjoy my life at present," he wrote. "I have my time fully occupied with work of which I am fond; and so have none of my usual restless, caged wolf feeling; I work two days out of three at my book or papers; and hunt, ride and lead the wild, half adventurous life of a ranchman all through it."[28]

Roosevelt did not feel at all threatened by the superior survival skills of the Badlands ranchmen or the abilities with the ax of his imported Maine woodsmen, Sewall and Dow, the primary builders of the Elkhorn ranch house. Roosevelt admitted he was an amateur woodsman who could not come close to matching their speed. As they cleared the lot of cottonwood trees before building, Dow took stock of a day's work of Sewall and Roosevelt in tree cutting. "Well, Bill cut down fifty-three, I cut forty-nine, and the boss he beavered down seventeen."[29] Sewall's humorous tone did not diminish his admiration for Roosevelt's remarkable physical transformation in the Badlands from sickly legislator to rugged outdoorsman. "He went to Dakota a frail young man suffering from asthma and stomach trouble. When he got back into the world again he was as husky as almost any man I have ever seen."[30]

While the wife of the marquis, the Queen of the Badlands, frittered away her days in a mansion of make-believe, the marquis evolved into a cutthroat businessman. He adopted Chicago meatpacker Gustavus Franklin Swift's innovation of slaughtering cattle on the range and then shipping fresh beef thousands of miles in refrigerated freight cars—thus cutting costs and undercutting competitors. The marquis beat Swift at his own game by eliminating the meatpacking middleman and selling directly from the ranch to the customer. De Mores invested the extravagant sum of $10 million to build a multifaceted beef enterprise that included a large herd of cattle, a packing plant in Medora, and a fleet of refrigerated railcars.[31] Although he single-handedly brought an economic boomlet to the Badlands and was the largest employer in the region, the outsider couldn't buy the respect of locals who, behind his back, referred to the Medora operation as "that crazy Frenchman's packing plant."[32] The marquis also hemorrhaged money at the plant, which suffered losses of more than $300,000 in three years of operation before it closed for good in 1887.

The fate of the marquis in the Badlands was intertwined with that of Roosevelt. The two driven, strong-willed men began to clash during entertainments that each sponsored, and it became obvious that the Badlands weren't big enough for two such force-ful, outsize personalities. One newspaper described them as "two very big toads in a small puddle."[33] Although the source of their animosity was unclear, the marquis and Roosevelt began a public feud that was mentioned in the press. It escalated into vague threats and counterthreats of a duel to preserve their reputations and sense of honor.

"I thought you were my friend," the marquis wrote to Roo-sevelt. "If you are my enemy I want to know it. I am always on hand as you know, and between gentlemen it is easy to settle matters of that sort directly."

Roosevelt shot back testily, "Most emphatically I am not your enemy; if I were you would know it, for I would be an open one, and would not have asked you to my house nor gone to yours. As your final words, however, seem to imply a threat, it is due to myself to say that the statement is not made through any fear of possible consequences to me; I too, as you know, am always on hand, and ever ready to hold myself accountable in any way for anything I have said or done."[34]

Ironically, for all that he idealized the cowboys, Roosevelt's descriptions of the Badlands' ranch hands, up to a point, resem-bled those of the men he had encountered in the Assembly. Both groups included thugs, ruffians, and brawlers. Roosevelt had learned early on to stand up to the bullies in the New York State Legislature, and he repeated this never-back-down approach in the Badlands, where he eventually earned respect as a rugged individualist. Yet while he saw the tough-guy legislators as cor-rupt and undesirable, he ascribed a sort of purity to similar behavior in the Badlands. He considered the fights among these "lean, sinewy fellows" as somehow ennobling and a positive test of courage.

There was a good deal of rough horse-play, and, as with any other gathering of men or boys of high animal spirits, the horse-play sometimes became very rough indeed; and as the men usually carried revolvers, and as there were occasionally one or two noted gunfighters among them, there was now and then a shooting affray. A man who was a coward or who shirked his work had a bad time, of course; a man could not afford to let himself be bullied or treated as a butt.[35]

There was a lesson lurking in the experiences: in politics, you have to work with the system and respect its politicians. That, as much as muscle mass, was what he gained out West.

Roosevelt made regular trips back to the East Coast but spent his time in New York City rather than visiting Albany. He managed to keep his hand in literary work and met with his publisher to deliver the 95,000-word manuscript for *Hunting Trips of a Ranchman.* On these return visits to New York, Roosevelt assiduously avoided meetings with the still-single Edith Carow, who maintained a close relationship with Roosevelt's sisters. In the fall of 1885, however, Roosevelt unexpectedly encountered her. Edith was a regular guest at Bamie's house in Manhattan but always discreetly vacated the premises when Theodore was due to arrive. On this occasion, however, he came earlier than expected and literally ran into Edith in the front hallway as she prepared to leave. It was a startling, but not altogether unpleasant, collision. The years of anger and regret melted away. Whatever was said between the two former lovers in that foyer, some form of latent love was reawakened, as her sapphire blue eyes peered into his steely grays. For several days afterward, the letter *E* was the only entry Theodore made in his diary. The couple rekindled their romance in secret, out of concern about public perception regarding the recent death of Theodore's wife. He called on Edith at her house at East Thirty-sixth Street. (Edith had managed to remain financially independent as a single woman because of a small annuity from a grandfather's inheritance.) Nobody seemed to notice that

Theodore spent longer than usual in Manhattan during his visits nowadays, delaying returning to his ranch.

On November 17, 1885, Theodore, his arm in a sling after a riding accident fracture, struggled to present Edith with a ring, a watch, and a pearl necklace as he asked her to marry him. She accepted. They didn't tell anyone, mainly because of fear of a negative public reaction. Theodore had been a widower for just eighteen months; Victorian mores frowned on an engagement or second marriage after such a brief interval. The betrothed agreed that they would wait a year or so to announce their engagement and set a date for the wedding. That would also give Theodore time to solidify his shifting interests and help him decide if he would settle on a job as rancher, writer, politician, or something else entirely. Roosevelt hadn't decided, after all, what he'd be when he grew up. Or in his case, perhaps, if he grew up.

Politics never disappeared entirely from his interests. Roosevelt followed closely the vicious 1884 presidential campaign in which New York Governor Grover Cleveland, a Democrat, overcame an embarrassing paternity scandal to defeat Republican James G. Blaine of Maine—putting into the White House Roosevelt's collaborator on civil service reform in Albany. It was a breath of fresh air for the Democratic Party, and it would not be Cleveland's only election victory, though he became the only president in U.S. history to regain office after losing an intermediate term.

Back in the Badlands, Roosevelt's infrequent trips into Medora were usually coordinated so that he could call on Arthur T. Packard, a University of Michigan graduate who had drifted West and become editor of the *Bad Lands Cow Boy*. Roosevelt made brief stopovers so that he could sit by a potbellied coal stove in Packard's newspaper office and soak up the editor's collected wisdom. The subtext was that life was a harsh struggle requiring moral soundness, mental toughness, and good judgment of character, estimating men on their merits rather than on their social backgrounds. The goal was to become, as the *Sioux Falls Press* described Roosevelt, "a whole-souled, clear-headed, high-minded gentleman."[36] Listening to stories and lessons in the grassroots, common-sense politics of the West, Roosevelt began to learn how to broaden his appeal from a New York regional politician to a national figure. Packard saw in Roosevelt's nature presidential timber. Roosevelt accepted Packard's rather fantastical assessment without disagreement.

Roosevelt's discussions with Packard also helped keep him abreast of national news and allowed him to wet a finger and hold it up to test the direction of America's political winds. The bitter and prolonged clashes between capital and labor from Maine to Texas in the spring of 1886—culminating in widespread strikes and mob violence during the Haymarket Square riots in Chicago—became a burr under the saddle of cattle rancher Roosevelt. He took a hard-line position against the mob and its call for shorter daily working hours with the rallying cry, "Eight-hour day with no cut in pay."

> My men here are hardworking, labouring men, who work longer hours for no greater wages than many of the strikers; but they are Americans through and through; I believe nothing would give them greater pleasure than a chance with their rifles at one of the mobs.[37]

Roosevelt knew the power of good press from his years in the Assembly and managed, through Packard and other western correspondents, to burnish the legend of "Teddy" in the remote reaches of the Badlands. Now that he let the cowboys call him Teddy, he benefited from the folksy charm of that moniker. A Teddy tale first told in the *Chicago Tribune,* and retold in numerous national journals, was related by Rudolph Lehmicke, a cowboy who participated in roundups with Roosevelt and later became a compositor at the *Tribune.*

This particular roundup was heading into its third week and had been uneventful, aside from two days of heavy and sustained rain that left the cowboys drenched and miserable. Some expected Roosevelt to complain of some phantom illness to get out of the sodden drudgery when they broke camp in the dark at three o'clock in the morning beneath a pelting rain. But Roosevelt was in the saddle with the others at that godawful appointed hour, and he did not complain. Roosevelt, Lehmicke, and Merle Bentley were assigned to drive the day herd, which is the cattle who have strayed away from their ranges during the winter. Stray cattle are gathered, their owners determined by their brands, and then they are driven in the direction of their appropriate ranges. At about noon, the men happened upon a cow with a calf that was just one week old and too small and weak to keep up with the others, causing the mother cow to lag behind. Lehmicke related the rest of the story:

> Teddy had been watching the feeble efforts of the calf to keep along with the mother, and he was touched by the little fellow's plucky struggle to follow . . . Teddy rode along slowly to accommodate the pace of the calf, but after half an hour's struggle the little fellow had to give up. With a bleat he fell from exhaustion. Teddy got off his horse, picked the calf up in his arms, put it on the saddle in front of him, and rode along for a couple of miles . . . The calf was put down after its rest in the saddle . . . This was repeated three or four times, I think, before it was decided to let the calf lie where it had fallen in the last brave struggle. Usually in such cases the mother cow is driven along with the day herd, and the abandoned calf soon dies of hunger and exposure. We were going to do this, when Teddy said, "What do you say if we leave the mother with the little fellow?" Bentley and I wanted to laugh, but we didn't and we rode away.[38]

Roosevelt liked to tell the story of an encounter with a band of five young Sioux Indians, who spotted him riding alone across a plateau near his ranch. They drew their guns and galloped directly at him, whooping and whipping their horses. Roosevelt dismounted his favorite horse, Manitou, and stood beside the unflappable animal with his rifle ready. Roosevelt knew that a marauding group of Indians like this had killed a white man on occasion, and he vowed to face the threat head-on. When the lead Indian rider was one hundred yards off and closing, Roosevelt expertly raised his rifle, drew a bead on his target, and exuded the steely resolve of a man who is cool and not afraid to shoot. The five braves quickly turned their horses around and raced away in the opposite direction. The Indians followed Roosevelt at a distance for a couple of miles before letting him go. "The worst thing a white man could do was to get into cover," he wrote to Bamie, "whereas out in the open if he kept his head he had a good chance of standing off even half a dozen assailants."

Another story that Roosevelt didn't mind recounting later involved his capture of boat thieves. A boat was a necessity on the Little Missouri, and having his own stolen was a personal affront. He was bound to find the perpetrators, and it was his duty, since he had volunteered as a deputy sheriff for the northern end of his county under Sheriff "Hell-Roaring" Bill Jones— who, according to Roosevelt, was "a thoroughly good citizen when sober." More important than doing his sworn duty for Jones, perhaps, was the promise of a bully adventure in giving chase to the thieves. Although the river was running fast and clogged with dangerous ice floes, Roosevelt did not listen to his ranch hands, who counseled him to let the larcenous act pass. Instead, he gathered up a posse. After a few days of tracking the boat thieves downriver in difficult and frigid winter conditions, Roosevelt and his gang, Sewall and Dow, caught up with the thieves at the mouth of Cherry Creek. Sewall recounted the arrest:

Will and I both were equipped with double barrel guns loaded with Buck shot and we were all three going to shoot if they offered to raise a gun. It is rather savage work but it don't do to fool with such fellows. If there was killing to be done we meant to do it ourselves . . . When Roosevelt called to him he hesitated as if he had a mind to try it . . . and he dropped it. So they were taken without danger to ourselves or harm to them . . . Mr. Roosevelt told them if they kept quiet and did not try to get off they would be all right but if they tried anything we would shoot them.[39]

Sewall called the one-hundred-mile return trip—upriver and against the current, with the boats bogged down by the added weight of the tied-up thieves and their gear—"the longest and dirtiest voyage we ever had." Sewall, Dow, and Roosevelt took turns keeping a watchful eye, with weapons trained on the captured crooks. Once they made it back to the ranch, though, the journey was not over. Roosevelt let Sewall and Dow return to their neglected ranching duties and commandeered another ranch hand for backup as they rode on to Dickinson, the nearest town, where the thieves were presented for arraignment and locked up in jail as they awaited a courtroom trial. Roosevelt was immensely satisfied. He knew too that it was the sort of story of courage and derring-do that any politician would relish adding to his campaign résumé. In order to make sure he didn't lose the opportunity, Roosevelt posed for photographs during a staged reenactment of the arrest. Roosevelt gave his own rousing version in a letter home:

My trip down the river after the three thieves was a grand succcess, as far as catching the men we were after goes . . . We came upon their camp by surprise and, covering them with our cocked rifles "held them up" and disarmed them in the most approved western fashion. Then we got caught in an ice jam, however, and had the pleasure of their company for eight days . . . Then I gave them up to the sheriff, and was heartily glad to get rid of them too.[40]

Thanks to good press, and recognition of his efforts at organizing the cattle ranchers, Roosevelt was becoming something of a local celebrity. In fact, he was invited to be the "orator of the day" during Fourth of July festivities in the town of Dickinson, which had a population of roughly seven hundred. A large number of Medora residents rode the train along with Roosevelt, and the combined crowd was considered the largest ever assembled in Stark County. The day's program began with a parade led by the Dickinson Silver Comet Band. One of the featured attractions was four white horses pulling a wagon filled with thirty-eight young girls dressed in white and representing each of the states in the Union at the time. Afterward, the Declaration of Independence was read, the crowd sang "America the Beautiful," and Roosevelt spoke:

> Much has been given us, and so, much will be expected of us; and we must take heed to use aright the gifts entrusted to our care . . . So it is peculiarly incumbent on us here today to act throughout our lives as to leave our children a heritage, for which we will receive their blessing and not their curse . . . It is not what we have that will make us a great nation; it is the way in which we use it . . . I am, myself, at heart as much a Westerner as an Easterner; I am proud, indeed, to be considered one of yourselves, and I address you in this rather solemn strain today, only because of my pride in you, and because your welfare, moral as well as material, is so near my heart.[41]

Roosevelt's cult of personality—a powerful magnetism that began in the Asssembly—grew in the Badlands. His chief accomplishment in this regard was to organize the Little Missouri Stockmen's Association. At first he rode through blizzards to discuss issues with other ranchers. There was consensus that the ranchers had to deal immediately with the problems of rustlers and inadequate protections under current range regulations. To reach those he couldn't speak to in person, Roosevelt took out an ad in *Cow Boy* calling for a meeting of the stockmen in Medora on December 19, 1884, to discuss the planning and bylaws of a membership association. The politician who had resisted the collective bargaining of unions early on in his tenure as an assemblyman, and who looked down on the Haymarket mobs, now tried to collectivize the most rugged individualists in the nation—successfully. Representatives of each of the eleven cattle companies attended the inaugural meeting and elected Roosevelt chairman of the fledgling organization. Although Roosevelt was considered a rather amateurish cattle rancher, he applied his organizational skills, indefatigable energy, and personal charisma to get the previously uncooperative stockmen to work together. Others before him had failed, but he persevered to gain consensus on drafting and enforcing new range regulations. He used his influence to hasten the firing of an incompetent livestock inspector in Medora.

He also kept his hand in New York politics, with a speech at Manhattan's Morton Hall in February 1886. His message was part proselytizing, part cheerleading. The *New York Herald* headline was "Keeping Them Straight." Roosevelt urged his fellow Republicans to take the moral high road in rallying together and working as a united front to defeat President Grover Cleveland and the rest of the Democratic slate on the national level and in the New York State Legislature—where Democrats held a majority. "Our men are of the best material, and we must get the best men of our party to represent us in the Senate and Assembly," Roosevelt argued. "They must be able to discuss all topics from the Silver question on down . . . We must win the fight of 1888 and we can do the best work by keeping our party and our representatives straight."[42]

He was more successful as a politician than a businessman. Roosevelt had entered the Badlands cattle industry when it was rapidly rising, and he was heavily invested when it plummeted due to the widespread loss of herds. The disaster began in the summer of 1886, when cattlemen from the drought-stricken south drove their herds in search of grass for grazing into the parched and already overstocked regions of the north. As chairman of the Little Missouri Stockmen's Association, Roosevelt sounded the alarm in a local newspaper interview:

> In certain sections of the West the losses this year are enormous, owing to the drought and overstocking. Each steer needs from fifteen to twenty-five acres, but they are crowded on very much thicker, and the cattlemen this season have paid the penalty. Between the drought, the grasshoppers and the late frosts, ice forming as late as June 10, there is not a green thing in all the region.[43]

The summer drought in 1886 was the start of a chain reaction of weather catastrophes that hastened the demise of the cattlemen. By late November 1886, the first severe snowstorm struck and wreaked havoc. A succession of violent blizzards and extended subzero weather during the winter of 1886–87 were "in many respects the worst on record," according to the Bismarck *Tribune.*[44] Roosevelt lost about 60 percent of his cattle. Overall, an estimated three out of four cattle in the northern Plains were lost. One after the other, ranchers folded their operations and moved away.

"I am bluer than indigo about the cattle," Roosevelt wrote his sister Bamie. "Everything was cropped as bare as a bone. The sagebrush was stripped by starving cattle . . . We had only a few hundred sick steers left, no cows."[45]

Roosevelt's herds and his optimism had reached a peak in 1886, when he owned in the range of three to five thousand head. He was a medium-sized cattle rancher with a large ambition.

> While I do not see any great fortune ahead yet, if things go on as they are now going and have gone for the past three years, I think I will each year net enough money to pay a good interest on the capital, and yet be adding slowly to my herd all the time. I think I have more than my original capital on the ground, and this year I ought to be able to sell two and three hundred head of steers and dry stock.[46]

After the terrible winter, however, his projections turned dark and foreboding. "Well, we have had a perfect smashup all through the cattle country of the northwest," he wrote to Lodge, after witnessing the devastation firsthand for the first time in the spring of 1887. "The losses are crippling. For the first time I have been utterly unable to enjoy a visit to my ranch. I shall be glad to get home."[47] In all, Roosevelt's losses in the Badlands totaled about $40,000, roughly half of his initial investment and one quarter of the entire inheritance his father left him. He did not sell out completely until 1898, but he did understand that his future lay elsewhere.

Indeed, during the disastrous winter, Roosevelt had reinvented himself back home in New York. His secret wedding plans had leaked to the press; a story running in September 1886 wounded Bamie greatly. Roosevelt had written her from the Dakota Territory,

> On returning from the mountains I was savagely irritated by seeing in the papers that I was engaged to Edith Carow; from what source it could have originated I can not possibly conceive . . . But the statement itself is true. I am engaged to Edith and before Christmas I shall cross the ocean and

marry her. You are the first person to whom I have breathed one word on the subject; I am absolutely sure that I have never betrayed myself in any way, unless some servant has seen the address on the letters I wrote.[48]

Without fanfare, the Oyster Bay estate's name was changed from Leeholm (in honor of Alice Lee) to the Native American name, Sagamore Hill. The engagement to Edith required much emotional juggling, familial finesse, and duplicity of the sort that straight-shooting Theodore was not used to pulling off. He castigated himself for not being more nimble at such matters, writing to Bamie, "You could not reproach me one half as bitterly for my own inconstancy and unfaithfulness as I reproach myself."[49]

Soon thereafter, he was home. Rather unexpectedly, in October, after he had spent three years out of the political arena, a succession of influential Manhattan Republicans met with Roosevelt at Oyster Bay and urged him to accept their offer to run him as their candidate for mayor of New York. It was a position he claimed he didn't want, but the appeals of the prominent Republican leaders and his own vanity got the better of him. To Lodge he described his acquiescence in almost apologetic tones, covering up his formidable ego and still-smoldering political ambitions.

> With the most genuine reluctance I finally accepted. It is of course a perfectly hopeless contest, the chance for success being so very small that it may be left out of account. But they want to get a united Republican party in this city and to make a good record before the people; I am at the head of an unexceptional ticket. They seemed to think that my name would be the strongest they could get, and were most urgent for me to run; and I do not well see how I could refuse.[50]

With just three weeks left until the election, Roosevelt threw himself into the campaign. He spoke a handful of times each

night at the end of grueling, eighteen-hour days. He was opportunistic enough to reconnect with Harvard alumni through the
Harvard Club, to which Roosevelt had been elected a vice president at the club's annual meeting in the spring of 1885. He
attended the club's dinner in the winter of 1886 at Delmonico's
and worked the room among two hundred "merry Harvard
lads"[51] who sang typical songs, "The Bull Dog," "Are You There,
Moriarty?" and "Nelly Was a Lady," after a speech by Chauncey
Depew, a veteran Republican insider. Roosevelt was, as he suggested to Lodge, entering the race as a sacrificial lamb. The
Democrats had an insurmountable edge, with forty thousand
more registered voters in the city than the Republicans, thanks to
Irish and Italian immigration. Roosevelt ripped the Democrats as
"men who fatten on public plunder." The Democratic candidate
was Abraham S. Hewitt, a congressman and elder statesman, a
wealthy steel magnate with moderate views. The Labor Party put
up a mayoral candidate for the first time, the radical Henry
George, author of *Progress and Poverty,* who pushed a popular single tax on land that would burden the wealthy and spare the
poor. Roosevelt once dismissed George and his radical socialist
theory of taxation as "an utterly cheap reformer." But George's
promise to fight for "the disinherited class" resonated with voters. Republican leaders positioned Roosevelt as a young reformer
with sound ideas, of course, yet at age twenty-eight he was far too
young to be mayor. Roosevelt made a point of going to the press
at the outset of his campaign to declare his candidacy independent from the party organization. He pledged to battle "against
the spoilsmen who are eating up the substance of the city." The
press played up his feistiness and underdog status. "Theodore
Roosevelt has gone into the fight for the Mayoralty wth his
accustomed heartiness. Fighting is fun for him, win or lose," read
an editorial in the *New York Sun.*[52]

Despite a survey early in the race that put him in the lead,
Roosevelt was certain enough of not winning that he booked a

passage to England on a ship that set sail a week after the November 2 election day. "Here, I have but little chance," Roosevelt wrote to Lodge the day before the election. "I have made a rattling canvass, with heavy inroads on the Democratic vote; but the 'timid good' are for Hewitt. Godkin, White and various others of the 'better element' have acted with unscrupulous meanness and a low, partisan dishonesty and untruthfulness."[53] William Allen White was an influential journalist and E. L. Godkin was a correspondent with the *New York Post* and later editor of the *Nation.* Roosevelt accused the two writers of spreading false accusations that he favored low wages and was unsympathetic to the grinding toil and grim conditions of the city's working-class masses. The truth was that Roosevelt's own perspective on labor reform was in flux. On one hand, he advocated that "the Chicago dynamiters be hung," referring to the Haymarket rioters. On the other, he retained a heartfelt concern for the hardships of workers such as the exploited cigar assemblers in shabby tenements whom he had tried to help as an assemblyman. With his campaign going nowhere and Republicans defecting to Hewitt and George, Roosevelt lashed out at the journalists as scapegoats. He threatened to "take a hack at the estimable Godkin" and wage "war with the knife with the whole crew."[54] Such outbursts only served to underscore his largest liability, a mercurial youthfulness. Even if Roosevelt had won over all reformers, it would have been an uphill battle, with George capturing the progressive vote amid a fractured, egotistical, and unruly culture of reform in New York. In the end, Roosevelt ran a distant third and received far fewer votes than the normal Republican tally of 75,000 to 80,000. Hewitt was elected mayor of New York with 90,552 votes, George received 68,110 votes, and Roosevelt polled 60,435 votes. Roosevelt was now damaged political goods, having suffered three defeats within two years, starting with the Chicago convention.

Theodore and Edith were married early in December 1886 in

a simple and brief ceremony in London with Cecil Spring-Rice, a young English diplomat whom Theodore had befriended on the ship voyage, standing in as best man. The only other guests were Bamie; Edith's mother, Gertrude; and her sister, Emily, who were living abroad at the time to save money following the death of Edith's father. The timing was right for Roosevelt's older sister, Bamie, who had planned to visit relatives of Theodore's deceased first wife, Alice, in Liverpool. At the church, Bamie signed the register as a thirty-one-year-old spinster without a profession and he as a widower of twenty-eight who supported himself as a ranchman.[55]

Bamie had spent a lifetime as her younger brother's protector, confidante, surrogate mother, booster, scheduling secretary, interior decorator, and manager, and it was no surprise that she and Edith competed for him now. In the three years preceding Theodore's engagement to Edith, Bamie's support had been indispensable. Her brother had essentially turned over his baby to her, and she had come to love Alice as her own. The reentry of Edith into her brother's life turned Bamie's comfortable and happy routine on its head. The two were not particularly close; Edith was a very dear friend of Corinne's, and the two Roosevelt sisters did not always concur with each other's choice of friends and social set. Bamie was threatened by the forceful Edith, betrayed by her brother, and threatened with the loss of "her" daughter. Edith pressed Theodore to take Alice from Bamie and to bring his daughter under their roof and into their household. Theodore's attempts at damage control and reassurances to Bamie about her continued role in raising Alice rang hollow. A private custody feud between the two women ensued.

"As I have already told you, if you wish to you shall keep Baby Lee, I of course paying the expense," he wrote in the fall of 1886.[56] Four months later, from his honeymoon in Rome, he wrote, "I hardly know what to say about Baby Lee. Edith feels more strongly about her than I could have imagined possible.

However, we can decide it all when we meet. Give my best love to the darling, and many kisses."[57]

The newlyweds returned from their honeymoon to a waiting group of family, friends, and a typically doting press.

> Mr. Theodore Roosevelt, the young reform legislator, author and ranchman, returned with his charming young wife from his bridal tour in Europe yesterday on the Cunard steamer Etruria. He looked as brown as a cowboy and as handsome as he always looks . . . In greeting his friends he placed both hands on their ribs and squeezed them so tightly that they well might have bet as if he were in combat with a bear.[58]

A cold war ensued. "Poor, dear Edith," Bamie swiped. "She never could make a home comfortable and attractive."[59] Theodore dutifully wrote Bamie each Sunday and visited her—whenever possible, alone—because, as he often told her, he had come to count on Bamie's insights and wise counsel on people and politics. Edith was icy to her, threatened by the larger woman with the formidable intellect.

Perhaps surprisingly, considering the financial disaster of the Badlands—together with Theodore's lack of income except as a freelance magazine writer, and the expensive construction of Sagamore Hill—Edith succeeded where Bamie had not, in controlling his finances. Theodore and his new wife considered tightening their belts and pursuing every possible contingency to put their household back on firm financial footing. (They could not, of course, bring themselves to live without a cook, a waitress, a chambermaid, and as Alice's governess, a Carow family friend they called Mame.)

> My financial affairs for this past year make such a bad showing that Edith and I think very seriously of closing Sagamore Hill and going to the ranch for a year or two; but if

possible I wish to avoid this . . . I *must* live well within my
income and begin paying off my debt this year, at no matter
what cost, even to the shutting up or renting of Sagamore
Hill.[60]

Roosevelt even came close to selling off Sagamore Hill during correspondence with his brother-in-law and financial adviser,
Douglas Robinson. As a compromise, Robinson suggested to
Theodore a way to save some money by reducing the tax burden
on Sagamore Hill. It involved the technical matter of having
Roosevelt change his legal residence from New York City to
Washington, D.C.—where he had taken a job with the Civil Service Commission—in order to decrease the state tax he paid. The
residency switch would play a significant role in Roosevelt's
future, but he couldn't realize it at the time. "I don't care whether
I change my residence from New York to Washington," he
wrote.[61] "I have not the slightest belief in my having any political
future." Thanks to Edith, he was newly responsible. "I am pondering very seriously over the question of ways and means; I have
got to alter my whole standard of living at once, very evidently."[62]

From the beginning of their courtship and marriage, Edith
showed the personality that had put off Bamie: alternately
moody, selfish, and sharp-tongued. Roosevelt family members
attributed her prickliness to an underlying resentment that she
had been Theodore's second choice. She could be a nag and a
scold when it came to finances; in her view, economic considerations should take precedence over Theodore's ambition for reviv-
ing his political career. It was not a bad lesson for him, and he
managed to have everything he really wanted. By the end of the
summer, he was satisfied with Sagamore Hill and declared it "in
beautiful condition."[63] Roosevelt was immune to architectural
snobs who mocked the muscular and utilitarian design befitting
its owner as "bastard Queen Anne."

With Edith pregnant and the arrival of their first child

imminent, Theodore was in the throes of an unspoken fear of repeating his earlier experience of the childbed death of his first wife. He tried to be a supportive and helpful spouse, but in the week preceding the expected delivery date, the stress caused Theodore to become ill to the point that he took to his bed with what he deemed the worst attack of asthma he had suffered for a long time. He also chose that moment to begin calling his daughter by the name he had shunned, his late wife's name.

Edith went into labor two days later, earlier than expected. A few hours after it began, Theodore's worries turned to elation.

> The small son and heir was born at 2.15 this morning. Edith is getting on very well; she was extremely plucky all through. The boy is a fine little fellow about $8^{1}/2$ pounds. We were pretty nearly caught badly. Of course the nurse is not here yet. Aunt Annie spent the night here and took charge of Baby. Little Alice is too good and cunning for anything, and devoted to "my own little brother"; she will not allow her rocking chair to be moved from alongside him. I am heartily glad it is all over so quickly and safely.[64]

They named the baby boy Theodore Junior. His father had been hoping for a son. "I am very glad our house has an heir at last!" he declared.[65]

Though his cattle herd was still struggling, Roosevelt's life back east was flourishing. He was doing some of the same things in both places: organizing people and overtly or indirectly politicking. In 1887, Roosevelt helped found the Boone & Crockett Club, a group of sportsmen whose goal was to preserve wilderness in the West in order to halt the decline in the quality of big-game hunting. Roosevelt had helped get the group off the ground during a visit to Manhattan that year when he had hosted a dinner for a dozen outdoorsmen friends at his sister Bamie's house at 689 Madison Avenue. One of the other catalysts for the group was George Bird Grinnell, editor of *Forest and Stream* and an influential arbiter of conservation in the United States.

Others whom Roosevelt invited to the dinner included friends from Harvard, such as Winthrop Astor "Wintie" Chanler and Owen Wister; political associates Henry Cabot Lodge and Cecil Spring-Rice; and writer and historian Henry Adams. The Boone & Crockett Club was formally established in January 1888 with objectives ranging from studying and recording field observations on the natural history of big game, to preserving forests so as to halt the trend of habitat loss and the extinction of species, to occasionally publishing articles and books to advance their progressive agenda on behalf of wildlife and wild places. Roosevelt agreed to be the first president, and he was a guiding force as members gathered for annual dinners and pushed legislation that supported their ideals, including a protection act to preserve Yellowstone National Park, establishment of zoological gardens in New York, the preservation of sequoia groves in California, and an Alaskan island reserve to enhance the populations of endangered species of salmon, seals, and seabirds. Members were oblivious to the contradiction implicit in their support of the slaughter of big-game animals by the wealthy elite, themselves, whose hunting trips often measured success by the sheer quantity of kills. Membership in the Boone & Crockett Club, at its peak, was fewer than one hundred men.

Roosevelt became the goad who kept the prosperous, busy men together in some semblance of an organization. One year, when Wintie Chanler suggested that he might not be able to make it to the annual dinner, Roosevelt shot him a fast reply:

> You unsatisfactory cuss, what do you mean by saying that you may not be at dinner, and that is all there is about it! More than that, I can't make out from your letter if you have engaged or will engage, the rooms at the Knickerbocker Club. Please attend to this at once, as I don't want to

have a hungry crowd of hunters gathered and no fare for them.[66]

Wintie Chanler responded with a witty verse that playfully put Roosevelt in his place, something that Chanler was not afraid to do:

Keep your shirt on little Teddy
And don't get in a stew,
The dinner will be ready,
The room is ordered too . . .
You enumerate the Crocketts,
I'll their appetites indulge,
Till their eyeballs from their sockets
Do incontinently bulge.[67]

Roosevelt would continue to visit the Badlands—in 1888, 1890, 1892, 1893, and 1896—before selling off in 1898. "Not only did the men and women whom I met in the cow country quite unconsciously help me. Working and living with them enabled me to get into the mind and soul of the average American of the right type," he later wrote.[68] He understood that the most important thing he learned there was, at bottom, political.

His worthy efforts at organizing the stockmen of the Badlands did not endure long. When he pulled out of the cattle business, many of the Dakota members in the Montana Stockgrowers Association, an outgrowth that replaced the Little Missouri Stockmen's Association, resigned or dropped out. Still, he held on to the memory of his work there and was the only member on the executive committee of the Montana Stockgrowers Association in 1889. He continued to pay his dues until 1890, when he officially resigned from the association. He had turned the page on his glorious chapter as a rancher. "He is one of the finest thoroughbreds you ever met," the *Sioux Falls Press* declared. "When he first went on the range, the cowboys took him for a dude, but soon they realized the stuff of which the youngster was built, and there is no man now who inspires such enthusiastic regard among them as he."[69]

As for the many thousands of cattle carcasses strewn about the Badlands after the killing winter of 1887, what the swirling sands of the canyons did not accomplish, the wolves, coyotes, vultures, and other predators did. After a few months' exposed to the harsh elements of the range, those rotting heaps of meat and piles of bones simply vanished—carried away by carrion feeders or covered up by blowing soil.

Chapter 6

★ ★ ★ ★ ★

WASHINGTON

Washington is just a big village, but it is a very pleasant village.

Theodore Roosevelt had made an art out of overcoming failure, and in the spring of 1888, he was in need of artistry. Fresh from a crushing financial loss in cattle ranching and a humbling defeat in the mayoral race, Roosevelt had written off business and politics. With the birth of his son and the expenses of Sagamore Hill, Roosevelt was facing tough financial challenges. His younger brother, Elliott, whom he had felt partly responsible for raising after their father's death, was following a wastrel's path of drunken carousing and womanizing that deeply troubled Theodore. "I do hate his Hempstead life; I don't know whether he could get along without the excitement now, but it is certainly very unhealthy and it leads to nothing," Roosevelt wrote in a big brother's scold.[1] Moreover, the secret lascivious life of Roosevelt's colorful and eccentric Uncle Rob was becoming public knowledge and "will publicly disgrace the family," Roosevelt feared. He confided to his sister Bamie, "How I wish he would die! He is a coarse brute—and yet he has once or twice shown curious traits of kindness, after his own fashion."[2] Edith was pregnant again, creating additional pressure, and he had recurring flare-ups of asthma. Roosevelt had depleted his inheritance. His fallback position once again was literary work. Writing articles and books had provided the most sustained positive cash flow for Roosevelt since he had graduated from Harvard, politics being a poorly paid profession in those days, except for the bosses.

Roosevelt threw himself into strenuous athletic pursuits, lavished time on his children, and immersed himself in work. Later that spring, after the five-foot snows from the Great Blizzard of 1888 had melted, Roosevelt hunted and took guests to a rifle range on Long Island. He helped organize a polo club in Oyster Bay and played with a team that included Frank Underhill, Harry Morgan, and other Long Island aristocrats. They played aggressively three times each week and Roosevelt took perverse pride in getting thrown from his horse, which he downplayed as "tumbles." Despite the spills, Roosevelt's vanity remained intact. "I look very swell in blue and white jersey, jockey cap, white breeches, and boots," he wrote of his polo outfit.[3]

Roosevelt described that springtime in idyllic terms. He packed a picnic lunch and took Edith on long, romantic rows along Long Island Sound. Despite the early phase of her pregnancy, Edith felt well enough to play tennis with women friends. Alice returned from an extended visit to the Lee household and Roosevelt found no deeper happiness than "playing Sagamore" on the piazza of Sagamore Hill: giving Alice a wild and galloping piggyback ride around the porch "until I feared I would incapacitate myself . . . Ted is too cunning for anything; he crawls about the floor just like one of Barnum's little seals; and loves to come to me and be tossed about."[4]

Roosevelt soon ratcheted up his polo schedule to play nearly every afternoon that summer against formidable teams. In late July, as time had almost expired in a match against a Meadowbrook team, Roosevelt was thrown from his horse and knocked unconscious. Edith looked on, shocked. One week later, she suffered a miscarriage. Theodore blamed himself. "The mischief of course came from my informal tumble at the polo match. The tumble was nothing in itself; I have had twenty worse; but it *looked* bad, because I was knocked perfectly limp and senseless, and though I was all right in an hour, the mischief had been done to Edith."[5] He did begin to play polo with a newfound caution, but refused to cancel his planned six-week Rocky Mountain hunting trip with his cousin, James West Roosevelt, which began in late August—less than four weeks later.

Above all, he worked. None of his previous writing prepared him for the complexity and challenge of his multivolume history, *The Winning of the West,* which he referred to in correspondence as his magnum opus. In the summer of 1888, Roosevelt tried to focus on researching and writing the first volume, which was due at Putnam's in 1889. "I do not get on fast with my work; it seems impossible to write more than a page or two a day, and my time is broken into. I *must* settle down to hard pushing soon. The polo continues to be great fun," he wrote his sister Bamie.[6] Roosevelt sent a fan letter to his literary idol, the eminent historian Francis Parkman, calling Parkman's *The Oregon Trail* a model "for all historical treatment of the founding of new communities and the growth of the frontier." Roosevelt told Parkman that he intended to write only two volumes (eventually they grew to four) and asked his permission to dedicate the first volume to him. "Of course I know that you would not wish your name to be connected in even the most indirect way with any but good work; and I can only say that I will do my best to make the work creditable."[7]

Roosevelt left the first volume of *The Winning of the West* less than half-finished during the six weeks of his Rocky Mountain hunting trip and complained that it "will take even more work than I had expected; it seems to draw out."[8] But there were no regrets when he finally felt the animal energy of the hunt. He reveled in the hardship of the terrain in the craggy peaks of Idaho, which caused his cousin West to turn back, exhausted and defeated by the elements. West was guided back to camp by Roosevelt's ranch manager, Bill Merrifield. Roosevelt loaded up packs and hiked up to the snow line with an Indian guide named Willis. "The climbing and walking were fatiguing beyond belief, and of course we had neither shelter, nor extra clothing . . . But I was never in better health."[9] Roosevelt thrilled at his killing of a bear and a caribou and described the hunting trip as the best he had taken in many years. "Now I will go back and fall to on my book with redoubled energy," Roosevelt wrote.[10] After the hunt, Roosevelt traveled to his ranch and managed to stanch his heavy losses by brokering what he called "pretty good sales of my cattle."[11] He also continued to accept writing assignments that would pay his family's mounting bills. That fall, still overwhelmed by *The Winning of the West*—"I am still struggling dismally with the final chapters"[12]—he agreed to write a book on New York for a British publisher who was putting together a series titled *Historic Towns.* Roosevelt's friend and political mentor Lodge took the assignment to write the volume on Boston. Roosevelt hustled writing projects wherever he could find them and wasn't afraid to work for hire on a broad range of topics. In 1888, the *North American* published his "Remarks on Copyright and Balloting." *Century* magazine serialized the first of his six essays on ranch life in the West, which were collected and published later that year as *Ranch Life and the Hunting Trail,* with illustrations by Frederic Remington. Roosevelt's biography, *Gouverneur Morris,* was published that spring. In the fall, Roosevelt published "A Reply to Some Recent Criticism of America" in *Murray's Magazine* and Putnam's reissued his *Essays in Practical Politics* in a book-length edition.

Roosevelt may have thought he was done with politics, but politics was not done with him. After spending just one day at Sagamore Hill in early October following the western trip, Roosevelt discovered he had to prepare for a twelve-day campaign swing with Edith through Illinois, Minnesota, and Michigan to stump for Republican presidential candidate Benjamin Harrison. He had been drafted by the party to help offset the cold and aloof personality of Harrison. Roosevelt heated up as soon as he launched into a speech amid patriotic bunting and cheering, enthusiastic crowds. The press attention that came with his vigorous canvass stroked Roosevelt's ego. He quickly became the big draw of Harrison's campaign, galvanizing the throngs that turned out to listen to the fist-pounding, teeth-chomping, hand-sawing, vein-bulging dynamo on the stump. Presidential candidates since Washington had followed a tradition of avoiding any appearance of active campaigning. Harrison conducted a "front-porch campaign" from his home in Indianapolis and made few speeches or appearances. Roosevelt himself would later invent the whistle-stop train tour and launch a very different tradition; the 1888 proxy campaign was an unrealized rehearsal. The effort wore him out. "I am now recuperating from the Presidential campaign—our quadrennial Presidential riot being an interesting and exciting, but somewhat exhausting, pastime," Roosevelt wrote to Cecil Spring-Rice. "I always genuinely enjoy it and act as target and marksman alternately with immense zest; but it is a trifle wearing."[13]

Harrison and running mate Levi P. Morton of New York faced an uphill battle against the incumbent Democrat, President Grover Cleveland. Although Harrison enjoyed name recognition as a decorated general and grandson of the ninth president, William Henry Harrison, he was coming off a disappointing upset loss in his reelection bid to retain his seat in the U.S. Senate. Harrison countered the defeat with humor: "I am a dead statesman, but I am a living and rejuvenated Republican." What Harrison lacked in interpersonal skills, he made up for in power as an orator. Harrison delivered stirring arguments on the campaign's central debate over the tariff question. Cleveland and the Democrats favored lower tariffs and freer trade on behalf of consumers, but "free trade" was far from the popular business it would eventually become. Harrison ran on a platform of raising tariffs, in part because his major campaign contributors—business owners and industrialists—controlled the Republican Party. The election was a fractious, eight-man race that helped dilute the potency of Cleveland's incumbency. Harrison narrowly lost the popular vote—5,444,000 votes to Cleveland's 5,540,000—but was elected president on the strength of 233 electoral votes. Harrison's divided victory was a surprise upset. Few pundits had picked him to defeat Cleveland (indeed, Cleveland won the presidency back again four years later), and there had been little speculation on whom Harrison would select as his cabinet. Roosevelt hoped that his efforts on the campaign trail would be rewarded, but the president-elect was not tipping his hand. "On Friday Harrison Jr.—the son of the grandson—lunches with me at the Down Town Club; Wise, who is one of the guests, suggests that we get him very drunk and find out about the cabinet," Roosevelt wrote in a playful moment.[14]

Lodge offered to lobby on Roosevelt's behalf in Washington, D.C., pushing for an appointment in the state department. Lodge had just won a Massachusetts seat in the U.S. Senate and would amass significant influence during a thirty-year congressional career. A decade older than Theodore, Lodge had become Roosevelt's deepest supporter and closest political confidant. Although their two personalities sharply contrasted—Lodge was typically aloof and rather dry—theirs was a meeting of the minds. They were both well-read, intellectual powerhouses. Both had grown up sickly and overcome illness through an iron will and commitment to building up their bodies. Both went to Harvard University, got married to Boston women at a young age, studied law, considered themselves writers, moved in literary circles, and eventually became drawn to politics. Yet nothing came of Lodge's lobbying. The months dragged on after the election and Harrison's inauguration, without Roosevelt's being tapped for a post in the new administration. "I would like above all things to go into politics; but in this part of the State that seems impossible, especially with such a number of very wealthy competitors," Roosevelt wrote Lodge.[15] "So I have made up my mind that I will go in especially for literature, simply taking the part in politics that a decent man should."

Roosevelt was too proud to grovel and too self-confident to sulk. He worked at an intense pace on *The Winning of the West* through the fall and finished the first volume just before Christmas. Satisfied with his accomplishment and feeling isolated, Roosevelt closed down Sagamore Hill for the winter and transferred his family to New York and Bamie's house at 689 Madison Avenue, which she had graciously offered for her brother's brood while she was on an extended European tour. Roosevelt had no time to fret about Washington. His publisher, George Haven Putnam, assigned him a desk at the publisher's office and cracked the whip so that Putnam's could issue a two-volume set of *The Winning of the West* in June 1889. While volume one was being edited and prepared for production, Roosevelt was madly writing new chapters, which were being typeset in the composing room upstairs at the publisher's office as quickly as he finished them. In a sustained burst, Roosevelt met Putnam's harsh deadline and completed the second manuscript on April 1. He spent a few weeks proofreading the first volume, struggling to contain his doubts. "It is wholly impossible for me to say if I have or have not properly expressed all the ideas that seethed vaguely in my soul as I wrote it," he said.[16] "I know I have hold of some good strains of thought; but I can't tell whether I have expressed them properly or not." He looked forward to relief from the drudgery, although his magnum opus eventually grew to four volumes and consumed nine years of his life. After finishing the first two volumes, he anticipated a dinner party he'd been planning for Lodge, Joseph Choate, Ernest Crosby, and a few other well-connected political friends. "I want to see and talk with you dreadfully," Roosevelt wrote Lodge a few days before the April 27 dinner.[17] "I do hope the President will appoint good civil service commissioners; I am very much discontented with him so far; in this state he has deliberately built up a Platt machine."

Thomas Collier Platt had staged a notable political comeback by 1888, following his disastrous decision to resign his U.S. Senate seat along with Roscoe Conkling, fellow New York senator and Republican boss, in a dispute over patronage in 1880. After taking the fall with Conkling, Platt regrouped and scaled the state's political hierarchy once more. He had become the power behind the Republican Party in 1888, when he backed Harrison in exchange for a promise to put Platt's people into federal posts. Although they moved in different social circles, the political fates of Platt and Roosevelt became intertwined, although Platt was twenty-five years Roosevelt's senior and their political styles were markedly different. Platt preferred to pull the strings behind the party machinery, instead of trying to sway public opinion by delivering animated speeches and wooing the press as Roosevelt did. Alongside Roosevelt's dynamic energy, Platt was a frail old man stooped by arthritis, whose movements were aided by a cane and limited to a slow shuffle. His infirmity was deceiving, though. Platt had gotten into politics before Roosevelt was born and his durability was only one indication of the savvy of the man they called "the Easy Boss." Roosevelt may have been as strong as a bull after his ranching days, but Platt had amassed the power of an army of loyal lackeys, and he possessed the instincts of a longtime survivor in the political wars. The reformer and the boss would one day clash across Republican battlegrounds in Albany and Washington, D.C.

Roosevelt's critical remarks about Harrison's appointments were soon silenced. Lodge came to Roosevelt's April dinner with more than good tidings; he brought an offer from the White House. The lobbying on Roosevelt's behalf from Lodge, Elihu Root, and others had paid off. President Harrison offered the exceedingly modest position of Civil Service commissioner. It was a job, but certainly not the one Roosevelt wanted. He had hoped to be appointed assistant secretary of state, but Roosevelt's reputation as a rabid reformer with a rash temperament made a position as second in charge seem like a poor fit indeed. Harrison's new secretary of state, James G. Blaine, whose presidential aspirations Roosevelt had initially opposed in 1884, politely rebuffed the suggestion of Roosevelt. Lodge tried to position Harrison's second-tier Civil Service offer as a generous one to his friend, but Roosevelt knew that others already had turned down the job. Roosevelt rapidly tallied up the drawbacks of accepting the Civil Service post. For starters, the salary was a paltry $3,500 per year—roughly equivalent to what he had made five years earlier as a seasonal assemblyman in Albany. Second, it was a full-time job that would preclude his literary projects and require paying Washington rent, thereby straining his finances. Third, he would have to uproot his family and pull Edith away from her friends in New York. Fourth, the political power of the office was diluted between three commissioners. Above all, the potential for making enemies and incurring the wrath of Republican Party leaders was considerable. Ironically, by succeeding on the Civil Service Commission, Roosevelt knew, he might be killing his future chances at elective office. "Yes, he ought to have it if he wants it," Lodge told a friend about the job offered Roosevelt. "But I can't see why anyone with his prospects should want a place like it."[18]

Against all these negatives and numerous other rational objections, Roosevelt did not hesitate. He accepted President Harrison's offer. He had spent time enough in the wilderness of the Badlands and the solitude of his writer's study and now he was itching to get back into the hurly-burly of politics. If anybody could make some noise in the dull quietude of the civil service realm, it was he.

Roosevelt's initial introduction to the Civil Service Commission offices set the tone for his tenure. An official with the commission at the time recalled the scene:

One bright, early May morning in 1889 an energetic young man entered my room in the office . . . and announced, "I am the new Civil Service Commissioner, Theodore Roosevelt of New York. Have you a telephone? Call up the Ebbit House. I have an engagement with Archbishop Ireland. Say that I will be there at ten o'clock."[19]

Roosevelt was no stranger to the delicate dance between upholding civil service requirements and doing his part as a loyal member of the Republican Party. He had worked with Grover Cleveland to reform the civil service laws in New York State by bridging partisan politics. That bipartisanship was among the lessons in practical politics he had learned in Albany. Five years later, age thirty, Roosevelt had grown up. "Before me stood an athletic man . . . slightly above medium height, broad shouldered, full chested, and wearing a close-clipped brown mustache," a commission official wrote in describing their first meeting. "Behind large-rimmed eyeglasses flashed piercing blue-gray eyes. He impressed me as a fine specimen of vigorous manhood."[20]

Roosevelt's job was to uphold the Civil Service Act, established by the Pendleton Act of 1883. It had been a long time coming and resonated strongly with President Harrison. His grandfather, President William Henry Harrison, the first Whig elected to the presidency, had been inaugurated on March 4, 1841. In his inaugural address, given on a cold, windy March day, he vowed not to employ patronage to enhance his authority. Exactly one month later, exhausted by the intense and insatiable demands of a flood of office seekers and a grueling social schedule, afflicted by pneumonia possibly caught at the inauguration, on April 4, 1841, he became the first president to die in office.

The Pendleton Act was much more immediately triggered by another presidential death, the assassination of President James A. Garfield in 1881 by a disgruntled job seeker, Charles J. Guiteau. Guiteau was a failed utopian in the Oneida colony, a lawyer, and a religious journalist who handed out around Republican headquarters in 1880 privately printed copies of a deranged speech in which he claimed to be entitled to a diplomatic post after Garfield's victory. Rebuffed repeatedly by the White House and State Department during contentious fights for political appointments in the administration, Guiteau received what he believed was a message from God that the new president must be eliminated in order to rescue the failing republic. Guiteau shot Garfield in the back at point-blank range in the Baltimore and Potomac Railroad station with a .44-caliber ivory-handled revolver. "I am a Stalwart," the assassin said upon his arrest. "Arthur is now president of the United States."

The Pendleton Act was a revolutionary piece of legislation that moved the spoils system toward a meritocracy. It mandated that the president appoint three Civil Service commissioners (no more than two from the same political party) with Senate approval. The president had the authority to remove any commissioner. The act set up competitive examinations for positions in the federal government that were to be filled by the top scorers on those exams—with a period of probation to test a candidate's fitness for the position. The act expressly forbade a civil servant from being forced to contribute to a political fund or to be coerced into political service in order to keep his or her job. The act also gave the Civil Service Commission the authority to investigate alleged violations of these provisions and required the commissioners to make an annual report to the president and Congress.

Roosevelt was appointed shortly after the removal of Alfred P. Edgerton, a Democrat from Indiana, and came on board in May 1889 along with Democrat Hugh S. Thompson, a former governor of South Carolina. The incumbent commissioner was Charles Lyman, a Connecticut Republican and three-year veteran. Roosevelt was idealistic about the position: "Civil Service Reform had two sides," he wrote.[21] "There was, first, the effort to secure a more efficient administration of the public service, and, second, the even more important effort to withdraw the administrative offices of the Government from the domain of spoils politics, and thereby cut out of American political life a fruitful source of corruption and degradation."

In New York State, the spoils system dated back to the Albany Regency in the early decades of the nineteenth century. The powerful Albany Regency, considered the country's original political machine, counted President Martin Van Buren, of Kinderhook, New York, and New York Central Railroad founder Erastus Corning, of Albany, among its members. The successful Albany template was transferred to the nation's capital by President Andrew Jackson for his federal appointments. The spoils system was called by a former Civil Service commissioner "an inevitable product of the union of discretionary appointments with party government . . . with elections largely controlled by personal and venal motives."[22] Roosevelt's goal was to destroy the spoils system with an aggressive and relentless attack. It prevents "decent men" from taking part in politics and "degenerates into a mere corrupt scramble for plunder," Roosevelt said.[23] Such rhetoric played well with the press, particularly editorial cartoonists like Thomas Nast, who portrayed the aggressive reformer as a wild cowboy reining in a bucking bronco—an allusion to his days as a cattle rancher and a useful addition to his mystique.

A political lightweight with a marginal position in Harrison's new administration, Roosevelt knew he faced an uphill battle. The Civil Service Commission was a paper tiger with few resources. In addition to the three commissioners, the only staff that Congress provided the tiny agency in Roosevelt's era was a chief examiner, a secretary, a stenographer, and a messenger. As outlined in the 1883 act, the secretary of the interior had the responsibility to provide the commissioners with office space, stationery, and supplies—a form of containment by bureaucratic pigeonhole. The commission did, however, have a largely unused power to remove certain federal employees for misbehavior.

Roosevelt reported for work on May 13, 1889, at the Civil Service Commission's headquarters in Washington's City Hall. Although Lyman had incumbency and the title of president and Thompson had age and experience on his side, it was the boy commissioner who simply assumed control of the trio and ran the commission with the same energy and sense of purpose with which he had rounded up cattle. It was a massive task. He exhorted his fellow commissioners, Chief Examiner William H. Webster and secretary John T. Doyle, to follow his aggressive lead. Machine bosses and veteran politicos resisted the merit system because it cut at the heart of their authority. When the commission was formed in 1883, just 10 percent of government positions, or 13,780 jobs, were covered under the Pendleton Act. Roosevelt worked hard to shift that balance of power, but it took one-half century, until 1930, before successive administrations had increased the percentage of federal government positions covered to 80 percent, or 426,083 jobs.[24] Still, after just two weeks on the job, Roosevelt wrote his sister Bamie with a sense of confidence that he could drive the commission in the right direction with a hard-charging style.

> I "went it strong" into the Custom House people, and did some pretty good work; I think it will have an excellent affect, and in addition there is some personal satisfaction to me in having shown that I did not intend to have the Commission remain a mere board of head clerks.[25]

Just one month after taking office, Roosevelt took the lead in issuing a scathing report that concluded that civil service examinations were characterized by great laxity, negligence, and fraud; that members of the local Civil Service Board ridiculed the act they were supposed to enforce; that one of the employees of the

commission should be removed and prosecuted for criminal violation of the law after cheating to get the job. He adopted a fire-
first-and-ask-questions-later attitude. Roosevelt immediately
terminated a postmaster in Indiana who had been operating a
gambling room at his station. Roosevelt rooted out scores of
newspaper editors who had been put on the government payroll
for supporting Harrison's campaign with favorable editorials and
positive coverage. Republican supporters who had been promised
jobs were brought in to replace Democratic postmasters at a rate
of one every five minutes in the early days of the new administration. President Harrison considered some of Roosevelt's tactics
heavy-handed, commenting that he "wanted to put an end to all
the evil in the world between sunrise and sunset."[26]

In choosing to attack the Custom House first, Roosevelt was
avenging his father's loss of his Custom House appointment at
Conkling's hands, as well as attacking a traditional symbol of
useless, well-paid jobs. Roosevelt likened opponents of the merit
system to "an organized band of drilled mercenaries who are paid
out of the public chest," compared to "ordinary good citizens"
who find themselves like "militia matched against regular
troops."[27] Roosevelt early and often railed to any members of
Congress who would listen about the inadequacies of the Civil
Service Commission workforce, which resulted in a large backlog
of unscored examinations for federal jobs. Moreover, Roosevelt
complained that the limited staff who were available were largely
incompetent and insubordinate, holding on to political loyalties
outside the commission.

Roosevelt's frustration at his new job in Washington did not
carry over into his home life. The Washington years were marked
by one of Roosevelt's most restful and serene stretches in which
he could devote more time and focus than ever before to Edith
and his children. Compared to the hectic speed of New York City,
the nation's capital moved at a casual, southern pace. Politicians
and high-ranking government officials lingered over late break-

fasts, broke for full-service lunches, closed their offices in late afternoon, made the rounds of lavish society dinners, took extended breaks for major holidays, and essentially shut down the operations of the Capitol during a lengthy summer recess. Roosevelt also welcomed the diversion of having his children visit him in his office. Their frequent arrivals were recalled as "a gala occasion indeed" by a commission official who worked during Roosevelt's tenure. "Whenever a circus or Wild West show was in town they would come in romping into his room," the colleague recalled.[28] "Alice, with flaxen braids down her back, would sit on one side of his desk and Teddy Jr., on the other, while the younger ones cuddled in his lap." Edith was fully occupied with the children; in a ten-year span, she gave birth to five.

Washington was just beginning to grow into a social mecca, drawing the moneyed class who summered in New York at Saratoga Springs and at Newport, Rhode Island. Outside its urban core and the impressive necklace of grand, gleaming, and columned marble government buildings that ringed the city center, it was a sylvan setting marked by a picturesque river and lushly forested hillsides. It had not yet begun to suffer the problems of population congestion, industrial discharge, and increasing air pollution that gripped New York City and caused flare-ups of Roosevelt's asthma. The fresh air and open spaces weren't the only attractions, of course; many were drawn by the aphrodisiac of power. Real estate prices were high, such that an estate equivalent to Sagamore Hill was out of reach to all save millionaires in the late 1800s, and even a modest furnished house for rent would have set Roosevelt back nearly $3,000 for the year—more than 85 percent of his annual salary. Luckily, Lodge, who had helped get the appointment for Roosevelt, offered a contingency housing plan. Lodge and his wife, Anna, were taking an extended European vacation, so they offered Roosevelt the use of their house on Connecticut Avenue rent-free—including the services of a cook and servants—for his first six months. Roosevelt could not invite his entire brood to camp out on Connecticut Avenue under Lodge's largesse, so Edith, who was pregnant, and the children remained in Oyster Bay through the fall—until the new baby was born. Edith leaned heavily upon longtime family governess Mame Ledwith, who was first hired by Edith's mother to care for Edith and her sister during their childhood in Manhattan. Mame remained in Edith's service for two decades, from the time her first child, Ted, was born, through the births of all her children. The strength and organizational skills of Mame helped put Theodore's mind at ease during his travels away from home. "Of course I feel a little homesick at being away from Edith and the children; but I have my hands fairly full of work," Roosevelt wrote in the first of his regular dispatches to the Lodges.[29]

Theodore's extended absence from Sagamore Hill would begin to weigh on Edith, who occasionally complained bitterly about the heavy domestic load she was expected to shoulder as the sole parent on the scene. Edith even called a truce with Bamie and accepted Bamie's visits and take-charge attitude in organizing household matters and pampering Edith during and after her labor and delivery. Meanwhile, Theodore allowed Edith to take control of their finances with her firm hand. "This commissionership, which has prevented my writing, has in consequence cut down my income by seven or eight hundred dollars," he wrote. "Now all my money will be turned over to Edith, and I will draw from her what I need."[30] Although Edith imposed more discipline on their finances than Theodore ever had, she was not about to go without the trappings of the upper class. Edith looked to consolidate and find employees who would work for lower pay at Sagamore Hill, where she employed a farmer, gardener, coachman, cook, nurse, maid, chambermaid, laundress, and furnaceman for a total payroll of $210 per month in 1891.[31] Her annual cash outlays included typically about $300 yearly for coal and wood; medical bills of roughly $550; and groceries of an additional few hundred dollars each month.

Roosevelt's restful introductory stretch at the Civil Service Commission was short-lived. Harrison's 1889 appointment for postmaster general was John Wanamaker, of Philadelphia, a brash and aggressive millionaire who had made his fortune in department stores. Wanamaker had been the primary fund-raiser and manager for Harrison's presidential campaign. Wanamaker was a defender of the spoils system and served notice early on that he would directly challenge Roosevelt's push for the merit system. Wanamaker had contributed a large sum to Harrison's campaign and the president had repaid him with the appointment in classic fashion. If Wanamaker—who snidely referred to Roosevelt as one of the "Snivel Service Reformers"—was to be muzzled and taken out of service, it would have to be Roosevelt's doing.

Commissioner Roosevelt wasted no time. Within one week of taking office, he investigated a recent round of Custom House tests and uncovered fraud. Job candidates with an inside edge were given answers in advance of the exam, after parting with a fifty-dollar bribe to the local examination board. Roosevelt fired three of the exam board members and served notice that he would not tolerate flouting of the Civil Service Act. Wanamaker fired back. One of the new postmaster's first major actions was to sack scores of assistant postmasters—who had the unfortunate mark of being Democrats, no matter how competent in their jobs—and to replace them with friends and those loyal to President Harrison's wing of the Republican Party.

Roosevelt did not intend to let Wanamaker get away with it, but the reformer was swimming against the current of party regulars. Harrison's five-month delay in appointing Roosevelt to the Civil Service Commission had given Wanamaker plenty of time to get a head start on dispensing patronage without regard to merit. Wanamaker was charming and forceful, and he had strong administrative skills, which helped him move fast. Roosevelt had little support from his fellow commissioners, the Harrison administration, or Republican members of Congress. "Oh, Heaven, if the President had a little backbone, and if the Senators did not have flannel legs!" he lamented.[32]

Nevertheless, he fought. Roosevelt brought his fellow commissioners on a Midwest road swing in June 1889 to investigate and prosecute allegations of corruption and civil service law violation at post offices in Indianapolis and Milwaukee. Roosevelt won a few of the skirmishes, resulting in removal of certain postmasters, but lost others. Roosevelt could usually convince his two fellow commissioners to capitulate and to agree to back his decision. While the commissioners did not have the legal authority to fire postal employees, Roosevelt's forceful nature often persuaded postmasters to institute his recommendations immediately—or face being dragged through the press by the quotable commissioner.

Roosevelt cut a wide swath through the top rungs of the Civil Service ranks; there were ominous whispers that Harrison's administration was upset by Roosevelt's heavy-handed ways. Roosevelt took Lodge's advice and vowed to reduce the high-profile, shrill volume of his crusade. Privately, he crowed about his quick and sweeping success as Civil Service commissioner. He saw the job as a form of manly combat, and he felt he was winning the first rounds. "I have been continuing my Civil Service fight," he wrote, "battling with everybody . . . the little gray man in the White House looking on with cold and hesitating disapproval, but not seeing how he can interfere . . . I am very glad to have been in this position; I think I have done good work, and a man ought to show that he can go out into the world and hold his own with other men."[33]

In several post offices across Midwest cities, from Indianapolis to Milwaukee, Roosevelt rooted out corruption. Incompetence, bribery, and the rewarding of party loyalty with jobs were systemic. One widespread infraction was to fraudulently score post office exams to make inferior Republican insiders appear qualified and capable, and intelligent Democratic candidates unfit. The postmaster of Milwaukee was George H. Paul, one of the more creatively corrupt managers, whom Roosevelt regarded as "about as thorough paced a scoundrel as I ever saw—an oily-Gammon, church-going specimen."[34] Roosevelt recommended Postmaster Paul's removal, and with a little help from a story leaked to the Associated Press and favorable newspaper coverage, he was about to make it so. But Wanamaker outflanked Roosevelt and preserved Paul's position, for the time being. After nearly two months of political wrangling, Harrison sought a compromise and asked for Paul's letter of resignation, which he got.

It became apparent, as time went on, that Harrison had appointed Roosevelt because he had to—he owed him the favor—but not because he had any interest in altering the spoils system. "The President actually refuses to consider the changes in the rules which are necessary to enable us to do our work effectively," he wrote. "He has never given us one ounce of real backing. He won't see us, or consider any method for improving the service, even when it in no way touches a politician. It is very disheartening to work under such a Chief. However, the very fact that he takes so little interest gives me a free hand to do some things."[35]

Roosevelt never lacked for self-assurance. "I have made this Commission a living force, and in consequence the outcry among the spoilsmen has become furious . . . They have shown symptoms of telling me that the law should be rigidly enforced where people will stand it, and gingerly handled elsewhere," he recounted in an 1889 letter.[36] "But I answered militantly; that as long as I was responsible the law should be enforced up to the handle *every where;* fearlessly and honestly . . . I am perfectly willing to be turned out—or legislated out—but while in I mean business."

He wasn't winning friends in Washington, but he was earning respect for his unwavering and equal enforcement of the civil service laws. "For the last few years politics with me has been largely a balancing of evils, and I am delighted to go in on a side where I have no doubt whatever, and feel absolutely certain that my efforts are wholly for the good; and you can guarantee I intend to hew to the line, and let the chips fall where they will."[37] Although Roosevelt had learned the lesson of practical politics in Albany, he had still chafed at the quid pro quo of the Assembly floor and the backroom dealing at national conventions. He hadn't gotten comfortable with political horse trading and wanted to believe his Civil Service work was a more pure form of public service, a chance to take the moral high road that his father had laid out for him.

When Congress broke for its recess each spring, Roosevelt's workload dropped off, and there would be "comparatively little to do until next December . . . It is rather disheartening to have to keep going down every day to the office, to do very little, and yet be unable to settle down to anything else."[38] He quickly discovered the doldrums of Washington in summer. "It is pretty dreary to sizzle here, day after day, doing routine work that the good Lyman is quite competent to attend to by himself; and I shall take my six weeks in the West with a light heart and a clear conscience," Roosevelt declared,[39] preparing to head not to Sagamore Hill but to the Rockies to hunt, where he enjoyed a "great bag" of game and was nearly mauled by a bear. He would take similar trips each summer without fail, from 1889 through his next six years in Washington.

He did manage to finish the book on New York, though he fell behind on the third volume of *The Winning of the West*. Roosevelt was especially pleased when he received a letter from the eminent historian Francis Parkman, who praised the first two volumes, which sold well and won critical acclaim. "I have always intended to devote myself to essentially American work; and literature must be my mistress perforce, for though I really enjoy politics I appreciate perfectly the exceedingly short nature of my tenure," Roosevelt replied.[40]

Roosevelt often felt that he inhabited a political no-man's-land as Civil Service commissioner, having taken what traditionally had been a somnambulant roost to reward a party hack and turned it into a lightning rod. The challenge was that, having staked out an unyielding position on reform, Roosevelt found few allies among Republican factions. Although he had done more in his two years to raise the profile of the position than previous commissioners with much longer tenures, Roosevelt would not conceal his frustration. "It is quite impossible to continue long to do much, between two sets of kittle-cattle as the spoilsmen and the mugwumps," he wrote.[41] He sought satisfaction in his writing and outside interests. He filled his social calendar with dinners at the Chanlers', lunches with Spring-Rice, and formal banquets at the Lodges'. Roosevelt also entertained informally at his home, mainly Spring-Rice; he had his cook, Millie, make dishes of chicken and rice and they enjoyed California claret. Roosevelt also eagerly took to the saddle again on a polo pony he rented for the summer from his Harvard pal, Winthrop Chanler, with whom he had a running competition from their days together on nearby family estates along the lower Hudson Valley. Roosevelt named the horse Pickle and described it as "a very nice pony, high spirited, and as handy as a jackknife."[42]

His work with the Civil Service Commission settled into a familiar routine, with each year between 1889 and 1892 blending into the other and little to distinguish one session from the next. He continued to clash with Wanamaker, but Roosevelt's labors to install a merit system within the postal service workforce and other large federal agencies failed to gain much traction as long as President Harrison failed to take up the crusade and allowed through inaction the status quo of spoilsmanship to remain in place. Roosevelt also was forced to contend with other matters. Much of his energy, in fact, was consumed by matters outside the office. During these years, his weekly letters to Bamie, the best barometer of his moods and concerns, focused less on work and more on troublesome private affairs.

The most consuming and painful situation involved his brother Elliott's descent into madness. What had been a low-grade family worry for years burst into a full-fledged crisis during Roosevelt's time with the Civil Service Commission. The accumulated damage from Elliott's lengthy abuse of alcohol and drugs reached a point of no return. Binges stretched out longer and intervals of sobriety disappeared; inebriation escalated into blackouts, hallucinations, and violent outbursts; previous strategies to coax Elliott back to a manageable level of alcoholism broke down as his behavior became increasingly erratic, bizarre, and dangerous. Theodore and Bamie's love for their brother and memories of Elliott's happy-go-lucky, brilliant, and kindly youth were tested time after time, until the concerned siblings reached their limit of patience. Through their correspondence, they managed Elliott's illness and the damage left in its wake—including trying to counsel his battered wife, Anna, across the emotionally complex landscape of domestic violence—as if the couple were a limited liability corporation. In the end, they oversaw Elliott's confinements in lunatic asylums, a variety of medical treatments, petitions to have him declared legally insane, and a paternity scandal. Elliott had fathered a bastard child with a maid, Katy Mann; she hired a lawyer who demanded ten thousand dollars. "The horror about Elliott broods over me like a nightmare," Theodore wrote to Bamie.[43]

Roosevelt faced unresolved problems in his marriage as well, although they were nowhere near as extreme or tragic as Elliott's corrosive dysfunction. Much of the vague unhappiness and strain between Theodore and Edith could be attributed to the fact that they were living parallel lives. He was busy with political and social engagements in Washington, D.C., while she raised the children in Oyster Bay. Lacking Theodore's forceful, energetic core, the household seemed adrift and distressed during his prolonged absences. Ted suffered from chronic health problems, both physical and emotional, that confined him to bed and a doctor's care for long stretches. Edith endured lingering maladies, which occasionally flared into debilitating headaches. Theodore gradually fell into a pattern of avoidance by making his annual hunting trip to the Badlands and staying behind in Washington during part of his summer recesses. The Roosevelts limped along, looking forward to the presidential election of 1892, since campaigns always seemed to reenergize and bring out the best in Theodore.

The election of 1892 would not be a happy one for Roosevelt, as his incumbent leader Harrison—who clearly did not share his politics—was crushed by the former incumbent, Grover Cleveland. Despite their opposing party affiliations, Cleveland was closer politically to Roosevelt in some respects, but not so close that he was likely to break protocol and keep Republican appointees in their cabinet posts. At least the campaign had started happily, in the summer, when Roosevelt stopped in Deadwood, South Dakota, on his return from hunting. A throng of local residents awaited him at his "rotten, shaky" hotel and though he was "sunburnt and in rough garb," he was greeted as a visiting dignitary. Roosevelt was thrilled when he "suddenly found myself a lion."[44] Although Roosevelt said he was "forced to open the campaign," it probably didn't require too much arm twisting on the part of Deadwoodians to convince him to follow a raucous marching band on an impromptu parade to the Deadwood Opera House and launch into a spirited stump speech for Harrison before a "large and enthusiastic mass meeting." Roosevelt conveniently neglected to mention to the surging crowd who carried him along during the speech and at a reception at the Deadwood Club afterward that, if he were following the letter of the civil service laws that he had personally helped shape, he technically should have recused himself from making a partisan political appearance. However, he followed the speech with a fact-finding mission to Indian reservations in order to ascertain and root out political corruption and civil service abuses, so the slip into partisanship was momentary. The spoils system functioned widely on reservations throughout the Dakotas and Iowa, but a New York cholera scare almost cut the trip short. After weighing the work he was doing against the potential threat to Edith and his children, he stayed put. "I am only prevented [from returning home] by the sense that I ought not to stop my work here without cause, for I am getting a mountain of valuable information—at some little cost of personal discomfort and feel I am earning my salary," he wrote.[45] In October he returned to Washington and a lackluster reelection campaign by President Harrison, who had managed to hold off a challenge by William McKinley at the Republican convention in Minneapolis. Harrison's popular support had eroded after he pushed a liberal and costly pension law through Congress in 1890. The law expanded the definition of those eligible for a federal government pension to all disabled military veterans, minors, dependent parents, and widows. The number of pensioners rose from 676,000 to 970,000 between 1891 and 1895, and the annual appropriation for pensions from Washington grew from $81 million to $135 million. Harrison was harshly criticized as the architect of the "Billion-Dollar Congress."

The election of 1892 was the first in U.S. history in which the nominees of both major parties had previously served as president. Harrison was distracted by the health problems of his wife, Caroline, who was gravely ill with pulmonary tuberculosis during the campaign, after she had been originally misdiagnosed with nervous prostration. Harrison's already low-key campaign style—his handshake was compared to encountering a limp petunia—essentially went underground as he cared for his dying wife. A week before the election, on October 25, 1892, Caroline died. Two days later, Roosevelt turned thirty-four and sat on the sidelines as the final days of the campaign rolled by. A recession gripped the nation. A third-party candidate, James B. Weaver of Iowa, representing the new People's Party (also called the Populist Party), splintered the vote. Demanding unlimited coinage of silver, he polled more than 1 million popular votes and twenty-two electoral votes. In the end, Cleveland crushed Harrison 277 to 145 electoral votes, winning nearly 400,000 more popular votes—the largest plurality in a presidential election since Grant defeated Horace Greeley in 1872. The Democrats also won control of both houses of Congress. Roosevelt was now a high-profile Republican appointee in a delicate position politically. Although he had crossed party lines and formed a friendly collaboration with New York Governor Cleveland on state civil service reform, they had parted on angry terms in the spring of 1884. Roosevelt had little leverage with the new Democratic administration. Republican spoilsmen hated him and he had made mostly enemies as Civil Service commissioner. Nonetheless, Cleveland did decide to allow him to retain his position and gave no signal that he intended to put Roosevelt on a short leash. His aggressive independence was viewed, at least for now, as an asset. "Well, my boy, you have been a thorn in our side during four years," Secretary of the Navy Benjamin F. Tracy told Roosevelt as he was replaced. "I earnestly hope that you will remain to be a thorn in the side of the next Administration."[46]

Cleveland's sparing Roosevelt the ax was a compliment and an honor, yet Roosevelt was beginning to get restless. Personal tragedy intruded too. Elliott's estranged wife, Anna, died on December 7, 1892. She was twenty-nine years old. The cause of death was diphtheria, although the years of anguish she suffered during Elliott's unraveling contributed. Their young daughter, Eleanor—who later married Franklin Delano Roosevelt and became the nation's first lady—was raised by relatives.

Roosevelt found a new passion in 1893 that forced him to look beyond his family struggles and the provincial skirmishes of his civil service work. "There is one thing that I personally feel very strong about, and that is about hauling down the flag at Hawaii," he wrote.[47] "I am a bit of a believer in the manifest destiny doctrine. I believe in more ships; I believe in ultimately driving every European power off of this continent, and I don't want to see our flag hauled down where it has been hauled up."

After centuries as a Polynesian kingdom and decades of economic domination of its sugar crop by the United States, Hawaii was ripe for plucking. Queen Liliuokalani, a popular leader, urged a movement for independence early in 1893 by calling for a government of "Hawaii for the Hawaiians." She was deposed by a native force, assisted by American troops, and negotiations began toward a treaty of annexation. Strategically, America could use a naval base in the Pacific to counteract the growing military strength of Japan. National debate stirred up by the four-month U.S. occupation in Hawaii typified the year's volatility, which pitted expansionists against isolationists and capital against labor. The government's opening of 6 million acres of Cherokee land in the Oklahoma Territory created a land rush by more than a hundred thousand white settlers eager to carve up usurped Indian property into homestead parcels. For the first time in nearly a century, a U.S. attorney ruled a strike by a labor union illegal under the Sherman Antitrust Act. A stock market crash left the nation in panic and financial turmoil after six hundred banks closed, seventy-four railroads went out of business, and fifteen thousand commercial businesses collapsed during 1893. The federal government switched its currency standard from silver to gold, causing silver prices to plummet and Treasury gold reserves to run dangerously low.

Although he was not progressing politically and seemed mired in his Civil Service work, Roosevelt had settled comfortably into Washington's lifestyle. His job left time to pursue his literary work, he enjoyed socializing with influential friends, and he was in close proximity to Senator Lodge, his best friend, who had bucked the trend of Republican losses and was elected to the

U.S. Senate in 1893 by the Massachusetts legislature. He was depressed after a trip to the Badlands in the fall of 1893 when he realized that the bright promise of his cattle-ranching days would never return, a loss symbolized by the sight of "the ranch house fast tumbling into decay."[48] As the year drew to a close, the volatile nature of 1893 left Roosevelt more uncertain than ever about his career direction, especially since his financial problems had worsened and, deep in debt, he worried about having to sell Sagamore Hill. He was forced to sell off a six-acre parcel and to take on any freelance writing assignment that came his way in a despererate scramble for cash. "My career has been a very pleasant, honorable and useful career for a man of means, but not the right career for a man without the means," he wrote.[49] Roosevelt also felt pressure to complete the third and fourth volumes of *The Winning of the West,* which were not progressing as quickly as he had hoped, given the distraction of freelance articles. He intensified his aggravation by simultaneously beginning to plan out the fifth and sixth volumes, which were never written.

Roosevelt managed to compartmentalize the welter of problems and issues that vied for his attention and to carve out a central place for his Civil Service Commission work, of which he took stock at the outset of 1894, his fifth year in the post. "I am trying to persuade the President to make some real extensions of the classified service," he wrote.[50] "I only wish he would make all that is possible now; if the Republicans do come in again, I hope they'll have as little patronage to quarrel over as possible." Roosevelt felt that he had forged a good, working relationship with Cleveland, despite their brief contretemps in Albany, and that the president "is really very cordial with me."[51]

Roosevelt exploited that alliance with Cleveland over an office flapdoodle. As the Civil Service Commission's star and driving force, Roosevelt clashed with General George D. Johnston, an elderly and cantankerous new commissioner who replaced Hugh Thompson. The two quarreled frequently over

routine functions of the commission that Roosevelt had established—which exams in the large backlog should be reviewed
first, and when to conduct press interviews—and they nearly
came to blows at times. The only factor that gave the former
boxer pause in mixing it up was the pistol that Johnston, a military man to the core, packed at work. Their animosity reached a
fever pitch when the general became outraged that Roosevelt
pulled rank and had new carpeting installed before Johnston's
office received a makeover. Tapping his friendship with Cleveland, Roosevelt met privately with the president and laid out the
brouhaha. Roosevelt was persuasive in his arguments, which
resulted in Cleveland's making Johnston an offer he couldn't
refuse—a diplomatic post in Siam or Vancouver. Johnston
refused. The president canned him.

Roosevelt couldn't gloat, given the enemies in the wings,
waiting for him to stumble. He kept his head down and pushed
an agenda that sounded like a broken record. Targeting a seemingly endless array of "mean, sneaky little acts of petty
spoilsmongering" in federal offices across the nation, he pressed
forward with investigations and leveraged his rapport with the
press as a way of lobbying Congress and the White House in the
forum of public opinion. He sought more staff, resources, and
stronger support in his drive to replace patronage with the merit
system. Despite periodic pleas from Lodge and others to tone
down his rhetoric, Roosevelt continued to shoot from the hip,
personally attacking those whom he considered the worst offend-
ers. He ripped Assistant Secretary of State Josiah P. Quincy as a
forager of spoils in the same vein "as a pig hunts truffles" and
slammed Secretary of the Interior Hoke Smith for scarfing up
jobs for his cronies at the government trough "with his twinkling
little green pig's eyes."[52]

Roosevelt thrived on a good fight, but his punches, after five
years, were losing some of their sting, so Roosevelt focused on
other parts of his life to bring him the same emotional lift that a

published book, a buffalo brought down with a single shot, or a family triumph brought him. His uplift arrived on April 9, 1894, shortly after midnight, with the birth of a baby boy, Archibald Bulloch, known as Archie. The labor and delivery were free of complications for Edith. The "bunnies," as their father called them, now numbered five. Edith's ripe fertility became a source of catty gossip among the Washington social set. "When I think of their very moderate income, and the recklessness with which she brings children into the world without the means to educate them or provide for them I am quite worked up," a society lady scolded. "She will have a round dozen I am sure. It is a shame."

When their father was with his bunnies at Sagamore Hill, his workaday worries and political uncertainty melted away. Alice had traversed a rocky adolescence and was at times outright rude and demeaning toward her stepmother, but the two were beginning to reach an equilibrium. "Altogether we're a very happy household," Roosevelt said.[53] There were times when his brood could use a referee. Kermit had been fitted with a steel leg brace to correct the weakness and deformity of his gait, and his favorite tactic was to fight back against his tormentors by standing on his head and fighting off the attacks of siblings by thwacking them with the steel leg contraption. Ethel's best defense was a strong offense: she terrorized the others by viciously biting them. Ted and Quentin, meanwhile, resorted to the more traditional methods of fisticuffs and wrestling.

Roosevelt's children were shielded from the frightening disintegration of their uncle Elliott, whose long, tortured derangement came to an end in the summer of 1894. After a drunken carriage wreck that caused a severe head injury, Elliott continued on a binge—six bottles of champagne in the morning, followed by bottles of brandy and anisette—that escalated into a suicidal rampage in the throes of delirium tremens. The demons would not be stilled. He tried to leap out an upper-story window of his house, raced crazily up and down the stairway, suffered a major epileptic seizure, convulsed, and died on August 14. Elliott was thirty-four years old.

Theodore rushed to New York. Finding Elliott's corpse on a bed devastated him. He sobbed and cried "like a little child for a long time" and "was more overcome" than his sister Corinne had ever seen him.[54] Theodore struggled to articulate his feelings to Bamie:

> I suppose he has been doomed from the beginning; the absolute contradiction of all his actions, and of all his moral even more than his mental qualities is utterly impossible to explain . . . He was like some stricken, hunted creature, and indeed he was hunted by the most terrible demons that ever entered into man's body and soul . . . Well, it is over now; it is fortunate it is over, and we need only think of his bright youth.[55]

By the end of August, Roosevelt was rescued from depression by a beguiling offer from the Republican leadership to run for mayor of New York City—a chance to avenge his humiliating loss in 1886. It came in an approach by Lemuel Ely Quigg, a congressman from New York and a Republican machine lieutenant, who possessed a persuasive, slightly sinister air that fit well with the role of Iago that Boss Platt had cast for him. Theodore wanted another go at the mayor's job, but Edith was adamantly against it and other friends counseled him not to run because if he lost, he'd be branded a two-time loser and his political career would be dead on arrival. Quigg continued to hiss in Roosevelt's ear about the sweet possibilities of becoming the mayor of New York, playing to Roosevelt's ambition and his love of the city of his birth.

Quigg's prey was susceptible to his overtures. Roosevelt had been staring into a psychological abyss similar to one that trapped his close friend and long-term houseguest, Spring-Rice, whose blue mood began to rub off on Theodore. Roosevelt had been pondering the approach of his thirty-sixth birthday and speaking in terms akin to Spring-Rice's, feeling like a failure in politics and uncertain about which career direction to pursue. At the party's offer, Roosevelt's vanity swelled immediately. Yet while he lusted after the mayoralty and saw it as a linchpin in achieving his ambitions for higher political office, there were practical concerns that prevented him from answering immediately in the affirmative. Edith would not budge in her opposition to another campaign after she and the children had finally settled into a comfort zone between Washington and Sagamore Hill. Moreover, a campaign for mayor would be a costly affair and the Roosevelt household was barely treading water as it was. In the end, largely because of Edith's strong objections, he decided not to run for mayor. He would forever regret what he called "the one golden chance which never returns."[56] He confided to Lodge soon after, "The last four weeks, ever since I decided not to run, have been pretty bitter ones for me; I would literally have given my right arm to have made the race, win or lose."[57] The stress of standing in the way of Theodore's powerful political ambitions caused an exacerbation of Edith's neuralgia—a sudden and severe pain along the course of a nerve. She required bed rest. She also tried to calm her frayed nerves by taking refuge in a thick arbor, known as "the Nest," a few hundred yards from the house, which provided a sanctuary of solitude. Theodore did not hide his anger and resentment toward Edith, and their marriage was severely strained for perhaps the first time in eight years. "I never realized for a minute how he felt over this, or that the mayoralty stood for so much to him," Edith wrote to Bamie,[58] who understood the growing hostilities and took all of their children on a brief vacation so that Theodore and Edith could be alone to work out their difficulties.

Roosevelt's finely tuned political instincts had been correct. "I made a mistake in not trying my luck in the mayoralty race," he wrote a week before the election.[59] "The prize was very great; the expense would have been trivial; and the chances of success were good." He realized that it was the Republicans' time. William L. Strong, a businessman and political neophyte, who brought to the race a substantial personal fortune, was nominated by the Republicans and elected. Mayor Strong immediately offered Roosevelt the position of police commissioner, which both surprised Theodore and once more tore at his loyalties, with so many civil service reform goals still unmet. "I have been dreadfully harassed over this offer of Strong's," he wrote.[60] "Finally I refused, after much hesitation. I should much have liked to help him, and to find myself again in close touch with my New York friends; but I was not willing to leave this work at this time, just when the ends are loose."

Instead of heading to an exciting new challenge in New York City, he returned to the old, familiar, and frustrating hassles of the Civil Service Commission. Going back to the job after turning down Mayor Strong's offer was "a little like starting to go through Harvard again after graduating."[61] But he plunged back into the bureaucratic mire.

Roosevelt took many unpopular positions as a Civil Service commissioner, including women's rights. "No distinction is made in the examinations, or in any proceedings under the Commission, between men and women," he wrote to a female college student and job applicant.[62] "The sole discretion whether men or women shall be appointed rests with the appointing officer." Roosevelt conceded, though, that currently men were hired at a rate of four to one over women by the appointing officer. In theory, Roosevelt wanted to make inroads toward equality, but the reality was that he was happy simply to continue a slow and incremental increase of jobs added to the competitive ranks and could not push women's rights without facing a backlash.

Enjoying the slowdown in the federal government's workload in the spring of 1895, Roosevelt rode horses every other afternoon with Lodge. When they weren't reading, the two friends were finishing writing a small book called *Hero Tales from American History.* Roosevelt also was making slow but steady progress on the fourth volume of *The Winning of the West* and making plans for the next phase of his willy-nilly political career. "I want to finish it before I leave this position, a year hence; then I shall have wound up all my work, and shall be ready for anything that arises."[63]

A month after making that earnest pronouncement, however, the mercurial reformer tore up his game plan. Mayor Strong made a second offer for the job of police commissioner—this time the mayor came in person instead of working through an intermediary—and the personal touch and passionate appeal were too much for Roosevelt to resist. Still, he kept his swelled head enough about him that he didn't give Mayor Strong a definite answer on the spot and instead asked for assurances that he would get "decent colleagues" on the Police Commission. Meanwhile, he conferred with Lodge and financial adviser Douglas Robinson. Both urged him to accept the position. Roosevelt felt a twinge of fear in giving up such a comfortable position in Washington, which provided a good balance between work and family, and he tried halfheartedly to talk himself out of accepting the job. Despite Edith's vote to remain in Washington, Roosevelt yearned to return to New York. There were signs that Roosevelt was maturing in deciding on his political future, thoroughly thinking out his moves and leading with his head instead of his romantic heart.

> I hated to leave Washington, for I love the life; and I shall
> have, if I go, much hard work, and I will hardly be able to
> keep on with my literary matters. Moreover it is a position
> in which it is absolutely impossible to do what will be
> expected of me; the conditions will not admit it. I must
> make up my mind to much criticism and disappointment.

But on the other hand, I am nearly through what I can do here; and this is a good way of leaving a position which I greatly like but which I do not wish permanently to retain; and I think it is a good thing to be definitely identified with my city once more . . . It was a rather close decision; but on the whole I felt I ought to go, though it is "taking chances."[64]

On April 21, Roosevelt met with President Cleveland and resigned as Civil Service commissioner. "We feel very melancholy at leaving here, where we have passed six such very happy years; but I feel very sure I am right in going back to my own city, to stay among my own people; and I shall not be disappointed, whatever the outcome, for I realize the dangers, and the disagreeable features of the work and the life."[65]

Surprisingly, relations with Edith improved. Their household was enjoying a rare moment of calm after so many storms—until a cable arrived to announce that Edith's mother had died. "It was a terrible shock to Edith, and has fairly broken her down," Roosevelt said.[66]

Roosevelt's last day in Washington was May 10, 1895, a Sunday. He settled back in Manhattan with his family at the Madison Avenue townhouse of his sister Bamie, who was still living abroad in England.

Roosevelt looked back at his six years in the nation's capital as a Civil Service commissioner—the longest he had remained in any job—with fondness, personal satisfaction, and a sense of professional accomplishment. His time in Washington had also served Roosevelt politically, for he made a name for himself there and forged important connections with leading members of the Republican Party on the national level. He grew particularly close to Thomas Reed of Maine, John Hay, and others. He also used the opportunity of the Washington social circuit to befriend the writers Henry and Brooks Adams, Hamlin Garland, and other literary figures. The goals of his reform drive at the Civil Service Commission were not complex or intellectually challenging, but leveling the playing field for federal government jobs was a never-ending challenge and long-term power struggle. He succeeded at least partially. "During my six years' service as Commissioner the field of the merit system was extended at the expense of the spoils system so as to include several times the number of offices that had originally been included," Roosevelt wrote, noting that the most powerful weapons in his reform arsenal were the introduction of competitive entrance examinations and the expansion of the system of job registration.[67]

Roosevelt indeed had managed to fashion a victory from a predicted defeat, as a Civil Service Commission official noted. "The office that was predicted to bury him in oblivion was the beginning of his fame," the bureaucrat wrote. "It gave Roosevelt an opportunity to employ his superior talents and indefatigable energy in the public interest . . . Tireless and unrelenting in his efforts, he placed the commission upon a secure footing, increasing its power and adding greatly to its prestige."[68]

Theodore "Thee" Roosevelt Sr. (above), a glass importer and patriarch of a wealthy and notable Dutch family that first settled in Manhattan in the 1640s, was a prominent philanthropist and civic leader. His stern moral certitude and public service on behalf of society's dispossessed were powerful influences on his son Theodore. The father avoided politics, considered an unseemly pursuit for aristocrats, until righteous indignation over the corruption of Boss Roscoe Conkling (right) spurred him to lead a reform group at the 1876 Republican National Convention to block Conkling. Roosevelt succeeded in pushing through the presidential nomination of reformer Rutherford B. Hayes, who tried to reward him with a customs job, but Conkling got his revenge by convincing the Senate to reject the appointment. The clash hastened Roosevelt's health decline and became a bitter lesson that his son never forgot.

Utica Observer-Dispatch, *Utica, N.Y.*

Martha "Mittie" Bulloch Roosevelt (above left) was a sickly and fragile southern belle and a vaporous presence as a mother who left much of the parenting to her husband. She imbued her son Theodore with a dreamy romanticism and encouraged his solitary pursuits of reading and gathering animal specimens in their elegant townhouse at 28 East Twentieth Street (above right) in the exclusive Gramercy Park neighborhood of Manhattan. Theodore's boyhood was marked by severe asthma and his family's division during the Civil War. By the time he was five, when this portrait (left) was taken in 1863, Teedie, as he was called, had endured electrotherapy sessions, forced rest, water cures, and vigorous massages in attempts to control his asthmatic attacks. During the Civil War, his mother's brothers fought for the Confederate side, his father paid to have surrogates take his place in the Union army, and his mother retreated from the Manhattan social scene during a tumultuous period that left a deep imprint on Teedie.

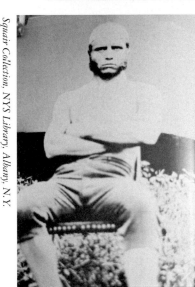

Hoping to leave his boyhood as a sickly weakling behind after undertaking a vigorous exercise regimen ordered by his father, Theodore entered Harvard in 1876; despite muttonchops and rippling biceps, he was mocked as an outsider and considered immature by the Boston Brahmins. He didn't let the teasing and hazing diminish his enthusiasm, and he joined numerous organizations, including the staff of the *Advocate* (above; upper right corner), where he was an editor, as well as the Finance Club, the Art Club, and the Natural History Society. As an athlete, he was a reckless competitor who emerged, bloody and battered, as a runner-up in the lightweight boxing championship. He also enjoyed pushing himself to the limit while sculling (left) on the Charles River. After grieving over the death of his father in his sophomore year, Theodore fell madly in love with Alice Lee, a cousin of a Harvard classmate. He aggressively pursued the tall, willowy, blond seventeen-year-old beauty (right) and the two were married on October 27, 1880, the day he turned twenty-two. She was nineteen.

National Park Service, TR Birthplace, NYC

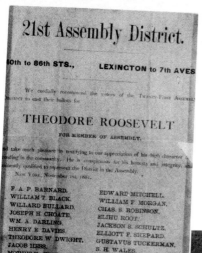

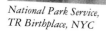

Newly married and back in Manhattan, Roosevelt finished the book he had begun at Harvard, *The Naval War of 1812,* and enrolled in Columbia Law School, but he lacked passion for a legal career. Out of curiosity, he began attending political meetings and was tapped by machine leaders Jake Hess and Joe Murray as their Republican candidate for the State Assembly in the Twenty-first District, securing an endorsement (top left) by prominent New Yorkers who included his father's friends. Riding his family name and a pledge of independence, Roosevelt was elected and arrived in Albany on January 2, 1882, as a freshman assemblyman (top right), where he was hazed for his arrogance and Harvard pretention. Despite being the youngest legislator, Roosevelt led a group of reform-minded colleagues (above; clockwise, from right corner): Walter Howe, a Brooklyn Republican; George Spinney, correspondent for the *New York Times;* and Isaac Hunt and William O'Neil, both young Republican assemblymen who were Roosevelt's closest friends and allies.

His First Political Experiences

GOVERNOR'S ROOM

REFORM WITHOUT BLOODSHED

Albany Times Union, Albany, N.Y.

Culver Pictures

Corbis-Bettmann Archives

"I rose like a rocket," Roosevelt said of his rapid ascent on the Albany political scene, where he became a leader of Republican assemblymen by learning to garner favorable press attention for colorful, quotable attacks on bossism and spoils politics. He was an opportunist when it came to reforming civil service laws and collaborated with Democratic governor Grover Cleveland, depicted in this 1884 Thomas Nast cartoon (above left) from *Harper's Weekly,* titled "Reform Without Bloodshed." Two of the biggest obstacles facing Roosevelt the reformer were "Honest" John Kelly (above right), the Tammany boss, and Republican Party leader Thomas Collier Platt (left), a U.S. senator from New York whose laconic style as the great manipulator behind the machine earned him the nickname "The Easy Boss."

Albany Times Union, *Albany, N.Y.*

After three single-year terms in Albany, a string of high-profile crusades against corporate malfeasance, and an attempted impeachment of a state supreme court judge, Roosevelt had gained a national reputation, but he abruptly quit politics after the sudden, shocking deaths of his wife and mother a few hours apart on Valentine's Day, 1884. Grief-stricken and dazed, Roosevelt retreated from public life and sought the desolation of the Badlands of the Dakota Territory (above) as a balm to his depression. The dude from New York reinvented himself as a western cowboy and cattle rancher, living in a crude log structure (below) on his Chimney Butte Ranch and spending long days in the saddle on roundups and hunting expeditions before harsh winters wiped out his herds and he returned to the New York political scene a changed man.

Squair Collection, NYS Library, Albany, N.Y.

National Park Service, TR Birthplace, NYC

National Park Service, TR Birthplace, NYC

Albany Times Union, *Albany, N.Y.*

Considered by some political pundits to be an appointment of anonymity and semiretirement, Roosevelt threw himself into the job of civil service commissioner (above left) with his usual gusto and became a formidable player on the Washington, D.C., political scene over the course of six years, beginning in 1889—the longest stretch he stayed in one job. In a cartoon from *Life* magazine (above right), he was depicted as a hero chopping down the unruly tree of patronage and graft in New York City. Nationally, he earned a reputation as a fearless reformer who fought for standardized testing, oversight in hiring, and professional standards that gave federal jobs to qualified applicants instead of political hacks under the thumb of Tammany Boss Kelly, shown in a *Harper's Weekly* cartoon by Thomas Nast (right) as being run off by Roosevelt.

When Roosevelt reported to work as New York police commissioner (above right) at 300 Mulberry Street on May 6, 1895, he took to heart the motto on the marble facade at headquarters: "Aggressive fighting for the right is the noblest sport the world affords." He took aim at crime, vice, and corruption both in Manhattan's notorious slums and within the Tammany-controlled police officers' ranks. Roosevelt became famous for his midnight patrols, as portrayed in a cartoon in the *New York Advertiser* (above left) in which he skulked incognito around town in order to roust sleeping patrolmen and impart to them a stern moralistic code derived from his Dutch Reformed Church upbringing. One of his many lifelong enemies, Tammany Boss Richard Croker (right), may have been most upset by this period in Roosevelt's career.

Roosevelt took great delight in instigating horseplay and conjuring memorable games and adventures for his children, whom he called his "bunnies." In a rare moment of repose, the Roosevelt family (top) poses for a formal photograph in 1895: from left, Roosevelt, Archie, Ted, Alice, Kermit, Edith, and Ethel. (Roosevelt's sixth child, Quentin, was born in 1897.) Roosevelt enjoyed indulging a case of arrested development at Sagamore Hill (above), the ruggedly masculine home he helped design in Oyster Bay, Long Island, whose interior (right) was decorated with trophy animals that Roosevelt shot, such as the pair of buffalo pictured, and sculptures by friend Frederic Remington that recalled his cowboy days.

National Park Service, TR Birthplace, NYC

Fulfilling a boyhood dream fueled by reading books of maritime history and hearing stories from his mother about her brothers fighting aboard Confederate warships during the Civil War, Roosevelt was appointed assistant secretary of the navy (top right) in 1897. He quickly began upgrading the inferior American naval fleet and overstepping his authority whenever his boss, John D. Long, was on vacation. Roosevelt benefited throughout his political career from the support of mentors, such as Elihu Root (above left), a powerful New York lawyer and Republican Party leader whose advice Roosevelt generally took because Root was older and more experienced. Roosevelt's closest political confidant was Henry Cabot Lodge (above right), a prominent U.S. senator from Massachusetts who used his influence to help Roosevelt secure federal appointments. The two were kindred spirits who shared a common passion for reform politics and literary work.

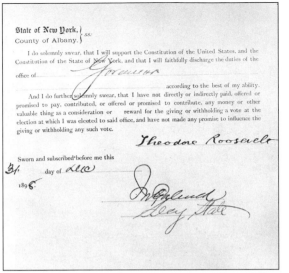

Albany Times Union, *Albany, N.Y.*

When Roosevelt signed the oath of office as governor of New York State on December 31, 1898 (above), he was just forty years old and was dubbed "the boy governor." He had ridden into the Executive Mansion in Albany as an illustrious war hero from the Spanish-American War and one of the most famous men in America as colonel of the fabled Rough Riders (right).

A collage of composite drawings taken from photographs (below) depicts the many guises of Roosevelt and the arenas in which he excelled: politician, orator, hunter, writer, reformer, conservationist, soldier, family man.

National Park Service,
TR Birthplace, NYC

Albany Times Union, *Albany, N.Y.*

TEDDY TO THE RESCUE OF REPUBLICANISM!

Roosevelt had cast himself as a reformer and an independent politician from the outset and, as governor, it became increasingly difficult to walk the political tightrope of
maintaining his maverick ways while still working with powerful machine bosses on
both the Republican and Democratic sides in order to advance his own legislative
agenda. In a cartoon (left) from *Verdict,* Roosevelt is seen in a tense standoff with Boss
Platt at the 1898 Republican state convention. Roosevelt's greatest ally in trying to
appease both the reform wing and Republican Stalwarts was a sympathetic press,
whom he cultivated through special attention and access, resulting in adoring cartoons like the one on the right, portraying a triumphant ride from the State Capitol in
Albany above the caption "Teddy to the Rescue of Republicanism!"

Roosevelt added to his reputation in Albany as the "cyclone assemblyman" by becoming a titanic force of nature as governor (right), meeting daily with legislative correspondents in his State Capitol office (below) to float new ideas and attack critics; visiting tenements and small factories (bottom right) in order to gain support for workplace improvements; and slaying corrupt remnants of the Tammany "tiger" as the cartooon on the bottom left depicts.

National Park Service,
TR Birthplace, NYC

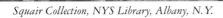

Squair Collection, NYS Library, Albany, N.Y.

National Park Service, TR Birthplace, NYC

National Park Service, TR Birthplace, NYC

National Park Service, TR Birthplace, NYC

While residing in the Executive Mansion in Albany, Governor Roosevelt denied presidential aspirations, but many political observers believed he had his sights set on the White House, as the above cartoon for *Judge* shows, with the looming shadow of the Rough Rider dominating the grounds outside the Capitol and flushing worried politicos from the rotunda. Meanwhile, Roosevelt had his hands full in Albany, where he learned to finesse Boss Platt and won a major victory over spoilsmanship by removing corrupt state superintendent of insurance Lou Payn, depicted as a rodent in the *Verdict* cartoon below.

National Park Service, TR Birthplace, NYC

Despite struggling to beat back Boss Platt's machinations to remove the mettlesome Roosevelt from the governor's office and shelve him as vice president, Roosevelt basked in his nomination as President William McKinley's running mate at the 1900 Republican National Convention. McKinley was shot by assassin Leon Czolgosz at the Pan-American Exposition in Buffalo, New York, on September 6, 1901, and Vice President Roosevelt (above) visited a recuperating McKinley in Buffalo. McKinley (right) succumbed on September 14 from his bullet wounds, and Roosevelt, six weeks shy of his forty-third birthday, became the twenty-sixth president—the youngest ever to hold that office.

Vice President Roosevelt, at Sagamore Hill, in one of the last quiet moments before his great—and peripatetic—presidency.

Chapter 7

★ ★ ★ ★ ★

POLICE
COMMISSIONER

I have the most important, and the most corrupt, department in New York on my hands.

The genteel brownstones and leafy serenity of Gramercy Park, where Theodore Roosevelt grew up, were only about a mile away from New York's Police Headquarters at 300 Mulberry Street. But socially and culturally, Roosevelt's milieu was worlds apart from the neighborhood of Little Italy, where he reported to work on May 6, 1895. The streets surrounding Police Headquarters were narrow and cobbled, crowded with grimy tenement buildings, riotous taverns, and bustling brothels. Just to the south lay the Five Points, still one of the world's most infamous slums. Instead of the elegant environment of servants and society dinners he had known in his youth, the gloomy and prisonlike Police Headquarters—where rats roamed the filthy basement and human vermin came and went on the ground floors—was located in a cauldron of crime and vice, peopled with street hustlers and hoodlums, grifters and con men, prostitutes and alcoholics.

At the top of this food chain of graft and corruption were the police officers themselves. Although the average patrolman possessed only rudimentary reading and writing skills, he was a highly evolved Tammany species who had perfected the art of intimidation, extortion, and bribery among shopkeepers and merchants—particularly newly arrived and illiterate immigrants, easily duped. A bronze tablet above the imposing marble façade of Police Headquarters was an ironic introduction to the corruption that filled the building: "Aggressive fighting for the right is the noblest sport the world affords."

Roosevelt did not know the full extent of the problems he was inheriting as a member of the Police Commission, but he had some forewarning about how much reform was necessary. The Legislature had established a committee chaired by Senator Clarence Lexow, a Republican from Nyack along the lower Hudson River, to investigate the Police Department. The commission had released a review that uncovered widespread corruption, administrative inefficiency, and systemic incompetence. It was the first in a long line of investigations of the Police Department by such commissions, including the Seabury hearings in the 1930s through the Knapp Commission in the 1970s. The 1894 report of the Lexow Commission's exhaustive probe exceeded ten thousand pages and documented millions of dollars in kickbacks to cops by brothels, saloons, gambling houses, merchants, and newly hired cops who essentially bought their jobs. The most damning finding was the institutionalized and routine criminality of payoffs involving Tammany politicians and police officials. Saloons were one source; they were supposed to remain closed on Sundays but saloon owners often bribed a cop in order to open. Press coverage of the Lexow Commission report was lurid, as typified by the *New York Tribune*'s description:

No one expected anything except insolence and brutality from any member of the force; from the bedizened inspector, brilliant in his brass buttons and glittering in gold lace, down to the swaggering patrolman who jeered at the seeker for information with uncouth language or coarse jests, or clubbed the inoffensive citizens with drunken profanity into the station-house. The whole public service reeked with brutality and bad manners.[1]

The population of New York was in the midst of doubling in a generation, between 1890 and 1910. At the turn of the century, more than 20 percent of the city's 1.6 million residents were immigrants, primarily from southern and eastern Europe. And the pace of immigration was still gathering speed. During Roosevelt's two years as police commissioner, an additional 1 million immigrants poured through the newly built main hall on Ellis Island. Hundreds of thousands of them decided to stay in the city. Each wave of foreign arrivals stirred the melting pot of Manhattan, straining inadequate resources and social services. The newcomers were easy marks for corrupt policemen, naive victims in a system of coercion and retribution.

Roosevelt felt he arrived with a mandate from Mayor Strong to clean up political corruption, as he described in his *Autobiography.*

> I was appointed with the distinct understanding that I was
> to administer the Police Department with entire disregard
> of partisan politics, and only from the standpoint of a good
> citizen interested in promoting the welfare of all good citi-
> zens. My task, therefore, was really simple.[2]

It was self-serving prose, but his description more or less matched his behavior as a Civil Service commissioner, where he had attacked Democratic appointees only because the previous administration had been Democratic and where he had made few friends on his own side of the aisle. Roosevelt envisioned a seamless progression in government service as he moved from Washington, D.C., to New York City.

As Civil Service Commissioner I had been instructing heads of departments and bureaus how to get men appointed without regard to politics, and assuring them that by following our methods they would obtain first-class results. As Police Commissioner I was able practically to apply my own teachings.[3]

Leaving Edith behind to pack and move with the family, Roosevelt traveled to New York City ahead of his wife and children. He would see little of them over the next few months. Since his sister Bamie was abroad, Roosevelt stayed initially at her home at 689 Madison Avenue—thus saving precious hours of commuting from Manhattan to Oyster Bay—and ate his meals at the Union League Club or at the Harvard Club. He was a member of both. At the Harvard Club, Roosevelt made famous a bowl-sized coffee mug he had custom made in order to satisfy his outsize thirst. "Theodore Roosevelt loved coffee and had been heard to remark that the first cup always seemed to taste better than the second," according to a Harvard Club history.[4] (The monstrous mugs soon became a club tradition.) He needed copious quantities of caffeine each morning to build up the energy to attack the problems at 300 Mulberry Street. Coffee coursed through his veins throughout the day. Roosevelt routinely grabbed a hasty lunch near Police Headquarters at the Old Vienna Bakery, washing down thick slabs of bread slathered with butter with tall glasses of milk and large mugs of *café au lait*.

The former "cyclone Assemblyman" created new twisters in the wake of the Lexow Commission. Newspaper correspondents had a front-row seat for the developing storm. A group of reporters shared space in a building at 303 Mulberry Street, across from Police Headquarters. They whiled away the hours lounging on the stoop across the street between briefings and arrivals of horse-drawn patrol wagons filled with assorted miscreants and ne'er-do-wells who promised a few paragraphs of titillating copy. Roosevelt seduced those reporters with unprecedented access. He invited them to follow him on after-hours patrols, in the courtroom at internal Police Department hearings and trials, even during meals. Wherever Commissioner Roosevelt went, a pack of reporters was sure to follow. It was a transparent scheme, captured in a subhead to a story in the *World* that summed up Roosevelt's approach in three words: "Publicity, publicity, publicity."

The openness of Roosevelt's tenure, however calculated, was a boon to copy-hungry reporters like Joseph Bucklin Bishop of the *New York Evening Post:* "The peculiarity about Roosevelt is that he has what is essentially a boy's mind. With it he has great qualities which make him an invaluable public servant—inflexible honesty, absolute fearlessness, and devotion to good government which amounts to religion. We must let him work in his own way for nobody can induce him to change it."[5] Roosevelt already had a formidable ally in the *Evening Sun*'s Jacob Riis, with whom a decade earlier he had toured tenement slums in the Five Points. Riis, in fact, had been crowing in his coverage about Roosevelt's appointment and predicted how Roosevelt single-handedly would clean up the nest of corruption at Police Headquarters. Roosevelt would also bring Lincoln Steffens, a rising young reporter with the *Evening Post,* into the confidence of his inner circle. Roosevelt went so far in ingratiating himself with Steffens as to write a letter of endorsement helping Steffens break into the *Atlantic* magazine, touting Steffens's education at the University of California and his having studied abroad in Germany and Paris. Steffens would go on to become the nation's most famous muckraker.

Roosevelt and the three other new police commissioners, two Democrats and two Republicans, walked from City Hall to Police Headquarters after their swearing-in. It was no easygoing saunter for the eighteen blocks. It was more like the cops' time-honored "perp walk," in which the perpetrator of a crime is paraded in front of the press for a public assessment. The spotlight shone on Roosevelt, whose reputation as a reformer and incorruptible crusader had been burnished to a high gloss by the press in their breathless advance stories. Roosevelt hadn't spent a day on the job and he was being hailed as the corrupt Police Board's savior, which only served to anger the overshadowed trio beside him. Roosevelt's fellow commissioners were Frederick D. Grant, son of the Civil War general; Avery D. Andrews, an amiable Democrat and West Point graduate; and Andrew D. Parker, a Democrat and well-connected lawyer with a personal animosity built up against Roosevelt for his scene-stealing ways. With vigorous strides, Roosevelt led the quartet, shouting a hearty hello to Riis as he caught sight of his old friend across the street. Roosevelt ran up the steep stairs of headquarters and beckoned reporters to follow. Riis was joined by a cast of notables at the cop shop, including Steffens and the *New York World*'s veteran correspondent Arthur Brisbane. Roosevelt broke protocol by bounding down the hallway to the boardroom, where he introduced himself to the outgoing commissioners. After calling a meeting of the new Police Board to order, he was named president. He immediately brought Riis and Steffens into his new office. Hardly stopping to draw breath, as Steffens recalled, he inquired of his guests, "Now, then, what'll we do?" The question was punctuated with the flash of Roosevelt's large, gleaming white teeth. "He shows a set of teeth calculated to unnerve the bravest of the Finest," Brisbane observed in the *World*. "His teeth are very white and almost as big as a colt's teeth. They are broad teeth, they form a perfectly straight line. The lower teeth look like a row of dominoes."[6] This set of exuberant chompers and the new commissioner's thick, round eyeglasses became new fodder for political cartoonists' pens. A caricature was born.

As in the past, Roosevelt wore an outlandish outfit. His unorthodox Mulberry Street summer outfit consisted of a pink shirt accentuated with a black silk cummerbund with long tassels and a straw English boater worn at a jaunty angle. The reporters covered Roosevelt's arrival like a play's opening night. Brisbane offered this description in the *New York World:*

> We have a real Police Commissioner. His teeth are big and white, his eyes are small and piercing, his voice is rasping. He makes our policemen feel as the little froggies did when the stork came to rule them. His heart is full of reform, and a policeman in full uniform, with helmet, revolver and night club is no more to him than a plain, ordinary human being. He is at work now, teaching the force that it is paid to work, not to boss . . . From his round bullet-head down to his square-toed boots, he looks like a man of strength. His jaw and chin are powerful. His chest is broad. His lungs and his liver are in good working order.[7]

Offstage, Roosevelt was privately lamenting the long hours he was putting in at Police Headquarters during his initial days and complaining of a growing unease at how formidable it would be to reform the police force. He wrote to Lodge,

> For the next six months I am going to be absorbed in the work here and under a terrific strain; I have got to move against the scandals in this Department, if my work is to be at all thorough; but my hands have been tied in a large measure, thanks to the action of the legislature.[8]

It was only in his letters to Bamie that he felt comfortable enough to discuss personal concerns that might be viewed by his enemies as signs of weakness. Roosevelt's mantra in these moments of honest reflection was that he had never worked so hard as he did as police commissioner; the long hours and prolonged absences from his wife and children made him melancholy. He felt frustrated that the job left him no time to write articles and books. In the next breath, though, he shifted away from personal worries and to his plans for fighting corruption.

> The actual work is hard; but far harder is the intense strain . . . I shall speedily assail some of the ablest, shrewdest men in this city, who will be fighting for their lives, and I know well how hard the task ahead of me is. Yet, in spite of the nervous strain and worry, I am glad I undertook it; for it is a man's work.[9]

Roosevelt had to work against an entrenched and corrupt police chief, the powerful and revered Thomas F. Byrnes. Byrnes, at fifty-three a generation older than Roosevelt, enjoyed a reputation as an oustanding detective. He also could count on support across the economic spectrum of New Yorkers, from the working class to Wall Street tycoons, because Byrnes had developed a seamless system of extortion in exchange for lax enforcement or protection against criminals. Byrnes set the pattern for the rest of his force. From patrolmen to captains, all paid a fee to win their positions and were then reimbursed by money extorted from grocers, gambling house operators, saloon owners, and brothel madams.

Roosevelt set his sights on toppling Byrnes, a thirty-year veteran of the department and a seemingly immovable object. "I thoroughly distrust him, and cannot do any thorough work while he remains," Roosevelt wrote to Lodge, to whom he announced his intention just ten days after joining the Police Board.[10] Pundits and Police Department observers predicted a long and bitter power struggle. Yet Roosevelt's judgment of character was unusually astute. He had intuited that although Byrnes's support was a mile long, it was only an inch deep. Two weeks after Roosevelt declared war, Chief Byrnes fell as easily as the trees Roosevelt chopped down at Oyster Bay. By the end of May, Byrnes turned in his resignation—albeit with a negotiated full pension and without having to face interrogation from a review board. Roosevelt didn't need to make any direct threats. The pragmatic Byrnes realized that the young commissioner had strong support from the mugwumps and reform-minded Republicans, and he didn't want to risk losing retirement benefits or to face possible criminal charges. (Byrnes also had an exit strategy; he went on to form a successful detective agency on Wall Street.) Roosevelt would go on to oust other departmental ciphers—notably the notorious advocate of police brutality, a nightstick-toting inspector dubbed "Clubber" Williams. (Once again, justice was fleeting; Williams set himself up in the insurance business and was a multimillionaire when he died.) Commissioner Andrews noted that these moves signaled a "top to bottom" shakeup of the force, which served as a corrective and deterrent to other police officials contemplating corrupt acts. In place of Byrnes, Roosevelt convinced Strong to appoint as acting chief his choice, Peter Conlin, a soft-spoken and malleable former inspector who would not impede the continued shakeup.

With the obstinate police brass removed, Roosevelt could turn his attention to his three fellow commissioners, assessing their vulnerabilities and exploiting each one's weakness to suit his purposes. Roosevelt liked Parker best.

> My queer, strong, able colleague Parker is far and away the most positive character with whom I have worked on a commission. If he and I get at odds we shall have a battle royal; but I think we can pull together; and though Grant and Andrews do excellent work, Parker is the only man from whom I get any real help in shaping a big measure of policy.[11]

Roosevelt plowed through a massive backlog of disciplinary actions against corrupt or poorly performing policemen. Headlines in the *New York Herald* tracked his fast-moving assault:

"The Reform Commissioner Tries Nearly One Hundred Police-men in One Day," "Men in Uniform Get Embarrassed," "Hearings to Be Continued Until the Overcrowded Trial Docket Is Cleared." At the same time, Commissioner Roosevelt could show mercy in special cases, particularly when it involved a close friend. Archie Chanler, brother of Wintie, Roosevelt's friend from Harvard, suffered a nervous breakdown and was becoming a dangerous lunatic who was threatening suicide in a New York City hotel. Two police detectives appeared with a warrant for him, after being given express orders from Commissioner Roosevelt to show Chanler every consideration and not to use excessive force. Chanler went calmly with the detectives in their carriage.

Commissioner Roosevelt began most days—when he didn't remain in the city overnight because of evening meetings or political functions—with a vigorous bicycle ride from Sagamore Hill to the Oyster Bay train station, beginning at 7:30 A.M., followed by "a perfect whirl of eight hours in New York, and returning just in time for a short play with the children before I get dressed for supper."[12] This daily routine led Roosevelt to develop the city's first bicycle patrol, working with fellow commissioner Andrews. It was in 1895, before the automobile's arrival. He took pride in the success of the bike squad and held public award ceremonies if squad members committed an act of bravery in the line of duty. Andrews said Roosevelt always supported his requests for more men and money. Roosevelt allowed Andrews to take credit for the unit, which Roosevelt referred to as "your bicycle police" in meetings with Andrews. Roosevelt also cited in his *Autobiography* another accomplishment that pleased him: establishment of a school of pistol practice and systematic training in firearms for all patrolmen. Roosevelt said the result was marked improvement in the marksmanship skills of the police force. Roosevelt also devised an incentive system that rewarded bravery and outstanding work among police officers with certificates and medals of meritorious service, as well as the awarding of additional points that could hasten a patrolman's promotion.

Commissioner Roosevelt's manifesto of reform was more than mere rhetoric. The numbers from the Police Department's *Annual Report* illustrate how forcefully he acted. In 1895, the year Roosevelt began in the post, there were 3,757 complaints brought against officers, compared to 6,134 in 1897. The total days officers were fined without pay, one measure of Roosevelt's crackdown, increased from 6,064 in 1895 to 10,217 in 1897, and the total monetary fines imposed for the infractions of officers showed a similar rise, from $23,139 to $35,759, over the same two-year period. The total number of officers dismissed from the force jumped from forty-one to ninety-eight during those years. Roosevelt also trumpeted one of his proudest accomplishments, nearly doubling the number of arrests by the Detective Bureau, from 1,384 in 1895 to 2,527 in 1896.[13]

One of Roosevelt's earliest and boldest moves was to demand that police officers begin to enforce a law that banned the sale of liquor on the Sabbath. Known as the Sunday Closing Act, it had long been on the books in New York State and either blithely ignored or used as an opportunity to solicit a tidy payoff. Roosevelt had supported strict enforcement as an assemblyman, and the idea was no more popular now. And it wasn't only Germans and other working-class immigrants who opposed closing saloons on Sunday. Even his fellow members of the Harvard Club were generally in favor of alcohol's being available all week. Many years after, the Rev. Dr. Richard S. Storrs of Brooklyn took tongue-in-cheek jabs at Roosevelt at the club's annual dinner. "I don't altogether approve of him. He has disturbed the moral equilibrium of the universe. We always knew that New York was greater than Brooklyn, but we used to think that Brooklyn was better than New York. Now, when a man wants to get drunk on Sunday, he has to cross to Brooklyn," Storrs said.[14]

In private, Roosevelt claimed to disagree with the law. "I

have now run up against an ugly snag, the Sunday Excise Law," Roosevelt wrote.[15] "It is altogether too strict; but I have no honorable alternative save to enforce it, and I am enforcing it; to the furious rage of the saloonkeepers, and of many good people too; for which I am sorry. I have a difficult task." Protesters against this newly aggressive enforcement of dry Sundays in Manhattan pelted Roosevelt from many quarters. "The howl that rose was deafening," Roosevelt said. "The professional politicians raved. The yellow press surpassed themselves in clamor and mendacity."[16]

The Sunday closing law was opposed especially bitterly by German Americans, for whom a popular cultural ritual was the intergenerational gathering on Sunday afternoon at beer gardens with music and dancing. Thousands of protesters, led by the German contingent, marched in opposition to Roosevelt's initiative. "The other day there was a great parade of the liquor men here," he wrote.[17] "They asked me to review it, in a spirit of irony; but I accepted, and rather non-plussed them by doing so." Roosevelt's nemesis, William Randolph Hearst, beat the drums against the police commissioner and likely increased circulation by a taunt in the editorial pages of the *New York Evening Journal:* "East Side, West Side, all around the town, yesterday went King Roosevelt I, ruler of New York and patron saint of dry Sundays."[18]

Roosevelt ordered police officers to shut down saloons illegally open on Sundays by padlocking the front doors, arresting the owners, and bringing charges in the courts. He also cracked down on taverns that stayed open beyond the legal daily closing time of one o'clock in the morning. Yet he had learned something about politics. Many of those prosecuted saloon keepers conveniently happened to be Roosevelt's political enemies. Indeed, saloons were central to New York's political life and had been for decades. The Sunday closing law was so thoroughly ignored that a survey in the 1890s estimated that the average sale of beer on the Sabbath across New York was about three million glasses.

Tammany ward chiefs were often saloon keepers, and voting stations were often inside their establishments. New York election history is filled with stories of gang battles among contending factions at these polling places. Going after a stalwart Tammany saloon keeper enabled Roosevelt to strike a public blow against his partisan enemies. Roosevelt often reiterated his estimate that up to two thirds of Tammany Hall's political leaders had been associated with the liquor business at some point. In a highly publicized case, Roosevelt faced down criticism from a phalanx of lawmakers by urging prosecution of a politically powerful saloon keeper and former assemblyman, Pat "King" Callahan, who had earned the nickname by his dictatorial style.

One Sunday evening, rookie cop Eddie Bourke was walking his beat in Chatham Square when he passed Callahan's saloon, which was in full swing. Bourke walked in and tried to arrest Callahan, who thought it was a prank. When Bourke assured him it was no joke, Callahan punched him. The saloon keeper's friends jumped in and kicked Bourke in the stomach when he was down. Bourke managed to fight back with a flailing nightstick and eventually subdued the King, who was transported to the police station. Callahan filled the courtroom with Tammany politicos in an attempt to intimidate the judge into releasing him. Tipped off, Roosevelt rushed to the courtroom and convinced the judge to hold Callahan until the trial. A short time later, having recovered from his wounds, Bourke was promoted. It was Roosevelt's way of serving notice that cops who worked to defend justice would be rewarded.

Although resourceful tavern owners created numerous scams for getting around the Sunday crackdown—spiking coffee with cognac, leaving a secret back entrance open for stealthy customers, providing liquor as a free accompaniment with meals to exploit a loophole in the law—Roosevelt's aggressive prosecution hurt the powerful liquor lobby in its pocketbook. That was the most effective blow of all; the *New York Times* estimated that members of the Wine, Beer, and Liquor Sellers' Association were losing $20,000 worth of revenues on average each week, and many establishments faced bankruptcy. Roosevelt's bold move drew not only national attention but international praise, which was generally effusive. "There has not been a more remarkable triumph of law in the municipal history of New York," the *London Times* said.[19] "The consensus is that to Theodore Roosevelt's courage and ability more than to any other single cause this victory is due."

Commissioner Roosevelt knew how to manipulate public opinion as well as any politician, though, and he eventually played the temperance movement like a grand piano. The crescendo came during a speech at the Catholic Total Abstinence Union's national convention on August 7, 1895. More than seven thousand fervent temperance supporters packed Carnegie Hall. Roosevelt drove them to a crescendo of religious zeal as his speech was interrupted frequently with thunderous applause.

> I hope to see the time when a man will be ashamed to take any enjoyment on Sunday which shall rob those who should be dearest to him, and are dependent on him, of the money he has earned during the week; when a man will be ashamed to take a selfish enjoyment, and not to find some kind of pleasure which he can share with his wife and children.[20]

Roosevelt later said the ovation was one of the most emphatic he'd ever received for a speech. It would still be twenty-five years before the passing of the Eighteenth Amendment to the U.S. Constitution initiated an ill-fated national experiment in temperance. Prohibition was in effect from 1920 to 1933, but already in the late 1890s a movement once relegated to a small fraction of religious reformers had spread to the newly powerful middle class, from towns to rural areas to cities.

Six months into the job, just before his summer vacation,

Roosevelt was exhausted. "I am almost worn out with the strain of the long uphill fight," he conceded to Bamie. "Thank Heavens there is only a week more, and then the exhausting six months will be over, and I can ease up a little, no matter which way the battle goes."[21] The militaristic imagery was apt, since the framework of Roosevelt's overhaul of the Police Department was based on the U.S. military's organization. He centralized control at New York Police Department headquarters and did away with the autonomy the precincts had previously enjoyed and abused. He also instituted a formal sealed-bid contract process for the purchase of equipment and supplies, removing a source of graft. Influenced by his time as a captain in the New York National Guard while studying law at Columbia, the rigid organizational structure Roosevelt instituted rewarded efficiency, order, and discipline—all of which were considered in the system for police promotions that Roosevelt fostered.

In the end, Roosevelt had no delusions that his efforts at the Police Board had earned him any kind of broad political support. For Lodge he assessed his status without a hint of his usual romanticism or hyperbole.

> I am very much touched by your persistence in far overestimating the position I hold; but you really make me a little uneasy for I do not want you to get false ideas of my standing. I undoubtedly have a strong hold on the imagination of decent people; and I have the courageous and enthusiastic support of the men who make up the back-bone of the Republican party; but I have no hold whatever on the people who run the Republican machine. Platt's influence is simply poisonous. I cannot go in with him; no honest man of sincerity can.[22]

Thomas Collier Platt had the sallow, wizened face of a tortoise and the sensibility to match. His patience and perseverance in politics were legendary. He had the ability to subsume his own ambition for years, even a decade or more at a stretch, slowly accumulating political capital until he had worked his way back up to a leadership role. He approached politics as a marathon and would wear down an opponent with the methodical constancy of water dripping on stone. Platt, elected a congressman when Roosevelt was an adolescent, moved up to the U.S. Senate in 1881. After his disastrous decision to follow Boss Conkling into obscurity over an ignominious spat with President Garfield, Platt dropped into the background of the Republican organization until he eventually cobbled together the political machinery that carried Strong into the New York mayor's office in 1894. Platt's quiet, forceful determination was best seen in his de facto office, the lobby of the Fifth Avenue Hotel in Manhattan. He made Republican supplicants travel to him; a steady stream came to genuflect before Platt. The laconic style of the Easy Boss belied an iron grip that demanded acquiesence. Platt's lobby perch was known as the "amen corner," so called because his operatives were said to utter "amen" to everything the boss said.

Commissioner Roosevelt soon faced personal attack, including a broadside by United States Senator David B. Hill, a Democrat and former governor (and Tammany man). In a letter published in the *New York Times,* Hill accused Roosevelt of being "a busybody and notoriety-seeking" and of being a class warrior. "A glass of beer with a few crackers in a humble restaurant is just as much a poor man's lunch on Sunday as is Mr. Roosevelt's elaborate champagne dinner at the Union League Club," Hill wrote.[23] The question of Roosevelt's alcohol consumption would dog him throughout his career in public service and elective office, even though he was not an excessive drinker by any standard. Despite a campaign of rumors and innuendo, numerous investigations confirmed that Roosevelt did not consume alcohol on a regular basis and rarely if ever to excess. Although there was some indication he had drunk more heavily at Harvard, throughout adulthood Roosevelt drank no more than an occasional glass of wine, by most accounts. Still, his moralistic crusading did leave Roosevelt legitimately open to criticism for minor abuses of his office. For instance, Roosevelt frequently used Police Headquarters letterhead to write personal letters and occasionally used his clerical staff to help him process personal correspondence. He also didn't mind using the perks of his office for his own enjoyment. In September of 1895, Roosevelt and his wife boarded a police patrol boat to watch *Defender* defeat *Valkyrie* in the first of the America's Cup races.

Such infractions never tarnished the reputation of Roosevelt, a perpetually moving target. In a kind of sequel to his field trips with Gompers to inspect cigar-making tenement operations as a young, reform-minded assemblyman, Roosevelt began making clandestine, late-night prowls around New York City in order to assess the performance of police officers and to confront and correct misbehavior or malfeasance. It was the sort of vigorous, hands-on scientific observation that had long thrilled Roosevelt. Roosevelt described his nocturnal ramblings to Bamie:

> I passed the night in tramping the streets, finding out by personal inspection how the police were doing their duty. A good many were not doing their duty; and I had a line of huge frightened guardians of the peace down for reprimand or fine, as a sequel to my all-night walk. At present I am in high favor with both the Republicans and the Good Government people; and I certainly have hold of the reins in this police department.[24]

The widespread incompetence and chicanery of the police force made for easy pickings as Roosevelt and Riis trolled for infractions on the Lower East Side. In their rounds of precincts, they quickly found a pattern of patrolmen absent without leave from their posts: slumbering while being paid, imbibing in saloons, sampling the services of prostitutes. Roosevelt carried a pocket notebook with him and jotted down names of patrolmen he found derelict in their duties. Alleged infractions were later reviewed and disciplined by hearings that Roosevelt, judge and jury, oversaw himself. On one midnight patrol, Roosevelt brought along Richard Harding Davis, the prominent correspondent for *Harper's Monthly.* It was the beginning of a long and varied association with the star journalist. On the whole, his trips received terrific coverage, with such headlines as "He Makes the Night Hideous for Sleepy Patrolmen." Cartoonists splashed his teeth and spectacles across many pages, depicting Roosevelt as a supernatural force ignored at one's peril. One peddler on Mulberry Street began hawking a toy whistle embedded in a set of false teeth that could be clipped onto the mouth of the purchaser and gleefully blown. The entrepreneur called his fast-selling conversation piece "the Roosey."

Avery Delano Andrews recalled a fabled story of Roosevelt's midnight patrol. Roosevelt found a patrolman, who was missing from his assigned post, at an oyster bar on Third Avenue with a large quantity of oysters on his plate. Without introducing himself, Roosevelt asked the patrolman why he wasn't at his post.

"What's that to you, and who are you anyway?" the officer asked.

The waiter behind the counter interjected, "You've got a good nerve, coming in here and interfering with an officer."

"I am Police Commissioner Roosevelt," he said, "and now you get out on your post where you belong!"

"Yes, you are," the patrolman shrugged, before devouring more oysters. "You're Grover Cleveland and Mayor Strong, all in a bunch you are. Move on now, or else—"

"Shut up, Bill," the oyster server said in a pained whisper. "It's his Nibs, sure! Don't you see his teeth and glasses?"[25]

Aside from dereliction of police duty, Commissioner Roosevelt, who was also an ex officio member of the city's Board of

Health, was looking out for signs of sanitary problems and living conditions that could lead to an outbreak of disease. Andrews recalled the ritual:

> We tramped steadily for several hours, interviewing patrol-men and wanderers like ourselves without disclosing our identity, occasionally finding a patrolman off beat or other-wise delinquent. It was an interesting study to observe the varied activities of the great city at the close of one day and the beginning of another. About daylight, we dropped into a large and busy restaurant in the Bowery, well filled with patrons even at that early hour.[26]

Andrews observed Roosevelt putting in ten to twelve hours at the office each day, followed by frequent speeches at night in front of a civic group, followed one or two nights per week on average of all-night patrolling.

Roosevelt complained often that he felt alone and without support because of his alienating positions. He adopted a woe-is-me pose.

> The party leaders, great and small, have come as near cast-ing me off as they dared; I only speak at outside meetings; but I attract huge audiences, and have a very good popular following. It is an entire mistake however to think that I have gained any strength politically. I have none whatso-ever.[27]

Roosevelt easily lost his temper and patience even with allies. His early praise of Parker, for example, disappeared in a letter to Bamie.

> My troubles on the Police Board are rendered very acute because the ablest of my colleagues, Parker, is an utterly

untrustworthy and lying schemer. Lord, it is hard work trying to accomplish anything in civic reform.[28]

Roosevelt took on the difficult task of attempting to convince Mayor Strong to oust Parker, setting up another delicate
power play. The internal struggle in the spring of 1896 was exacerbated by the death of Roosevelt's beloved uncle, James Roosevelt, in April of that year after a lengthy illness exacerbated by
weak lungs, alcoholism, and morphine dependency. Kermit's
response to the passing of his grand-uncle struck a deep chord in
Roosevelt. "Oh, Mother," the boy said, "I wish we had the water
of life to give to our friends."[29] Just a few months earlier, Roosevelt had offered a rare moment of reflection on difficult circumstances in a heartfelt letter to Bamie. Indeed, he had known many
deaths of family and friends.

> There does seem to be a veritable fatality in our family; so
> many have died in the last eight years—Hilly, Uncle Com-
> erl, Alfred, Weil's children, Aunt Annie, Anna, Elliott, Lit-
> tle Ellie, and now Jack Elliott's poor little wife and
> Frank . . . This letter seems to dwell only on death and sick-
> ness; but that is what there has been this week.[30]

Yet Roosevelt never wallowed in personal grief and—following a pattern set in the wake of the deaths of his father, wife, and
mother—assuaged his sorrow over his uncle by immersing himself in work. Roosevelt's skirmishes with the other members of
the Police Board took his mind off the losses. "I am having one of
my perennial rows with Parker," he wrote, "and Grant is rather
more of a muttonhead than usual."[31] A few weeks later, he added,
"My own work is becoming of almost intolerable difficulty; for
Grant is proving himself a mere dolt, a bit too cunning for
unscrupulous, shifty Parker. The depraved scoundrel of ability,
and the dull fool who thinks he is cunning, and has no high stan-

dards, make a horrible combination."[32] He referred to Grant as a "chuckle head" and also noted that "Parker's tortuous soul loves the welter of corrupt intrigue which the present system encourages."[33]

Parker was a former assistant district attorney with the savvy to build a base of support among a non-Tammany faction of the Democratic Party. Parker had resented Roosevelt from the outset, not only because of party affiliation, but for the blustery way in which Roosevelt assumed control of the Police Board, placed the other commissioners in subservient positions, and trumpeted his own accomplishments in the press. Parker, assigned to reorganize the Detective Bureau, did so with sinister effect, approving the head-busting methods of its thuggish cops and making pacts with brutal underworld figures. Parker's underhanded behavior sharpened the "snake in the grass" characterization by Joseph Bishop, an editor of the *Evening Post* and Roosevelt's buddy, who tried to warn his friend.

Roosevelt found out for himself when Parker began boycotting meetings of the Police Board, openly challenged Roosevelt's promotion recommendations, and became an obstructionist who forced a deadlock on Mulberry Street. Newspaper editorials turned on Roosevelt and criticized him for the board's inaction. Roosevelt moved to have the obstinate commissioner removed and convinced Mayor Strong to begin an administrative trial against Parker, which included a signed affidavit from a patrolman who had paid four hundred dollars to Parker for a promotion. But the snake bit back, attempting to entrap Roosevelt at a high-society bachelor's party, where several dancing girls were performing. Parker's goons burst in, did not find Commissioner Roosevelt—who was at home with his children—and left without making any arrests. Although he was never officially implicated, there were suggestions that Parker had a hand in a letter bomb that arrived for Roosevelt at Mulberry Street, which was intercepted and defused by police officials.

Roosevelt wanted Parker gone, and their clashes reached a showdown at the departmental trial. Roosevelt convinced Elihu Root, a friend and Republican Party ally who was one of New York's leading lawyers, to prosecute the case against Parker. Dragging on for months in the spring and summer of 1896, the trial tainted the entire Police Board, depressed Roosevelt, and deepened Parker's belligerence. After eight months of posttrial waffling, in which the scandal made the Police Board the butt of endless jokes, Mayor Strong determined that Parker should be removed for proven neglect of duty. But the mayor's ruling was subject to gubernatorial approval and, despite Roosevelt's lobbying, Republican Governor Levi P. Morton refused to dismiss Parker, because Morton and Roosevelt had clashed in the past. The snake slithered away, while Roosevelt looked for a new job.

Roosevelt had some relief from larger fights in the form of playful skirmishes—at home. Commissioner Andrews recalled one encounter with Roosevelt's rambunctious brood.

> On one of these drives through some woods near Sagamore Hill, I was suddenly greeted by several well-directed volleys of green apples, coming from the woods nearby . . . I jumped quickly to the ground, picked up a few of their apples and opened a counter offensive in the direction from which the volleys came. There was at once a general scattering of boys and girls in all directions, hastened and accompanied by my return volleys . . . On the following morning Theodore Jr. came to me and said his father had told him to apologize to me for pelting me with green apples; that he was very glad to do so because, although they were merely following their usual sport, they would not have pelted me if they had known I was their father's guest![34]

When Roosevelt was home, Sagamore was transformed into a raucous place where the children raced after their dad as he swam in the Sound, raced down a bluff, galloped a horse, tramped through the woods, and caroused through the house in games in which he imitated the charge of a grizzly bear. Injuries were commonplace for kids and father alike. Edith had long ago learned to take in stride the profuse bleeding of Theodore's head wounds suffered during falls in polo matches. Occasionally he suffered a home repair mishap. When the windmill that pumped water for the house got stuck, Roosevelt swung into action with an oilcan and tools. He climbed carefully up the sixty-foot tower and was about to make the needed repair when the wind abruptly changed direction; the blades swung around and whacked Theodore so hard in the head that "it took a slice of my scalp," as he later reounted. Bleeding profusely, his vision obscured, Roosevelt felt his way back down and, dripping with the gore, met Edith in the front hall. His wife did not flinch. "Theodore," she said, affecting boredom, "I wish you'd do your bleeding in the bathroom. You're spoiling every rug in the house."[35]

At work, he faced hatemongers who made death threats and sent suspicious packages, including a second failed firebomb that smoked and burned when postal workers intercepted and opened it. Moreover, the wars of Progressivism were heating up. A Pullman railworkers' strike, in which seven were killed, scores wounded, and hundreds of railway cars burned, continued for five months, until the beginning of 1895, and set the tone for labor clashes in the years ahead. Growing labor unrest in New York City was often blamed on the Progressives, whose standard Roosevelt proudly wore. Discontent among workers found fertile ground in the city's unsanitary living conditions amid grim tenements in overcrowded slums. The immigrant tide, which showed no sign of slacking, exacerbated ethnic conflicts as well.

In particular, an influx of Jewish immigrants created a kind of litmus test for religious and cultural tolerance. Roosevelt endeavored to put himself on the side of righteousness in this divisive issue. He went out of his way to delineate his support of Jews in his

Autobiography, including a fawning portrait of Jewish officer Otto
Raphael. Roosevelt adopted Raphael as a kind of protégé, promot-
ing him and becoming friendly with Raphael's family to a degree
that almost smacked of tokenism. The Jewish vote was becoming
an increasingly important factor in New York City electoral politics, and Roosevelt's official accounting of his relationship with
Jews seemed a calculated move. In private correspondence he
made occasional cutting or mocking asides about Jews to family
members or friends. Few Jews were admitted during the years of
Roosevelt's membership to the Boone & Crockett Club, the Union
League Club, the Harvard Club of New York City, or the National
Arts Club. Still, Roosevelt's self-congratulatory acknowledgment
of his attitude toward Jews was responsible for an amusing anecdote in his *Autobiography.* While he was police commissioner, an
anti-Semitic preacher from Germany, Rector Ahlwardt, traveled
to New York to lead a crusade against Jews.

> Many of the New York Jews were much excited and asked
> me to prevent him from speaking and not to give him
> police protection. This, I told them, was impossible; and if
> possible would have been undesirable because it would have
> made him a martyr. The proper thing to do was to make
> him ridiculous.[36]

Roosevelt assigned to Rector Ahlwardt's security detail a Jewish
sergeant and several other Jewish policemen. As a result,
Ahlwardt made his anti-Semitic speech under the protection of
nearly forty policemen, every one of them a Jew. "It was the most
effective possible answer," Roosevelt said.

On another front, by going after Tammany saloon keepers
and enforcing the ban on Sunday liquor sales, he was striking at
political junior officers who answered to committeemen. It was
worse than when he had gone after assistant postmasters. "In the
New York political world just at present every man's hand is

against me; every politician and every editor," he wrote in a typically hyperbolic letter to his sister Bamie. "I live in a welter of small intrigue."[37]

But at age thirty-seven, Roosevelt's fabled strength and endurance were showing signs of a gradual decline. He often complained in letters of how tired and worn out he was, not just from the strain of the infighting and political pressure, but from the long hours and relentless physical grind. In a revealing moment, he also conceded the work of police comissioner had begun to depress him.

> I work—and fight!—from dawn until dark, almost; and the difficulties, the opposition, the lukewarm support I encounter, give me hours of profound depression; but at bottom I know the work has been well worth doing, and that I have done it as well as it could be done . . . It is a grimy struggle, but a vital one.[38]

Roosevelt finally took a break from the grind of his job with a monthlong trip to the Badlands in the middle of August 1896 "to spend time out on the plains among my cattle and after occasional antelope."[39] It had been a particularly trying period. As an overseer of the city's Health Board, he had faced a crisis. The unit had been stretched to the limits of its resources during the deadly heat wave of the summer of 1896.

> The death rate trebled until it approached the ratio of a cholera epidemic; the horses died by the hundreds, so that it was impossible to remove their carcasses, and they added a genuine flavor of pestilence; and we had to distribute hundreds of tons of ice from the Munition houses to the people of the poorer precincts. I had to be in town several nights; and I ran into some strange and pathetic scenes when the ice was distributed. Now a cool wave has come.[40]

What Roosevelt encountered in the Badlands was hardly more encouraging. His cattle operation had suffered severe losses from a harsh previous winter.

> I also enjoyed my trip, though a little disheartened to find that our cattle were not doing well—in fact a good deal disheartened. But I grew burly and sunburned riding over the great plains and sleeping in the open at night.[41]

That fall brought a new presidential election, new opportunities for work in Washington, and the chance to escape the grind of the Police Commission. The newly coined "yellow journalism" of Joseph Pulitzer's *New York World* and rival publisher William Randolph Hearst's *New York Journal* ratcheted up pressure on President Cleveland to intervene in Cuba, where a rebellion against Spain was turning violent. During a twelve-day campaign swing across New York and west to Ohio, Roosevelt stumped for William McKinley. The candidate's strategist, Ohio Senator Mark Hanna, had enlisted Roosevelt, whose hard-charging personality contrasted with McKinley's low-key, folksy style. Hanna's masterful stroke was to magnify the dichotomy of the '88 campaign. McKinley stayed home, in a "front porch" campaign, receiving visitors in Canton but acting the noble, becoming role of a reluctant suitor. Roosevelt stumped hard to counter the formidable Democratic candidate, William Jennings Bryan—nicknamed "the Great Commoner" for his ability to connect personally with voters through skillful oratory. The Nebraskan electrified Democrats with a stirring "cross of gold" speech in which he pushed for the free coinage of silver. The Republicans, taking nothing for granted, invested huge cash and personnel resources to recapture the White House. The party paid for trainloads of supporters to arrive in Canton each day and march to McKinley's house to the beat of brass bands. Roosevelt enlisted Lodge to barnstorm with him throughout upstate New

York, whipping up the crowds for McKinley in packed auditoriums. Hanna sent Roosevelt solo to shadow Bryan on a whistle-stop train tour across Illinois, Michigan, and Minnesota. Roosevelt likened Bryan and other free-silver Populists to "the leaders of the Terror of France in mental and moral attitude." Hanna's masterly tactics routed the Democrats.

A weary Roosevelt expressed relief over McKinley's victory— his crushing defeat of Bryan was the largest majority ever recorded in a presidential contest—and took pride in the role he played in the Republican landslide. It was time to consider his options. He felt that his reform work in the police department had hit a dead end, he was stymied in his war against Parker, and his effectiveness had stalled.

> As for my own police work, we have the force at a very high
> point of efficiency, and we gave the city the most honest and
> orderly election it has ever had. I have done nearly all I can
> do with the police under the present law; and now I should
> rather welcome being legislated out of office.[42]

Alas, the inherent problems of the Police Board were still there when Roosevelt returned from his trip out west. Continuous squabbling and a contentious working environment hastened Roosevelt's departure. He complained that the job wore him down with the constant infighting and undercutting of his authority. "I doubt if any man now has a much harder task than I have, with the police, taking everything into account," he said. "The grinding labor, and the worry, have been very great."[43] Roosevelt still managed to retreat to Sagamore Hill two or three days out of each week, where he worked on the fourth volume of *The Winning of the West,* consumed his long-time diet of two or three books daily (accomplished by skimming madly and enhanced by a near-photographic memory), chopped wood with Ted, and enjoyed long walks and horseback rides with Edith. He was cranky and downcast, even as new options were possible.

> The victorious Republican leaders have taken to feasting themselves, and especially Mark Hanna, and I have been at several Capuan entertainments, from which I have emerged in a condition of plethora only reduced by fighting Parker, or endeavoring to make Grant's brain less like a sweetbread. One was a huge lunch by the Seligmans where at least half the guests were Jew bankers; I felt as if I was personally realizing all of Brooks Adams' gloomiest anticipations of our gold-ridden, capitalist-bestridden, usurer-mastered future.[44]

Among several positions he desired in the new administration, the one that seemed the best fit—combining his own intense personal interest in the nation's naval forces and the enjoyment Edith and his family had found in Washington, D.C.—was assistant secretary of the navy. But it was by no means a lock. In the spring of 1897, Roosevelt still seemed at loose ends and uncertain of his next career move. "I have no idea what I should do next," he wrote Bamie, "but I should enjoy, and should feel I deserved, three or four months' holiday at Sagamore; and surely there is something I can turn my hand to."[45] Roosevelt encouraged all his friends, social and political, to push his name for the navy post. His good friends Bellamy and Maria Storer, socialites and Washington insiders, agreed to lobby on his behalf, as did John Hay, Henry Cabot Lodge, Speaker Tom Reed, and Judge William Taft. But McKinley remained unconvinced. Finally, after some pause, New York State Republican boss Thomas Platt let go of his misgivings and gave his endorsement of the police commissioner to McKinley. Platt's push was an act of self-preservation on behalf of his machine. Platt reasoned that Roosevelt would be likely to "do less harm to the organization as

Assistant Secretary of the Navy than in any other office that could be named."[46]

McKinley appointed Roosevelt assistant secretary of the navy. Edith was pregnant at the time, so Theodore went to Washington at first by himself and stayed with the Lodges. Roosevelt was as giddy as a Groton first former.

> I was even more pleased than I was astonished at the appointment. McKinley rather distrusted me, and Platt actively hated me; it was Cabot's untiring energy and devotion which put me in; and [Navy Secretary John D.] Long really wanted me. Of course until next Wednesday the Senate, where I have very bitter enemies, may reconsider the confirmation; but there is only a very small chance of this.[47]

The press hailed the announcement of Roosevelt's new post and predicted great things. "He is a fighter, a man of indomitable pluck and energy, a potent and forceful factor in any equation into which he may be introduced. A field of immeasurable usefulness awaits him," said the *Washington Post*.[48]

Even among Roosevelt's New York critics, there was a begrudging respect for his extraordinary energy and fearsome commitment to reform. Commissioner Andrews wrote,

> What emerged for New York City from Roosevelt's turbulent years as Police Commissioner was a police force with a morale, a faith in a square deal for "the man with the night stick," and a tradition of law enforcement which survived the corruption of succeeding administrations and made the men, admitted to the force in Roosevelt's administration, who wore, like a medal of honor the designation of "Roosevelt cop."[49]

A few small newspapers, including central New York's *Ithaca Daily News,* had actually endorsed Roosevelt for the Republican presidential nomination in 1896. At the reporters' shop on Mulberry Street, Riis had been convinced that Roosevelt aspired to be commander in chief and was of presidential timber. Steffens wasn't so easily persuaded. Each argued his case, until the two correspondents agreed to go directly to the source. They marched across the street, into Roosevelt's office, and asked if he was actively working toward the presidency.

The question produced a startling rage in Roosevelt, who hurtled himself around his desk and got up into the reporters' faces with hands balled into a boxer's fists and teeth clenched maniacally. According to Steffens's autobiography, Roosevelt exploded at Riis, "Don't you dare ask me that. Don't you put such ideas into my head. No friend of mine would ever say a thing like that, you—you—" Roosevelt then recovered his composure, and with a friendly arm around the shoulder of Riis, he drew the two newspapermen close into his confidence and softly spoke these telling words, according to Steffens:

> Never, never, you must never either of you remind a man at work on a political job that he may be President. It almost always gives up the very traits that are making him a possibility. I, for instance, I am going to do great things here, hard things that require all the courage, ability, work that I am capable of . . . But if I get to thinking of what it might lead to . . . I must be wanting to be President. Every young man does. But I won't let myself think of it; I must not, because if I do, I will begin to work for it, I'll be careful, calculating, cautious in word and act, and so—I'll beat myself. See?[50]

In fact, if he had stayed on as police commissioner, he probably would have beaten himself. Mayor Strong had pushed for Roosevelt's resignation, as had Platt and other Republican leaders. German Americans, a formidable voting bloc in New York

City, had bolted their traditional allegiance to the Republican Party in droves and voted Democratic as a result of Roosevelt's temperance work. No beer, no vote. The huge swing cost several Republicans their seats. The pressure on Roosevelt to resign was growing, as was Platt's willingness to send him to Washington just to get him out of the way.

As he had so often and resolutely done in the past, Roosevelt would recast the circumstances and finesse his personal defeat into victory. Already, while he was still police commissioner, Roosevelt had offered unsolicited opinions on foreign affairs to the president and other leading adminstration members who cared to listen.

> We ought to drive the Spaniards out of Cuba; and it would be a good thing, in more ways than one, to do it. Congress ought to take more decisive action; I always hate words unless they mean blows.[51]

Now, as assistant secretary of the navy, he could help do something about it. Roosevelt was ready to remedy what he perceived as a sickening situation: the United States' status as a nation with a second-class navy. The author of *The Naval War of 1812* was ready to push to expand the fleet into something that would have been unimaginable in President Madison's day.

Chapter 8

★ ★ ★ ★ ★

ROUGH RIDER

My men were children of the dragon's blood!

Roosevelt had sounded the alarm for years that the United States had only a second-rate, ill-prepared navy. The facts backed him up. By 1894, the United States Navy ranked a dismal sixth, behind those of Great Britain, France, Italy, Russia, and Germany. Despite the fact that the country was nearly an island power, with only two bordering neighbors, America had neither built its navy nor even maintained much of an army after the Civil War. Its economic base was world-class, but its decentralized political system had produced a generally peaceful policy before McKinley. All that was changing, however, as the government increasingly looked beyond its borders and a group of influential nationalists clamored for attention. Within the navy, they were represented by Alfred Thayer Mahan.

Mahan was a soft-spoken, stern, and underutilized Navy officer who had previously had command of the USS *Wasp,* a captured Civil War blockade runner. He was bored and unhappy handling odd assignments in the run-down South Atlantic Fleet. Mahan filled his prolonged periods of waiting between assignments by writing articles and books on the critical role of sea power in global events. In 1886, Mahan was promoted to head the newly established Naval War College in Newport, Rhode Island. But Mahan's writings, curricula, and addresses at the college often seemed like a cry in the wilderness—until answered by Roosevelt, a like-minded proponent of naval superiority who shared Mahan's literary bent. The two corresponded after Roosevelt devoured in a single weekend Mahan's seminal 1890 study, *The Influence of Sea Power upon History.* Roosevelt also wrote a glowing review of the book for the *Atlantic* magazine, which further endeared him to the naval commander turned author. The two men corresponded regularly about the need to upgrade, modernize, and expand to keep pace with advances in industrialization and technology. Mahan advocated that a strong U.S. Navy be deployed at strategic spots around the world that controlled the circulation of global trade. Both Mahan and Roosevelt agreed on the notion that navies could be more effective than armies in enforcing the sovereignty of a nation.

Upon accepting the appointment as assistant secretary of the navy, Roosevelt was eager to test the theories of his friend. Roosevelt's new position was also a culmination of his childhood fantasy of becoming a naval war hero along the lines of his mother's colorful brothers, Jimmy and Irvine Bulloch.

This time—in contrast to the angry repercussions a few years earlier after he passed up the chance to run for mayor of New York City—the career move satisfied both spouses. Edith was back in her favorite city, among a circle of friends, and her children were enrolled in the local public schools they had previously attended. Roosevelt's sixth child—the couple's fifth—was born in the fall of 1897 while Theodore served in the navy post. Theodore was so busy with his work and Edith so involved with the other children and setting up her household that they cut it a bit close when Edith commenced labor. Theodore hopped on his bicycle and pedaled furiously to summon a doctor and nurse, who arrived just in time for the delivery. "We are very glad and much relieved," wrote the proud father, who decided planning for the

future could not be started too soon.[1] Less than two hours after
Quentin was born, Roosevelt completed the paperwork and
enrolled him in Groton, the prestigious boys' prep school in
Massachusetts. The rigors of childbirth caused health problems
for Edith and lingering complications that confined her mostly
to bed rest for a few months after Quentin's arrival. His wife's lingering ailments wore on Theodore, who stayed home on some
evenings and lashed out at Edith's invalidism in correspondence.

At work, Roosevelt faced long-simmering tension with Spain
over its closest remaining colony, Cuba. As far back as 1873, the
SS *Virginia,* based in New York, had been loaded with a shipment
of arms intended for Cuba's rebel insurgents, only to be captured
by the Spanish gunboat *Tornado.* The Spaniards bound forty-three
passengers and crew of the *Virginia,* lined them up, and executed
them. The HMS *Niobe* arrived just in time to save some other
passengers. The incident inflamed U.S.-Spanish relations and
could have sparked a war.

Yet U.S. threats were empty because of the weakness of the
American navy. While the navies of the major European powers
were anchored by armored ships driven by steam, the Americans
had only wooden ships that relied upon sail power. In addition,
the U.S. secretary of the navy's office was riddled with political
corruption and incompetence. Finally, in 1890, Congress authorized the building of the nation's first modern steam-powered,
steel-hulled battleships. The result was three of the finest warships
anywhere in the world: *Indiana, Massachusetts*, and *Oregon.* Roosevelt wanted more. He advocated for a two-ocean navy capable of
attacking in both the Pacific and Atlantic simultaneously. It
would require three to four times the resources that Congress had
approved. Roosevelt delivered a major address at the Naval War
College in Newport in May 1897 in which he proclaimed, "No
triumph of peace is quite so great as the supreme triumph of war."

Through their speeches and writings, Mahan and Roosevelt
were instrumental in shifting the U.S. Navy away from slow,

bulky, short-haul monitors guarding the home shores and swift, light cruisers that shot out of protected ports to attack enemy ships. The new paradigm relied on heavily armed steel warships that combined strength, speed, and reach. These new warships would be able to travel further and faster, deliver more punishing fusillades, withstand greater enemy bombardment, and stay at sea longer during patrols. Roosevelt and Mahan's campaign benefited from the fact that their boss, Navy Secretary John D. Long, was an elderly career bureaucrat whose best days as a leader were behind him and who delegated much of his workload to subordinates during his frequent and extended absences from the department. Roosevelt saw his opening and he took it.

Twenty-five years after the Spanish attack on the SS *Virginia,* a still-unexplained incident over another U.S. ship served as the pretext for war. The battleship *Maine* exploded on February 15, 1898, while on a visit to Havana. A total of 262 sailors aboard were killed, and the ship sank, leaving only a mast and a few burned, twisted sections of the superstructure visible above water. The *Maine* was a strikingly sleek and powerful steel warship of recent vintage, painted a dazzling white and considered one of the Navy's best midsize battleships. Roosevelt had personally assisted with outfitting the *Maine* and had spewed bellicose rhetoric shortly before its ill-fated voyage. Along with other naval officers, he had ignored warnings that anchoring in Havana, recently rocked by rioting, would inflame already heated tensions with Spain. While Spain denied responsibility for the catastrophe, many Americans, including Roosevelt, felt that the deadly explosion was grounds for a declaration of war. An investigative committee concluded that the fatal blast came from outside the ship and was, therefore, an act of sabotage—although its report stopped short of charging Spain with the attack. A second inquiry also settled on a theory of an external explosion from a submarine mine, although a third disputed those findings and pointed to a malfunction in the engine room. Military leaders, politicians, and a wide swath of the American public weren't waiting for even the first investigation; circumstantial evidence was enough to fuel war fever against Spain. While Congress debated, delayed, and weighed the nation's options, Roosevelt sent a message to Capitol Hill requesting special wartime legislation from Congress. President McKinley also put off a decision while Hearst and others shouted for war. "He has no more backbone than a chocolate eclair," Roosevelt said of McKinley.[2] The cry "Remember the *Maine!* To Hell with Spain!" swirled. Rhyming headlines and editorials were used to full effect by those clamoring for a fight. One can only wonder if a war would have been fought had it been the *Oregon* that exploded.

Roosevelt wouldn't wait for presidential approval or even departmental orders. Just ten days after the sinking, Roosevelt found his opening for action when Secretary Long left the Navy Department for half a day on February 25. Long had given his assistant secretary explicit instructions not to take "any step affecting the policy of the administration without consulting the President or me." But Roosevelt conveniently ignored the directive and secretly ordered Commodore George Dewey in Hong Kong to prepare the Asiatic Squadron for attack and to keep the fleet full of coal—ready to strike the Spanish squadron in the Philippines quickly and forcefully in the event of a declaration of war. Long was furious and likened Roosevelt to a bull in a china shop. "He has come very near causing more of an explosion than happened to the *Maine,*" Long wrote in his diary. But the secretary did not rescind his assistant's order to Dewey, and so it was Roosevelt who sparked the navy to war.

Roosevelt also was willing to cross the political aisle in his effort to persuade President McKinley to wage war. He turned to a leading New York State Democrat, Willie Chanler, brother of his friend from Harvard Wintie Chanler. "I know you are as strong in your views of foreign policy as Cabot and I are," he wrote to Chanler. "It seems incredible that the Democratic party, the historic party of annexation, should be so inclined to go against the annexation of Hawaii . . . I think this is the time when you could use your influence in a way that would be invaluable to America."[3]

Hearst sent well-known western artist Frederic Remington to Cuba to make sketches of Cuban insurgents fighting for independence in Spain as a way for the newspaper publisher to generate public support for war. Remington found little to draw, grew bored, and sent a telegram to Hearst that read, "Everything quiet, no trouble here. There will be no war. I wish to return." Hearst sent the following fabled reply to the artist: "Please remain. You furnish the pictures and I will furnish the war." Remington stayed. Soon Hearst and his rival, Roosevelt, would have their wish.

President McKinley affirmed war with Spain in April 1898 by signing a joint resolution of Congress that authorized the United States military to liberate Cuba. As the great white fleet was repainted a dull gray for combat, the ships were loaded with a full complement of armaments, equipment, and ammunition—courtesy of the foresight and badgering of Assistant Secretary Roosevelt. In a clutch of months, Roosevelt felt he had already achieved his three basic goals: to improve morale, streamline administration, and enhance the tactical efficiency of the U.S. Navy. Ultimately, Dewey and his seven warships defeated the Spanish fleet at Manila Bay in May in a swift, lopsided victory, and U.S. forces seized the Philippine capital of Manila three months later. America joined the ranks of colonial powers.

In the single most important decision of his prepresidential career, Roosevelt made the extraordinary move to leave his desk job in the navy behind and leap directly into combat in Cuba. Not only did he believe he had accomplished his goals with the navy, but he also carried a romantic notion of war from his mother's brothers, the desire to put behind him a lingering sense of familial shame over his father's not serving in combat in the

Civil War, and his own lust for testing his mettle in combat. "An incurable Sancho Panza," his critics called him. There was also, to be sure, his strong sense of patriotism and desire to serve his country.

Yet at home there were obstacles. The lingering physical troubles that had left Edith bedridden for months after Quentin's birth remained a mystery, as doctors failed to pinpoint the source of her illness. Eventually, specialists were consulted who determined that Edith had a large abdominal growth. They urged emergency surgery, which was performed on March 5, 1898. The tumor was successfully removed and Edith's prognosis was good, but she faced a long recovery period. Moreover, their son Ted's years of health problems and recurring psychosomatic symptoms had deteriorated further into an invalidism not unlike his mother's, with stretches of days in which the boy was confined to bed with so-called nervous headaches. Over the years, Ted had suffered bouts of boils, double pneumonia, tonsillitis, and other maladies. This latest stretch had not at first overly concerned his parents. But the ten-year-old's symptoms persisted and deepened.

Finally, Ted suffered what amounted to a nervous breakdown. To the family friend and physician, Dr. Alexander Lambert, the boy confided the crushing pressure he felt from trying to follow his father's example. Lambert diagnosed mental exhaustion and "nervous prostration," prescribing a personal nurse and a regimen of exercise and nutritious eating. The nurse was also there to act as a buffer so that the father would not try to push his son too hard. The doctor's diagnosis was a bitter pill to swallow, but Roosevelt accepted the criticism. "Hereafter I shall never press Ted either in body or mind," he wrote to Lambert.[4] "The fact is that the little fellow, who is peculiarly dear to me, has bidden fair to be all the things I would like to have been and wasn't, and it has been a great temptation to push him."

Many years later, when he was a grown man, his mother confided to Ted that he had received the most intense scrutiny from his father out of all his siblings. "As I look back, you fared worst, because Father tried to 'toughen' you, but happily was too busy to exert the same pressure on others," Edith said.[5] His mother's later confidence was small comfort at the time, as the two Theodores rarely managed to strike a happy balance after the doctor's intervention.

Roosevelt had no business going to war. It was both personally irresponsible and professionally ill-advised. He had a critical position in Washington for which he was especially well suited and could have had a large impact as a navy strategist; he was a father to six children and husband of a convalescing wife, who did not want him to go. Even Navy Secretary Long and President McKinley tried to dissuade him from raising his own regiment and leading it to war in Cuba.

Others tried to discourage him, including the antiwar advocate and Roosevelt's former Harvard professor, the psychologist and philosopher William James. James published several articles and letters to the editor in newspapers arguing against warmongering and imperial expansionism. James became vice president of the Anti-Imperialist League and gave prominent speeches to that group. He also personally attacked his former student's enthusiasm for combat by describing Roosevelt as "still mentally in the *Sturm und Drang* period of early adolescence" and as spewing a "flood of abstract bellicose emotion."[6]

None of it, not even Edith's surgery, mattered. "I would not allow even a death to stand in my way; that it was my one chance to do something for my country and for my family and my one chance to cut my little notch on the stick that stands as a measuring-rod in every family," he confided to a friend years later.[7] "I know now that I would have turned from my wife's deathbed to have answered that call."

To Edith, he argued that he could not afford to become what a later era would call chicken-livered. Since he had been a leading proponent of going to war with Spain, if he backed out and did not serve on the front lines, he would be be criticized as hypocritical and the political fallout would be devastating. "It does not seem to me that it would be honorable for a man who has consistently advocated a warlike policy not to be willing to bear the brunt of carrying out that policy. I have a horror of the people who bark but don't bite," Roosevelt wrote to his brother-in-law.[8] Eventually, mindful of the price she had paid for going against his wish to run for New York City mayor, Edith acquiesced. Secretary Long also tried to talk Roosevelt out of volunteering for combat duty. "His heart is right, and he means well," Long wrote in his diary. "But it is one of those cases of aberration-desertion-vainglory; of which he is utterly unaware." Meanwhile, Roosevelt's friends tried to convince him to remain in Washington, but he would not listen even to those whose advice he most respected, including Henry Cabot Lodge, Douglas Robinson, John Hay, and Henry Adams. Some friends criticized Roosevelt's gung-ho preparations behind his back. "I think he is going mad," Wintie Chanler wrote. "Theodore is wild to fight and hack and hew. It is really sad. Of course, this ends his political career for good. Even Cabot says this."[9] As usual, reports of his political demise were greatly exaggerated.

President McKinley made a patriotic pitch that he was looking for 125,000 volunteers to boost the army's regular ranks of 28,000 soldiers. There was a specific request for volunteers to raise three cavalry regiments of men who had been at home on the range and were skilled with horse and rifle. The raising of volunteer regiments became a sort of Harvard intramural match, between Roosevelt and Willie Chanler. Willie was a Harvard dropout who had wrestled alligators in Florida, explored East Africa, run guns in Cuba, and associated with a criminal element in the Wild West. Lately he'd become bored and complacent as a New York legislator, and he saw the war in Cuba as yet another adventure and a chance to break away from the doldrums of Albany politics. He resigned from the Assembly and devoted himself to the task of regiment raising. Roosevelt, looking over his shoulder, responded to a letter from Chanler in mid-March:

> This is the first letter of yours that I have ever hated to receive, for I have been on the point of writing to you to know if you were going to raise a regiment, and to know if I could go along. I shall chafe my heart if I am kept here instead of being at the front.[10]

Chanler intended to raise an infantry regiment of volunteers; Roosevelt asked to be chosen to help lead it as a lieutenant colonel. Roosevelt also proposed that Dr. Leonard Wood, another Harvard man and his friend, be installed as the regimental major. "We will have a jim-dandy regiment if we are allowed to go," Roosevelt said.[11] He was also hedging his bets and was not terribly upset when Chanler's plans stalled.

Chanler, a Democrat, was facing roadblocks because Republicans controlled both Albany and Washington at that time. Chanler's repeated requests for an official blessing were met with resistance. Chanler appealed directly to President McKinley, who repeated the Republican line that no additional volunteers were being sought. Chanler tried to get Roosevelt to break the logjam, but Roosevelt claimed he had exhausted all avenues.

Roosevelt's real aim was to beat Chanler to the punch as a regiment raiser. He succeeded, since he had the inside track as a Republican and member of McKinley's inner circle. Roosevelt took pleasure in breaking the news in late April to Willie Chanler that Congress had authorized the raising of three regiments of volunteer cavalry—not infantry as Chanler had proposed—and that Secretary of War Russell A. Alger had offered Roosevelt the command of one of them.

Roosevelt's announcement on May 6 that he had resigned as assistant secretary of the navy in order to accept a commission to organize the First Volunteer Cavalry Regiment struck a chord with able-bodied men across the country. Applications poured in, more than twenty-three thousand for one thousand slots, representing men from all walks of life. One of the most widely represented groups, of course, were cowboys. Hundreds volunteered, many of whom had known of Roosevelt from his time as a cattle rancher. Roosevelt's connection to Harvard also drew many applicants from his alma mater and other Ivy League institutions, particularly former college athletes. Numerous New York City policemen, some of whom had worked under Commissioner Roosevelt, also asked to join.

Roosevelt soon decided he was unqualified to command a regiment himself and offered to serve under Wood. Instead he was named lieutenant colonel for the First United States Volunteer Cavalry—both the first and only regiment of volunteers raised, as it turned out. The Republicans were happy to take credit for this historic feat. Chanler reluctantly dropped plans to raise a regiment and instead joined the regular infantry troops under General Jose Miguel Gomez at the training camp in Tampa, Florida.

Dr. Leonard Wood, personal physician to President McKinley, was a professional soldier who fought bravely and showed great leadership with cavalry troops against Indian warriors during the Apache uprising in the West. Wood was awarded the nation's highest military honor, the Medal of Honor, for his relentless pursuit of Apache Chief Geronimo. He and Roosevelt had become friends; they now got along well with Wood in command. "He was always thoroughly subordinate," Wood said of Roosevelt many years later.[12] "People used to come and say, 'Well, you are going to have a good deal of trouble with Theodore as a subordinate.' There was absolutely nothing of the sort . . . He knew perfectly the line between subordination and servility; there was nothing of that."

Roosevelt joined his regiment at training camp in San Antonio, Texas. Lieutenant Colonel Roosevelt proved himself a taskmaster who earned the respect of even the most hardened cowboy. "Theodore has been drilling us the last few days," a cousin to Roosevelt's brother-in-law wrote from San Antonio. "The men always do their best when he is out. He would be amused if he heard some of the adjectives and terms applied to him, meant to be most complimentary but hardly fit for publication."[13]

Roosevelt normally pushed his men hard, but one afternoon he instead invited them to a pleasant, shady wooded area and treated them each to a big mug of beer. Colonel Wood came back to the training camp that day after learning of Roosevelt's beer session. In a talk to his officers that night, Wood said that officers were not permitted to drink beer with their men and any officer who did so must be considered unfit to hold a commission. The words of warning were met with silence. Wood left and went to his tent. A few minutes later, there was a scratching on his tent and a request by an officer to speak with the colonel. Roosevelt had come to confess.

"I wish to tell you sir, that I took the squadron, and without thinking about this question of officers' drinking with their men, I gave them all a schooner of beer," Roosevelt said.

Wood listened without replying.

Roosevelt continued, "I wish to say, sir, that I agree with what you said. I consider myself the damndest ass within ten miles of this camp."

Wood said nothing. Roosevelt bid Wood goodnight and walked out into the night.

Wood later recounted that he struggled to keep a stern face throughout.[14]

Wood's thousands of troops ran the gamut across every ethnic, sociological, economic, and educational level—and remained remarkably free of friction and clashes. At least part of that successful blending of personalities must be attributed to strong leadership from officers such as Roosevelt. There were arguments and fisticuffs in the barracks, according to soldiers' memoirs, but they were focused on which troop was the most efficient at drills. These rumbles were occasional and short-lived, and they did not fester into lingering grudges. "All in all, the troopers were well behaved; everyone was trying to conform to regulations and become a good soldier, and the very few who failed to enter the spirit pervading the camp were quietly dropped," a volunteer soldier recalled years later.[15] After two weeks in San Antonio, Roosevelt and his soldiers were reassigned to a training camp in Tampa Bay, Florida, where they would join other elements of the Fifth Army Corps.

Their regiment's initial arrival in Tampa was tangled in "a perfect welter of confusion," Roosevelt wrote in *The Rough Riders.* "We had to buy the men food out of our own pockets, and to seize wagons in order to get our spare baggage taken to the camping ground." In short order, though, behind Colonel Wood's strong organizational skills, Roosevelt helped get "order out of confusion" in setting up a tent city with officers' quarters, company kitchens, and toilet areas. Roosevelt started drilling the troops as soon as the tents were pitched.

Meanwhile, Edith's worries about her husband were assuaged, at least temporarily, during a trip she made to Florida. Theodore received special approval to stay with his wife at the Tampa Bay Hotel. "It has been delightful to have Edie here for the four days, and I think she has enjoyed it too," Roosevelt wrote to his sister Corinne. "We have had a regular spree here, for Col. Wood has let me be with her at the hotel from before dinner until after breakfast each day."[16]

Shortly after Edith's departure, the long-awaited orders from President William McKinley arrived on the night of June 7. Major General William R. Shafter read the terse instructions: "You will sail immediately as you are needed at destination." McKinley's command touched off a frenzy of confusion as the large volunteer army tried to move en masse to a flotilla of steamers in Port Tampa, nine miles away. Each regiment tried to elbow its way to the front of the line. Roosevelt's Rough Riders—who stood out in brown trousers, slouch hats, and neckerchiefs chosen by Roosevelt amid a sea of thirty thousand soldiers in blue—were among them. Although they had just arrived "very tired and very dirty"[17] after four days and sleepless nights tending to the horses on a train from San Antonio, Roosevelt roused his regiment in the early morning hours. He pushed his troops to pack quickly, corral all their baggage, and assemble for a train at midnight in order to get a jump on the other regiments. The train did not show. The Rough Riders settled in among their piles of gear and rested. Roosevelt and Wood returned at three o'clock in the morning, roused their men from sleep, and told them to trudge through the blackness to a different track. They waited some more. "It was a strange sight to see the dark figures of men moving about, like shadows on a curtain, getting ready for departure," one observer wrote.[18] But that train never showed either. Roosevelt fumed as the wan light of sunrise illuminated his regiment, and a growing anger infused the troops, who complained they were going to miss the battle. Suddenly he spotted a string of coal cars swinging into view. He stopped the train, told the Rough Riders to pile into the dusty, empty rigs, and demanded that the locomotive engineer throw the train into reverse and run backward for nine miles to Fort Tampa. Streaked with coal dust, Roosevelt's weary regiment unloaded their belongings at the dock and waited once more among thousands of troops, each unit as confused and lost as they were. Wintie Chanler chronicled the scene of confusion with particular disdain.

> Nothing here, except the gross incompetence of our transport officers of all grades from Shafter down, has impressed me so much as Theodore sitting at a table in a little hotel at the pier unable to get anything he wanted, in the uniform of a Lieutenant Colonel, dry and hungry. Colonel Wood on one side, his boss, on the other a naval officer, doting on

him. He gnashing his teeth at the whole disgraceful performance of embarkation. When he might have been running the best part of the show either in his office at
Washington or with the Fleets at Santiago. I cannot but feel
that his political future has been benefited rather than hurt
by his sacrifice.[19]

Nobody knew which among the cluster of troopships was
theirs to board. Roosevelt, who dismissed the turmoil as "a good
deal of higglety-pigglety,"[20] finally learned that the *Yucatan* was
the Rough Riders' assigned vessel. The problem was that the
ship, at anchor in the middle of the canal connected to the bay,
had also been promised to the Second Regular Infantry and the
Seventy-first New York Volunteers. Roosevelt, the former law
student, knew that possession was nine-tenths of the law, and so
he marched his cavalry double-time. He noted with pride that
the Rough Riders moved to the front of the line and held their
spot because the other two units were "a shade less ready than we
were in the matter of individual initiative."[21] In the end, the
Rough Riders ended up sharing their transport with some troops
of the Second Cavalry. Unfortunately, the *Yucatan* did not contain
all the cargo space the Rough Riders needed, and they were
forced to leave not only their horses but some of their troops
behind to wait for a later transport. "We would rather crawl on
all fours than not go," Roosevelt wrote.[22]

The thirty-six transport ships included coal-powered tenders
and lighters that could make about nine knots an hour at top
speed. There was also one sailing vessel at the mercy of the winds.
Soldiers shared space with 831 private horses (including two of
Roosevelt's), 578 government horses, 294 mules, 114 complete
sets of six-mule harnesses, 114 army wagons, 84 complete sets of
four-mule ambulance harnesses, 81 escort wagons, and 7 Red
Cross ambulances. There were bales of hay, sacks of oats, and
other forage for the animals. Provisions for the men included

hard bread, coffee, beef, flour, beans, bacon, rice, tomatoes, onions, salt, pepper, sugar, baking powder, vinegar, and candles. There was also the bulky tonnage of ordnance, rifles, and ammunition. In all, it was a costly flotilla of war making: about $80 million to purchase the ships from foreign countries and private shipping companies, an additional outlay of $151 million for equipment and supplies, and an estimated operating cost of $2 million per day—with Congress making piecemeal appropriations.[23]

Leaving their horses behind was disheartening. Only Roosevelt and a few officers were allowed to take their mounts aboard the *Yucatan*. The Rough Riders' anger at the miscues turned to embarrassment when they were given the nickname "Wood's Weary Walkers." A correspondent described the scene:

> Such a set of disappointed men one seldom has seen. The fates of war have certainly their disappointments. To think of Theodore Roosevelt leaving the position of Assistant Secretary of the Navy and organizing a regiment of expert cavalrymen, at least one company of which is made up of young men of high social standing in New York, every man in the command having furnished himself with expensive mounts, suddenly by an order to be dismounted is certainly hard luck.[24]

As it was, the *Yucatan* was extremely overcrowded, with one thousand men stuffed aboard a boat meant for a few hundred. Yet as waiting soldiers from the Second and Seventy-first regiments were turned away, the opportunistic Roosevelt squeezed aboard a pair of documentary filmmakers, who planned to make moving pictures of the war in Cuba and, of course, the brash lieutenant colonel's role in it.

As General Shafter in the flagship *Seguranca* finally weighed anchor and led the invasion fleet out of the canal, Secretary of

War Alger called the ships back to anchor because of a report of enemy warships waiting in ambush in the Gulf of Mexico. Shafter would not let the sixteen thousand troops go ashore, since Alger might give the order to steam into battle at any moment. They all spent the next several days in a holding pattern, crammed into the fetid ships with rising resentment at Shafter and the other commanding officers. Roosevelt lashed out in a letter to Lodge:

> No words could describe to you the confusion and lack of system and the general mismanagement of affairs here. We have been here two days now; the troops jammed together under the tropical sun on these crowded troop ships. We are in a sewer; a canal which is festering as if it were Havana harbor . . . Four or five days of this will reduce the efficiency of the landing force just about ten percent, and must inevitably shake the morale of the men . . . Do, old man, try to see that the expedition is not longer deferred, because the bad effects of so deferring it are evident to everyone.[25]

For six interminable days Roosevelt and his men milled about the crowded decks. The sun beat down on the ship, spoiling the already insufficient rations. Most of the water supply aboard, it turned out, was not potable. The only relief would have been to jump into the bay, but large sharks circled the flotilla. Roosevelt had plenty of time to write more long screeds to Lodge. "The mismanagement here is frightful . . . Confusion partly due to their own dilatory inefficiency and partly the utter incompetence . . . At least it may be possible to prevent such blunders in the future." He added, "I see Bronson and my old aide Sharp both got into the fight at Santiago. Lucky fellows . . . I do most sincerely hope we shall yet be able to get in."[26]

Finally, on June 14, the forty-eight ship invasion force—the largest American military armada ever to leave U.S. shores—

steamed out of Tampa Bay and into the Gulf of Mexico. "It is a great historical expedition," Roosevelt wrote Corinne. "And I thrill to feel that I am part of it." Almost before he finished his thoughts, though, the ship came "within an ace of a bad collision with another transport."[27] The Rough Riders' campaign in Cuba had nearly ended before it began.

After an uneventful five-day passage across smooth seas, as the Rough Riders received their battle orders, Roosevelt waved his hat in the air, set a hand on his hip, and danced around the deck in the manner of his celebrations to mark the killing of a big-game trophy animal. He shouted a ditty he'd learned in the Badlands: *"Shout hurrah for Erin go Bragh. And all the Yankee Nation!"* The Rough Riders watched Roosevelt's impromptu war dance with amusement and offered a wry toast: "To the Officers—may they get killed, wounded, or promoted."[28] Roosevelt used his pull in the Navy Department to get approval from a former naval colleague to allow the *Yucatan* to steam ahead of the other thirty troopships and to move first within a few hundred yards of shore.

Luckily, the June 21 landing at Daiquiri on the southern coast of Cuba was uncontested, as the village already had been deserted. Logistics remained a nightmare. "We did the landing as we had done everything else—that is, in a scramble," Roosevelt wrote in *The Rough Riders.* "There were no facilities for landing, and the fleet did not have a quarter of the number of boats it should have had for the purpose." Some of the ships, due to their deep draft, were forced to anchor a mile from shore beyond a shallow coral reef. Troops jumped in the water and tried to wade to shore rather than wait for too few landing boats. Each soldier carried fifty pounds on his back, as well as 105 rounds of ammunition and a spade or ax among his gear. A few men were pulled under by the weight of their equipment and drowned. Two Rough Riders were among those who died before they ever had a chance to fight. A cargo boat capsized in the turbulent waters and, although no men were lost, a critical load of blankets and cartridge belts sank to the bottom of the bay.

Roosevelt jumped into the water a few hundred yards out from shore and lost most of his gear in the frightening scramble to safety. The landing was farce, interspersed with high drama and sporadic tragedy. The sea was choppy and the small landing craft that attempted to unload at the pier were in harm's way as the gunwales rose and fell wildly alongside a rotting, slippery pier. One misjudged step and soldiers would be crushed in trying to disembark. Other troops tried to beach their boats in the crashing surf, often pitching soldiers into the breakers when they ran aground. There was no plan for the mules and horses, which were shoved into the surf and expected to beach themselves. Some became disoriented and swam out toward sea. Roosevelt's two horses, Rain-in-the-Face and Little Texas, received special treatment. They were placed into a harness and winched into the water on booms. But as Rain-in-the-Face was lowered, breakers crested and caused the animal to choke and retch on seawater. He drowned. Roosevelt screamed and cursed in a purple rage at the incompetence. The sailors took extra care with Little Texas, who dangled in the harness for long moments until Roosevelt screamed, "Stop that goddamned animal torture!" The horse eventually was lowered safely to shore. Before they could take stock of their troops and gear, the *Yucatan* was headed out again to open waters—although much of the Rough Riders' equipment had never gotten unloaded. Roosevelt came up empty-handed save for a toothbrush, a yellow rain slicker, and some waterlogged rations stuffed into the pockets. The lieutenant colonel kept his most critical supplies under his slouch hat: extra pairs of spectacles sewn into the lining. Fearful that his poor eyesight could prove fatal in battle, Roosevelt had packed a dozen pairs into the hat.

The disembarkation debacle was reported by a battalion of nearly ninety correspondents who'd been invited to accompany the invasion, including influential newspaper publisher and Roosevelt enemy William Randolph Hearst. Roosevelt and Hearst resumed their Harvard rivalry on Cuban soil. Hearst had brought along an American flag he planned to plant with great pomp (and self-aggrandizing coverage in his own papers). But Roosevelt and the Rough Riders declared Hearst's standard not suitably impressive and instead ran a much larger flag up the pole of an abandoned Spanish blockhouse.

The Spanish-American War had a decidedly Ivy League tinge to it. At least sixty-two members of the Harvard Club participated in the war, including nine Harvard men who fought with Roosevelt's Rough Riders. The quintet most responsible for getting the United States into the war were Harvard men all: Roosevelt; Senator Henry Cabot Lodge; Hearst (a dropout member of the class of 1886); Navy Secretary Long; and Roosevelt's commander, Colonel Leonard Wood (M.D., class of 1884). President Eliot, however, came out strongly against invading Cuba. His name headed a petition with the signatures of eighty-six Harvard administrators and professors opposed to the war.

At Daiquiri, after the chaos, Roosevelt calculated that the frustration of the seven-day layover in Tampa had reduced his men's fighting desire and energy by nearly one half. Roosevelt led a thousand Rough Riders, now horseless, on an eighteen-mile march from the landing area west to Santiago. The brutally relentless tramp up steep hills, amid clouds of insects, and through a blazing heat was rough medicine for the cavalry-turned-infantry regiment. Their progress was hampered by the only uniforms they had, made of heavy wool—a serious logistical error in the tropics. The searing temperatures also had caused much of their food to spoil. Having not estimated well how much potable water they should carry, they were forced to drink from contaminated streams—which put them within the largest swarms of mosquitoes and increased their risks for contracting malaria and cholera. In addition, they had not packed enough medical supplies and were already running low on quinine, the primary medicine for treating infectious tropical diseases. Against these trying circumstances, Roosevelt set an example by refusing to ride Little Texas. He slogged along west toward Siboney while his soldiers shed blanket rolls, cans of food, and clothing along the trail. Roosevelt felt at home in the harsh landscape, which he described as "high barren looking mountains rising abruptly from the shore, and at this distance looking much like those of Montana."[29]

At sunrise on June 24, Roosevelt and his troops started through the pass over the mountains known as Las Guasimas toward Santiago and a Spanish stronghold protected by the San Juan heights. "It was very beautiful and very peaceful," Roosevelt recalled in *The Rough Riders,* "and it seemed more as if we were off on some hunting expedition than as if we were about to go on to a sharp and bloody little fight." They were fighting ostensibly on behalf of the Cuban insurgents, who had been subjected to "hideous misery" at the hands of their Spanish colonial rulers. He would not be satisfied with anything less than "driving the Spaniard from the New World." Roosevelt marched alongside two pet reporters who had provided sympathetic coverage of his term as New York City police commissioner. Despite the thick mud and primitive conditions, Richard Harding Davis sported a dandified outfit of white tropic suit and matching white helmet. The less stylish but similarly favored correspondent was Edward Marshall of the *New York Journal.* The more meddlesome Stephen Crane, still some years away from writing *The Red Badge of Courage,* was relegated to the back of the long, advancing column. Upon reaching the hilltop, Roosevelt gave his men a rest and reminisced with Marshall about a luncheon the two had attended with Hearst at the Astor Hotel. Roosevelt paused in his reverie and picked up a piece of barbed wire fencing on the side of the trail. Roosevelt told Marshall it had been freshly cut, based on the former rancher's observation that the end was bright and not rusted as it would have been after even one night. Roosevelt's deduction was confirmed by the sharp crack and shrill whistle of a fired bullet. The Rough Riders were under attack. The Spaniards had set up an ambush at Las Guasimas.

Roosevelt hastily stepped over the cut fence and took on a new role, as warrior. Marshall wrote of this rite of passage:

> It was as if that barbed-wire strand formed a dividing line in his life, and that when he stepped across it he left behind him in the bridle path all those unadmirable and conspicuous traits which have so often caused him to be justly criticized in civic life, and found on the other side of it, in that Cuban thicket, the coolness, the calm judgment, the towering herosim, which made him, perhaps, the most admired and best loved of all Americans in Cuba.[30]

His father had chosen not to fight during the Civil War and instead, at least in his son's eyes, bought his way out of the danger of combat. The son now wiped away that stain on his father's résumé. In Cuba, Roosevelt was in his element, describing the Spanish bullets "singing through the trees over our heads, making a noise like the humming of telephone wires . . . They began to get the range and occasionally one of our men would crumple up." Roosevelt ordered a few of his sharpshooters to fire on the enemy positions. The Spaniards jumped out of their cover and bolted, pursued by the Rough Riders. A bullet smashed into a palm tree next to Roosevelt, momentarily blinding his left eye with flecks of bark. Others were not so lucky, as Roosevelt recounted in a letter the following day to Corinne, enumerating casualties from the two-and-one-half-hour skirmish:

> We lost a dozen men killed or mortally wounded, and sixty severely or slightly wounded. Brodie was wounded; poor Capron and Ham Fish were killed. Will you send this note

to Fish's father? One man was killed as he stood beside a tree with me . . . The last charge I led on the left using a rifle I took from a wounded man; and I kept three of the empty cartridges we got from a dead Spaniard at this point, for the children. Every man behaved well; there was no flinching. The fire was very hot at one or two points where the men around me went down like ninepins . . . It was a good fight. I am in good health.[31]

It was an unexpected assessment, given the four days Roosevelt had just endured: soldiers killed and wounded, the regiment sapped by heat and humidity, bitten by insects, sleeping on the hard ground, wearing the same clothes through torrential rains, limited to hardtack, bacon, and bitter coffee, continuously famished and parched after climbing steep mountains and thrashing through the dense tropical jungle vegetation. "I have no blanket or coat; I have not taken off my shoes even; I sleep in the drenching rain, and drink putrid water," Roosevelt wrote to Lodge.[32] Dysentery and stomach cramps were a constant concern because they had no time to boil their water. He continued to Corinne,

> The morning after the fight we buried our dead in a great big trench, reading the solemn burial service over them, and all the regiment joining in singing "Rock of Ages." The vultures were wheeling overhead by hundreds. They plucked out the eyes and tore the faces and the wounds of the dead Spaniards before we got to them, and even one of our own men who lay in the open. The wounded lay in the path, a ghastly group; there were no supplies for them; our doctors did all they could, but had little with which to do it; a couple died in the night.[33]

After a few hours of intense fighting, the Americans had routed the Spaniards in the battle of Las Guasimas and sent the enemy into full retreat. Eight Rough Riders were killed and 34 wounded. The first casualty for the Rough Riders was Sergeant Hamilton Fish Jr., a member of a prominent old Knickerbocker family from the lower Hudson Valley. In all, of the 964 American troops, there were 16 dead and 52 wounded. Nonetheless, Roosevelt said the fighting was "aside from Edith, *the* time of my life."[34]

The number of Spanish casualties was disputed. The enemy said seven were killed, but Roosevelt said he counted eleven dead. Roosevelt himself took credit for one Spanish kill, claiming that upon approaching the crest of Kettle Hill, he shot a fleeing Spaniard dead with his revolver. Roosevelt later disputed the newspaper accounts of Las Guasimas written by Harding Davis and Marshall, who characterized the battle as a Spanish ambush and Roosevelt and his regiment as having blundered into a trap. What was not under debate, though, was the way in which his unit had acquitted itself. They had adjusted to difficult and unfamiliar terrain and their fighting spirit did not break despite the days of privation that preceded the battle. "They accepted the most dangerous work with the utmost eagerness," Roosevelt said years later.[35] Also, Roosevelt's men accomplished their mission without a full complement of weapons and gear. Furthermore, they faced a superior Spanish force that was entrenched and fought with the extraordinary advantage of smokeless powder, firing at the Americans in stealth. "I commanded my regiment, I think I may say, with honor," Roosevelt wrote to Lodge.[36] A member of a New York regiment recounted,

Later, and further along the road, when the Rough Riders and other cavalrymen passed by our brigade, we having been ordered to rest, and our men cheered the popular Colonel Roosevelt . . . he said almost pettishly, "Don't cheer, but fight, now's the time to fight."[37]

There certainly was no inspiration to fight coming from the commanding general for the United States in Cuba, Major General William R. Shafter. Shafter struggled to sift the confusing and contradictory orders from Secretary of War Alger. Shafter was in his fifties and in poor health. Weighing more than three hundred pounds, he could not move his gout-ridden bulk about the battlefield without great difficulty. After arriving in Santiago with only a portion of the troops and supplies he expected, Shafter became ill during the invasion and was unable to command the troops firsthand. John D. Miley, Shafter's aide-de-camp, shuttled between the convalescing Shafter and the front with messages from the commander. Miley's own skills in the shuttle command would be severely challenged.

There were more pressing concerns. The lack of attendants and a shortage of medicine made care deplorable for wounded troops in field hospitals behind the lines. Roosevelt described seeing men lying in the mud, feverish and hungry, because there were no cots or blankets and very little food left. Roosevelt therefore kept as many injured soldiers as possible at the front and had them patched up the best he could. Dodging enemy bullets was apparently a better option than acquiring an additional tropical disease and starving.

The Rough Riders camped for a week on a ridge near Las Guasimas. Roosevelt was happy to receive a second bundle of gear to replace the one lost in the bungled landing, and he gushed in letters about his regiment's camp alongside a picturesque stream in the jungle. His men washed their foul and bloody uniforms in the stream, fried mangoes, and traded army beef for local rum, while Roosevelt lost his patience with the bureaucratic confusion. His mood brightened when he was informed that he had been promoted from lieutenant colonel to colonel and was finally, fully, and officially in charge of the Rough Riders as a result of illness among the commanding officers' ranks. Wood had been placed in charge of the entire brigade.

An assault on Santiago was set for July 1. At 6:30 in the morning, the Americans opened up with a battery of heavy artillery, scattering tropical birds in waves and leaving a thick cloud of cannon smoke hanging over their heads, easily marked by the Spaniards. Enemy mortars exploded over the Rough Riders, wounding four and raising a large bump on Roosevelt's wrist. At one point, before the charge, while Roosevelt surveyed the battlefield on horseback with bullets whizzing around him, Chanler jeered, "Don't move, Teddy! That's a bully place to be photographed."[38]

The newly promoted colonel did not wait for orders. He led his regiment down the hillside and took cover in the jungle foliage at the base of Kettle Hill, beyond which rose San Juan Hill and their ultimate objective, Santiago. The hillside finally grew quiet after two hours of cannon fire. Roosevelt rode Little Texas—a symbol of courage to his men but also a tall, obvious target for the enemy—as he led his men closer to the slope of Kettle Hill in one-hundred-degree heat. Roosevelt had attached a Rough Riders' blue polka-dot scarf to the rear brim of his hat to protect his neck from the punishing sun. The Rough Riders came to San Juan Creek and became jammed up at a pile of dead bodies at a crossing christened Bloody Ford. Roosevelt's words to his recruits when he was forming the regiment rang grimly prophetic: "I told the boys who enlisted with me it would be no picnic—and the place of honor was the post of danger, and that each must expect to die."[39] The whistle of Spanish Mauser bullets started again. Roosevelt's regiment lost several men at the base of San Juan Hill, including Captain Bucky O'Neill, who was killed, and a gravely wounded Lieutenant Ernest Haskell. "The Spanish Mauser bullets made clean wounds; but they also used a copper-jacketed or brass-jacketed bullet which exploded, making very bad wounds indeed," Roosevelt wrote.[40] The death of O'Neill was especially difficult for Roosevelt. O'Neill had swaggered about in the hail of ricocheting bullets, puffing a cigarette and recklessly blowing plumes of smoke, bragging that "the Spanish bullet ain't made that will kill me." A moment later an enemy round struck him in the mouth and came out the back of his head. "Even before he fell, his wild and gallant soul had gone out into the darkness," Roosevelt later wrote.

Roosevelt was stuck without orders. He dispatched a young soldier to find a general to get approval for an advance, but the runner was killed by a shot to the neck as he stood up to salute Roosevelt upon his return. General Wood finally passed the order to advance in support of the regular cavalry in the attack on the entrenchments and blockhouses. Roosevelt described in extensive detail what he later referred to as "the great day of my life" in a letter to Wood:

> We continued to move forward until I ordered a charge, and the men rushed the blockhouse and rifle pits on the hill to the right of our advance. They did the work in fine shape, though suffering severely . . . Meanwhile we were under a heavy rifle fire from the intrenchments along the hills to our front, from which they also shelled us with a piece of field artillery until some of our marksmen silenced it. When the men got their wind we charged again and carried the second line of intrenchments with a rush. Swinging to the left, we then drove the Spaniards over the brow of the chain of hills fronting Santiago . . . The Spaniards made one or two efforts to retake the line, but were promptly driven back.[41]

Meanwhile, even as he urged on his troops with praise and positive messages, he begged for supplies in a testy letter to Lodge:

> Tell the President for Heaven's sake to send us every regiment and above all every battery possible . . . We are within measurable distance of a terrible military disaster; we *must*

have help—thousands of men, batteries and *food* and ammunition . . . Our General is poor; he is too unwieldly to get to
the front.[42]

At the same time, Miley, facing his own frustrations, delivered three urgent appeals during the multipronged assault on
Santiago:

> I think another battery would be of advantage. Cavalry
> pressed on right. Have sent regiment to assist. Ammunition
> absolutely necessary, and must be brought here . . . I will
> hold my present positions and make them as strong as pos-
> sible, but ammunition is being rapidly exhausted . . . My
> losses have been heavy in both officers and men, and the
> troops are much exhausted.[43]

Brigadier General J. F. Kent's troops ground out their bloody
progress up San Juan Hill a short distance to the southwest of
Kettle Hill. At the same time, Roosevelt pushed his Rough Riders through a treacherous expanse of about one-half mile across
waist-high grass with little cover and moved slightly up the
flank of Kettle Hill. Roosevelt described the landscape as "covered with a dense tropical jungle. This was what made it so hard
for us in the fight. It was very hard trying to stand, or advance
slowly, while the men fell dead or wounded, shot down from we
knew not whence; for smokeless powder renders it almost impossible to place a hidden foe."[44] Spanish snipers clad in camouflage
were difficult to spot burrowed in the thick crests of royal palm
trees. Nonetheless, Roosevelt refused to cede to common sense
but stayed tall in the saddle of Little Texas. "Teddy was the only
one up on a mule," recalled Rough Rider William Bickford. "He
claimed it was a horse, but it was a mule. He wasn't up there to
be a hero, either. Up there, the snipers had a better chance of
spotting him. He was up there so the men could see him—so

they'd know which way he was headed. He said 'Forward!' That's what he said. And as we were moving along, he'd call out, 'Up the hill!' and 'Let's go!' things like that."[45]

From up in the saddle, Roosevelt ordered a detail of his sharpshooters to target the snipers—who incensed Roosevelt by ignoring Red Cross bandanas and shooting at surgeons and assistants carrying the wounded in litters. The sharpshooters managed to kill thirteen of them.

Roosevelt finally dismounted his horse and took cover in the tall grass. It was now past noon and Roosevelt's regiment had been exposed to the blistering sun and withering fusillades since early morning. Roosevelt sent several messages to General Wood and Brigadier General Samuel S. Sumner asking permission to advance to the top of the hill. Easy targets pinned down near the base of Kettle Hill, the Rough Riders were at a deadly disadvantage as they awaited orders. Finally, at about one o'clock in the afternoon, Roosevelt received the order he had been hoping and waiting for. "Move forward and support the regulars in the assault on the hills in front," the message said. "The instant I received the order I sprang on my horse and then my 'crowded hour' began," Roosevelt recalled in the *The Rough Riders*.[46]

Roosevelt wrote in his diary for July 1: "Rose at 4. Big battle. Commanded regiment. Held extreme front of firing line."[47] Roosevelt began his charge up Kettle Hill with 490 men, of whom 86 were killed or wounded, 6 were missing in action, and nearly 40 soldiers were incapacitated by heat exhaustion—including many Roosevelt considered the best in his regiment.

Clutching their rifles tightly to their chests, the Rough Riders strode through the tall grass as if through crashing waves during their disastrous beach landing—slipping, scrambling, stumbling, and churning forward in the savage, crippling heat. It was crude, elemental warfare, trying to capture high ground through grinding toil. Richard Harding Davis observed Roosevelt and his thin invading force of about 350 men—hot, tired, and weak from hours of intense fighting. "One's instinct was to call them back," Davis wrote. "You felt that someone had blundered and that these few men were blindly following some madman's mad order." A Spanish prisoner later remarked on the gritty determination of the Americans: "They kept pushing forward as if they were going to take us with their hands."[48] Stephen Crane's earlier critical opinion had disappeared; he also expressed amazement at their gutsy charge. "Yes, they were going up the hill," Crane wrote. "It was the best moment of anybody's life."[49]

Others were less sanguine about the situation, as one member of New York's Seventy-first Regiment described the battle scene:

> To go into the fight as part of the charging column, meant that one out of every four was to drop, wounded or killed . . . For the next fifteen minutes the interchange of shrapnel between the batteries was quite lively . . . horses and men tangled up on the hillside and everybody dodging and yelling . . . awaiting one's turn to be hit with the flying shell.[50]

Roosevelt's Rough Riders were blocked on their ascent of Kettle Hill by another regiment whose captain had not received orders to attack. Roosevelt explained that they could not overtake the Spaniards entrenched atop the hillside by merely firing at them. A full-scale rushing attack was the only way to seize the crucial high ground. The captain did not move. Rough Riders continued to be harrassed by snipers and other enemy fire. Roosevelt would wait no longer on protocol. "Then I am the ranking officer here and I give the order to charge," Roosevelt told the captain. The captain still hesitated, unsure of Roosevelt's authority or battlefield experience. "Then let my men through, sir," Roosevelt said.[51] Astride Little Texas, he rode through the lines, followed by an energized regiment eager to complete its mission. "By this time we were all in the spirit of the thing and greatly excited by the charge, the men cheering and running forward between shots," Roosevelt recalled.[52]

Roosevelt's Kettle Hill account grew in drama and intensity over the years. His descriptions of battles in *The Rough Riders* are more heroic and gallant than the measured, unemotional prose of his letters from Cuba. It's not so much that the two versions differ substantially in their particulars, but the book is clearly a more romanticized and embellished version. At least one of Roosevelt's Rough Riders hadn't succumbed to such nostalgia six decades after the battle of San Juan Hill. "We were just a mob that went up a hill," Jesse D. Langdon recalled. "If the Spaniards had been able to shoot, we'd never have made it to the top . . . Teddy's glasses were shot off and in the confusion of the attack many American casualties resulted from American bullets. In my belief, even Teddy's glasses were shot off from behind, but Teddy was always too much of a politician to admit it."[53]

From the top of Kettle Hill, named for the huge iron kettle used in sugar making, the conquering regiment had a good view of Kent's siege of San Juan Hill, where fierce fighting still raged about one-half mile away. Kent's troops were outnumbered. They desperately needed reinforcements. Roosevelt didn't waste time waiting for orders. After laying down a volley of artillery, he rushed toward San Juan Hill. He eventually looked back, only to find that there were just five men following him to the heights overlooking the city of Santiago. The battlefield mix-up appealed to Roosevelt's self-deprecating brand of humor.

> Meanwhile, I ran back, jumped over the wire fence, and went over the crest of the hill, filled with anger against the troopers, and especially those of my own regiment, for not having accompanied me. They, of course, were quite innocent of wrong-doing; and even while I taunted them bitterly for not having followed me, it was all I could do not to smile at the look of injury and surprise that came over their

faces, while they cried out: "We didn't hear you, we didn't see you."[54]

Roosevelt was not in a forgiving or humorous mood when he saw a few infantrymen, who were African Americans, grow uneasy at the heavy enemy fire and their exposed position on the top of a grassy hilltop during their rush to join the battle in progress on San Juan Hill. These black soldiers, who served in segregated regiments, were fighting without any of their officers in sight, so they tried to move back from the front line of combat toward the rear—either to assist the wounded or to reconnect with their own regiments. Roosevelt saw that the departures were depleting his already thin line and eroding the morale of the rest of his men. Roosevelt drew his revolver and strode to the rear. He said he would not hesitate to shoot the first man who went to the rear, regardless of his excuse. "Now, I shall be very sorry to hurt you and you don't know whether or not I will keep my word," he said, "but my men can tell you that I always do." Roosevelt's Rough Riders somberly nodded their assent.[55] Roosevelt described the incident in *The Rough Riders:*

> This was the end of the trouble, for the "smoked Yankees"—as the Spaniards called the colored soldiers—flashed their white teeth at one another, as they broke into broad grins, and I had no more trouble with them, they seeming to accept me as one of their own officers.[56]

In *The Rough Riders,* Roosevelt said his men from the Southwest, in particular, managed to overcome strong racial prejudice and, along with the rest of his regiment, to accept the black soldiers as comrades. This acceptance could be seen in the Rough Riders' willingness to "drink out of the same canteen" as the black soldiers, as they put it. Still, Roosevelt was not entirely willing to accept the notion of complete racial equality.

No troops could have behaved better than the colored soldiers had behaved so far; but they are, of course, peculiarly
dependent upon their white officers. Occasionally they produce non-commissioned officers who can take the initiative
and accept responsibility precisely like the best class of
whites; but this cannot be expected normally, nor is it fair
to expect it.[57]

Eventually Roosevelt regrouped his troops, fragments of six
cavalry regiments, black and white. As the highest-ranking officer in the vicinity, Roosevelt led a unified and effective attack
against what was left of the Spanish resistance atop San Juan Hill.

Long before we got near them the Spaniards ran, save a few
here and there, who either surrendered or were shot down.
When we reached the trenches we found them filled with
dead bodies in the light blue and white uniform of the
Spanish regular army. There were very few wounded. Most
of the fallen had little holes in their heads from which their
brains were oozing; for they were covered from the neck
down by the trenches.[58]

Whether riding tall in the saddle of Little Texas, or dodging
enemy fire as he led a charge, Colonel Roosevelt seemed invincible. The morning following their capture of San Juan Hill, Roosevelt had just finished setting up headquarters near a tree, when
an artillery shell exploded so close it blackened Roosevelt's skin
with burnt powder and fatally wounded several soldiers nearby.
Roosevelt, unscathed, stood up and wiped the dirt of the artillery
explosion off his uniform. Rough Rider Bob Ferguson, who had
been a family friend since meeting Bamie in England, witnessed
the near-hit on Roosevelt and wrote to Edith, "I really believe
firmly now they can't kill him."[59]
From their vantage point atop San Juan Hill, Roosevelt and

the Rough Riders could see for the first time their ultimate military objective: the city of Santiago. Enemy casualties were strewn about the battlefield; Roosevelt invited visitors to "look at those damned Spanish dead."[60] Roosevelt's men secured their position, exhaustedly dug trenches and—wrapping themselves in blankets they salvaged off dead Spaniards—collapsed into a deep sleep. Stephen Crane extolled Roosevelt's virtues as a leader in Pulitzer's *New York World.* "This fellow worked for his troops like a cider press. He tried to feed them. He helped build latrines. He cursed the quartermasters and the—'dogs'—on the transports to get quinine and grub for them. Let him be a politician if he likes. He was a gentleman down there."[61]

Other observers of the political scene were calling Roosevelt more than a gentleman; the first stirrings were beginning among those who believed Roosevelt's courage and leadership in Cuba would make him a perfect candidate for governor of New York. Edith clipped a letter to the editor from the *New York Sun* in mid-July and mailed it to Cuba. It was written and signed by three prominent New York Democrats who recommended that New Yorkers look past party affiliation and nominate Roosevelt, a Republican, as a candidate for the upcoming gubernatorial election.

Back home at Sagamore Hill, Edith took comfort in her husband's correspondence. "Last night I slept better because I held your dear letters to my heart instead of just having them under my pillow. I felt I was touching you when I pressed against me what your hand had touched," she wrote to him.[62] Edith tried to keep life as normal as possible for her children, despite her worries and fears. The children sensed her anxiety and offered comfort, particularly when she read one of her husband's letters. "I began to cry, and Alice came to pat my hand and console me, while the boys, two very interested little beneficiaries, put their heads in my lap and sobbed bitterly."[63]

Roosevelt, meanwhile, was carefully composing a long letter

to his commanding officer, Leonard Wood, describing in great detail the noble and gallant fighting by the soldiers in his regiment—both living and dead. Of all the regiments in Cuba, the Rough Riders arguably suffered the highest rate of men killed, wounded, or incapacitated by disease. Roosevelt followed up a few days later with a letter lobbying Lodge on behalf of his regiment, whom he believed fought the toughest battle of the war and lost a heavier percentage than any other.

> If it is judged that other men in the field have shown greater efficiency, why we have nothing to say; but we ought to receive the promotions rather than men who have not been in the fight. Gen. Wheeler says he intends to recommend me for the medal of honor; naturally I should like to have it. And, when we take Santiago, do try to see that we are sent to the front again, and not kept at garrison. I think we have shown we can fight.[64]

Newspaper correspondents, who had succumbed to Roosevelt's generous access and considerable charm, had already drowned the leader of the Rough Riders in flattering ink and dubbed him "the hero of San Juan Hill." It was more than a slogan, at least to his men. On more than one occasion, a wounded Rough Rider, allowed to return to the United States on furlough, made the effort to stop at Sagamore Hill to tell their commander's wife how much they respected and adored Theodore and how he led a charmed life and cared enough for his men that he would give them his all, including trudging through the mud for eight miles and over a mountain carrying a bag of beans on his back to feed them.[65]

The Rough Riders were dug into entrenchments on San Juan Hill for two weeks following their capture of the Spanish stronghold. They grumbled but were not allowed to march on Santiago, so tantalizingly close. Hunkered down, they were harassed by sporadic shelling and sniper fire despite several truces. By July 3, the American navy—a stronger, better prepared version thanks to Assistant Secretary Roosevelt—had destroyed the Spanish fleet in Santiago Harbor. As negotiations dragged on, the Rough Riders stayed on alert in the trenches. They finally celebrated a full Spanish surrender on July 17, without so much as a single advance in weeks. When word reached them that the Spanish formally surrendered the city of Santiago, the Rough Riders stood atop their trenches in a victorious pose. "When the American flag was hoisted the trumpets blared and the men cheered, and we knew that the fighting part of our work was over," Roosevelt wrote in *The Rough Riders.*

The endgame of Roosevelt's crowded hour was anticlimactic. The Americans agreed to a phantom shelling of Santiago, safely aiming high, so that the Spaniards could surrender their firearms with *Pundonor,* the Spanish term for military honor.

The Cuban campaign may have been finished for the Rough Riders, but in other ways the deprivation and hardships were just beginning for the native islanders. Thousands of poor and destitute Spanish noncombatants, mainly women and children, were expelled from Santiago. The ragged stream of starving refugees flowed through the lines of American soldiers, begging for food. "My men gave them a good deal out of their own scanty stores, until I had positively to forbid it and to insist that the refugees should go to headquarters; as, however hard and merciless it seemed, I was in duty bound to keep my own regiment at the highest pitch of fighting efficiency," Roosevelt wrote in *The Rough Riders.* The colonel also forbade his men to relieve the weakened refugees by carrying their bundles because of the fear of infectious diseases. Despite this order, by the end of July, nearly 80 percent of the Fifth Army Corps had fallen ill and the fearsome yellow fever was racing through the military ranks.

Three days after the Spanish surrender, Leonard Wood was appointed military governor of Santiago and Roosevelt assumed his former position as commander of the Second Cavalry Brigade. It was a big title with a small responsibility. "There was literally not one thing of any kind whatsoever for the army to do, and no purpose to serve by keeping it at Santiago," Roosevelt wrote in *The Rough Riders.* Acting as ringleader, Roosevelt got the other senior officers to sign a forceful letter telling General Shafter that their work was finished and they should be allowed to leave Cuba. There was some internal fallout over this brazen ultimatum to the army commanders when it was leaked to the press. Within three days, General Shafter finally gave the order to bring the soldiers home.

On cue, Spain ended its colonial rule and started its pullout from Cuba. The United States stepped right in, installing Wood to oversee an occupying force. The victory over Spain set off a domino effect between the rising new imperial power and the eclipsed one. Within the next four weeks, seven thousand Spanish soldiers on Puerto Rico gave up and the island surrendered to the American army. The capital of the Philippines, Manila, also fell to American troops as the Spanish surrendered after a mock show of force. The sovereignty of the island republic of Hawaii was transferred to the United States as well. "It's a good time to be alive," Roosevelt told reporters. "A bully time."

Roosevelt had reached the point of exasperation with the incompetence he encountered in the military leadership. He wrote a reckless letter of condemnation to Lodge that, if it had reached the press, would have been punishable for insubordination:

> It is criminal to keep Shafter in command. He is utterly inefficient; and now he is panic struck . . . The mismanagement has been beyond belief. We have a prize fool . . . We are half starved; and our men are sickening daily. The lack of transportation, food and artillery has brought us to the very verge of disaster; but above all the lack of any leadership, of any system or any executive capacity.[66]

Meanwhile, General Calixto Garcia, commander of the allied Cuban Army, wrote angry letters to General Shafter complaining that his troops were being left out of the loop and essentially forgotten:

> The number of bodies washed ashore has been considerable. I desire to inform you that the forces camped here are entirely out of rations and we have no base . . . All the families that reside in Santiago have left this morning, seeking refuge amongst us. The number is very large, and they have not been able to bring provisions of any kind, so they will have to face starvation unless we take measures to prevent it.[67]

Within a few weeks after the surrender of Santiago, the alliance between the Cuban and American armies had broken down. The motivations of the United States and the ultimate military purpose of what Secretary of State John Hay famously called "a splendid little war" were being challenged among Cubans. General Garcia wrote forcefully to Shafter, withdrawing his troops and quitting as commander of the Cuban Army:

> I have not been honored, Sir, with a single word from yourself informing me about the negotiations for peace or the terms of the capitulation by the Spaniards . . . A rumor, too absurd to be believed, General, ascribes the reason of your measure and of the orders forbidding my army to enter Santiago, to fear of massacres and revenges against Spaniards. Allow me, Sir, to protest against even the shadow of such an idea. We are not savages ignoring the rules of civilized warfare. We are a poor ragged army, as ragged and poor as the army of your forefathers in their noble war for Independence . . . We respect too deeply our cause to disgrace it with barbarism and cowardice.[68]

New York State paid a high price for its involvement in the Spanish-American War. The Empire State sent nearly 30,000 men, Roosevelt included, to the war in Cuba. In all, a total of 442 of them were killed—429 enlisted men and 13 officers.

By July 18, the day after the negotiated surrender at Santiago, Roosevelt toured Morro Castle with General Fitzhugh Lee. Roosevelt focused on the sunken wreckage of the collier *Merrimac* a few hundred yards offshore, downed by Spanish cannon fire in May, and challenged Lieutenant Jack Greenway to a swimming race out to inspect the shipwreck. The lower-ranking officer couldn't decline his colonel, who quickly shed his clothes and dived into the sea. Greenway halfheartedly followed. The two swimmers weren't out far when General Lee began to yell frantically from the wall of the fort. He had seen sharks following Roosevelt and Greenway, who was petrified. As he continued making strong, overhand strokes, the colonel reassured his subordinate that such sharks were harmless. "I've been studying them all my life and I've never heard of one bothering a swimmer," Roosevelt told Greenway in between breaths. "It's all poppy cock."[69] A pack of sharks, some twelve feet long, swam alongside. Roosevelt and Greenway inspected the hull of the *Merrimac,* then turned back. General Lee paced nervously the entire time, gesticulating wildly, but both made it back safely. It was another chapter in Roosevelt's growing legend.

To his fourteen-year-old daughter, Alice, he reflected,

I have had a very hard and dangerous month. I have enjoyed it, too, in a way; but war is a grim and fearful thing . . . Worse still is the awful agony of the field hospital where the wounded lie day and night in the mud, drenched with rain and scorched with the terrible sun; while the sky overhead is darkened by the whirling vultures and the stream of starving fugitives, the poor emaciated women and the little tots of children, some like Archie and Quentin. One poor little mite still carried a canary in a little cage. My men are not well fed, and they are fierce and terrible in battle; but they [gave] half they had to the poor women and children. I supposed a good many of them thought, as I did, of their own wives or sisters and little ones. War is often, as this one is, necessary and righteous; but it is terrible.[70]

The Rough Riders steamed out of Santiago Harbor on August 8, fueled by coal and the burgeoning celebrity of their colonel. Newpapermen dubbed Roosevelt "the most popular man in America." They may not have been far off. Already, days before his arrival, political bosses were salivating at his potential as a returning war hero turned candidate for governor of New York. "He is a rare combination of originality, unconventionality, candor, self-confidence, alertness, fearlessness, aggressiveness, positiveness, and nervous energy, and it is no doubt this combination which has made him the popular hero he is today," observed a Wyoming newspaper publisher.[71] Privately, Boss Platt hoped that a viable Republican candidate for governor other than Roosevelt would emerge—realizing the Rough Rider would be difficult to control—but Platt said nothing in public that could be interpreted as a negative view of the popular colonel.

Three weeks earlier, William Randolph Hearst returned to New York after a month on assignment covering the war in Cuba. The brilliant self-promoter liked to take credit for drawing the United States into the conflict, and with his dispatches from Cuba had sensationalized the evil of the Spaniards while attempting to knock Roosevelt down a peg. Hearst had taken aim at Roosevelt for years, jealous at first of his success in literature and politics and now of the colonel's battlefield glory—all arenas in which Hearst was merely a vain aspirant. Yet now Hearst returned to New York City, overlooked, without the parade or fanfare or adoring public that greeted Roosevelt. The publisher had failed to benefit personally, professionally, or politically from his involvement in Cuba, and his papers were losing more money than before he left. "I guess I'm a failure," Hearst wrote to his mother after Cuba. "I made the mistake of my life in not raising the cowboy regiment I had in mind before Roosevelt raised his. I really believe I brought on the war but I failed to score in the war. I had my chance and failed to grab it, and I suppose I must sit on the fence now and watch the procession go by."[72]

And what a procession it was for the man Hearst loathed. Colonel Roosevelt felt "strong as a bull moose" when he arrived at Camp Wikoff on Montauk Point 133 days after shipping out to Cuba. An outbreak of yellow fever among some of his troops forced a quarantine of all the officers and enlisted men. Roosevelt managed to enjoy several hours of free time each afternoon at his temporary detention on Long Island. He would lead a group of officers for a "gallop down to the beach and bathe in the surf, or else go for long rides over the beautiful rolling plains, thickly studded with pools which were white with water-lilies." Edith managed to get close by volunteering to tend to injured soldiers in the camp's hospital. Roosevelt paid for and had delivered to his wife, the volunteer nurse, a case each of brandy, whiskey, and champagne, as well as baskets of eggs, sacks of sugar, and cans of milk. Edith mixed therapeutic eggnogs for the wounded warriors and passed them out with Colonel Roosevelt's compliments.

Edith even managed to elude the security precautions of the quarantine and visit her husband for an hour or so. She convinced a junior officer to smuggle Roosevelt out of the camp proper for the visit. "Theodore looks well but very thin," she wrote.[73]

While Roosevelt rested and waited out the quarantine, his mentor, Senator Lodge, urged McKinley not to budge in negotiations but to claim as victor over Spain all the spoils of war—including Cuba, Puerto Rico, Guam, and the Philippines (for a $20 million indemnity payment). The U.S. triumph in the Spanish-American War underscored the long-held position of Mahan and Roosevelt on the need for naval superiority and spurred urgent discussions regarding a canal to be built across Panama as a deterrent against the restless imperialist European powers Germany and France.

As mustering-out approached at Camp Wikoff and Roosevelt and his regiment received medical approval for discharge, the Rough Riders took up a collection. They gathered on September 13 and presented their commander, Colonel Roosevelt, with a surprise: a bronze broncobuster sculpture by Frederic Remington. Private Murphy called the gift "a slight token of the admiration, love, and esteem in which you are held by the officers and men of your regiment . . . Your heart of hearts was ever with your men."[74]

Tears welled up in Roosevelt's eyes, and he spoke in a choked voice as he addressed the men of his regiment for the last time:

> Nothing could possibly happen that would touch and please me as this has touched and pleased me . . . I have never tried to coddle you, and have never hesitated to call upon you to spend your best blood like water . . . I have also a profound respect for you because you have fighting qualities, and because you had the qualities which enabled us to get you into the fight. Outside of my own immediate family, as I said before, I shall never know as strong ties as I do toward you.[75]

Someone called out, "Three cheers for Colonel Roosevelt!" The men shouted them out in cowboy fashion, with an extra "Tiger!" at the end of each cheer. Captain Curry of H Troop shouted out a call for "Three cheers for the next governor of New York!"[76] They offered an even more resounding trio of cheers. Roosevelt asked each soldier to file past him so that he could offer each a personal thank-you and a firm handshake. Roosevelt, who knew each soldier by his first name, added a private recollection of the wartime service of each man who passed. Afterward, Roosevelt said he considered it a triumph that he got a smile out of Polluck, the Pawnee Indian, something they'd never seen Polluck produce before. As they mustered out, each Rough Rider received his last pay, about $120 each, with an additional $40 for noncommissioned officers.

Roosevelt had one of the shortest trips home of any member in his regiment, from Long Island's Montauk Point to Sagamore Hill at Oyster Bay. As he reached town, the train station was crowded with fifteen hundred people, a cannon blasted a welcome, revolvers and muskets fired, and a band struck up a tune. "The crowd seemed mad with enthusiasm," the *New York Herald* reported. "The station platform was a solid mass of howling, pushing humanity."[77] He made his way through the throng, left the station, and as he rode up the drive at Sagamore, Roosevelt saw all his children clustered around a flagpole. They'd made a pole out of a stick and attached a flag they made themselves and inscribed "In Honor of Colonel Roosevelt's Return." They positioned it where their father could see it as he approached the piazza of his beloved home. He called it the most touching tribute he was to receive.

The Rough Riders' three cheers for the next governor of New York rang in his ears. The gubernatorial election was just two months away.

Chapter 9

★ ★ ★ ★ ★

GOVERNOR

In spite of everything, I am thoroughly enjoying my experience as Governor.

Colonel Roosevelt's reentry into politics began with missteps. The triumphant war hero, one of the most famous men in America, wasn't above playing hard to get, and he had ample reason to tweak Boss Platt and a Republican machine that had long viewed Roosevelt as trouble. In the days after mustering out, Roosevelt met on more than one occasion with a reform group led by John Jay Chapman, who offered to make Roosevelt the Independent Party's gubernatorial nominee. The party already had released a statement in New York City on September 9, 1898: "While Roosevelt is a party man, he is one in whom the masses of the people of both parties feel a confidence amounting to devotion, and who in his person represents independence and reform."[1] It was not quite a declaration of independence from Platt by the candidate, since the colonel was still at Camp Wikoff. Meanwhile, Edith urged her husband to consider a real reason to play hard to get. *Scribner's* magazine and other publications had offered Roosevelt a substantial sum to write a memoir about fighting in Cuba. The Roosevelts continued to owe monthly rent on their house in Washington and heavy mortgage payments on Sagamore Hill.

Theodore not only earned less as a Rough Rider than he would have in his navy post, but he had laid out hundreds of dollars on his own to pay for food and supplies for his troops. Yet Edith had little chance against her husband's ambition.

Platt, meanwhile, faced the problem of a dark cloud of scandal that hung over Republican Governor Frank S. Black. A lawyer from Troy and a Platt protégé, deeply loyal to the boss, Black became a convenient conduit for the machine's spoils as governor. He had been a popular leader, particularly across rural upstate New York, until a special state investigation in August discovered that more than a million dollars in "improper expenditures" were made on the project to widen and deepen the Erie Canal. The massive government enterprise was a long-running boondoggle, $9 million over budget and several years behind schedule, with less than two thirds of the canal improvements completed when the improprieties tainted Black and his administration. Platt needed a potential replacement as a contingency plan if Black couldn't clear his name, and Roosevelt was an obvious choice.

Platt sent trusted lieutenant Lemuel E. Quigg to the Rough Riders' encampment at Montauk Point. They met in Roosevelt's tent along with the colonel's political adviser, his brother-in-law Douglas Robinson. It was a smart choice of messenger. Platt himself had criticized the Spanish-American War and Roosevelt's role in agitating for the United States' entry into it. Quigg, on the other hand, had been friendly with Roosevelt from his days as editor of a Montana newspaper and as a reporter with the *New York Tribune.* A former congressman, Quigg worked amicably with Civil Service Commissioner Roosevelt in Washington, D.C., and had lobbied vigorously for Roosevelt's appointment as New York City's police commissioner.

Quigg laid out his mission in plain language. "He simply wanted a frank definition of my attitude towards existing party conditions," Roosevelt recalled.[2] The colonel's reply was frank but equivocal.

I said that I should not make war on Mr. Platt or anybody else if war could be avoided; that what I wanted was to be Governor and not a faction leader; that I certainly would confer with the organization men, as with everybody else who seemed to have knowledge of and interest in public affairs . . . I should have to act finally as my own judgment and conscience dictated.[3]

When Roosevelt failed to close the door on the courting of Chapman and the Independents, Boss Platt demanded exclusivity by saying that he would not run Roosevelt with dual endorsements. It was Republican only, all or nothing. Platt's ultimatum was in large part a bluff. Frank Black was damaged goods; Platt planned to dump the incumbent governor at the earliest opportunity. Yet he would not be able to control Roosevelt, already being extolled by the press as the antidote for all that ailed the party. "An honest and fearless Governor—a combination of conscience and backbone—is a mighty good thing to have at Albany!" gushed the New York World.[4]

The Platt-Roosevelt negotiations caused the Independents to feel that they had been badly used. They began to undercut Roosevelt's candidacy, and he felt himself in a bind not unlike that of the 1884 Republican National Convention. "The first installment of trouble is already at hand . . . but I am being as circumspect as possible and am trying to commit as few mistakes as possible," Roosevelt wrote to Lodge on September 19.[5] Indeed, he refused the Independents' endorsement in order to get Platt's backing.

"By accepting Platt he becomes the standard bearer of corruption and demoralization," the New York Evening Post declared, echoing criticism by the Independents.[6] Roosevelt hit back against the Independents' barbs and said he planned to accept the Republican nomination because that was his best chance at emerging victorious. He derisively labeled the Independents "prize idiots" and "Goo-Goos." The latter term had been used as a put-down since the early 1890s, after the City Club of New York established local action groups called Good Government Clubs. The writer and fierce Independent Party leader John Jay Chapman had been married to Willie and Wintie Chanler's sister, Elizabeth, and had been friendly with Roosevelt. Both were politically active Harvard alumni. Chapman became so angry and embittered that he did not speak to Roosevelt for the next twenty years and mocked his former friend as "muddle-headed and at the same time a pigheaded young man."[7] Roosevelt countered by dismissing Chapman's notions and place in politics as residing "on the lunatic fringe"—a celebrated phrase that became a Roosevelt hallmark.

Edith managed to get out from under the lease on the Washington house. Theodore was reimbursed seven hundred dollars by the Red Cross for what he spent on supplies for his men in Cuba. He also took the *Scribner's* assignment; the series of articles was eventually published in book form as *The Rough Riders*.

Unlike his first foray into politics, this time there was across-the-board support among family and relatives. His sister Corinne became actively involved in the campaign and recalled "all kinds of amusing, although sometimes unpleasant, contretemps that occurred."[8] Corinne described a miserable day of campaigning, in which Theodore—going along with his advisers who recommended a last-minute change of schedule—left Oyster Bay "at an abnormally early hour" to speak at a country fair near Troy. But the newspapers in Albany and Troy had already announced that Roosevelt would not be there because of a scheduling conflict, and "the attendance at the fair at the time he was supposed to speak was almost nil." He rushed back to New York that evening to attend "a large colored meeting," where she joined him.

The colored people were especially enthusiastic about my brother's candidacy, because the Tenth Regiment of regulars, a colored regiment, had stormed San Juan Hill side by side with the Rough Riders . . . My brother and I waited in the little room near the platform, anxiously peering out every now and then, hoping that the hall would soon be filled to overflowing, but no one came.[9]

Despite what she called her brother's "distinct distress of mind," he could laugh with his sister as they left the empty meeting hall after having spoken earlier at a nearly deserted country fair 170 miles away. Roosevelt jokingly quoted from a novel of manners by the Irish writer Maria Edgeworth, a childhood favorite of theirs. "Little Rosamund's day of misfortunes," Roosevelt said in self-deprecating humor. "From that day on," Corinne wrote, "through the strenuous campaign, my brother was known by the family entirely as 'Little Rosamund.'"[10]

He at least had the theatrics down pat. At all campaign stops, Roosevelt wore a soft black slouch hat modeled after the one he had worn in Cuba. Colonel Roosevelt was often escorted onto the platform by seven Rough Riders in full dress uniform, accompanied by a rousing brass flourish by Emilio Cassi, Rough Rider bugler, whose piercing notes caused the crowds to cheer raucously. It was a far more blatant trading on his service than any modern candidate would ever attempt.

Roosevelt had no shortage of jealous rivals. Lou F. Payn, a backer of Black and a corrupt party hack who was hoping to secure his own standing as the state's superintendent of insurance and enjoy a continuing flow of graft from insurance companies, dropped a bombshell. Three days before the opening of the Republican State Convention in Saratoga Springs, a copy of Roosevelt's affidavit of residence was leaked to the press. The insinuation that the self-righteous war hero had purposely tried to dodge paying some of his state taxes on Sagamore Hill made a sensational splash, with headlines trumpeting the news that Roosevelt was technically ineligible to run for governor. New York law required state residency of at least five continuous years preceding a candidacy. Just six months earlier, Roosevelt had executed the affidavit, declaring that since 1897, when he was assistant secretary of the navy, his legal residence had been Washington, D.C., where taxes were lower than in New York. Roosevelt's only defense was a weak one. He had left Robinson in charge of his business affairs when he went to fight in Cuba. Publicly, Roosevelt dismissed the charge and pretended to be unconcerned about the political fallout. Still, he was angry and depressed enough by the news to consider pulling out of the race. He paid $995.28 in Oyster Bay back taxes (changing his legal residence back to New York) and set up a meeting with Platt at his Fifth Avenue headquarters to announce his decision to quit the campaign.

Platt recalled that Roosevelt met privately with him and "with a trepidation I had never before and have never since seen him display" told the Easy Boss he felt he had to withdraw from the race.[11] Platt urged Roosevelt to remain in the campaign. Platt said he tried "brutal frankness," goading Roosevelt: "Is the hero of San Juan a coward?" Roosevelt responded, "No, I am not a coward," with his "customary vehemence."[12]

Roosevelt lay low, staying away from the Republican convention in Saratoga Springs that fall, as was customary for candidates in those days, while worrying whether the damning affidavit would undermine his chance at the governor's seat and cripple his political career permanently. Prominent attorneys Elihu Root and Joseph H. Choate were enlisted to investigate the tax matter on behalf of the Republican Party in an attempt to find a loophole that would exonerate Roosevelt. They discovered that Roosevelt had also executed an earlier tax dodge to escape paying taxes in Oyster Bay by declaring himself a Manhattanite, which did not help.

At the Saratoga convention, Chauncey Depew, the president of the New York Central Railroad and a powerful figure in

Republican politics, placed Roosevelt's name in nomination for governor with a compelling speech that managed once again to trade on Roosevelt's war hero status without seeming to be so transparently opportunistic:

> The times require constructive statesmen. As in 1776 and 1865, we need architects and builders . . . If he were only the hero of a brilliant charge on the battlefield, and there was nothing else which fitted him for this high place, I would not put him in nomination. But Colonel Roosevelt has shown conspicuous ability in the public service for ten years . . . Give him the chance and he leads to victory . . . The candidate of candidates is the hero of Santiago, the idol of the Rough Riders—Colonel Theodore Roosevelt.[13]

Depew's speech buttressed Root's maneuvering, which parsed multiple meanings of the term "resident" and reams of other supporting details meant as legal obfuscation, including Roosevelt's correspondence and the misinformed legal advice he received from relatives. Root had created enough reasonable doubt to clear the candidate; with Platt's support, the Rough Rider was nominated by an overwhelming margin, 753 votes to 218 for incumbent Black. Congratulatory telegrams from Saratoga poured in to Roosevelt at Oyster Bay. "May your march to the Capitol be as triumphant as your victorious charge up San Juan Hill," was the message from his future running mate, Timothy L. Woodruff. Even as he reveled in the victory, he would not forget the underhanded tactic by Payn that had almost cost him the nomination. He would seek revenge when the moment was right.

The press celebrated. "Honest, intelligent, capable, patriotic and fearless," proclaimed the *New York Sun*. "There is neither humbug nor vainglory, nor again the guile of self-seeking, in his composition."[14] The public also embraced him. "You are going to make a good Governor of the state," one man was quoted as telling Roosevelt at a campaign stop in Utica. "You are a good man and a good American." Roosevelt replied, "I'll try."[15]

It was Roosevelt's first statewide election, and the stakes were high. Democratic Boss Richard Croker vowed to stop Roosevelt at any cost. He had already sent one of his ward heelers to Depew's New York Central office to deliver the threat that if Depew made the nominating speech for Roosevelt, Croker and Tammany would retaliate against the railroad. "I know Mr. Croker's power and the injury he can do the road," Depew told Croker's messenger. "You can say to him that I am amazed at such a message . . . a blow below the belt."[16] Croker only backed off after Depew posed a counterthreat: to resign as president of the New York Central and to explain publicly why he stepped down.

Capitulation was rare for Richard Croker, a street brawler who brought muscle to the leadership of Tammany in the post-Tweed era. Croker emigrated from Ireland in 1846 at age three, had little formal education, and worked in the Harlem Railroad's machine shop and as a steamboat engineer. They were tough trades, and Croker didn't mind mixing it up with ruffians twice his age. He earned a reputation as a good boxer and put his pugilistic skills to good use as leader of the Fourth Avenue Tunnel Gang. Gang membership was a pipeline into Tammany; Croker first gained attention of the sachems by voting seventeen times in an 1864 election. It was the sort of bravado that caught the attention of Jimmy "the Famous" O'Brien, who liked Croker's toughness. City Comptroller "Slippery" Dick Connelly got Croker a job as a court attendant, and O'Brien, when he was elected county sheriff, left his seat on the Board of Aldermen warm for Croker. An alderman by age twenty-five, Croker rose swiftly in the organization's ranks. Turning against O'Brien when the political winds changed, Croker became a protégé of Boss John Kelly, who helped him win election as coroner of New York and, later, appointment as fire commissioner (both posts laden with ample graft). Croker eventually stepped into the role of

Tammany boss after Kelly died in 1886. He became known as "Master of Manhattan," so prodigious were his powers.

Taking aim at Tammany, Roosevelt charged across New York as if it were Kettle Hill. "He fairly pranced about the State," Platt said.[17] Roosevelt's Democratic opponent was August Van Wyck, whose political obscurity was offset by a reputation as an honorable politician with integrity—despite his nomination's being engineered by Croker and despite the fact that his brother, Robert, was the Tammany-backed mayor of New York City.

Hearst had explored a possible campaign for governor as a Democrat; he was thirty-five years old, with terrific name recognition, and he had access to funds to invest in the race. Yet after living in New York for just three years, Hearst had not made inroads on the Tammany organization, and Democratic leaders did not ask him to run. This second disappointment, so soon after the Cuba failure, stiffened Hearst's resolve to attack Roosevelt with the best weapon at hand—his newspapers. Hearst ordered up a three-pronged assault across news columns, editorials, and political cartoons, which mocked Roosevelt as a power-hungry, toothy, bespectacled, and opportunistic buffoon who would get into bed with Republican bosses if it meant winning the gubernatorial nomination. "There is no humiliation to which Mr. Roosevelt will not submit that he may get the nomination for Governor," Hearst's *Journal* editorialized on September 22. "The Theodore Roosevelt that was, was a humbug. The Theodore Roosevelt that is, is a prideless office-seeker."[18]

Roosevelt barnstormed the state by railroad car, bringing along his Rough Riders entourage and flag color guard. Relentlessly attacking Croker, he settled on a theme he knew resonated with the public: protecting the integrity of the judiciary from Croker's manipulation. The issue arose when a State Supreme Court judge and Tammany appointee, Joseph F. Daly, did not hire a Tammany-picked man for his court clerk. Croker, outraged, got even when Daly's judgeship came up for renomination in 1898. Croker did not couch his action in euphemisms when the media queried the Boss about his decision regarding Judge Daly. "Justice Daly was elected by Tammany Hall after he was discovered by Tammany Hall, and Tammany Hall had a right to expect proper consideration at his hands."[19] The issue exploded during a large gathering at Carnegie Hall in which Bourke Cockran, a former Croker aide, railed against bossism run amok. "Croker was a powerful and truculent man, the autocrat of his organization, and of a domineering nature," Roosevelt said later. "For his own reasons he insisted upon Tammany's turning down an excellent Democratic judge who was up for reelection. This gave me my chance."[20]

Jacob Riis recalled helping Roosevelt on the stump. At a stop in Dunkirk, along Lake Erie, Roosevelt stoked the passions of the crowd by calling Croker "a wild man" and challenging him to a fight. He must have thought he was back in the Badlands threatening to duel with the Marquis de Mores. "Let him take thirty of his best men, I don't care how well they're heeled, and I will take my gang and we'll see who's boss. I'll shoot him so full of holes he won't know himself from a honeycomb," Roosevelt told the crowd in the town square in Dunkirk. The throng cheered madly. There was such "wild enthusiasm," Riis recalled, "no one could hear a word of what was said for the cheering."[21] Croker did not square off with his fists, but he continued a war of words with Roosevelt.

Campaigns for high office in that era were often accompanied by songs and poems. "We Want Yer, Ma Teddy!" imitated a cowboy dialect and was served up with a thick twang:

> When de 'lection bells am pealin',
> An' de Democrats am squealin',
> Den we want yer, ma Teddy, yes we do!
> When de bonfires am a-burnin',
> Croker green wid rage am turnin',

Den we'll all be glad we voted straight for you!
You will teach 'em honest doin',
When in Albany yer rulin',
We'll get straight goods from you!
Den you'll go a little higher,
Cos dey want yer, ma Teddy, yes dey do![22]

On November 3, Roosevelt took the stage in Albany's Harmanus Bleecker Hall, the city's largest public auditorium, just three blocks west of the Capitol. An enthusiastic crowd filled the nineteen hundred seats and overflowed the standing room capacity for an additional three thousand people. His opponents weren't above planting a few hecklers in the crowd on such occasions, though, and did so in Albany. Someone in the audience shouted out an accusatory question about Roosevelt's tax dodge. By then he anticipated the question, and he angrily shouted back, "I paid it!"

Roosevelt made as many as two dozen whistle-stops in a single day. During a six-day stretch of the campaign in late October, he delivered an astonishing 102 speeches. "Teddy is a wonder," his old Assembly colleague Billy O'Neil wrote to J. S. Van Duzer on November 1, after accompanying Roosevelt's train campaign entourage for two days. "I feel as you do that he will be elected . . . My confidence is not based on any figures but is simply the conclusion arrived at in watching the crowds at the stations as we went along."

Boss Platt described Roosevelt's campaign: "He called a spade a 'spade,' a crook a 'crook.' During the final week of the canvass he made the issue Richard Croker, the Tammany boss."[23] It was payback for Roosevelt's failed campaign for mayor of New York City twelve years earlier. Croker had been the one to persuade the elderly and respected Abraham Hewitt to run on a combined Tammany–New York County Democratic ticket.

In spite of his frenetic campaign schedule, Roosevelt lacked conviction about the outcome. He didn't want to appear too confident or overeager. He cast his vote at Oyster Bay and awaited the results in seclusion at Sagamore Hill. He sent word to his campaign workers that he did not wish to be disturbed by telegrams or a messenger on election night. He planned to retire to bed at his usual hour. "If I am elected, I will know it in the morning," he reasoned. "If I am defeated, I don't want to know it any sooner."[24] It was an order meant to be disobeyed. He was awakened at two o'clock in the morning with rousing cheers and loud applause. Roosevelt emerged on the porch, still in the red long johns that served as his pajamas, ready to revel with the celebratory throng.

O'Neil's astute assessment of the 1898 political landscape proved correct. In a year in which Republicans were all hurt by the canal scandal, Roosevelt managed to defeat Van Wyck by a margin of slightly less than 18,000 votes out of 1.3 million cast. "I have always maintained that no man besides Roosevelt could have accomplished that feat in 1898," Platt wrote.[25] Roosevelt's old political mentor, Joe Murray, whose imprimatur won Roosevelt his seat in the Twenty-first Assembly district and a foothold in state politics, sent Edith a telegram: "Your husband won the nomination at San Juan Hill. His personality won the election."[26]

The vote did not break entirely on traditional lines. Two days after his inauguration, Roosevelt would take the time to challenge a constituent who urged the governor to "remember the Negro" in his appointments. Roosevelt testily replied, "I was a little disappointed in the fact that I was the first Republican candidate for Governor against whom there was considerable Negro opposition, although I had while Civil Service Commissioner done more for them than any other public man whom I know."[27]

Roosevelt gloated in a letter, which never mentioned Van Wyck, that he had defeated archenemies Croker, Carl Schurz, Joseph Pulitzer, Hearst, and others he called "the most corrupt" within the Republican Party, along with "the silly 'Goo-Goos' and the extraordinarily powerful machine of Tammany Hall," which had raised "a gigantic corruption fund on behalf of my opponents."[28] All in all, he marveled to Spring-Rice, "I have played it in bull luck this summer. First, to get into the war; then to get out of it; then to get elected . . . I know perfectly well that the luck will not continue, and it is not necessary that it should. I am more than contented to be Governor of New York, and shall not care if I never hold another office." He was already thinking, of course, of the White House.

Secretary of State John Hay predicted great things for Roosevelt. "While you are Governor, I believe the party can be made solid as never before. You have already shown that a man may be absolutely honest and yet practical; a reformer by instinct and a wise politician; brave, bold, and uncompromising, and yet not a wild ass of the desert."[29]

Roosevelt was not alone in parlaying his war hero status into political glory after the conflict in Cuba. His old foe Willie Chanler had been wounded in action in Santiago and honored for his gallantry. His name recognition was put to use by the Democratic organization in the campaign of 1898, in which Chanler managed to upset Roosevelt's candidate and Platt's messenger, incumbent Lemuel Ely Quigg, for a seat in the House of Representatives from Manhattan's Fourteenth Congressional District. Roosevelt tried to bury the hatchet with Willie, as he wrote to his brother, Wintie:

> I am awfully glad he is in Congress. I do not like his party associates at all, but on the great questions of foreign policy and the army and the navy, he is just the man to do good work in Washington.[30]

Roosevelt also took simple steps to underscore his integrity by not abusing the privileges of his office while at Sagamore Hill.

For instance, he employed at his own expense a local woman, Miss Amy Cheney, as his secretary instead of using a state employee from Albany while he was at home.[31] He also made good on his campaign pledge not to accept any favors from corporations, turning down his ally and friend, New York Central Railroad President Chauncey Depew, who had sent a pass that permitted free travel over all the lines of his railroad. It was sent to each newly elected governor by tradition. Roosevelt broke with custom and returned it.

Jacob Riis described in epic images the triumphant arrival by train—Roosevelt paying his own ticket—of the governor-elect at daybreak in Albany. "The whole big state shouted with us. Theodore Roosevelt was Governor, elected upon the pledge that he would rule by the Ten Commandments, in the city where, fifteen years before, the spoils politicians had spurned him for insisting upon doing the thing that was right rather than the thing that was expedient."[32]

Roosevelt took the oath of office at noon on December 31 before Secretary of State John Palmer. That same day, his first installment of *The Rough Riders* was published in *Scribner's*. That night, he stayed out late at dinner with friends. By the time he returned to the Executive Mansion, his children and Edith—who had been ill and declined the dinner invitation—were long asleep. The doors to his new residence had been inadvertently locked by the staff, and the governor hadn't bothered to bring a key. Roosevelt was locked out. He had to break a window to gain access.[33] It made for a great story to tell his children and friends.

At the inaugural, two days later, the press estimated there were six thousand well-wishers, an unusually large crowd, waiting to meet and greet the Roosevelts. Roosevelt thrived on the frenetic shaking of hands (he had once been described as one of the fastest handshakers in politics by a *New York Times* reporter). Correspondents estimated that Roosevelt could pump fifty palms per minute, hour after hour. For her part, Edith clutched a bouquet of flowers that allowed her gracefully to avoid the work.

Edith was less excited about the relocation of her family to Albany than her husband, although she did find a certain charm in the capital city because of what she considered its resemblance to an English cathedral town. Edith, who still harbored some of the anxiety and social uncertainty she had carried since girlhood, was acutely aware that it would be human nature among his old Assembly colleagues to compare Edith with Roosevelt's first wife, Alice. She was ambivalent about her public role as New York's first lady. The three-story, turreted, sprawling governor's mansion that Edith was in charge of rearranging and adapting for use by her family was considered the most ornate and impressive house in the city. She would come to appreciate its spacious interior, solidity, and informal comfort.

On January 4, Governor Roosevelt laid out his reform agenda as he delivered his first annual message to the Legislature, a document that ran thirty pages and was filled with robust language and a parade of specific proposals arranged by department. Roosevelt began with a theme that propelled him to that spot, his by-now-familiar drumbeat of patriotism that "has carried to a brilliant triumph one of the most righteous wars of modern times."[34] His first priority, surprisingly, was to bolster a Naval Militia that "did admirable work in the last war . . . The State should carefully preserve and build up this arm of the service."[35] Similar to the New York State National Guard, the Naval Militia was made up of workers in the merchant marine who trained part-time at weekend military drills and could be called up to active duty to supplement full-time professionals in the U.S. Navy if need be in time of war. By focusing his remarks on the Naval Militia, Roosevelt avoided a political vulnerability with the state's National Guard, whom he had criticized in Cuba for being poorly trained and weak fighters—a censure they wouldn't forget, costing him votes in the election and ongoing clashes during his governorship.

In his other initiatives, Roosevelt drew heavily from his experience as an assemblyman and carried through on business left unfinished after his three terms in the State Legislature. Reform of civil service headed the list. Roosevelt thumbed his nose at Boss Platt's system. "The methods of appointment to the civil service of the State are now in utter confusion, no less than three systems being in effect—one in the city of New York, one in other cities, and one in the State at large."[36] He recommended passage of a law that would create a single, uniform civil service code for the entire State of New York and asked the Legislature to put teeth into the constitutional provision that required proper enforcement of civil service regulations. He also took a shot at the Mugwumps, Half-Breeds, and Black Horse Cavalry. "I invite the attention of the Legislature particularly to the evils of over-legislation. The tendency to pass laws which are utterly unnecessary . . . enacted purely to favor certain special private interests, seems to grow instead of diminish."[37]

The Progressive movement had more than its share of radical new ideas, and Roosevelt was amenable to many of them. He called upon the Legislature to "gradually extend the sphere in which the suffrage can be exercised by women,"[38] and he articulated for the first time a vision for forest conservation that would become a hallmark of his governorship and a legacy of his later presidency. Roosevelt proposed laying aside vast acreage across New York, particularly in the Adirondack and Catskill mountains, of untouched wilderness and virgin stands of forests as a gift to future generations. "The Forest Preserve will be a monument to the wisdom of its founders," Roosevelt said.[39]

Progressivism was utterly opposed to machine politics, yet Albany remained as much a machine as ever. Boss Platt made all appointments, including judges, and was his own one-man law-making body with clout equal to the leadership in the Legislature. He replenished his party's coffers by extortionate tactics aimed at corporations, which paid under the pretense of campaign contributions. He spread these funds around to Republican candidates to pay for their campaigns for the Legislature. Platt's cash came with the proviso that the legislators elected with the boss's funding would do his bidding with utmost loyalty when requested. It was an unbroken circle of *quid pro quo*, a self-perpetuating system that kept Republicans in power.

Roosevelt understood and accepted these political realities for perhaps the first time in his political career. Maturity had brought a newfound sense of his limitations. "I had neither the training nor the capacity that would have enabled me to match Mr. Platt and his machine people on their own ground," Roosevelt conceded.[40] He also realized he had been elected as a popular war hero, not as a reformer given a mandate for change by the voters. "They had no definite and clearly outlined conception of what they wished in the way of reform," Roosevelt wrote about the populace who elected him governor. "They on the whole tolerated, and indeed approved of, the machine."[41]

He offered compromise and negotiation to Platt, but Croker was fair game for assault. Wielding executive powers for the first time in his elective career, Roosevelt quickly launched a preemptive strike by ordering an investigation into Tammany's influence and manipulation of New York City's government. It was another in a long line of Tammany investigations, which had focused on corruption within city government in general and the police department in particular. Roosevelt responded to a public outcry for an investigation into what newspapers dubbed "Mr. Croker's Punch and Judy Show Government." Roosevelt appointed trusted Republican Assemblyman Robert Mazet as chairman of the investigation and Frank Moss—a lawyer Roosevelt had known since their days together on the Police Board of New York—as chief counsel. Moss had continued to fight corruption as Roosevelt's successor as president of the Police Board. The Mazet investigation called dozens of witnesses to its hearings over the course of several months, including Croker himself.

Moss used legal and linguistic jujitsu to score a knockout against the brawling former gang leader.

"So we have it, then, that you, participating in the selection of judges before election, participate in the emolument that comes away down at the end of their proceeding; namely, judicial sales?" Moss asked.

"Yes, sir," Croker said.

"And it goes into your pocket?"

"I get—that is, a part of my profit—"

"Then, you are working for your own pocket, are you not?" Moss asked.

"All the time, the same as you," Croker said.[42]

Croker's arrogant and stunning admission echoed across the state in large-type, front-page headlines and raised the profile of the Mazet investigation. "I think we may be able to wake the voters up, after all," Roosevelt wrote to Moss. The Mazet investigation expanded upon the 1890 Fassett investigation, an anti-Tammany probe set up by Platt in the Legislature. Many of the Mazet targets were carryovers, but nonetheless raised fresh outrage among the public. The investigation exposed extravagant increases in official salaries of city government employees (with presumed kickbacks to Tammany) and corrupt connections with Wall Street. Contributions of stock to Croker were a common way for companies that had to do business with the city to ingratiate themselves with the powerful boss. One firm that constructed a rapid transit tunnel in the 1890s reportedly gave $500,000 worth of stock to Croker, an allegation he refused to discuss by uttering a standard reply to Moss and his investigators: "Any questions you ask me about my personal business, I decline to answer." The Mazet investigation confirmed how Tammany muscled out companies that refused to pay the requisite graft, such as the Manhattan Elevated Railway Company. Croker owned stock in the New York Auto Truck Company, which stood to rise in value exponentially if Manhattan Elevated signed a contract for the truck company to attach a pipe to the elevated tracks to carry compressed air around the city to service its fleet. When Manhattan Elevated rejected the contract, Croker called on his minions in the city's Board of Health, Parks Department, and various other city agencies to attack Manhattan Elevated with bogus code violations, sabotage, and other dirty tricks.

The street fighter Croker knew when to cut his losses. A reform bill with backing of both the State Assembly and Senate, introduced in mid-April at the height of the Mazet investigation, was his sign to pull back. The State Constabulary legislation would completely revise police administration in the state's largest cities. The bill called for abolishing the police boards or commissions of New York, Buffalo, Rochester, Syracuse, Albany, and Troy, and transferring supervisory duties to a new official whom the governor would appoint for a six-year term—removable only upon criminal charges and an administrative hearing. Also, future applicants to these cities' police forces would be subject to state civil service laws and regulations. Local police chiefs would become state employees in the centralized police system proposed. Public reaction and newspaper editorials were against this usurpation of "home rule," so it was never enacted, but the bill's introduction was enough to force Croker, already weakened by the Mazet revelations, to negotiate. In the end, the outcome of the Mazet investigation was somewhat anticlimactic; all of its findings and proposed changes to city governance were deferred and passed along to a nonlegislative commission that would form the following year, with an equal number of Republican and Democatic members appointed by the governor and legislative leaders.

Roosevelt's role in the Mazet investigation at the beginning of his governorship was only the beginning of several encounters with Tammany. Near the end of his brief tenure, on December 23, 1900, Governor Roosevelt issued an executive order removing New York City's Tammany-backed district attorney, Asa Bird

Gardiner—best known for his motto, "To Hell with reform!" And to hell with Gardiner, Governor Roosevelt declared. Momentum against Gardiner's corrupt practices had been building since the City Club of New York released a five-hundred-page report the year before that alleged the district attorney had manipulated indictments to favor his friends and Tammany and had failed to account for $183,900 in forfeited bail bonds. Roosevelt replaced Gardiner with Eugene A. Philbin, a Roman Catholic and a Democrat who was a prominent New York City lawyer. Philbin had earned a reputation as a reformer by cleaning up corruption within retirement homes and hospitals as head of the State Board of Charities, and he brought the same integrity and fearlessness to the job of district attorney. "There are few things in my two years' term as Governor to which I shall look back with more unalloyed pleasure than the removal of Gardiner and the appointment of yourself," Roosevelt wrote to Philbin five days after Gardiner's ouster.

Roosevelt, sensing he had Croker on the ropes, kept pounding away at Tammany. The cumulative effect of the Mazet investigation, the removal of Gardiner, and the incompetence of Croker's candidate, New York Mayor Van Wyck, brought an end to Croker's ability to rule as boss. The death knell for Croker was sounded in the New York mayoral campaign of 1901, when Roosevelt's ally, Seth Low, an independently wealthy Republican, defeated Van Wyck.

Roosevelt juggled numerous projects in the office of the governor. "I've never worked so hard in my life," the governor's chief secretary, William Loeb Jr., declared. "At times the Governor keeps three of us busy."[43] Loeb described a typical morning in which Roosevelt dictated a lengthy and complex position paper on a particular issue, replied to a thick stack of correspondence to a different stenographer, and handed the draft of a speech or magazine article or book chapter to a third assistant to type. During the early months of his governorship, Roosevelt juggled three book projects: publication and promotion of *The Rough Riders,* proofreading and revisions for his first volume of *The Winning of the West,* and the research and initial writing of *The Life of Oliver Cromwell.* One of his staffers in the Executive Chamber described Roosevelt's restless energy and personal management style as "Biff-bang-do-it-right-now-can't-wait-another-minute."[44]

Everyone, even Governor Roosevelt, had to come to Boss Platt for support, however. Roosevelt attended regular Saturday morning breakfast meetings at the Fifth Avenue Hotel in New York City, where Platt lived. "A series of breakfasts was always the prelude to some active warfare," Roosevelt surmised.[45] In Albany, Roosevelt worked through political matters with one of Platt's lieutenants, such as Quigg or Benjamin Odell, the State Republican Party chairman.

Compared to Cleveland, whom Platt loathed because as governor he "repudiated every contract ever made with me," the Boss had qualified praise for the consistent manner with which Roosevelt negotiated. "Roosevelt had from the first agreed he would consult me on all questions of appointments, Legislature or party policy," Platt wrote. "He religiously fulfilled this pledge, although he frequently did just what he pleased."[46] Roosevelt spoke of his battle of wills with Platt and the Republicans in terms of his vulnerability to political ambush. "Face to face, I can defend myself and make a pretty good fight, but any weakling can murder me," he said. "If I am hit that way very often, I will take to the open, and the blows from the dark will only help me in an out-and-out battle."[47]

He was far from the hotheaded young man who first took his seat in the Assembly. He gave way to Boss Platt on the most important matter of party organization: patronage appointments. In a letter to Roosevelt in August of 1899 regarding the nomination of John P. Grant, of Stamford, New York, as Delaware County judge and surrogate, Platt described Grant as "an old time Republican. As you will see, he is endorsed by the Organization and by nearly the whole Bar of the County. It is a good appointment, and I think the sooner it is disposed of the better."[48] Roosevelt duly appointed him. But Roosevelt had won some concessions in what amounted to a prenuptial agreement with Platt hammered out with Quigg in the colonel's tent at Camp Wikoff. The most critical was the provision that allowed Roosevelt to seek advice with Republicans other than Platt—most notably Lodge, Root, Low, and Choate.

Although the process of selecting appointees to head state agencies was generally brief, efficient, and partisan, with Platt primarily taking the lead, there were clashes. Roosevelt chose his battles carefully. He went over the head of the Easy Boss in naming his trusted ally from the New York City Police Board, Avery D. Andrews, a Democrat and West Point graduate, as adjutant general of the New York State National Guard. Roosevelt needed a man he could count on to handle that sensitive post, given Roosevelt's criticism of the Guard's soldiers in the Spanish-American War and that group's lingering distrust of his governorship.

There was more friction over the appointment of a new superintendent of Public Works. Platt's handpicked choice was Francis J. Hendricks, of Syracuse, whom Roosevelt rejected on the grounds that "the Administration was my Administration and no one else's but mine"[49] and that he would not be dictated to in personnel matters by anyone, including the boss. This was one of those infrequent battles with Platt in which Roosevelt dug in. He considered Hendricks an Onondaga County hack whose appointment would be seen by Independents as Roosevelt's breaking his campaign promise to clean up the canal scandal and, magnified by the press, would symbolize that Roosevelt's new administration was little more than a Platt rubber stamp. In shock that Roosevelt would create a public showdown, Platt blew up at the challenge. Roosevelt responded astutely, providing Platt a choice of four candidates. The plan worked. Colonel John Nelson Partridge was nominated within two weeks of Roosevelt's taking office. "My strength has consisted very largely in the fact that I have never begun a fight save with extreme caution; that by constant consultation I have kept the Machine, without which I was powerless, on my side, save in two or three exceptional cases," Roosevelt wrote.[50]

In Roosevelt's first term, the matter upon which all eyes were trained was the canal scandal. Roosevelt immediately hit the explosive issue head-on in a January 3 letter to Odell. "I would like to appoint a counsel to represent me in this canal business, and in view of the possibility and even probability of a failure, I want to get a strong man, one who is not identified in any way with my interests." Six days later, having received a nod of assent from Platt, Roosevelt designated a special counsel to investigate the canal matter. Anticipating complaints, Roosevelt selected two prominent and well-respected Democratic lawyers to head the investigation. Roosevelt also appointed a bipartisan commission of business leaders and respected engineers to conduct their own investigation of the canal issue and to report what steps the state should take in order to put the troubled canal system on sound footing.

Roosevelt next turned his attention to another inherited boondoggle, the construction of the State Capitol, a long-running debacle that had already consumed thirty-two years and expended $25 million of taxpayer funds. One of the most lavish structures produced in nineteenth-century America, it was ridiculously over budget and long past deadline, a marble monolith Governor Black described in 1897 as "an affliction from which time affords but little hope of relief." Black had vowed to finish the job during his administration but failed, as had ten previous governors. The huge pile of construction materials and debris at the Capitol site that greeted Roosevelt in 1882 had been replaced with lawns and landscaping, giving the exterior, at least, a sense of completion. Inside, though, was another matter. Several monumental features, including a proposed grandiose tower dome that promised to be "the landmark of the capital city," remained on the drawing boards, while squabbles had flared up over plans among the three teams of architects who oversaw construction. Roosevelt nevertheless declared the unfinished Capitol complete. On February 4, he formally fired Commissioner Isaac G. Perry, the architectural force known as "the grand old man of the Capitol." Workers left tools and equipment behind, quickly vacating the massive building after nearly four decades—much of that time under the direction of Perry, whose forced retirement sent him back home to Binghamton and anonymity in the Southern Tier. Roosevelt became the first governor to occupy the Capitol in quietude, without the constant cacophony of hammering, chiseling, sawing, and the thumping of large stone blocks into place. After Roosevelt pulled the plug, the ornate tower was never built; it remained a phantom apparition on early architectural drawings and a few period postcards that never corrected the error—leaving Albany one of the only state capitol buildings in the nation without a central dome.

From the south-facing windows of his Executive Chamber, Roosevelt could gaze across a few blocks of row houses to another Albany property that required his attention—the Executive Mansion. The governor's official residence didn't exist for the first century of New York State's history. At that time, governors had to secure housing on their own. In 1874, Samuel J. Tilden rented as his official residence a grand mansion on a hillside south of the Capitol on Eagle Street at the exorbitant rate of $9,000 a year. Tilden entertained lavishly and the elegant home earned such high praise that Tilden's successor, Governor Lucius Robinson, continued the tradition of renting the Eagle Street mansion until he persuaded the state to purchase it in 1877 as New York's official governor's residence. In 1882, as Roosevelt began his first term in the Assembly, newly elected Governor Grover Cleveland decided the Executive Mansion was not imposing enough and planned an expansion. Vacating the house to become president, he left his successor, former lieutenant governor David B. Hill, a bachelor, to persuade the Legislature to renovate and enlarge it. The Capitol architect, Perry, in good graces at that point, drew up the plans and sent over some of his craftsmen from the Capitol construction to execute the overhaul. They got carried away with architectural flourishes and added a jumble of dormers, balconies, turrets, and gables—an eclectic style the *New Yorker* magazine later described as "Hudson River helter-skelter."[51] The house accumulated a trove of political lore over the decades, some of it pure invention, such as the false legend that President William McKinley slept in the Executive Mansion the night before he was shot by an assassin in Buffalo on September 6, 1901. (McKinley was at home that night in Canton, Ohio.) McKinley was an overnight guest of Governor Levi P. Morton at the Executive Mansion in Albany in 1895 when, as governor of Ohio, he visited the capital city to give the Lincoln's birthday address at the Unconditional Republican Club. The room at the head of the stairs on the second floor, where McKinley is believed to have slept as Morton's guest, is called the McKinley Room by tradition and features his portrait.

The Executive Mansion was a gloomy place when the Roosevelt family moved in. Theodore likened the shabby interior to a downtrodden Chicago hotel. Alice Roosevelt later recalled the place as "a big, ugly, rather shabby house, larger than any house we had heretofore lived in, hideously furnished."[52] Edith took charge, replacing the old and musty paintings with fine works by her favorite artists, including John La Farge. She scoured the attic and basement, resurrected long-lost matching pieces of furniture, and showed off the few heirloom-quality pieces to best effect. "[Edith] is making changes which are distinctly diminishing the general resemblance of the lower floor of the house to the meeting room of a board of directors of a wealthy railroad, or to a first-class Chicago hotel. The children revel in the size of the house and have great games," Roosevelt wrote.[53] Edith's refurbishing was at state expense, not that she was as deeply worried about the household budget anymore. Her husband's salary of $10,000 as governor doubled his Washington pay and came with the mansion and added perks.

Roosevelt enjoyed his rich surroundings, but felt he was going soft. He complained of weight gain and lack of strenuous exercise and urged Edith to have a third-floor billiard room converted into a gymnasium. The Roosevelt children transformed the basement of the governor's mansion into a wild kingdom for their ever-growing menagerie of pets, which included rabbits, hamsters, guinea pigs, and other animals, twenty-one in all. One of the guinea pigs was named Bishop Doane, after the prelate who headed the Episcopal diocese in Albany and the Episcopal All Saints Cathedral, which Edith attended. That led to a favorite Roosevelt story. One evening, while his parents entertained guests, Archie ran into the room and shouted with glee, "Father! Father! Bishop Doane has had twins!"[54] Two of their more unusual house pets were the eagle Roosevelt brought back from Cuba and a bear cub that was a gift from West Virginia Republicans. The basement could smell quite foul, especially in warm weather, and the family's dogs occasionally broke free by digging under the fence and tearing up neighbors' gardens—which the governor dutifully assigned his grounds crew to repair.

A downstairs wing of the Executive Mansion was cleared and transformed into a schoolroom. Edith hired an English governess, Miss Young, for Alice and Ethel. Mame Ledwith took care of Quentin and Archie. Ted and Kermit were enrolled at Albany Academy, a prep school featuring military training located across the street from the Capitol; past students included Henry James and Herman Melville. In order to continue her own education and to stave off boredom amid an Albany social scene that didn't approach the sophistication of Washington or New York, Edith joined the Friday Morning Club. It was an Albany group whose members were well-bred and highly educated young women who researched and wrote reports akin to term papers that they read aloud to their fellow members. In warm months, Edith joined her friend Fanny Parsons, author of a popular book about wildflowers, on botanical walks in the countryside outside Albany.[55]

The Roosevelt children became a familiar presence to Albany residents, particularly Ted and Kermit. To toughen them up, their father demanded that his sons walk the five blocks each day between the governor's mansion and Albany Academy. Sharing their father's boyhood propensity for natural history, they used the walk to collect stray cats, dogs, and other critters. There were other distractions on their walks to school. One day Ted returned from Albany Academy covered with mud and cuts on his face and hands. His father asked what happened. "Well, a boy up the street made a face at me and said, 'Your father's a faker.' He was a good deal bigger than I, but I wouldn't stand that, you know, so I just lit into him, and I had a pretty hard time. But I licked him," his son said. "That's right. That's right," his father replied. "I'm glad you licked him."[56] The governor occasionally happened upon fighting youngsters in his rambles around Albany. One scuffle was broken up by an Albany cop, whom Roosevelt cautioned, "Let 'em fight it out. It's good for them."[57]

In the converted gym at the Executive Mansion, the governor pushed himself to his physical limits and to the edge of recklessness. He wrote to Bamie,

> Recently I have been having a little too much strenuous life with a large gentleman whom I have had up to wrestle with me. First of all, he caved in my ribs. When I got over those, I fetched loose one shoulder blade, while endeavoring to give him a flying fall. I think I shall take to boxing as a gentler sport.[58]

Roosevelt took his own advice and hired a sparring partner, Mike Donovan, a former lightweight champ. Donovan took it easy on the governor in their first go-round. Roosevelt told the boxer not to pull his punches. "You're not hitting me. I'd like you to hit out," he said.[59] Donovan agreed and came in swinging, landing heavy blows to Roosevelt's ample midsection. When Donovan swung a bit wildly with a left hook to the head, Roosevelt expertly ducked inside and got his weight behind a crushing right that caught Donovan squarely on the ear and rocked the boxer back on his heels. "I realized from that moment that the Governor was no ordinary amateur," Donovan noted. "If I took chances with him, I was endangering my reputation."

Curiously, Roosevelt as governor took a strong stance against prizefighting, making a distinction between boxing, which he called "a fine sport," and prizefighting, which he considered "in danger of losing much that is valuable, and of acquiring some exceedingly undesirable characteristics" because of all the gambling on the fights.[60] With the drive of Roosevelt to offset Democratic opposition and the lobbying of prizefighting interests, a ban on professional boxing passed by a single vote and kept prizefighting out of the Empire State for the next decade—even as its governor continued to spar and praise the amateur, sporting version of "exercise that tends to develop bodily vigor, daring, endurance, resolution and self-command."[61]

Edith entertained visiting dignitaries and other notable guests, who were often treated to unexpected entertainment courtesy of the Roosevelt children. The brood occasionally escaped boredom and upstairs confinement during formal dinners by climbing down a drainpipe from their bedrooms and engaging in snowball fights on winter nights—typically in their pajamas. One night they played a practical joke by hiding a purple billiard ball in a bowl of plums on a table before a reception. A preoccupied guest bit into the plum-colored ball and nearly cracked a molar.[62] The Roosevelt kids were also forever chasing pets escaped fom their basement menagerie.

Unlike other offspring of politicians, the Roosevelt children did not put on a goody two-shoes act for guests. Alice in particular could be sullen and droll, since she pined for the social whirl of New York and Washington and found Albany parochial and dull. "She cares neither for athletics nor good works, the two resources of youth in this town," Edith wrote. During a moody and stubborn adolescence in Albany, Alice could be as pugnacious as her father. Her parents discussed sending her to a finishing school, Miss Spence's School in New York City. Alice dug in her dainty heels. "The thought of becoming one of them shrivelled me," Alice wrote. "I practically went on strike. I said that I would not go—I said that if the family insisted, and sent me, I should do something disgraceful."[63] In the end, her parents gave in. Alice would have the freedom to be a self-taught scholar, roaming the family's extensive library—her father had carted to Albany boxes of books from Sagamore Hill—as long as she was productive in her reading and could tell her father something new she had learned the previous day at the breakfast table each morning.

The governor, who did not take himself too seriously, taught his children to laugh at themselves as he had done. His sister Corinne recalled how he would draw a large set of teeth in a self-mocking way on the envelope of his personal letters in place of a return address. "Those strong white teeth, which had been the terror of the recreant policemen, were quite as much a factor at the Capitol on the hill at Albany," she wrote.[64]

The Roosevelt children were not timid with their opinions about guests. They considered rude and boorish a young newspaper correspondent who accompanied Lord Minto, the governor general of Canada. This reporter slouched insouciantly in his chair and puffed on a cigar during dinner, and most atrocious of all, he refused to rise when ladies came into the dining room. The uncouth young fellow's name was Winston Churchill.

Roosevelt also could count on visits from the colorful and endearing Rough Riders. One of Roosevelt's regimental soldiers had read a newspaper account in which the governor complained about sycophants and office seekers who ingratiated themselves into his life at the Executive Mansion. As Roosevelt explained in a letter, "Dear old Happy Jack read, way out in Arizona, about the annoyance I was having with these people, and he just packed his kit and came all the way from Arizona to offer to be 'bouncer-out' of the Executive Mansion!"[65]

Roosevelt understood the power of the press to sustain his exceptional popularity. Governor Roosevelt held press conferences twice each day, summoning correspondents to his office on the second floor of the Capitol for a wide-ranging briefing. He sat on the edge of his desk, parrying and thrusting with reporters. He knew when to go off the record, leaking information to reporters in strictest confidence, or pointing them in the direction of behind-the-scenes maneuvering or conspiracy. Roosevelt used the press to advance his agenda, test ideas, signal displeasure at pending legislation, and counterpunch enemies. The correspondents were both pleased for the access and obviously enthralled by the ebullient, gregarious monologist who gave them so much material. The fact that he provided such extensive press access was seen as a universal good, although few seemed to ask at what cost to objectivity. "He has torn down the curtain that shut in the Governor and taken the public into his confidence," the *New York Times* gushed.[66]

At times, though, Governor Roosevelt took Capitol correspondents by the scruff of the neck and gave them a good shake, the way one might discipline an errant puppy. Roosevelt's secretary, Amy Cheney, recalled one incident in which Roosevelt had promised to give a joint interview with all statehouse reporters. One of the attendees who worked for an evening paper, wary of being scooped, asked the governor pointedly whether he had already provided the information to the morning newspapermen. Roosevelt pivoted sharply and snapped, "Look here, my friend, don't think because you're a fool, I'm one!" The reporter tried to mumble a defense suggesting that he was only relaying what he had heard, when Roosevelt tore into him again in front of the other correspondents. When the interview had finished, Roosevelt stepped up to the quaking young scribe and said in a reassuring and gentle voice, "My good fellow, I allow no one to question my word, but as you seem only to be overanxious in fulfilling your duty, I forgive you."[67]

Not every issue was publicized. Roosevelt believed he deserved the Medal of Honor, the nation's highest military commendation, for his leadership in the Spanish-American War. He was convinced that he had been wrongfully passed over because he had written letters highly critical of his superiors and their mismanagement of military logistics in Cuba. Roosevelt decided to mount a campaign for the medal, despite the fact, as he complained to Platt shortly after his inauguration, that he did "not have one minute's rest from morning until night."[68] In a letter to the captain of the Rough Riders, William H. H. Llewellyn, on January 9, 1899, he wrote, "The War Department has refused to grant me the medal of honor for which I was recommended by every General in the Cavalry Division, Wood, Summer and Wheeler, as well as Shafter. It is possible I may ask you to give me a certificate as to what I did on that July First day in leading our men through the lines of the Regulars and in heading the two charges." He would continue to lobby unsuccessfully for the rest of his life. "I do not believe the War Department has the slightest intention of granting it, and I have really given up thinking about it," he wrote in 1899. "You see I cannot blame the War Department for feeling bitterly toward me now, for I have hit, and intend to hit them, hard for what they have done and left undone."[69]

The drumbeat of Roosevelt's daily schedule as governor carried distinct patterns, which grew intense only at certain times of the year and eased off during long stretches of uneventful weeks punctuated by regular commutes between Albany and New York

City. Still, Theodore never rested. He dictated letters, signed or vetoed legislation, negotiated with legislators, scheduled meetings, and met with party regulars from early morning until evening—a long day followed by formal dinners, a heavy schedule of speeches, and reviewing reports prepared by his staff and memos from legislative leaders late into the night.

The business of the state was agriculture, even as the business of the city was anything but. The Progressives worried greatly about urban working conditions; the farmers protected themselves, as can be seen in some of the laws that consumed Roosevelt during his first few months in office. The Ambler Dairy Products Act, which became law on March 27, 1899, after much effort by Roosevelt, prohibited the sale of artificially colored oleomargarine. The following month saw the approval of an amendment to the Beet Sugar Act, which authorized a bounty for manufacturers of sugar made exclusively of beets grown in New York State. On April 1, 1899, Roosevelt signed two labor laws; the first provided for the inspection and regulation of the conditions of work in tenements, while the second was a far-ranging amendment to the labor law that increased the authority of factory inspectors and the number and scope of safety rules and also limited the working hours of women and minors.

As governor, Roosevelt also presided over issues of life and death. Just three months into his first term, he faced the difficult decision of ruling on the fate of a Brooklyn woman, Martha Place, in a capital punishment case. As the first time a woman faced death by the newly devised form of "electric execution" in New York State, it was a historic case upon which the nation focused. Roosevelt had been positioning himself as a champion of women and an advocate of women's suffrage. Capital punishment had long ago fallen out of favor among the gentry, who pushed to ban the spectacle of public hangings in 1835, although yellow journalism revived interest in prison executions in the 1890s by running lurid accounts by reporters who served as witnesses. Martha

Place had been confined to Sing Sing Prison and sentenced to death for killing her stepdaughter and attempting to kill her husband with an ax on February 7, 1898, in an act "of particular deliberation and atrocity" that included premeditated torture, according to Roosevelt. Place's attorney and her supporters had petitioned Roosevelt for a commutation of her sentence on March 15, 1899. That same day Roosevelt wrote to Platt, "Since you left I have had one exceedingly painful and disagreeable duty to perform, in the case of the convicted murderess, Mrs. Place."[70]

Roosevelt was deeply affected by the decision demanded of him. "No more painful case can come before a Governor than an appeal to arrest the course of justice in order to save a woman from capital punishment, when that woman's guilt has been clearly established and when there are no circumstances whatever to mitigate the crime," he would write in his opinion.[71] That opinion, that there were no mitigating circumstances, had been contested. Mrs. Place claimed to have no memory of the murders, and her legal defense team and supporters urged a reprieve on the basis that she was mentally incapacitated.

Roosevelt had been flooded with petitions for a pardon or a lighter sentence for Mrs. Place, including an appeal from Jacob Riis. Political advisers also weighed in. "If you do not pardon this woman, you will never be President," one wrote. "You must rest assured that the last thing that will influence me will be any statement that no man can become President if he allows a woman to be executed," Roosevelt replied, to which he emphatically added that he had no thoughts of the presidency anyway. "I should heartily despise the public servant who failed to do his duty because it might jeopardize his own future."[72]

Still, Roosevelt appointed two doctors to examine Mrs. Place and to assess her mental health. Both found her sane. In very deliberate, legalistic prose, then, Roosevelt ran through his options. Since she was completely and absolutely guilty and also fully rational at the time of the murder, "All that remains is the question as to whether I should be justified in interfering to save a murderess on the ground of her sex when no justification would exist to interfere on behalf of a murderer," he wrote. Martha Place was set to be executed.

The method of the execution would be controversial as well. Roxie Druse, who murdered her husband in 1884, became the first woman executed in New York State in four decades when she was hanged in Herkimer County Jail during the winter of 1887. Rather than suffering just a quick snap of the neck, she moaned, wept, and writhed for fifteen minutes at the end of the rope, dying slowly of strangulation. She wore a pretty dress sent by her daughter. The public was outraged, though men had suffered similarly for decades.

The botched hanging of Druse became a *cause célèbre* and spurred Governor David B. Hill to urge the Legislature to reform New York's capital punishment laws and to look into whether a new technology of death, "electric execution," might be more humane.[73] Ironically, the technology was still in a complicated infancy. A decade after Thomas Edison introduced the lightbulb, he devoted substantial resources and laboratory staff to create the electric chair—all the more controversial because Edison was a strong opponent of the death penalty. The backdrop of Edison's race to build the death machine was a bitter competition between his own direct current lines and his rival George Westinghouse's alternating current system. Edison got the jump by wiring Manhattan and other cities with direct current first, while Westinghouse gained quickly on his enemy because his alternating current was cheaper. At the peak of the battle for market dominance between Edison and Westinghouse, several accidental electrocutions in the alternating current system gained public attention at the same time that state legislators were debating about alternatives for capital punishment after the gruesome Druse hanging. Edison was called before a legislative committee, and his testimony persuaded legislators to put aside proposals of a guillotine and lethal injection and instead to back electricity as the favored method for capital punishment. After tests of an electric chair on animals, Edison said execution by electricity was quick and safe, but only if Westinghouse's alternating current were used. Edison thus smeared Westinghouse as the inventor of the "death current," while playing up the propaganda of the dangers of the supposedly uncontrollable current in order to boost his own direct current sales.

The law that made electric execution the state's official method of capital punishment went into effect on January 1, 1889. Compared to the frequently grotesque outcomes of hanging, it was considered a technological improvement and a macabre source of pride for New York, the first government in the world to harness electricity for execution. The first electrocution (although that word was not commonly used then) was carried out at the Auburn State Prison in March of 1889. William Kemmler, a fruit vendor from Buffalo, had murdered his common-law wife with a hatchet in the presence of her young daughter. Alternating current was a "success," although Kemmler was not killed by the first surge from Westinghouse's dynamo. The second time, the powerful alternating current was turned on so long that the stench of burning hair and flesh filled the execution room. A witness vomited, a reporter fainted, and the district attorney rushed out of the room in horror. (The electric chair was transferred to Sing Sing Prison in 1891, where Martha Place was one of 614 people electrocuted between 1891 and 1963.)

Roosevelt wrote to Omar V. Sage, warden of Sing Sing, on March 16, 1899, asking to have a woman attendant and a "reputable woman physician" for Mrs. Place. The district attorney, his assistant, a clergyman chosen by Mrs. Place, and other witnesses would be present. Roosevelt would not permit a press spectacle, but he did allow one representative from the Associated Press, one reporter from the *New York Sun,* and one each from the very few papers that were not AP members and thus not entitled to run the wire service account. By modern standards, it would guarantee a spectacle, with descriptions of Martha Place's final moments, but Roosevelt was limiting access by the standards of that era. "I particularly desire that this solemn and painful act of justice shall not be made an excuse for that species of hideous sensationalism which is more demoralizing than anything else to the public mind."[74]

Overall, Roosevelt's term would reveal him to be far more mature and calculating than in the past. He still attacked the Legislature: his first veto, on March 27, 1899, slapped down a bill to regulate the gowns worn by attorneys in State Supreme Court. "This bill is obviously and utterly unnecessary," Roosevelt wrote.[75] "The whole subject should be left and can safely be left where it properly belongs—to the good sense of the judiciary."

Roosevelt still took up politically difficult reform issues. But he relied far more on expert advice; he allowed Platt to make full use of party patronage, and he compromised often. He would veto one bill to reduce the hours of drug clerks, trading his Progressive friends' interests against Platt. Early in his administration he established Progressive credentials by decisively cracking down on factory polluters. He took aim first at pollutants fouling the water sources for the spa tourist town of Saratoga Springs. On March 10, Roosevelt ordered the State Board of Health to investigate complaints that residents and property owners on Saratoga Lake were discharging sewage, domestic waste, and manufacturing refuse that endangered public health. Kayaderosseras Creek, the inlet to six-mile-long Saratoga Lake, was the pollution conduit. Roosevelt received a report that called the creek "practically an open sewer from Ballston Spa to the lake," carrying refuse from paper plants, leather tanneries, and a factory that produced sulfite pulp. In addition, Saratoga Springs, with a year-round population of ten thousand that swelled to many times that size in summer, directly discharged its sewage into the lake. The result was large fish kills that caused rotting fish carcasses to wash up on shore that "during the warm summer months, with ferment and decay, produced stenches more or less offensive."[76]

Roosevelt's executive order said that owners of properties along the lake must stop discharging waste and sewage into the lake and must collect and dispose of it in a sanitary manner beginning July 1, 1899. He gave the villages of Ballston Spa and Saratoga Springs, as well as the mills and factories along the creek, until April 1, 1900, to comply with proper sewage disposal. Failure to do so by those deadlines would result in a monetary fine and possible jail sentence. It was one of the first and by far the toughest antipollution statutes adopted by a state anywhere in the nation.

Roosevelt's maturity was evident in the measured tone of his executive orders. By relying on the findings of a State Board of Health report that Roosevelt had ordered, he gave himself cover. No longer did Roosevelt shoot from the lip first and gather his facts later. Roosevelt had created a new forum for gathering advice at weekly meetings of his agency heads and leading state officials, who formed a kind of *de facto* cabinet. Roosevelt also corresponded with, and solicited advice from, a wide range of academics and experts on the difficult decisions that faced him regarding canal improvements, labor, education, conservation, and taxation. One of them, invited for a weekend at Sagamore Hill, was Woodrow Wilson, a political science professor at Princeton, whose intellect was gaining him a national reputation.

When it came to conditions of the working class, Roosevelt turned to his old friend Jacob Riis for direction. As in the past, Roosevelt accompanied Riis on exhausting marathon tours of New York City sweatshops in the swelter of summer. Roosevelt was not simply scoring political points. "The Governor went carefully through every room, observing its condition and noting the number of the license on the wall, if anything was wrong," Riis recalled.[77] Riis noted that Roosevelt didn't abandon the issue after the laudatory press coverage faded. He pressed ahead with an emergency executive message for passage of the Tenement House Commission Bill, which challenged "the mercenary hostility of the slum landlord" and demanded "decent and cleanly living and fair play to all our citizens."[78]

The friendship between Roosevelt and Riis survived ideological gaps and a political divide—Riis was an ardent Democrat—as well as geographical distance, which Riis closed with frequent visits to Albany. The capital city began to grow on the New Yorker, as it had on Roosevelt. "I never liked Albany before, but I grew to be quite fond of the queer old Dutch city on the Hudson in those two years," Riis wrote.[79] "It is not so far away but that I would run up after office hours and have a good talk with the Governor before the midnight train carried me back home."

Roosevelt also relished sharing stories about how the power of being governor had not made him forget the little guys. His sister Corinne remembered a time when he had invited more guests to a breakfast meeting at her house than her table and fourteen chairs could accommodate. Corinne said her brother went into the hall, passed over an important guest, and returned with a Rough Rider. Both were smiling. Corinne asked what had happened with the two guests competing for the one chair left, which the Rough Rider claimed. "Yes, there were two," he said, "the other was the president of the University of ——. I told them to have a toss up, and the Rough Rider won."[80]

Thanks to the weekly breakfasts with Platt, and regular meetings with Odell and others for conferences on legislation and appointments in Albany, Roosevelt was frequently in touch with Platt to keep him abreast of developments. Roosevelt claimed to be pleased with the relationships. He wrote to an old friend,

> So far, Senator Platt, and above all, Ben. Odell, the Chairman of the State Committee, have treated me as "white" as any man could have been treated. I have had to do a great many things they did not want and leave undone quite as

large a number which they did want, and yet they have stood up to me perfectly straight, and profess to be, and indeed I think are, entirely satisfied.[81]

From Platt's point of view, the relationship was not so satisfying. Early on, they squared off in what Platt called "the great dispute" between himself and Roosevelt.[82] At the start of Roosevelt's term, Senator John Ford, a New York City Democrat, had introduced a bill and opened the door for taxation of public service corporations by redefining utility franchises as real property assets. Up to that point, street railway companies, gas and electric lighting companies, and other public service corporations had enjoyed unlimited and perpetual franchises with no obligations and no strings attached. These corporation franchises were awarded to private companies, which amassed fortunes. Roosevelt had learned about this system while an assemblyman, and it had rankled him at the time that public service corporations did not pay their fair share. Now he saw Ford's bill—and his own amendments of it—as the most important piece of reform legislation of his tenure as governor. Roosevelt realized that the defeat of William Jennings Bryan and his populist platform in 1896 did not silence the demands of taxpayers who felt overburdened and who urged large corporations to pay their share. The country was simmering with nascent class warfare. The State Treasury estimated that if Ford's bill passed, the new tax revenue would total more than $26 million in six years.

Roosevelt sounded out his confidant and adviser Elihu Root on the issue. "I don't want to be misled by any demagogic cry against capital on the one hand, nor on the other do I want to sign a bill and find that I have either given away a franchise for which money should be paid to the public treasury or granted too extensive powers."[83] Root was hardly objective, since he had been retained as counsel by the Astoria Gas Company to lobby against the franchise tax bill. Root argued that the state had operated without a franchise tax for many years and that it had become "the immemorial custom" of New York. Roosevelt's relations with Root cooled considerably after their disagreement; a rumor grew that Roosevelt was going to drop Root as a political adviser, causing Roosevelt to write his old friend a conciliatory letter even as he marched forward on the matter. At a March 18 press conference, Roosevelt told reporters that he looked favorably upon the bill. "I was hardly prepared for the storm of protest and anger which my proposal aroused," Roosevelt claimed in his *Autobiography,* meaning his amendments.[84] Platt's Republicans and Tammany's Democrats, however, needed a full public spigot. The transformation from horsepower to electric power in the streetcar lines of New York City brought a fresh wave of graft and corruption, and taxing it was akin to taxing Tammany.

In truth, the utilities were already taxed: they pumped large sums into Platt's Republican coffers with what amounted to extortion payments masquerading as campaign contributions. In return, however, Platt had to be able to guarantee noncompetition and tax freedom.

Platt immediately and publicly announced his unequivocal opposition to the idea. Privately, during a meeting with Roosevelt, he gave the "boy Governor" a blunt lesson in the boss's version of practical politics. "If that becomes a law, no corporation will ever again contribute a dollar to any campaign fund when you are a candidate," Platt told Roosevelt.[85] "The people will give three cheers for your independence and then forget all about it. The corporations have long memories; they don't forget." The divisive issue received a spirited airing in the press. Roosevelt didn't think he could push the Ford bill through the Legislature over Platt's objection, and yet he had already voiced his support. He proposed a governor's favorite fallback position: appointment of a joint legislative committee to study franchise tax as part of a comprehensive look at tax reform. Roosevelt felt he had shelved the problematic issue until the following year, when the report would be due. That was an eternity in legislative terms and bought Roosevelt room to maneuver.

"I don't know whether you have realized how entirely during my administration I have had the kernel and Mr. Platt the husk," Roosevelt wrote to a friend. "I am only too glad to call on Mr. Platt, or to have him to dinner, or take breakfast with him, and to discuss with him first and at length all projects, provided, in the end, I have my way about these same projects."[86] The reformers did not see it this way, and criticized Roosevelt for shelving the franchise tax fight.

In response, Roosevelt took the offensive and stated at a press conference that if the Ford franchise tax bill were approved, he would sign it. Politically, Roosevelt assumed it was an empty promise because of Platt's blockade. But the bill was carried forward on a wave of favorable public opinion, stirred up by newspaper editorials and labor leaders who were more vocal than the machine's leaders. The press also goaded Roosevelt into standing up against Platt by insinuating that if he sat on the sidelines on the bill, he was a puppet of the boss. The Senate swiftly passed the measure and sent it on to the Assembly. Platt managed to get the bill stalled in the Assembly's Rules Committee, a legislative black hole, while backing a diluted rival bill that exempted steam railroads and created other loopholes that would waive the tax for certain industries. The Senate stood its ground and refused to take up the Assembly's sleight-of-hand legislation, however, and the two houses were at a standoff. Less than a week remained in the session.

Roosevelt decided to make a last stand on the franchise tax measure in the final days of the 1899 session, realizing its potential as the most important victory of his gubernatorial term. The *Brooklyn Eagle* called it "an epoch-making measure." He arm-twisted assemblymen and made public demands to bring the Ford bill to the floor for a vote. Roosevelt argued privately that a franchise tax was a politically astute move for Republicans because it would be a signal to voters that they were the party of the people and not in the pocket of big business. A public survey released on April 27, a day before the scheduled end of the legislative session, showed a two-to-one majority of New Yorkers in favor. Still, Platt's forces resisted and "hoisted the signal of rebellion," against which Roosevelt "clenched his fist and gritted his teeth, and drove through the legislature the franchise tax law," according to Platt.[87] As with the Senate, the Assembly caved to publicity and the bill was passed by an overwhelming margin of 109 to 35. "Well, I suppose this ends my political career," Roosevelt said offhandedly to legislators after the vote, anticipating Platt's retaliation.[88] "You're mistaken," a prescient senator replied. "It's only the beginning."

The Easy Boss conceded that battle but took some comfort that the franchise tax law could be fought in the courts. Further diminishing Roosevelt's victory was the fact that he called the Legislature back to Albany into special session to approve further amendments to the Ford bill that gave the authority to levy franchise taxes to state officials rather than local ones. The amendments were seen as an appeasement to Platt. Eventually, the State Supreme Court saw the matter Roosevelt's way, it denied the claims of the corporations, and the bill became law. Roosevelt, as well as historians, considered the franchise law his most important gubernatorial achievement.

In his first year, Roosevelt's governorship had become his most effective political office to date. He won passage of several pioneering pieces of labor and education legislation, including an eight-hour workday for state employees and raises for New York City schoolteachers. Roosevelt began to build a national reputation as a conservationist by replacing the political hacks on the state's five-member Fisheries, Game, and Forest Commission with a single commission head with established professional credentials; he also closed legal loopholes in order to keep loggers out of forest preserves and protect vanishing wilderness. "All that later I strove for in the Nation in connection with Conservation was foreshadowed by what I strove to obtain for New York State when I was Governor," he wrote.[89]

In addition, he gave eighteen major speeches across the state, in Chicago, in Ann Arbor, Michigan, and elsewhere in his first five months as governor, while writing thousands of letters and continuing to write articles and books. Above all, Roosevelt restored the integrity of the office after the canal scandal taint on his predecessor, Governor Black, and established a national reputation as a man of character.

His Chicago speech, at the Hamilton Club on April 10, was called "The Strenuous Life." Roosevelt advocated physical strength, bold risk-taking, and fierce competitiveness, as well as a supreme military and a willingness to use it to achieve American domination across the globe. Roosevelt wrote the speech not only as a politicking document, but as a means to future income through publication. Indeed, the following year Roosevelt published with the Century Company a book titled *The Strenuous Life: Essays and Addresses.* The title piece begins,

> I wish to preach not the doctrine of ignoble ease, but the doctrine of the strenuous life; the life of toil and effort; of labor and strife; to preach that highest form of success which comes, not to the man who desires more easy peace, but to the man who does not shrink from danger, from hardship or bitter toil, and who out of these wins the splendid ultimate triumph.[90]

Among the thousands of addresses and speeches Roosevelt made, it was perhaps his most famous and endured the longest.

At the end of the legislative session, Governor Roosevelt embarked on a wide-ranging speaking tour that concluded in Las Vegas, New Mexico, at the first reunion of the Rough Riders. His men welcomed back their leader with a massive celebration that included an elaborate salute with twenty-one bomb blasts and an extravagant fireworks display featuring Roosevelt's familiar caricature likeness of spectacles, mustache, and big teeth burning across the New Mexico sky in the rockets' red glare.[91] A bully sight, indeed.

Chapter 10

★ ★ ★ ★ ★

VICE
PRESIDENT

*There is more work to be done in the Governorship in
two years than in the Vice-Presidency in four.*

Roosevelt began his second year as governor riding high after a
string of legislative victories and a wave of enthusiastic public
approval. The Rough Rider mystique had given him nationwide
popularity. On his trip to attend the first reunion of his regiment,
he had bathed in adulation. "All the way out and back I had a
perfect ovation from the people along the road—as much so as if
I had been a presidential candidate," he wrote to a friend in
Washington, D.C.[1] As usual, Roosevelt claimed to fear "the bitch
goddess success" and labored to downplay his rising national
political fame by predicting the worst. In homage to William
James's pessimism, Roosevelt wrote, "Life is a long campaign
where every victory leaves the ground free for another battle, and
sooner or later defeat comes to every man, unless death forestalls
it."[2] His egocentric ability to claim modesty grandiosely is evident in a response to a feeler from a literary friend about assum-
ing the editorship of *Harper's Weekly.*

Of course, I cannot be an editor while I am Governor, but with my ways of looking at politics, and my unwillingness to refuse to say the truth because of its effect even upon bodies of decent voters, it is only a question of one year or another when I shall have to leave politics, and then I might be able to do first-rate work in just such a position as editor of the *Weekly*.[3]

With such boundless self-confidence, it is hard to take seriously his repeated insistence that he had no political ambitions, as in this letter to his Maine hunting guide, Bill Sewall, at the start of his second year as governor: "I am proud of being Governor and am going to try to make a square and decent one," he wrote. "I do not expect, however, to hold political office again, and in a way that is a help, because the politicians cannot threaten me with what they will do in the future."[4]

The governor of New York found himself frequently touted by pundits as presidential timber. "He is more than a presidential possibility in 1904, he is a presidential probability," wrote William Allen White, editor of the *Emporia Gazette*.[5] "Heaven forbid!" Roosevelt wrote to Lodge.

Lodge, however, urged that he aim for a wholly different position: vice president. Lodge argued it would return Roosevelt to the national arena of Washington, D.C., rescue him from what he often referred to derisively as the "parochial politics" of Albany, and position him for a presidential run in 1904. Roosevelt brushed aside Lodge's suggestion for two practical reasons. First, President McKinley's current vice president, Garret A. Hobart, was not making any signals that he intended to step down. Secondly, less believably, Edith had reminded her husband of their precarious financial situation. He'd have to take a pay cut for the vice presidency, which paid $8,000 annually compared to the governor's salary of $10,000, and (in those days) had no free housing. "The money question is a serious one with me . . . My means are very moderate. Thanks to the fact that the idiots of the magazines now wish to pay me very large prices for writing, on account of my temporary notoriety, I was enabled to save handsomely last year and will be enabled to do so again this year."[6] Yet financial concerns had never stopped him in the past.

On November 22, 1899, Vice President Hobart died suddenly of heart disease. Roosevelt issued a gubernatorial proclamation of grief on behalf of New Yorkers and ordered all American flags on public buildings to be lowered to half staff for three days, until Hobart's funeral on November 25. "He was a public servant of tried capacity and stainless integrity, who in his high office exerted an influence for good."[7]

Privately, of course, he immediately thought of himself. "It seems so difficult to accomplish even a little" in the vice presidency, Governor Roosevelt wrote to Lodge, "and I have encountered so much unreasoning stupidity and sinister opposition from men on whose support I should be able to count."[8] Yet he apparently shut the door quickly on the job, at least in his own mind. He wrote Bamie a curt dismissal: "I have told Cabot that I did not want, and would not take, the Vice-Presidency; also Platt. The latter assures me that he is for me for a renomination [as governor]; and that there will be no opposition to me."[9] There is a long tradition in American politics of acting coy precisely when one most wants to become a candidate. Roosevelt had broken other traditions, by campaigning for himself on a whistle-stop tour, but this one mattered more. Still, the will-he-or-won't-he scenario became an ever-present background noise to Roosevelt's second year as governor and, eventually, an irritating distraction. Roosevelt's name had surfaced immediately in the speculation over who would fill the vice presidency on the Republican ticket with McKinley as the 1900 presidential campaign approached. Since 1800, just one vice president, Martin Van Buren, had been elected directly to the presidency, and Roosevelt knew it. He was only forty-one years old and had the luxury of waiting for a politically opportune moment for the White House. He enjoyed national exposure as governor of New York—a position of prominence in the nation's most influential state that made him an automatic contender for future campaigns. Roosevelt was also a doer who thrived on the closure of completing a task, and he had plenty of unfinished business on his gubernatorial agenda. Yet Washington beckoned, and Albany could not compete. Boss Platt was based in Washington, too, although they conducted their political business at Platt's hotel in Manhattan. "Compared with the great game of which Washington is the center, my own work here is parochial, but it is interesting too," Roosevelt wrote to John Hay, the U.S. Secretary of State. "So far I seem to have been fairly successful in overcoming the centrifugal forces always so strong in the Republican Party."[10] Perhaps, at some level, it was not a question of Roosevelt's seeking office or a particular office's seeking him; it was an entire country that sought him as he sought it. On the cusp of the new century, America was roiled by new conflicts and old ones with new intensities: capital versus labor, new immigrants versus established residents, rural areas versus urban ones, farming versus industrialization, blacks versus whites, and liberals versus conservatives. Editor William Allen White said of Roosevelt, "He is the coming American of the twentieth century,"[11] and he proved correct. Roosevelt appealed across many lines, as a progressive but a Republican, an aristocrat but an antimonopolist, an easterner beloved in the West.

Roosevelt certainly wasn't waiting for political and literary glory to find him. He worked harder than sometimes seemed humanly possible; he "had Napoleon's qualities," in the words of English writer and critic Christopher Morley. He continued his prodigious literary output while running the state. Each morning, Roosevelt carried down to his study in the Executive Mansion a stack of notes, reference books, and a sheaf of research material. Once settled, the governor began to dictate the text of his biography of Oliver Cromwell to his secretary, William

Loeb—with "hardly a pause."[12] Roosevelt couldn't afford writer's block; he was under contract with *Scribner's* to publish the Cromwell biography serially between January and June 1900. He also continued to contribute to *Century* magazine, including a piece at the beginning of that year titled "Fellow-Feeling as a Political Factor." Later that year, the Century Company published *The Strenuous Life: Essays and Addresses.* Meanwhile, Roosevelt's voracious reading of newspapers, magazines, and the latest books made him keenly aware of the prevailing sentiments in mainstream American culture. Roosevelt used his second annual message to the Legislature to promote the upcoming Pan-American Exposition in Buffalo and to make fin-de-siècle pronouncements.

> The beginning of a new century would seem to be a peculiarly fitting time to gather up the results of investigation and experience in the preceding century by which to help the peoples of North and South America up to a higher plane—physical, mental and moral.[13]

Roosevelt had a deep understanding of history and its complexities, and he looked back over the receding nineteenth century as a time of profound change. Even more profound challenges lay ahead for America as a new and growing world power. He wrote his friend the English diplomat Spring-Rice toward the end of 1899,

> Do not think me a mere optimist. I do not pretend to be able to see into the future . . . most certainly there are evil forces at work among us in America. The diminishing birth rate among the old native American stock, especially in the north east, with all that that implies, I should consider the worst. But we have also tremendous problems in the way of the relations of labor and capital to solve. My own belief is

that we shall have to pay far more attention to this than to any question of expansion for the next fifty years, and this although I am an expansionist and believe that we can go and take our place among the nations of the world, by dealing with the outside problems without in any way neglecting those of our internal administration . . . While the future is dim and uncertain . . . in any event we have all of us got to face it and do the best we can, with conditions as they actually are.[14]

Roosevelt's second-year agenda as governor carried over much from the previous year, but with a new initiative: to take on the trusts as a way of reining in the runaway power and control of large corporations in collusion. "Our laws should be so drawn as to protect and encourage corporations which do their honest duty by the public and to discriminate sharply against those organized in a spirit of mere greed, for improper speculative purpose," Roosevelt said, throwing fuel on the fire raging between himself and Platt over the Republican Party's symbiotic relationship with business.[15] Roosevelt proposed mandatory public reporting for corporate profits, reaffirmed a state's right to take action to break up a monopoly, and pushed for strong accounting and reviews to make certain that corporations paid an appropriate amount of taxes. Roosevelt concluded his message with a call for restraint on fiscal matters and legislation run amok with a proposal to place a limit on advancing pet projects through private legislation. "I again call the attention of the Legislature to the undesirability of cumbering our statute books with a mass of needless legislation," he said. "I also again call the attention of the Legislature to the need of economy [and the Legislature's] steady tendency to increase expenses beyond the limit that can be afforded by the taxpayers."[16]

Roosevelt's gubernatorial message received extensive press coverage, of course, but the governor was angry about the way the

New York Mail & Express secured an advance copy, broke the press embargo, and printed the details of Roosevelt's message the night before he delivered it on January 3. Roosevelt fired off a furious letter to the editor of the *Mail & Express* on January 4 and followed it up the next day with a letter to Frank W. Mack, superintendent of the Associated Press, in New York City. "It flagrantly violated faith," Roosevelt complained to Mack about the *Mail & Express,* a member of the AP's cooperative wire service. "I suppose that what we shall have to do is sometime when there is an important bit of news for New York to give it out specifically to the individual correspondents of the other New York evening papers and not to the *Mail & Express.* As I say, the Associated Press has always treated me so fairly that I do not want to do anything that will embarrass them." Beneath this typed text, Roosevelt scrawled a personal appeal to Mack in a postscript: "I am in a quandary; won't you give me your advice? By character and experience you are peculiarly fitted to advise me in this matter."[17]

Of course Roosevelt used the press more than vice versa. In November 1899, before the speech, Roosevelt had written John Huston Finley, editor of both *Harper's Weekly* and *McClure's,* to propose a discussion of the canal matter, which he said he would focus on in detail in his annual message. "But I want you to know the whole thing from the inside," Roosevelt wrote, "both for the sake of *Harper's Weekly,* and because, my dear sir, you are the type of man with whom I wish to work."[18] A second letter on the same day dangled unprecedented access and cooperation. "Would you not like to come up here and see the whole administration of the State Government from the inside with a view to writing an article upon it? You shall see the head of every department and as much of the work as you want."

Roosevelt had an ability to ingratiate himself with people of every class and station, quickly establishing a connection that left a lasting, at times rhapsodic, impression. One political observer whom Roosevelt had invited to the Executive Chamber to discuss pending legislation recalled his meeting with the governor in florid detail. "He had walked over to the window and lifted one foot upon the sill, and he put around me an arm which had the strength of a grizzly bear's paw and the tenderness of a woman pressing her babe to her heart."[19]

The seduction and flattery were balanced by intense anger and grudges, and against Tammany and machine hacks of his own party he was able to indulge the latter. Lou F. Payn, the insurance superintendent who had tried to undercut Roosevelt's 1898 gubernatorial campaign, a scoundrel Elihu Root once called "a stench in the nostrils of the people of the State of New York,"[20] was serving a three-year term that finally expired. Payn had been a swindler as a lowly politico in Columbia County, where he was accused of "voting tombstones." In a classic proud-pol response, he quipped, "We always respect a man's conviction," claiming he cast the ballots in the way the deceased would have done.[21] The fact that the rascal Payn was a Platt machine operative and backed by a majority of the Senate did not dissuade Roosevelt from turning him out of a job now. Platt recalled that Roosevelt "threw Payn out of his job so quickly as to send that official to me with a cry: 'I warned you that this fellow would soon have you dangling at his chariot wheel. You would not believe me. He has begun by scalping members of your Old Guard. He'll get you soon, too, soon.'"[22]

Platt's recollection in his autobiography was slightly hyperbolic when he stated that Roosevelt acted in "whirlwind fashion to clean house in Albany" right after his inauguration. In reality, the process had been a year in the making and Roosevelt expended plenty of political capital to clash with the Easy Boss. He began with Payn, whom Platt battled to retain. "Just at present I am in a horrid fight over the Payn business," he wrote to his brother-in-law, William Sheffield Cowles. "All that I reasonably can do to stay in with the organization I will, but I will not renominate Payn because he is a crook pure and simple."[23] Platt was hardly the only defender of Payn. Billy Barnes, the Republican boss of Albany County and editor of the Albany *Evening Journal*—whose personal animosity for Roosevelt led to frequently critical editorials against his governorship—wrote in outraged tones. And as the stooge of corrupt insurance companies and unsavory businessmen, Payn was the darling of many of New York's business titans, including Jay Gould. A rising chorus of objection to Roosevelt's unilateral dismissal of Payn was squelched, however, with revelations that finally pinned on Payn the corrupt dealings of which he had long been suspected. The State Trust Company of New York City was discovered to have made $5 million worth of improper loans, one of them for $435,000 to Lou Payn—who couldn't hide the windfall behind his $7,000 annual salary. Behind the scenes, Roosevelt now maneuvered to protect the McKinley administration and his old friend, Elihu Root, then McKinley's Secretary of War. As legal counsel for the State Trust Company, Root had approved the $435,000 payoff to Payn. Roosevelt buried a report of the state banking superintendent that was critical of Root's role in the scandal.

Roosevelt tried to fill Payn's position with Francis J. Hendricks of Syracuse, after consulting Platt, of course, rather than rubbing the boss's nose in his defeat. Hendricks was a conciliatory candidate since he was an organization man and Platt's recommendation for superintendent of public works the previous year. Hendricks didn't get that job, however, and now he would not accept Roosevelt's offer of insurance superintendent, saying he was too busy with business affairs—an indirect slap from Platt. In the end, after a thrust-and-parry duel with Republican Party Chairman Odell, Platt acquiesced and Hendricks accepted. Roosevelt greeted his major political victory with his most famous apothegm, according to biographer Henry Pringle. Roosevelt wrote to Henry L. Sprague, an ally in the fights of his

Assembly days: "I have always been fond of the West African proverb: 'Speak softly and carry a big stick, you will go far.'"[24] Roosevelt's confidence had morphed into a cocky arrogance. He had "won out in a very ugly fight" over Boss Platt. "With his [Payn's] retirement I am able to say that I have carried out every pledge I made on the stump and that my entire household is composed of clean, able men, who are doing their work . . . in accordance with ideal standards," Roosevelt wrote to an old friend.[25]

Two weeks after Roosevelt's reform-minded message to the Legislature, Platt, who had been plotting behind the scenes to yank the Rough Rider from the governor's bully pulpit, made his first public statement in support of Roosevelt for vice president after a breakfast meeting with Roosevelt and Odell in Manhattan. Roosevelt shot right back with a denial that same evening following speeches at the Union League Club dinner and at the Boone & Crockett Club banquet. There was a tradition in city machine politics of sending useless or annoying men to state jobs, to get them out of the way of the real business of politics. Platt undoubtedly hoped the vice presidency would be a graveyard far from New York, and by tradition, it should have been.

As governor, Roosevelt had watched the wave of support that swept him into the highest office in the state slowly recede as his victorious charge up Kettle Hill became a distant memory and he took a series of unpopular stands in which he alternately disappointed Independents for being too partisan, angered Platt for being too autonomous, and irritated Mugwumps for failing to consult them. After less than two years, Roosevelt found himself occupying a thin isthmus politically. Looking ahead, Roosevelt envisioned three possible routes that might eventually lead to the White House: renomination as governor, his first choice, which Platt was now trying to block; secretary of war, removed from his equation when McKinley appointed Root; and vice president, a consolation prize that would be death for a reformer of his energies but nonetheless a job with a steady paycheck, as his wife often reminded him. On the battlefield and in the corridors of power, Roosevelt always prepared a plan of retreat, but with one of his options killed and another mortally wounded, he was running out of choices. Further clouding the picture was Republican National Chairman Mark Hanna, who loathed Roosevelt, didn't want him on the ticket with McKinley, and was plotting to close off the escape route of the vice presidency.

Platt, meanwhile, gave mixed messages. "I want to get rid of the bastard," the boss told a crony. "I don't want him raising hell in my state any longer. I want to bury him."[26] Those sentiments echoed the vociferous objections Platt was receiving from insurance executives and leading business owners to renominating Roosevelt as governor for the 1900 campaign (terms were two years instead of four in that era). Also, Roosevelt had served Platt's purpose of tapping the Rough Rider's popularity to reinvigorate the Republican Party after the canal scandal and, with his machine returned to top form, no longer needed the headache of repeatedly clashing with a freethinking governor. Yet in his *Autobiography,* Platt claimed the high road:

> I believed that the death of Vice-President Hobart had weakened the Republican party, and that some strong, popular personality should be added to the ticket to be nominated in 1900; and I firmly believed that the virile personality of Mr. Roosevelt, supported by his war record in Cuba and by his administrative record as Governor of New York, would add great strength to the national ticket that year.[27]

Hokum was never stronger in a politician's autobiography, despite all the competition. Roosevelt wrote Lodge with only slightly more honesty, deceiving himself rather than the public:

He [Platt] is I am convinced, genuinely friendly, and indeed I think I may say really fond of me, and is personally satisfied with the way I have conducted politics; but the big-monied men with whom he is in close touch and whose campaign contributions have certainly been no inconsiderable factor in his strength, have been pressing him very strongly to get me put in the Vice-Presidency, so as to get me out of the State.[28]

There were several months to go before the national convention in Philadelphia. After Vice President Hobart's death the previous November, McKinley, in typical fashion, moved slowly on naming a replacement. Privately, he had asked both Senator William B. Allison of Iowa and Elihu Root to become his running mate, but both turned him down—Root holding out for secretary of war.

At home, Roosevelt fancied himself the center of the family's attention, despite his long absences. In the spring, he took time to visit his sister Corinne, as she lay sick with an attack of grippe. "He seemed to bring the whole world of spring sunshine into the room with him, and before I could say anything to greet him he called out: 'Pussie, haven't we had fun being Governor of New York State?'" she recalled.[29] Roosevelt's letters to his old Washington friends, Bellamy and Maria Storer, were full of newsy items from the home front:

Ted is stiff today, the result of playing tackle in a football match yesterday, in which, as he remarked to me, 'there was a good deal of slugging,' and as he was the smallest and lightest boy on either eleven, he got his fair share of knocks. Kermit is so chivalrous and tender and protective towards his mother . . . Ethel is a real little mother. Archie and Quentin are as cunning as they can be, though they still do not know any more than the innumerable Guinea pigs which the little boys are at present breeding in the cellar.[30]

That wasn't the extent of the Executive Mansion menagerie. The Roosevelts also had dogs, including a terrier named Jack and a Chesapeake Bay retriever called Sailor Boy. There was also Eli the macaw, "with a bill that I think could bite through boiler plate, who crawls all over Ted, and whom I view with dark suspicion," Roosevelt wrote to a friend. "And Jonathan, the piebald rat, of most friendly and affectionate nature, who also crawls all over everybody; and the flying squirrel and two kangaroo rats."[31] Although friends considered Roosevelt as rambunctious and playful as his children, he knew when to assert himself as a mature parent and a father who would impart life lessons. He closely scrutinized the performance of his children in school and would discipline them when they lost sight of the goals he had set for them. He wrote letters of reprimand to them at boarding school, typified in a stern note to Kermit at Groton. "I do not like your having so many black marks," Roosevelt wrote. "Please try to see that the number is never again as great as it was the last month. As you know, I have much sympathy with some kinds of mischief, but there are other kinds with which I have no sympathy at all."[32]

Of course, much of Roosevelt's belief that he was at the center of domestic matters or the primary influence on his children's behavior was a happy illusion. When he was at home, Roosevelt had a knack for immersing himself in the moment and making each child, family member, and guest feel like the most important person in the world. Yet his political, literary, and sporting careers kept him away for a large number of days each year. Edith was the family anchor. "She managed TR very cleverly without his being conscious of it," said Roosevelt's cousin, Franklin Delano Roosevelt. "No slight achievement as anyone will concede."[33]

Roosevelt also made time to follow his own advice regarding the strenuous life. He continued to take long, vigorous walks around Albany and into the hinterlands of the Pine Bush a dozen miles west of the Capitol. He also studied and practiced wrestling based on the advice given in a book by Hugh F. Leonard, an instructor at the New York Athletic Club. Given a copy of Leonard's wrestling book, Roosevelt wrote the author that he was "delighted with it and would not miss it for anything . . . Wrestling gives more concentrated exercise in less time than any other [sport]."[34]

Roosevelt pushed his son Ted to excel in all of his physical and mental pursuits. It became an unspoken expectation that Ted would re-create the ruggedness of his father in miniature, and the boy tried mightily to live up to that difficult assignment. Roosevelt proudly wrote to his brother-in-law about one incident at Albany Academy:

> Ted came home in his soldier suit with a puffed eye, which he explained to me as due to a battle with a "Mick" who had sneeringly referred to him as a toy soldier. I am afraid Ted did not fight wholly in accordance with the rules of the prize ring, for he explained that when he got the Mick down, he sat on his chest and pounded his head until the Celt agreed that he had had enough.[35]

The spring was consumed with maneuvers and worries about the vice presidency. Platt began planting statements in the press about how Governor Roosevelt was the best possible candidate for vice president and was creating momentum for his putative campaign. Roosevelt continued to decline the drafting effort, saying privately that he would not accept the nomination for vice president under any circumstances, although Lodge and other advisers were urging him to reconsider and he played coy by not issuing a Sherman statement to the press, meaning he had

not made an irrevocable statement about not accepting if nominated and not serving if elected. "I knew how stoutly he had opposed the offer, how he had met delegation after delegation with
the frank avowal that he could serve the party and the country
better as Governor of New York and I knew that was his ambition," Jacob Riis wrote. "He was fully advised of the plans of his
enemies to shelve him in the 'harmless office' of Vice-President,
and how they were taking advantage of his popularity in the
West and with young men on the ticket."[36] It was a battle Roosevelt wanted to win, for the vice presidency was widely agreed
to be useless and, although Root and Allison had turned it
down, Theodore had been in a similar position before with the
second-tier appointment of Civil Service commissioner and
making something substantial out of a passed-over and lightly
regarded job.

An utterly determined Platt declared, "Why, Roosevelt
might as well stand under Niagara Falls and try to spit the water back as to stop his nomination [for vice president]."[37] President McKinley remained neutral, at least publicly, and avoided
being drawn into a press statement about whom he preferred as
his running mate. As the convention approached, Governor
Roosevelt had the greatest name recognition and an overwhelming edge in public support compared to others mentioned for the
post: former secretary of the interior Cornelius Bliss; John D.
Long, former secretary of the navy and Roosevelt's onetime boss;
and Roosevelt's lieutenant governor, Timothy L. Woodruff. In
public speeches and private correspondence, Roosevelt was consistent in his low opinion of the office of the vice president. "It
would be an irksome, wearisome place where I could do nothing," Roosevelt wrote to Bamie. "My being in politics is in a
sense an accident; and it is only a question of time when I shall
be forced out. The best thing I can do is to strive to get the position in which I can do the most work, and that position is
surely the Governorship."[38]

Despite the distraction of Platt, Roosevelt managed to shepherd some significant legislation into law. On March 14, an amendment to the stock corporation law was approved that required the stock books of all corporations to contain full information and to be open for inspection by stockholders and creditors—as he had urged in his annual message. Two weeks later, he created the Palisades Parkway, which provided land, funds, and a commission of management for the interstate park along the Palisades. On April 2, Roosevelt approved a law that prohibited commercial prizefighting across New York State. Two days after that, he signed the Tenement House Commission Act, a law close to his heart, which gave the governor power to appoint a commission to examine tenement houses and their condition in large cities and to report to the next Legislature a code of tenement house laws. In April, Roosevelt learned that Platt had made the governor one of New York's four delegates-at-large to the Republican National Convention in Philadelphia in June. Roosevelt could have blunted the vice-presidential draft movement by declining and remaining in Albany, two hundred miles away, but he did not take that clear-cut step or any other that took himself out of contention as McKinley's running mate. Platt anticipated that Roosevelt's enormous popularity, his galvanic presence, and the desire of delegates would carry him right into the vice presidency during the convention. Roosevelt put up a front of not budging and reiterated that he would refuse any attempt to make him vice president.

In May, five weeks before the convention, Roosevelt went to Washington, D.C., to make a final stand. He planned to inform President McKinley and National Chairman Hanna that he would not accept the nomination. Instead, the two men told a stunned Roosevelt that he was not being considered for the office. Secretary of State John Hay mocked Roosevelt's overzealousness in a letter to a friend: "Teddy has been here: have you heard of it? It has been more fun than a goat. He came down with a sombre resolution thrown on his strenuous brow to let McKinley and Hanna know once and for all that he would not be Vice President, and found to his stupefaction that nobody in Washington except Platt had ever dreamed of such a thing."[39]

Roosevelt was meeting with Platt, Odell, and other Republican leaders in New York on a weekly basis as jockeying for the vice presidential opening heated up. His plate of gubernatorial duties was full. Roosevelt had a lot of work left if he wanted to complete a comprehensive overhaul of the state's forest, fish, and game regulations and the new revisions to the law passed on February 19. "Delirious with activity" is how the educational reformer John Dewey once described him, and the phrase never seemed more apt.[40] Roosevelt pushed for protection of public health with several important initiatives in the spring of 1900. He issued an emergency order in March that mandated clean drinking water for residents in Rensselaer, a city directly across the Hudson River from Albany, and set tough punishments for violators. He was the guiding force behind establishment of a state tuberculosis hospital in the Adirondacks—his own lung problems had been helped by clean mountain air during summer vacations in his youth—near where Dr. Edward Livingston Trudeau had established a tuberculosis sanitarium in Saranac Lake a few decades earlier.

In political affairs, the governor often felt as if there was nobody he could depend upon. "I wonder if you realize how very much alone I am here in the way of advisers upon whom I can trust," Roosevelt wrote to a political supporter from Newburgh after a lunch with Odell and before an evening speech at Trinity Episcopal Church on "Good Citizenship."[41] He worked alone— most brilliantly, when he was campaigning—whether it was for reelection as governor or for a vice presidency he claimed not to want. He now picked up the pace on speeches. Roosevelt delivered more than twenty major addresses across New York State and beyond in the three months preceding the Philadelphia convention. On February 21, in New York City, Roosevelt tested his vocal cords by giving three speeches in one evening: to the Harvard Club, Buyers Association, and Press Club. The following day, Roosevelt was in Buffalo to give two more speeches, to the Daughters of the American Revolution and the Saturn Club dinner. Although Roosevelt made noise that he was not interested in the vice presidency, the topics and venues of his speeches belied that resistance.

In the run-up to the Republican National Convention, Roosevelt reversed his take-no-prisoners approach and tried to play it safe and preserve political capital. One messy matter that erupted into an upstate versus downstate controversy involved the highly publicized "water steal" of Ramapo by New York City officials. During the summer of 1899, the Municipal Board of Public Improvements of New York quietly inked a forty-year contract with the Ramapo Water Company to furnish the greater metropolitan area with 200 million gallons of water daily at a cost of about $5 million annually. This contract was overseen by William Dalton, a former butcher appointed commissioner of water supply by Tammany Hall. A press investigation revealed that several prominent Republican politicos had a financial stake in the Ramapo Water Company. William Randolph Hearst and something called the Vigilance League, as well as several New York newspapers, led the charge to cancel the water contract and disband the company. They accused Tammany leader Croker and Republican boss Platt of cutting a deal that enriched their organizations while defrauding New Yorkers through exorbitant and unnecessary fees. None of the dirt flung at political leaders directly stuck to Roosevelt, but he couldn't sit out the fray. Three bills taking action against the Ramapo Water Company were stalled in committee, and newspapers began taunting Roosevelt to get involved to resolve the controversy. "I suppose I have got to begin to take an active part in the Ramapo business," a reluctant Roosevelt wrote to Seth Low on March 7. "But the theory and the practice of our Constitution do not always coincide, and if in the course of the next ten days definite action is not taken in the legislature, I suppose I shall have to try to help."[42] Roosevelt tried to find a private resolution by meeting with the legal counsel for the Ramapo Water Company in Albany on February 17. Meanwhile, the goading continued in the papers, including this dig in the *New York Tribune:* "A year ago he rushed into the arena a perfect hero, to prevent the same band of jobbers from strangling franchise taxation. It cannot be that he is less opposed to such methods now. It cannot be that he lacks courage for such a fight."[43] In his second annual message to the Legislature, Roosevelt had urged that "New York must own its own water supply" and, moreover, that "legislation permitting private ownership should be annulled." Now, he had to act.

Finally, Croker, Platt, and therefore the Legislature, worked out a compromise that fell short of entirely repealing the Ramapo Water Company's 1895 charter, a settlement that preserved veto power for the state comptroller—a critical safeguard against unchecked "Ramapo jobbers." Roosevelt discussed these agreements at a March 10 breakfast with Odell and Platt, and the governor took credit for setting "the Organization all straight on the Ramapo business, but it took blood to do it."[44] The stopgap measure bought time for Roosevelt until there was a critical mass of opposition in the Legislature and the charter of the Ramapo Water Company was repealed in 1901. Construction began on a permanent water system, the Ashokan Reservoir and Catskill Aqueduct, in 1907. It was completed after a decade at a cost of more than $150 million.

At the end of March, Roosevelt wrote a letter to a political supporter that was both an assessment of his record as governor and a contemplation of his future:

> It would be impossible for me not to go to the National convention. It seems to me that I can help the party more

by running for Governor of New York State than by being a candidate for the Vice-Presidency, and we simply have got to make the people at Washington and elsewhere understand it. Personally I have kept out of the rows with the Machine very satisfactorily and my administration has literally been as clean as a hound's tooth, as I said it would be; and I can say conscientiously that it has been the most efficient and best administration that I have seen during the twenty years that I have followed New York politics.[45]

Jacob Riis described returning to Albany many years after Roosevelt's time as governor. He reminisced with a veteran state official who had observed many governors pass through, hardly leaving any trace. Not so with Roosevelt and his legacy, as the official recounted:

The place seemed dreary when he was gone. But I know that he left something behind that was worth our losing him to get. This past winter, for the first time, I heard the question spring up spontaneously, as it seemed, when a measure was up in the legislature: "Is it right?" Not "Is it expedient?" Not "How is it going to help me?" Not "What is it worth to the party?" Not any of these, but "Is it right?" That is Roosevelt's legacy to Albany.[46]

Of course, he wasn't gone yet. The Republican National Convention opened in Philadelphia's Exposition Hall on June 19. Edith had returned from a tour of Cuba and Puerto Rico and, with a newfound interest in global and political affairs involving her husband, decided to attend. "I am expecting to have a good time," she told Judge Alton B. Parker, a dinner guest at the Executive Mansion a few days before she and her husband left for Philadelphia on June 16. Parker predicted a draft scenario: "Just a bit late, you will see your handsome husband come in and bedlam will at once break loose, and he will receive such a demonstration of applause from the thousands of delegates as no one else will receive . . . You will see your husband unanimously nominated for the Vice-President of the United States," the judge said.[47] "You disagreeable thing," she said playfully, reiterating her husband's stock denunciation that he was not interested in becoming McKinley's running mate. Although at heart a private person, Edith was not immune to the overwhelming press attention. A *New York World* correspondent wrote of her, "She is not according to artistic standards a beautiful woman, but she would be at any time an interesting one."[48] Roosevelt also brought his sisters along to the convention. "One of the most endearing characteristics of my brother was his desire to have my sister and myself share in all of his interests, in his glory, or in his disappointments, and so, when the convention at Philadephia met, we hurried to his side to be near him during the fray," Corinne wrote.[49]

As Hanna gaveled the convention to order, Roosevelt arrived as if with a cavalry charge, sporting a Rough Rider–type, wide-brimmed black hat amid a sea of straw boaters. "Gentlemen!" one pundit announced. "That's an acceptance hat."[50] Roosevelt remained consistent in his lack of interest in the vice presidency, but his statements were becoming less convincing. His old friend Nicholas Murray Butler, a Columbia professor who had been sent ahead by Hanna to head off any Roosevelt draft rumblings, joined with Edith to draft a disavowal for Roosevelt to issue that would once and for all shut down a nomination drive. Instead, Roosevelt rewrote the statement in such a way that left the door wide open for his nomination by the Philadelphia delegates.

In view of the revival of the talk of myself as a Vice-Presidential candidate, I have this to say. It is impossible too deeply to express how touched I am by the attitude of those delegates, who have wished me to take the nomination . . . I understand the high honor and dignity of the office, an office so high and so honorable that it is well worthy of the ambition of any man in the United States.[51]

Much further down in his remarks, by the time Roosevelt got around to mentioning that he thought he could be most effective for the national ticket by remaining governor, it was obvious for all to see that he protested too much. Roosevelt was not simply swept up by the vanity of realizing the delegates were squarely behind him, ready to choose him as their nominee. He had learned practical politics as an assemblyman. Platt had the power and control of a machine that could outmaneuver him on the state level and block his renomination as governor. That left only the path to the vice presidency, which tipped to Roosevelt's advantage when none of Hanna's proffered candidates met with McKinley's approval.

Roosevelt's backpedaling was enhanced when the chairman of the Iowa delegation, LaFayette Young, withdrew the name of Iowan Jonathan Dolliver and placed Roosevelt's name in nomination for vice president. The convention crowd of eighteen thousand erupted into cheers and wild applause as the hall mysteriously bloomed with Roosevelt banners and placards. The band struck up "There'll Be a Hot Time in the Old Town Tonight" as delegates jumped up on chairs, tossed their hats in the air, and screamed. The governor of New York sat rigid in his seat, his jaw clenched, eyes expressionless, among his state's section of delegates, momentarily unable to admit even to himself what he had been inexorably edging toward for months. Eventually, Roosevelt caught a glimpse of Edith in a box high above the floor. "With just a little gasp of regret, Mrs. Roosevelt's face broke into smiles," a *New York World* correspondent wrote.[52]

For a man who supposedly would not stoop to conquer the vice presidency, he did not hesitate to accept the nomination. He ascended to the podium in Exposition Hall the following morning to deliver, with his towering oratorical skills, an acceptance speech for the ages.

> We stand on the threshold of a new century big with the fate of mighty nations. It rests with us now to decide whether in the opening years of that century we shall march forward to fresh triumphs or whether at the outset we shall cripple ourselves for the contest . . . Our nation, glorious in youth and strength, looks into the future with eager eyes and rejoices as a strong man to run a race.[53]

Roosevelt was swiftly and raucuously nominated with every single delegate's vote—except his own. The final tally was 926 for McKinley and 925 for Roosevelt. Despite voting against himself—a final show of anti-Platt autonomy—the vice-presidential nominee rode the crowd's fervor. Roosevelt accepted the nomination and tried to put a positive spin on the reversal of his heretofore adamant position in a letter to Lodge three days after the convention ended:

> I am completely reconciled and I believe it all for the best as regards my own personal interests and it is a great load of personal anxiety off me. Instead of having to fight single-handed against the trusts and corporations I now must take pot luck with the whole ticket and my anxiety on behalf of the nation is so great that I can say with all honesty there is none left.[54]

He was trying to convince himself that the nomination was a spontaneous groundswell of support and that he had not been "shelved" by Platt. Gamely, he told Hanna, "I am as strong as a bull moose and you can use me to the limit."[55]

Taking Roosevelt at his word, Hanna pushed him at an unprecedented pace on the campaign trail. If Roosevelt had been a cyclonic state assemblyman in Albany, he was nothing short of a hurricane now. A *New York Times* correspondent calculated the extent of Roosevelt's crisscrossings of the country and figured he covered 21,209 miles and addressed a total of 3 million people. On a single speaking swing toward the end of the campaign, Roosevelt visited 24 states and 567 towns, in which he delivered a total of 673 speeches.[56] The vice-presidential candidate traveled by train and coach in an era when transportation difficulties were common, and he overcame the lack of speaking amplification by drilling the crowd with his high, reedy voice as forcefully as he pounded palm with fist. His schedule on July 2 was typical. He spoke in a single day at Newkirk, Holliday, Lawrence, Osage City, Emporia, Florence, Peabody, and Newton, Kansas. Reporters were won over completely and hoodwinked. One said that Roosevelt never displayed a dark side in private and his public persona appeared to be genuine. "It is the unanimous judgment of the reporters who made the long journey with Governor Roosevelt that at no time on the long trip, under no circumstances, did he show the possession of a bit of off color," a correspondent noted.[57]

In late September, the western part of the campaign swing took Roosevelt through Wyoming, with stops in Rawlins, Laramie, and Cheyenne. A pack of cowboys rode to his appearances and Roosevelt made a point of personally greeting each one, pinning a Rough Riders button on the jacket lapel of each. "It was wonderful to see how quickly those boys were at ease in his presence," observed a Wyoming newspaper publisher.[58] "Children and animals understand quickly the character of a man. I have never known a person a horse seemed more pleased to carry than Colonel Roosevelt."

A contingent of Rough Riders who accompanied Roosevelt were once pressed into action beyond mere political ornamentation. On September 26, there was a brief and unsuccessful attack by bandits upon Roosevelt's campaign train at Cripple Creek, Colorado. The Rough Riders quickly repelled it. Roosevelt was never in danger and the incident did not alter his busy schedule. Roosevelt's campaign entourage filled a special train with six sleeper cars, a diner, and a private car occupied by the candidate. When the train stopped at the Daley Ranch in Cheyenne after nightfall, despite the darkness, Roosevelt bounded onto the platform and shouted, "Come on, boys, let us go and take a ride!" Roosevelt, his entourage, and several onlookers saddled horses along with a group of newspaper reporters. Roosevelt led this horse caravan to a dinner of elk, venison, sage chickens, and luxurious accompaniments. Dinner was followed by a torchlight parade and Roosevelt's stump speech at the Cheyenne Opera House with "perhaps the largest campaign meeting ever held in Cheyenne."[59]

Roosevelt's national recognition brought a lot of gossip, speculation, innuendo, and mudslinging from his opponents. One of the rumors that came to the fore after years of persistent background whispering was the allegation that Roosevelt had a drinking problem. Anonymous sources claimed Roosevelt consumed vast quantities of alcohol on hunting trips and the campaign trail. He angrily refuted these attempts to smear his character.

> I have never been drunk or in the slightest degree under the influence of liquor. I do not drink either whiskey or brandy, except as I shall hereafter say, as I drink it under the direction of a doctor; I do not drink beer; I sometimes drink light wine. I have never drunk a highball or a cocktail in my life . . . At home, at dinner, I may partake of a glass or two glasses of white wine with dinner. At a public dinner, or a big dinner, if they have champagne I will take a glass or two glasses of champagne.[60]

If Roosevelt needed a cautionary tale to teach him about the ravages of alcoholism, he had to look no further than his brother,

Elliott, whose years of heavy drinking devastated his family and eventually killed him. Yet the rumors of Roosevelt's own drinking persisted and made good newspaper copy. The issue was explored in a lengthy article titled "Rum, Rumor and Roosevelt," by Frederic Sturdevant, a correspondent for the *New York World*. "It is such an infamous lie that it is a little doubtful to know what to do regarding it," Sturdevant quoted Roosevelt as saying.[61] He noted that Roosevelt did not dispute an addiction to coffee. Roosevelt also drank large quantities of milk with a simple meal of bread and tea after dinner. It was Roosevelt's frenzy as a speaker that led some wags to suggest he performed at the rostrum under the influence of alcohol. All the rumors were unfounded. Roosevelt needed no artificial stimulants, Henry Adams once dryly suggested: "Theodore is never sober—only he is drunk with himself and not with rum."[62]

Fueled by coffee, Roosevelt's manic energy on the campaign trail helped reelect President McKinley with a plurality of 850,000 votes and 292 electoral votes compared to 150 for William Jennings Bryan and Adlai Stevenson. Republican Party Chairman Mark Hanna, who made no secret of his contempt for Roosevelt, told McKinley, "Your duty to the country is to *live* four years from next March."[63] Hanna had been opposed to Roosevelt's nomination from the outset. The two had clashed repeatedly over Roosevelt's lack of deference to the chairman's position and the Rough Rider's outspoken contempt for McKinley's hesitation over invading Cuba. Months earlier, Hanna had been overheard trying to raise an alarm about the reform governor in a fabled warning: "Don't any of you realize that there's only one life between that madman and the Presidency?"[64]

The madman and President McKinley took the oath of office on March 4, 1901. "Theodore took the oath with great dignity & looked so young and handsome," Edith wrote in her diary.[65] At a presidential reception afterward, Edith accompanied her husband, leaving son Quentin with Roosevelt's valet, Pinckney:

nobody could be expected to watch all of the vice president's off-spring single-handedly. Apparently Ted roamed freely after the president's soiree and swigged down two glasses of what he thought was sparkling water. "Happily it had no effect whatever which speaks volumes either for Ted's head or the President's champagne," his mother wrote.[66]

There was no hangover to sleep off from Roosevelt's two years as governor. He had not allowed Tammany or Republican spoils-men to loot the state, as earlier generations had done in rolling over for Boss Tweed. He had stood up to Boss Platt, although somewhat less after the stridency of his first year at the Executive Mansion. More important, the most popular man in America—lifted into the governor's seat on the strength of his glorious Cuban campaign—had actually carried out the people's business as he had promised in the breakneck campaign of 1898. Governor Roosevelt had signed into law more strict licensing regula-tions for textile factories; increased the power and scope of factory inspections and prosecuted safety violations; and regulated the hours of drug clerks and state workers to an eight-hour shift. He had made significant headway in fighting to stiffen labor laws and closing loopholes for employers' liability. Fearless in the face of powerful corporations, Roosevelt had championed the fran-chise tax bill and fought business collusion regardless of the hit his party took in campaign donations. Above all, he had grown into a leader who possessed grace under pressure and made the act of governing New York State seem like a matter of simple com-mon sense. "All I want to do is cautiously feel my way to see if we cannot make the general conditions of life a little easier, a little better," he said.[67]

Beyond offering temporary relief to the grim working condi-tions facing families in New York tenements and clearing up other labor abuses, Roosevelt produced visionary legislation that improved future workplace standards for generations to come. In the area of conservation, he professionalized the state's Forest,

Fish, and Game Commission and increased protected forest preserves in the Catskills and Adirondacks. Moreover, he spearheaded preservation of the Palisades, pushed for the cleanup of municipal water supplies, and insisted on stringent regulations in the production of food products.

And, despite his occasional acquiescence to the authority of Boss Platt in his second year as governor—angling for organizational support of his renomination—Roosevelt saved the best for last. In late December 1900, during his final days as governor, Roosevelt stuck it to the Easy Boss by firing Platt appointee Peter M. Wise as president of the State Commission on Lunacy on account of "gross impropriety" for using state labor to build his own icehouse business. He also dumped Tammany's Asa Bird Gardiner as New York district attorney on December 22, 1900, on charges of "malfeasance, misfeasance and misconduct."

Although he was looking ahead to the vice presidency and a homecoming of sorts in Washington, Roosevelt assessed his time as governor in his *Autobiography* thus: "For my two years I have been able to make a Republican majority in the Legislature do good and decent work and have prevented any split within the party." It wasn't the most resounding boast for a victory tour, but, in the fractious world of Albany politics, where things fall apart, Roosevelt had made sure that the center would hold.

Chapter 11

⭐ ⭐ ⭐ ⭐ ⭐

RIDE TO THE PRESIDENCY

*I have about as heavy and painful a task put upon me
as can fall to the lot of any man in a civilized country.*

Once the excitement of the marathon campaign was finished, Roosevelt's prediction of the boredom he expected to find in the vice presidency quickly became true. Socialites in Washington anticipated the return of "the fabulous Roosevelts," who brought a rare level of energy and excitement with them. Edith had enjoyed earlier years in Washington, but she expressed ambivalence about coming back to the nation's capital and remained particularly wary of her husband's growing dejected and restless in "such a useless and empty position."[1] The vice president himself suggested that the largely ceremonial position "ought to be abolished."[2] The idle time and boredom weighed heavily upon Roosevelt, who welcomed the colorful diversion of visits from his Rough Riders—so full of mischief and mayhem that Edith said she felt that she and her husband were "parents of a thousand very large and very bad children."[3] The Rough Riders usually arrived only when they were in a bind and needed a special favor or handout from their beneficent colonel. Often, they'd appeal by letter.

"Dear Colonel. I write you because I am in trouble. I have shot a lady in the eye. But Colonel I did not mean to shoot that lady. It was an accident, for I was shooting at my wife."[4]

Roosevelt was flooded with letters and in-person appeals by his Rough Riders for government positions or other special assistance. Their colonel tried to take care of as many requests as possible—his loyalty to his men was unwavering ——but he began to feel a twinge of guilt over abusing his office. "I have asked so many favors for men of the regiment that I am positively ashamed to go to a single department in Washington, and above all, to the War Department," Roosevelt wrote.[5]

Roosevelt's new role did serve to temper some of his wildness and to put on hold his pursuit of dangerous, thrill-seeking sports. He was willing to adopt the cautious, sedentary lifestyle appropriate to the office. He was called upon, after all, to preside over the Senate for five consecutive sessions beginning the day after his swearing-in. At the time of his inauguration, Roosevelt received a letter detailing Wintie Chanler's most recent riding injury. "They talk of me leading a 'strenuous life,'" Roosevelt wrote to Chanler. "Good Heavens, I would not face the risks you continually run for a good deal! My days of chamois hunting and fox hunting are over."[6] As a man who had reached his forties, Roosevelt was preparing to enter middle age, and he looked back sentimentally to past adventures, writing to Chanler that they were men "who have warmed both hands before the fire of life."

The vice president wasn't the only one feeling uncertain about his new position. Gripped by debilitating attacks of anxiety, Edith began eating less and dropped a noticeable amount of weight. Moving out of the governor's mansion in Albany and uprooting her family once again left Edith in a melancholy mood, because she had fashioned a comfortable and happy life for herself and her children in the state capital. Theodore, at least, enjoyed far more time for leisure pursuits than he ever had before in elective office. In the winter after the campaign, with his duties as a lame duck governor winding down, Roosevelt embarked on an ambitious seven-week Colorado hunting trip for cougar and lynx in the dead of winter over dangerous terrain with horses and tracking hounds. Edith wrote with unmasked bitterness to her sister Emily that Theodore had left her with all the kids while he went off to stalk big game.

By August, nine months into his vice presidency, Roosevelt felt unchallenged and restless for adventure. He spent extended periods at Sagamore Hill, where he had ample time to contemplate the family motto carved above a doorway on the west side of the house: *Qui plantavit curabit.* "He who has planted will preserve." In Roosevelt's mind, though, his political career was withering on the vine in his trifling position as McKinley's understudy. He made a second, two-week hunting trip to Colorado. The pretext was a political speech, but his primary objective was to spend as much time as possible hunting and fishing in the Rockies. Roosevelt was traveling and giving more speeches as vice president than he had as governor; it was one of his tactics for staving off boredom. The new job was looking to Theodore more and more like a political dead end. Perhaps Platt had shelved Roosevelt, after all. "[It is] very unlikely that I shall be able to go on in politics after my term as Vice-President is over, and when I have gone out of public life I shall be able to do very much less in trying to steer straight young fellows of the right type, who ought to take an interest in politics," he wrote.[7]

Desperate to feel he still possessed political vitality, Roosevelt considered no diversion too small to warrant his attention. He accepted an invitation to be initiated into the Masons at a lodge in Oyster Bay. He made trips to New York City and to Harvard to deliver requested speeches. He accepted an invitation to speak at the twenty-fifth anniversary of Colorado's statehood in early August. He willingly took assignments as McKinley's stand-in when the president could not attend functions—McKinley often remaining behind to tend to his sickly wife.

Later in August, Roosevelt traveled to Springfield, Illinois, for a political dinner and then, on the way back, gave an address at the opening of the state fair at Minneapolis.

As Roosevelt's backers laid the groundwork for a presidential candidacy in 1904—with the planning done quietly so as not to anger President McKinley—both the vice president and president embarked on late-summer speaking tours. The lecture circuit was a way for Roosevelt to connect with voters in a forum that was, in theory, not overtly political. Roosevelt had accepted an invitation to speak on September 6, 1901, at a reception of the Vermont Fish and Game Club in Burlington and at a private party hosted by Vermont Lieutenant Governor Nelson W. Fisk on Isle La Motte in Lake Champlain. It was a region Roosevelt knew from summer vacations during his youth in the Adirondack Mountains to the west. Roosevelt was keen to rekindle his fond memories of the North Country and to share his love for the northern woods with his wife and children. The Isle La Motte lecture was the conclusion of a series of talks Roosevelt had scheduled to dovetail neatly with an Adirondack family vacation. Early September was an ideal time in the Adirondacks, after the summer tourists had gone and long after the bothersome blackflies had finished their springtime assault.

By late summer, meanwhile, President McKinley, sworn in to a second term six months earlier, had completed an extensive tour of the western states. McKinley was greeted by enthusiastic crowds along the way, and the tour was a success, except for his wife's getting sick in San Francisco. After she recovered, the McKinleys returned home to Canton, Ohio, to rest before traveling to New York State in September, where the president was scheduled to deliver a major address at the Pan-American Exposition in Buffalo. Because of his wife's illness, McKinley had sent Vice President Roosevelt in his stead several months earlier to open the exposition on May 20. Roosevelt had spent that night in Buffalo with Edith and his daughter Alice, and had written to his remaining children a letter describing how impressed he had been by the exposition. Edith was especially enamored of the Saint-Gaudens statue of Sherman and Cecilia Beaux's painting of the Gider children. Theodore took the opportunity to reconnect with his interest in Indian rituals and joined in a powwow, while Alice couldn't get enough of the exotic dromedaries and literally "rolled around on the backs of camels," according to her step-mother.[8] The exposition became a small city that never slept, thanks to the engineering marvel of new electrical circuits that drew power from the hydroelectric plant at Niagara Falls and turned night into perpetual daytime. The most gaudy bauble on this unprecedented, illuminated, twenty-four-hour pleasurescape was the Edison Company's shimmering Tower of Light.

Essentially, the exposition was an attempt in the era after the Spanish-American War to display unity and harmony among the Americas—North, South, and Central—and to show off techno-logical advances. It was also an opportunity for the United States to boast about its reach and flex its developing global muscle. Having rescheduled their appearance after missing the opening, the McKinleys arrived on September 5 to great fanfare for what was christened President's Day. John G. Milburn, president of the exposition committee and a prominent Buffalo attorney, hosted the McKinleys. Mrs. McKinley had recovered from her illness, but her constitution was aggravated again when the train carrying the couple suffered a bizarre accident. Soldiers alongside the track fired a twenty-one-gun salute, and the percussion of the blasts shattered the windows of their railroad car. Mrs. McKin-ley's fear and agitation were not quickly calmed. One year earlier, authorities had uncovered a plot to assassinate the president. Investigators tracked down a group of anarchists in Paterson, New Jersey, who had already been linked to the murders of two statesmen in Europe as part of a scheme to kill six leaders from around the world. The anarchists had placed President McKinley fifth on their hit list.[9]

Despite Mrs. McKinley's protests and the misgivings of his Secret Service officers, the president—whose presence had drawn more than a hundred thousand people, the largest crowd of the exposition so far—would not be cowed. He decided to go ahead and speak in the Esplanade. His theme was the power of peaceful commerce. "Commercial wars are unprofitable," he said. The onetime booster of protective tariffs preached a new kind of global market. "The period of exclusiveness is past," McKinley said, urging a policy of commercial reciprocity and free trade. Realizing that the U.S. economy needed new markets to continue to grow, McKinley noted that "the expansion of our trade and commerce is the pressing problem."[10]

The next day, September 6, President McKinley and his wife took a trip to Niagara Falls. Afterward, Mrs. McKinley was sent in a separate carriage to the house of their host, John G. Milburn, to rest. She tried once more to dissuade her husband from going ahead with his plan for an afternoon reception and public receiving line. Even McKinley's secretary, George Cortelyou, tried to convince the president to cancel the reception because of the large crush of well-wishers anticipated. McKinley, who loved to connect with common folks, would not hear of it. After his wife departed, the president, Milburn, and Cortelyou returned to the exposition grounds and its ornate Temple of Music to greet a large gathering of McKinley's supporters. The president held something of a record for the large number of hands he could shake in a single minute—approaching one per second. He never seemed to tire of this press-the-flesh routine. The crowds this afternoon were huge and pushed in fiercely to meet McKinley. Courtelyou grew concerned about the situation; he felt that McKinley had not been assigned adequate protection given the size of the crowds. Some off-duty Buffalo police officers had been hired for crowd control, but Cortelyou wanted more personal bodyguards assigned to the president. He got reinforcements in the form of an army corporal and ten men from his unit. "Keep your eyes open and watch every man approaching the President," Cortelyou told them.[11]

Political violence was in the air. Just a few days earlier, Vice President Roosevelt had been threatened by Christopher Miller, an apparently demented man in Berlin, New Hampshire. A thirty-one-year-old French-American using an alias, Miller had been making statements to the effect that he had a mission to kill Roosevelt, according to a report in the *New York Herald.* Miller attempted to purchase a train ticket to Washington, D.C., but found no direct route and instead took a train to New York City, where he was arrested on September 11. At the time of his arrest, Miller carried an explosive device known as a "railroad torpedo," as well as books on anarchism printed in French and German and fifty-five dollars in cash. Miller was taken to Bellevue Hospital, where physicians and psychiatrists deemed him criminally insane.[12]

On that fateful Friday, September 6, another deranged man attracted to anarchism and brooding over social injustice in the United States took his place in the receiving line to meet McKinley. The line had grown so long that Cortelyou had had the doors to the reception area closed, but the anarchist made it into the room. He was "pleasant-faced and mild-mannered" and had "a kind and intelligent face," according to Louis L. Babcock, an exposition marshal and a witness.[13]

Leon Czolgosz considered it his duty to assassinate McKinley. He said he was inspired by the speeches and writings of the radical Emma Goldman. Czolgosz carried a .32-caliber Iver Johnson revolver. It was a hot and humid late-summer day, and the crowd fanned itself and mopped brows with handkerchiefs. Czolgosz concealed the revolver in a handkerchief draped over his gun hand, as if his hand were wrapped in a dressing for an injury. Czolgosz waited in line, biding his time, and pressing up close to hide the handkerchief. When Czolgosz drew close enough to reach out and shake McKinley's extended hand, the anarchist fired the pistol twice from point-blank range into the abdomen of the president. One bullet struck the button of McKinley's waistcoat and was deflected harmlessly. But the second hit between the second and third ribs, just right of the sternum, and ripped deep into McKinley's stomach. The bullet's downward trajectory created a life-threatening, front-to-back abdominal perforation.[14]

Several guards lunged at Czolgosz and wrestled him to the ground. McKinley crumpled in shock, his sagging body propped up by Secret Service men, the hemorrhaging gut wound searing with pain. The crowd set upon Czolgosz, prepared to rough him up. McKinley managed to utter a plea not to savage his attacker. As Cortelyou bent down to listen, McKinley whispered, "My wife—be careful, Cortelyou, how you tell her—oh, be careful!" The hall was cleared and the room secured by a phalanx of soldiers and policemen.[15] "I done my duty," the assassin wrote in a signed statement taken by a police clerk after the shooting. "I didn't believe one man should have so much service and another man should have none."[16]

The gravely wounded president was taken away by motor ambulance. At 4:18 P.M., eleven minutes after the shooting, he arrived at the exposition's simple first-aid station. It was ill-equipped for serious medical emergencies and certainly not outfitted for major surgery. Dr. Herman Mynter and Dr. Eugene Wasdin of the United States Hospital Service were the first to arrive. The pair of physicians, although not surgeons, examined the president's wounds and determined that an immediate emergency operation was needed. They elected not to test recently invented X-ray machinery on display at the exposition. Instead, Milburn telephoned for Dr. Matthew D. Mann, a gynecologist and the closest specialist to a surgeon available, who arrived at 5:10 P.M. After conferring with the other medical personnel on the scene, at 5:20 P.M., the doctor administered ether to McKinley so that an operation could commence. Led by Mann, the physicians cleaned the bullet wound and stitched the damage to the stomach and abdominal walls as best they could. The single bullet that deeply perforated McKinley's abdomen was not recovered. While their patient was still asleep from the effects of ether, the medical team decided to transfer McKinley by motor ambulance once more, to Milburn's house on Delaware Avenue in Buffalo—where the president's wife, and the world, awaited a report on his condition.[17]

On that Friday morning, Vice President Roosevelt had been at the Van Ness House in Burlington, Vermont, at the reception sponsored by the Vermont Fish and Game Club. Afterward, Roosevelt had joined a group of notable citizens and cruised on Lake Champlain. They made their way to the estate of Vermont Lieutenant Governor Nelson W. Fisk at Isle La Motte, so Roosevelt could make a speech. But just before his time came to speak, Roosevelt was interrupted.[18]

A phone call from Buffalo had reached Fisk, who brought over Senator Redfield Proctor. The two leaders conferred before deciding they must give the vice president the news right away. They pulled Roosevelt aside and beckoned him into the library. Fisk said the wife of J. C. Butler, general manager of the New England Telephone Company in Burlington, Vermont, called in the second leg of a relay to alert them to a wire news bulletin reporting that President McKinley had been shot by an assassin at the Pan-American Exposition in Buffalo. "Stunned amazement" was the vice president's initial reaction.

Soon another call came to Fisk's house that confirmed the assassination attempt. Roosevelt asked Proctor to tell the rest of the party outside on the lawn the news before the vice president dictated a telegram. An update followed reporting that McKinley's wound was not fatal. Roosevelt gathered himself and made an announcement from the veranda to reassure the group before he boarded a yacht owned by Dr. W. Seward Webb, a Rutland Railroad trustee. Roosevelt's party motored south on Lake Cham-

plain, crossed the channel and docked at Burlington on the eastern shore. It was eight o'clock in the evening and growing dark.
A special train was waiting in the gloaming, an ominous hulk
and a harbinger of a historic train journey to come.[19]

As he prepared to board the train, Roosevelt's entourage plied
the vice president with political advice. He was counseled to stay
clear of Buffalo, given the delicate matter of succession, and to go
instead to Washington, D.C., or Sagamore Hill and await further
news on McKinley's condition. Roosevelt discarded their advice,
though, and decided to do what in his heart felt right. Even
though they'd had their differences politically, Roosevelt was
genuinely fond of McKinley and he wanted to make a personal
visit.

Roosevelt shared none of McKinley's feelings of forgiveness
toward the assassin. "It was in the most naked way an assault not
on power, not on wealth, but simply and solely upon free government, government by the common people, because it was government and because it yet stood for order as well as for liberty,"
Roosevelt wrote.[20] Three days later, in a letter to Lodge, Roosevelt railed against the anarchistic climate of the times that led
to the unthinkable act on the part of Czolgosz, whom he called a
"Judas-like dog" and wanted to punish in the most severe way. In
less than four months, the assassin would be executed in the electric chair at New York State's Auburn Prison and buried in a
grave with fifteen bushels of quicklime and a sulfuric acid mix-
ture to dissolve all remains swiftly. Roosevelt expressed incre-
dulity to Lodge about how "it did not seem possible that just at
this time in just this country, and in the case of this particular
president, any human being could be so infamous a scoundrel, so
crazy a fool as to attempt to assassinate him." Roosevelt issued a
call to battle against anarchy, the authors of its nihilistic tracts,
and those who supported the philosophy of lawlessness: "We
should war with relentless efficiency not only against anarchists,
but against all active and passive sympathizers with anarchists.

Moreover, every scoundrel like Hearst and his satellites who for whatever purposes appeals to and inflames evil human passion, has made himself accessory before the fact to every crime of this nature, and every soft fool who extends a maudlin sympathy has done likewise."[21]

Roosevelt was alluding to Hearst's newspapers' relentless attacks on President McKinley's policies and on the politician personally. Hearst's *Journal* reached a nadir in its barrage against McKinley in April 1901, shortly before McKinley's second inauguration, by editorializing in favor of political assassination. "If bad institutions and bad men can be got rid of only by killing, then the killing must be done."[22] The scorn heaped upon Hearst was swift and overwhelming from Republican-affiliated newspapers, which blamed the publisher's editorials for spurring the assassin to pull the trigger against the president. Groups began boycotting Hearst's papers and the publisher received death threats. Hearst tried to extract himself from the maelstrom by claiming he pulled the offensive editorial after reading it in the first edition—an assertion made long after the fact and unverified. In any event, he had sent an emissary to apologize personally to President McKinley after the editorial generated a controversy.[23] But the damage was done. One magazine editorialized, "As for Hearst personally . . . he will always remain the degraded, unclean thing that he is, shunned by every honest citizen, and for whose wandering feet there shall be no resting place where the American flag rises and falls on the breeze."[24] The scandal forced Hearst to retreat from electoral politics and dogged the publisher the rest of his days. There was no love lost on the part of Roosevelt, who had despised Hearst since Harvard. "He preaches the gospel of envy, hatred and unrest," Roosevelt wrote of Hearst. "He cares nothing for the nation, not for any citizen in it . . . He is the most potent single influence for evil we have in our life."[25]

The president had at first seemed to come through the operation well. His pulse improved, the pain subsided, and he slept comfortably through the first night. The president's condition was stable and improving slowly by the time Roosevelt arrived. McKinley's wife had been allowed to visit with her husband, as had Cortelyou and just a few others—and then only briefly. As McKinley's fever abated, his kindly and convivial spirit returned. He enjoyed speaking with visitors and ignored doctors' orders to remain quiet. "It's mighty lonesome in here," McKinley said of his sequestered recovery room. Just outside Milburn's house, a large number of reporters milled around an impromptu press encampment with tents pitched across Delaware Avenue as they waited for hourly news updates. Telegraph operators sent their dispatches out across the United States and around the world. Straw was laid in a thick mat along Delaware Avenue to muffle the clip-clop of horses' hooves from the steady stream of people arriving and departing in carriages.[26]

Roosevelt was joined at the president's recovery room by Hanna, who came from Cleveland; Colonel Myron T. Herrick, who had planned to host the president at his home in Cleveland; Judge William R. Day from Canton, Ohio; and members of McKinley's cabinet. Reports coming from the press corps outside the Milburn house shifted from grim and guarded to cautiously optimistic as McKinley continued to gain strength. Members of McKinley's political inner circle were encouraged when the president asked how his speech at the exposition had been received around the country and abroad. His strength had improved and his mind was alert. "More and more satisfactory" was Monday's bulletin carried in newspapers worldwide. By Tuesday, McKinley had passed "the most comfortable night since the attempt on his life," according to dispatches. "Continues to gain" was Wednesday's optimistic synopsis.[27] The remarkable rebound by McKinley was obvious not only to his relieved physicians but to those close aides allowed access to his recuperation room. Roosevelt wrote to Lodge on Monday, September 9, "Things are now progressing so favorably that I believe the President will be out of danger before you receive this letter."[28] Yet the bullet was still deep in McKinley's gut. The bullet track and the lodged lead, in fact, invited infection. But on the scene, with the president increasingly verbal, his vice president declared to a friend in a September 10 letter, "Thank Heaven, the President is now out of danger."[29]

Roosevelt remained wary of the perception of appearing overeager and hovering at the wounded president's bedside. The second in line to the White House decided that a four-day vigil was sufficient, especially given McKinley's apparent rally. Roosevelt left Buffalo on September 10 "with a light heart" and the belief that he had accomplished his natural duty without paying a political price. It seemed entirely appropriate for the vice president to rejoin his family on a delayed Adirondack vacation. Roosevelt stopped briefly in Oyster Bay before riding a train north to the Adirondacks. Roosevelt's private secretary, William Loeb, left the train in Albany and remained at the state Capitol in order to be in direct communication with McKinley's staff in Buffalo. Roosevelt continued one hundred miles northward from Albany alone, arriving at the small train station of North Creek on the morning of September 11 without an entourage or any attendant hoopla. Roosevelt had arranged for local coachman Frank Kelly to pick him up at the train station and to transfer his luggage to a one-seat buckboard driven by Kelly.[30]

Roosevelt was bound for the Tahawus Club, where he had booked his family for a stay. Edith badly needed a getaway, given the travails of her brood. Archie was just getting over a bout of chicken pox and Edith had to care for her children while suffering the itch and discomfort herself, or at least a psychosomatic version of the disease. Alice, returning from a stay with a friend, required hospitalization for a painful abscess in her jaw and two loosened front teeth, probably suffered in an accidental kick at a dance. Edith rushed Alice to Roosevelt Hospital in New York City—it helped to have a hospital named in honor of Theodore's philanthropist father—and received immediate treatment. Edith overruled doctors who wanted to remove Alice's teeth, but recovery would be slow. Moreover, when her husband had returned from his Colorado hunting trip in August, he had been feeling sick with bronchitis. Illness enveloped Edith. Perhaps the most challenging patient was Quentin, who not only managed to stuff a mothball up his nose—requiring medical attention to remove it—but also had to be admitted to the hospital, to a room beside Alice, because of an infected ear. The cause was an errant pebble that was eventually removed.[31]

The invitation for the Roosevelts to the Tahawus Club was a special opportunity, since the converted mining camp was not open to the public. It was a destination for sportsmen whose membership bought them private, unsurpassed hunting and fishing opportunities on 105,000 acres of prime wilderness owned by the McIntyre Iron Works. It was the first of its kind in the Adirondacks, an exclusive fish-and-game club that catered primarily to wealthy outsiders. The Roosevelts were guests of the club's founding president, James MacNaughton, an Albany physician, who had married one of ironworks owner McIntyre's daughters, Caroline. The vice president had a familial connection to the private club, since original Tahawus members included his uncles Emlen and James. "The choicest spot, to one who loves the woods, in the Empire State," a late governor, Charles Evans Hughes, said of the club.[32]

MacNaughton's camp at the Tahawus Club was known as MacNaughton Cottage, a large farmhouse-type structure of white clapboard, designed with rustic simplicity. The Roosevelt clan filled the space and then some. Roosevelt's six children—the teenage Alice, Theodore Jr., Kermit, Archie, Ethel, and Quentin—made quite an impression on the club's guests, who dubbed the lively brood "the little Indians." Ethel recounted the Tahawus vacation years later: "We were enjoying every minute of the day, its activities so different from those at home. We heard of the attack upon President McKinley with no real understanding of its implications in my case. Then our cup of happiness was full, for my father, ever the most beloved of companions, arrived. We always knew there would be expeditions and adventures."[33] One of the games their father encouraged was known as "chase the squirrel," which involved shinnying up the porch columns to the roof and then sliding off the cottage's shingles and swinging back onto the porch. The kids splashed through the upper Hudson River, collecting frogs, snakes, and other animals they kept on the porch. Ted spent his time hunting; he killed a two-year-old buck. Edith made time to socialize and was visited one day by an old Albany friend, Mrs. Dean Sage, who was staying nearby. Theodore was happy to reunite with his Adirondack guide, Noah LaCasse, who had led Roosevelt on wilderness trips when he was governor.

Roosevelt had been looking forward to climbing Mount Marcy, the highest peak in the state at 5,344 feet, and he organized the group that left the Tahawus Club on the morning of Thursday, September 12. His sister Corinne's sons, Beverley and Herman Robinson, both students at Harvard Law School, joined the hikers and guide E. J. Dimmock. Edith and all the children except four-year-old Quentin, who stayed behind at the cottage with a governess, set out on the first leg. Their progress was slowed by a cold, driving rain, which turned the trail to mud as they passed the Hudson River and Calamity Brook, where the route steepened sharply. They passed some loggers; woodsman John Galusha, introduced to the vice president, entertained them by singing a lumberjack tune, "The Bells of Long Lake." Roosevelt referred to these vigorous hikes with his family as "yarning." He still worried about President McKinley's recovery, but there was nothing like a good yarning with his little scamps to clear Roosevelt's head.

At Lake Colden, they canoed across to two primitive log cabins on the western shore of the lake. The soggy entourage was happy to take refuge in their dry shelter.[34] Ethel later wrote of the Colden trek that the rain "made us feel like really hardened woodsmen."

Early the next morning, after polishing off a hearty breakfast and bidding adieu to his wife, who went back down with a guide, Roosevelt and the others broke camp. LaCasse recalled that Roosevelt always dipped water from a stream and handed it up to his guide, so that LaCasse wouldn't have to bend down with a heavy pack when they stopped for a rest and a drink.[35]

By late Friday morning, while Roosevelt was churning upward toward the Marcy summit, President McKinley's condition plunged precipitously. A special train had been summoned for Senator Hanna and a group of McKinley's close confidants, when they were awakened by grim news. Physicians administered medication to counter the rapid weakening of the president's heartbeat, but it seemed to have no positive effect. McKinley knew that he had run out of options, and hope, by noontime Friday. He indicated to the medical team that their ministrations appeared fruitless. It was time for prayer, the president said through half-closed eyes. The nurses and doctors grew silent around McKinley's bed as he strained to mouth the words of the Lord's Prayer. Hanna and a few other close friends left the room when McKinley's wife arrived, assisted by the president's secretary. Cortelyou left the couple alone for their final moments together.[36]

Meanwhile, shortly before noon, Roosevelt, his guide, his children, and their cousins reached a clear summit after a rainy, foggy climb. Roosevelt, rarely at a loss for words, was uncharacteristically humbled by the magnificent view. "Beautiful country! Beautiful country." It was cold, though, so they started back down after a brief rest.

In Buffalo, President McKinley's room fell silent. He clutched his wife's hands. There was nothing more that medicine or his powerful friends could do. McKinley's breathing had grown weak and shallow and his life seemed to be slowly seeping out. "It is God's way," he murmured, almost inaudibly. Cabinet members, congressmen, and other friends stood vigil outside. His strength drained away throughout the late afternoon and evening.[37]

Roosevelt's private secretary, William Loeb, took a special train to the Adirondack station at North Creek—the closest stop to Mount Marcy—at the request of cabinet members. Just a few years earlier a long-distance telephone line had been built linking Buffalo, Utica, and Albany, and just recently a single-wire circuit had reached Aiden Lair, near North Creek, but only telegraph could reach remote sites near Mount Marcy.[38] While Roosevelt was climbing, Loeb placed an emergency call to the Tahawus Club's Lower Works clubhouse, the nearest phone, and asked for a message from Elihu Root to be relayed in person to the vice president: "President appears to be dying and members of the Cabinet in Buffalo think you should lose no time in coming." Given the remote wilderness location, nothing was simple. The manager of the club's Lower Works relayed the message by wagon to the Upper Works and David Hunter, superintendent of the Tahawus Club. Hunter chose guide Harrison Hall for his strength and stamina to deliver Root's verbal message and a sealed telegram from McKinley's personal secretary, George Cortelyou. Loeb stayed put at the North Creek train station. Edgy, he paced along the tracks. "It was mighty tiresome, but he wouldn't go farther than the American Hotel, which is in sight of the station," recalled Lee Waddell, a North Creek businessman who waited with Loeb. Gradually, they were joined near the station by a small knot of villagers who had caught wind of history in the making.[39]

Having successfully descended the steep rock face of the summit, Roosevelt discovered new muscle soreness in his quadriceps. He was happy to stop for a rest beside Lake Tear-of-the-Clouds when the most strenuous part of the descent was over. He was famished. The group unpacked the lunch. Roosevelt made quick work of the food and watched the gathering gloom of stormy weather approaching, while calculating how many hours it would take them to hike nine miles back to the trailhead and comparing that number with the handful of hours of daylight remaining. They didn't have much time to tarry.[40]

Lake Tear-of-the-Clouds, source of the Hudson River, is nothing more than a mere comma in the massive flank of Marcy, a slight indentation of rock almost hidden from view by stands of evergreen and the slope of the mountainside. On a clear day, the sight lines are obscured; someone approaching cannot be seen until almost at hand. On a foggy afternoon, such as that Friday, the man who came up the trail at nearly a gallop must have appeared wraithlike as he materialized out of the mists. Given the vice president's poor eyesight and the way his glasses became obscured by condensation in high humidity, Roosevelt had to squint to decipher the vision. The only sounds were of the runner's thudding footfalls and heavy breathing at the labor, which mingled with a whisper of water cascading down from the summit. Roosevelt's eyes were drawn to the man's hand, which clutched a telegram that flashed yellow in the grayness. "I felt at once that he had bad news," Roosevelt recalled in his *Autobiography*.

Just how bad was confirmed when Hall handed Roosevelt the telegram from Cortelyou. Instinctively, without discussion, Roosevelt packed up the remains of his lunch and shouldered his pack. The other hikers followed his lead. It was one-thirty in the afternoon when the group immediately set out down the trail to Tahawus.[41]

After long hours of hiking, as dusk enveloped him, Roosevelt arrived at the Upper Works clubhouse spent. It was about five thirty in the evening, and a numb exhaustion had set in on the trail over the final couple of miles. Roosevelt struggled to rouse his exhausted mind to the intensity of the moment, but there was no additional news awaiting him. News had not yet reached them that President McKinley was at death's door.[42]

By nine o'clock that night, with Roosevelt's strength revived by a meal and rest, there was still no word. The vice president was torn over what course to take. Since there had not been another message, he assumed that McKinley might have rallied again as before. But the afternoon telegram sounded grave. Should he stay or should he go?

"I'm not going to go unless I'm really needed," he told Edith as they prepared to retire for the night. "I've been there once and that shows how I feel. But I will not go to stand beside those people who are suffering and anxious. I'm going to wait here." He and his wife went to bed.[43]

The Roosevelts' sleep was interrupted in the middle of the night by a sharp knock at their door. It was MacNaughton. "They said it was absolutely imperative that my husband leave at once," Edith recalled. "He took a most terrifying ride in the middle of the night."[44]

The guides and others at the clubhouse, familiar with the terrain, urged him to reconsider the risky trip in darkness, with the rains making the route especially slick and dangerous. Roosevelt was the only person against putting off the start until dawn. He threatened to take a lantern and set out on foot if no driver stepped forward with a horse and coach. Hunter, the club superintendent, finally relented and offered to start out. The train station lay forty miles away, beyond the capabilities of any single team of horses without rest. The journey was planned in a three-part relay. Time was wasting and Roosevelt was anxious to set out. He gulped down a quick meal as Hunter hitched a big, bay horse that had been skidding logs all day to a light wagon, or buckboard. Hunter tied a lantern to the rear axle in a futile attempt at illumination. Ten miles of dark, pitted wilderness road stretched between the Upper Works and the next pocket of human settlement at the Lower Works.

The road was "full of mud holes and corduroy," Hunter later recalled. The corduroy—logs laid together transversely as a road across swampy ground—was overwhelmed by the wet weather.

"It had been raining a lot during the last few days and the road was in terrible shape," Hunter said. "So we started out down through the mud—plunk, plunk, plunk."[45]

In the memories of Adirondackers, Roosevelt's midnight ride to the presidency has taken on near-mythic proportions. Hunter's big bay was a powerful creature built for strength, not speed. Roosevelt kept urging Hunter to go faster, but the driver kept his speed within the limitations of the conditions and the abilities of the horse. The pair traveled alone. Averaging a steady five miles per hour, they reached the Lower Works roughly two hours after they set out. It was now just past two o'clock in the morning. Roosevelt drank coffee and made a telephone call. He was ready to go after a short pause. All the vice president wrote in the Tahawus Club register were these words: "Went up Mt. Marcy."[46]

Hunter passed off to Orrin Kellogg, who drove the second leg of the relay. He had a two-seat wagon and a team of horses that had not rested much, having already traveled twenty-five miles that day. Roosevelt got in the back seat with a rucksack, his only luggage. It was raining, so Kellogg offered the vice president an old raincoat to cover his legs from splashing mud churned up by the wagon wheels. "He talked but little," Kellogg recalled.[47]

Kellogg formed a lasting impression from his brief encounter with the vice president. "Mr. Roosevelt was a very plain man—he was plain spoken, and he wasn't any afraid," Kellogg said. "You could drive as fast as you'd a mind to and nothing scared him a bit." During their hours together in the middle of the night, talk eventually got around to their reaction to the assassin. "I think I'd have guzzled him first," Kellogg recalled Roosevelt telling him.[48]

Two and one-half hours later, Roosevelt reached Aiden Lair. Mike Cronin was anxiously awaiting to begin the third and final leg. Cronin had received a call from Loeb, who told Cronin that President McKinley had died. Loeb asked Cronin to keep that information to himself so that he could break the news to Roosevelt at the North Creek train station.[49]

Cronin had two horses hitched to a small, covered surrey, and as they prepared to set off, a man handed the driver a lantern, which he'd have to hold with one hand. Cronin hesitated over whether it was worth the trouble to take. "Here, give it to me," Roosevelt said firmly. They were off, a wan pool of light cast by the lantern glinting off Roosevelt's spectacles, dappling the reins, and etching the heaving horses' flanks.[50]

Sixteen more miles of treacherous mountain road stood between them and the special train awaiting Roosevelt's arrival at North Creek. The horses slid around tight turns and stumbled along a particularly slippery and steep stretch. Cronin reined in the team. "Oh, that doesn't matter," Roosevelt told his driver. "Push ahead!"[51] Cronin turned in a record time of one hour and forty-one minutes over the sixteen-mile stretch. It had been touch and go at times.[52] "I tell you, Mr. Roosevelt is the nerviest man I ever saw, and I ain't easily scared," Cronin told the *New York Herald*.

The first light of dawn softly suffused the roof of the station and the waiting train, wreathed in steam from its idling engine. Faces of townsfolk alerted to the historic arrival pressed to windows in shops and houses along Main Street. A knot of men stood on the station platform alongside Loeb. Cronin pulled his team of heavily lathered horses to a stop at the platform; Roosevelt hopped down and was immediately handed a telegram from Loeb. It was from Secretary of State John Hay, issued from Buffalo, and postmarked September 14, 1901. Roosevelt read the news for the first time: "The President died at 2:15 this morning." It was now just before five o'clock in the morning.

Roosevelt's midnight ride quickly became the stuff of legend in the Adirondacks, where Bill Hall, a great-grandson of Harrison Hall, composed this ballad:

With the North Creek Station 40 miles south
And with a dark road they moved on out.
His friends pleaded, "Please wait till morn."
"Give me a lantern, I'll go by foot," he scorned.
The clatter of hooves broke the still of night
And the midnight ride stood for what seemed right.
By 4:46 he arrived at the station.
It was clear by now he would address the nation.
His train was waiting to roll
To take Ted back to Buffalo.
He turned as he moved down the tracks
To bid farewell to the Adirondacks.[53]

"The Roosevelt Special," as the train was dubbed, and its crew had been waiting at North Creek for long, anxious hours by the time Roosevelt stepped down from Cronin's muddy carriage. Roosevelt's mackintosh was mud-spattered and his light-colored fedora hat was darkened by rain. A Delaware & Hudson Railroad executive personally oversaw the crew and offered his private car for the special. At 5:23 A.M., the engine puffed, rumbled a few times, and got under way "as fast as an old and experienced engineer could manage it." A crowd of correspondents had rushed out from the freight house, but Roosevelt made no statement, leaving the reporters to watch the rear of the train receding in the distance to the south.[54]

The crew made every effort to clear the track, but it was a heavily traveled stretch and Roosevelt's train had to wait on a few occasions until another train was shunted out of the way before the special could pass. The train's progress was not as intense from moment to moment as the buckboard relay, but there were moments of high drama. On a flat, open stretch south of Stony Creek, a handcar being pumped by two men appeared on the track. "The President's train was tearing along and the fog was still close to the ground," according to the *Albany Evening Journal* account. "The men on the handcar saw the engine just in time. They jumped and a minute later their car went hurtling into a ditch. There was a stiff jar, and the President, the superintendent and the President's secretary hurried to the platform."[55] Crew members checked but found no serious damage. Fifteen minutes later, the train was under way again.

Much was made in press accounts at the time that the "mile a minute" pace for the stretch from Saratoga to Albany amounted to a new speed record. Certainly, Roosevelt would have urged the engineer to proceed at the greatest haste. He had enough time while on the train to answer the stack of letters and telegrams that had been loaded on at North Creek. One was from his old Harvard friend, Wintie Chanler, who had fought in Cuba and tried to beat Roosevelt over many years in various forms of competition, but he now wished the new president only the best as he undertook the major challenges ahead.[56]

Waiting in Buffalo, none of McKinley's cabinet members on hand knew the proper protocol for replacing a president who died in office. The particulars of planning Roosevelt's swearing-in fell to Secretary of War Elihu Root, who was the senior cabinet member on the scene. In order to answer questions of procedure, Root sent an aide to the Buffalo Public Library to consult newspaper accounts of the induction of Chester Arthur as the twenty-first president on September 20, 1881, in his Manhattan home by a New York State judge the day after President James Garfield died of the effects of blood poisoning, following months of illness and complications from an assassin's bullet.[57]

A large crowd gathered at the Albany train station. The city's entire police force was called out for crowd control. Detectives moved vigilantly through the crowd, looking for suspicious behavior.[58]

At 7:56 A.M., the Roosevelt Special pulled into the capital city. All eyes were on the private car and the nation's next president, but he made no appearance. Loeb emerged briefly and told reporters there would be no press access. He had arranged for a formal suit in Roosevelt's size to be brought to replace the wet and mud-spattered clothes Roosevelt wore. Loeb also secured a top hat for Roosevelt to don for his date with political destiny.

There were no traces of the Theodore Roosevelt who had arrived in Albany nineteen years earlier as an impetuous young man full of Harvard arrogance, uttering the improbable pronouncement that he "intended to be one of the governing class." Tammany's thugs and machine bullies had hazed, intimidated, and run out of the Legislature plenty of cocky, dilettantish freshman assemblymen after a single term—sent them packing back to their fathers' Wall Street firms or law school or some other patrician pursuit. What had been a rather vague and aimless urge to honor his beloved father's memory and a convenient way to put off an uncertain career choice for Roosevelt was forged in the crucible of Albany politics into steely political ambition. Rejecting the advice of his family and their aristocratic friends to stay away from the coarse and low affairs at the state Capitol, Roosevelt instead discovered a transforming experience and his true calling amid the hurly-burly of the State Legislature.

His three years in the Assembly, more than any other experience in his early years, set the course for Roosevelt's incomparable career in politics. For the first time, he was exposed to a wide spectrum of the human condition and gained firsthand insights into the grim fate of the urban poor, the struggles of new immigrant groups, the deplorable working conditions of laborers—and how a responsive government could alleviate their suffering. It was a political education he could not have gotten anywhere else. His time in Albany was equally revelatory for how it opened a window onto the venality of politics and set Roosevelt on a path as reformer, corruption fighter, and trustbuster. It was also there, and in the Adirondack Mountains to the north, that a seed was planted and he began to grow into the towering conservationist that he would become.

The lessons he learned as an assemblyman were deepened during Roosevelt's governorship, and those cumulative experiences taught him how to work simultaneously as an outsider and an insider—how to use the press to bully the machine, but also how to work with the machine on things that mattered less, in order to get through the things that mattered more. Roosevelt had "come an awful cropper" in Albany, as he admitted, but his years as assemblyman in his early twenties and as governor in his early forties formed bookends to the narrative of his political development.

His mixed record on legislative issues and the way in which he gave in to the interests of corporations and capital to appease Boss Platt and a Republican organization to which he was beholden suggest that he was better suited for the presidency than for any other office, since only the commander in chief has such a strong "bully pulpit" (the phrase is his, of course) that he can campaign against Congress and the bureaucracy and still win. The former cyclone assemblyman remained a force of nature whose intellect, vitality, and depth of experience—he had single-handedly excelled in a variety of careers that would have taken a half-dozen merely brilliant men to accomplish—could not be contained in a job that was anything less than the highest in the land.

The train was now stopped in the city where he first "rose like a rocket" in politics, but it did not stay long. He was being thrust into a new trajectory. There had been press speculation that Roosevelt was to be sworn in at Albany. Large crowds had begun gathering at the train station before daybreak. That symmetry was not to be, though. The ultimate destination that pundits, political insiders, and friends had long ago predicted awaited Roosevelt in Buffalo at his inauguration as the twenty-sixth president.

In the railbeds along the Hudson River, looming in the shadow of the shimmering granite façade of the state Capitol atop State Street Hill, the special's engine was quickly uncoupled and, within a few minutes, another engine had been backed up. The coupling pin dropped into place. At 8:02 A.M., the train was off and bound due west.

"Nearly a thousand people saw the train leave Albany," according to the *New York World*. "But it quickly disappeared from their view. As soon as the houses of the suburbs were left behind the engineer opened the throttle wide and the new President flew across the country at the record rate of a mile a minute."[59]

NOTES

Unless otherwise noted, all TR letters cited in the text are from the Theodore Roosevelt Collection in the Houghton Library at Harvard University.

PRELUDE: PRACTICAL POLITICS

1. Nathan Miller, *Theodore Roosevelt: A Life* (New York: William Morrow, 1992), 10.

2. Harold Howland, *Theodore Roosevelt and His Times* (New Haven: Yale University Press, 1921), 20.

CHAPTER 1: BEGINNINGS

1. Theodore Roosevelt diary entry, undated, TR Collection, Harvard.

2. D. Willis James, "Theodore Roosevelt Memorial Meeting of the State Charities Aid Association," New York, February 15, 1878, 34.

3. Kathleen Dalton, *Theodore Roosevelt: A Strenuous Life* (New York: Alfred A. Knopf, 2002), 37.

4. Hermann Hagedorn notes, TR Collection, Harvard.

5. Interview with Mrs. Robert Bacon, Hagedorn notes, TR Collection, Harvard.

6. Theodore Roosevelt, *An Autobiography* (New York: Da Capo Press, 1985), 8.

7. Interview with LeGrand B. Marshall, Hagedorn notes, TR Collection, Harvard.

8. Dalton, 41.

9. Interview with Mrs. Young, Hagedorn notes, TR Collection, Harvard.

10. Roosevelt, *An Autobiography*, 4.

11. Copy of the book Bamie inscribed in 1871 "To Theodore Roosevelt Jr. From his sister Bamie" is in the private collection of Peter Scanlan, a noted TR collector who lives in Albany, N.Y.

12. Hagedorn notes, TR Collection, Harvard.

13. Theodore Roosevelt, "My Life as a Naturalist," *Natural History*, April 1980.

14. TR letter to William Randolph Hearst, April 15, 1916, in David Nasaw, *The Chief: The Life of William Randolph Hearst* (Boston: Houghton Mifflin, 2000), 249.

15. Douglas Brinkley, "Theodore Roosevelt and Conservation," address at the Theodore Roosevelt Association centennial symposium, Canisius College, Buffalo, N.Y., October 19, 2002.

16. Theodore Roosevelt diary entry, from the country, July 4, 1870, TR Collection, Harvard.

17. Interview with Mr. Putnam, Hagedorn notes, TR Collection, Harvard.

18. Interview with Mrs. Robert Bacon, Hagedorn notes, TR Collection, Harvard.

19. Theodore Roosevelt diary entries respectively from July 6, 1870, and September 10, 1870, TR Collection, Harvard.

20. From Daniel Henderson told to Henry Beech Needham, Hagedorn notes, TR Collection, Harvard.

21. Hagedorn notes, TR Collection, Harvard.

22. Roosevelt, *An Autobiography*, 5.

23. Author interview with National Park Service staff at Roosevelt birthplace, May 2002.

24. Roosevelt, *An Autobiography*, 6.

25. Ibid., 9.

26. Sylvia Jukes Morris, *Edith Kermit Roosevelt: Portrait of a First Lady* (New York: Coward, McCann & Geoghegan, 1980), 43.

27. Ibid., 47.

28. Anecdote from Mrs. Uriel Doane of West Harwich, Mass., Hagedorn notes, TR Collection, Harvard.

29. Louise Lee Schuyler, "Theodore Roosevelt Memorial Meeting of the State Charities Aid Association," 6.

30. Joseph H. Choate, "Theodore Roosevelt Memorial Meeting of the State Charities Aid Association," 17.

31. Charles Loring Brace, "Theodore Roosevelt Memorial Meeting of the State Charities Aid Association," 24.

32. Stephen O'Connor, *Orphan Trains: The Story of Charles Loring Brace and the Children He Saved and Failed* (Boston: Houghton Mifflin, 2001), 78.

33. Mrs. C. R. Lowell, "Theodore Roosevelt Memorial Meeting of the State Charities Aid Association," 30.

34. Choate resolution in "Theodore Roosevelt Senior: A Tribute," Union League Club, February 14, 1878, 22.

35. "The Roosevelt House Bulletin," spring 1926, 5.

36. George Emlen Roosevelt, "Theodore Roosevelt," *The Christian Endeavor World,* October 24, 1912, 67.

37. "President Theodore Roosevelt's Speech as President at Roswell, Georgia, on October 26, 1905," *Atlanta Constitution,* October 27, 1905.

38. Dalton, 26.

39. Ibid., 32.

40. Ibid., 27.

41. Ibid.

42. Choate, 19.

43. Dalton, 28.

44. William Henry Harbaugh, *Power and Responsibility: The Life and Times of Theodore Roosevelt* (New York: Farrar, Strauss and Cudahy, 1961), 8.

45. David M. Jordan, *Roscoe Conkling of New York: Voice in the Senate* (Ithaca, N.Y.: Cornell University Press, 1971), 239.

46. Jordan, 281.

47. Letter of Theodore Roosevelt Sr. to Joseph H. Choate, from New York, April 16, 1877. Private collection of Peter Scanlan.

CHAPTER 2: HARVARD

1. Edgar L. Murlin, Theodore Roosevelt official biography in *The New York Red Book: An Illustrated Legislative Manual* (Albany: James B. Lyon,1900), 31.

2. Carleton B. Case, *Good Stories about Roosevelt: The Humorous Side of a Great American* (Chicago: Shrewsbury Publishing, 1920), 9.

3. Richard Welling, "Theodore Roosevelt at Harvard: Some Personal Reminiscences," *The Outlook,* October 27, 1919, 366.

4. Daniel Henderson oral history, Hagedorn files, TR Collection, Harvard.

5. William Hooper oral history, Hagedorn files, TR Collection, Harvard.

6. Case, 9.

7. TR letter to Bamie, from Cambridge, October 28, 1877, TR Collection, Harvard.

8. Sylvia Jukes Morris, 55.

9. David McCullough, *Theodore Roosevelt Association Journal,* Summer 1980, TR Collection, Harvard.

10. Letter from Theodore Roosevelt Sr. to TR, September 28, 1876, TR Collection, Harvard.

11. Harbaugh, *Power and Responsibility,* 10.

12. Ibid.

13. TR letter to Bamie, from Cambridge, September 30, 1876, TR Collection, Harvard.

14. William Harbaugh, review of Lilian Rixey's *Bamie: Theodore Roosevelt's Remarkable Sister,* in *Book Week,* December 8, 1963.

15. McCullough, *Theodore Roosevelt Association Journal,* Summer 1980, 15.

16. TR letter to Bamie, from Oyster Bay, August 6, 1876, TR Collection, Harvard.

17. TR letter to Bamie, from Cambridge, December 11, 1876, TR Collection, Harvard.

18. TR letter to Bamie, from Cambridge, November 12, 1876, TR Collection, Harvard.

19. TR letter to Bamie, from Cambridge, December 11, 1876, TR Collection, Harvard.

20. Bradley Gilman, *Roosevelt the Happy Warrior* (Boston: Little, Brown, 1921), 30.

21. Noel F. Busch, *TR: The Story of Theodore Roosevelt and His Influence on Our Times* (New York: Reynal, 1963), 25, quoting William Roscoe Thayer.

22. President Charles William Eliot oral history, Hagedorn files, TR Collection, Harvard.

23. TR to Bamie, from Cambridge, January 22, 1877, TR Collection, Harvard.

24. Classmate John Woodbury oral history, Hagedorn files, TR Collection, Harvard.

25. Busch, 25, quoting William Roscoe Thayer.

26. William Roscoe Thayer quoted in Gilman, 35.

27. Classmate Henry E. Jackson oral history, Hagedorn files, TR Collection, Harvard.

28. Welling, 366.

29. Ibid.

30. Ibid., 367.

31. TR classmate William Hooper oral history, Hagedorn files, TR Collection, Harvard.

32. Gilman, 30.

33. Roosevelt, Theodore, "My Life as a Naturalist," 87.

34. Harbaugh, *Power and Responsibility,* 13.

35. Saul K. Padover, *The Genius of America: Men Whose Ideas Shaped Our Civilization* (New York: McGraw-Hill, 1960), 290.

36. Miller, 130.

37. TR diary entry, November 2, 1878, TR Collection, Harvard.

38. TR diary entry, June 17, 1878, TR Collection, Harvard.

39. Letter from TR Harvard classmate Dr. Samuel Delano (class of 1879) to Perry, in Ralph Barton Perry, *The Thought and Character of William James* (New York: George Braziller, 1954), 247.

40. Recollection of Harvard student Rollo Walter Brown, in Gay Wilson Allen, *William James: A Biography* (New York: Viking Press, 1967), vii.

41. Sylvia Jukes Morris, 57.

42. TR letter to Henry Minot, from New York, February 28, 1878, in H. W. Brands, ed., *The Selected Letters of Theodore Roosevelt* (New York: Cooper Square Press, 2001), 14.

43. TR to newspaperman Oscar K. Davis, in Busch, 15.

44. Quoted in *TR: An American Lion,* a documentary broadcast on the History Channel, January 19, 2003.

45. Harbaugh, *Power and Responsibility,* 7.

46. TR letter to Bamie, from Cambridge, March 3, 1878.

47. Sylvia Jukes Morris, 57.

48. TR diary entry, June 16, 1879, TR Collection, Harvard.

49. Sylvia Jukes Morris, 60.

50. Henry F. Pringle, "The Forgotten Woman in the life of T.R.," *Syracuse Herald-American,* July 24, 1960, reprinted from *American Heritage* magazine.

51. Thomas Lee, Alice's brother, oral history, Hagedorn files, TR Collection, Harvard.

52. Harbaugh, *Power and Responsibility,* 15.

53. "TR: An American Lion."

54. Harbaugh, *Power and Responsibility,* 14.

55. Gilman, 37.

56. Physical inspection report by Dr. Dudley A. Sargent, in Gilman, 34.

57. Harvard classmate Harry Champion Jones, oral history, Hagedorn files, TR Collection, Harvard.

58. *TR: An American Lion.*

59. John W. Burgess, *Reminiscences of an American Scholar* (New York: Columbia University Press, 1934), 212–14.

60. Roosevelt assessing his career to newspaper correspondent Oscar K. Davis, in Busch, 11.

61. Harbaugh, *Power and Responsibility,* 18.

62. Lawrence F. Abbott, *Impressions of Theodore Roosevelt* (New York: Doubleday, Page, 1919), 40. Abbott was a longtime friend and literary colleague of Roosevelt's and editor at *The Outlook* who interviewed Joe Murray in his office there about TR.

63. W. Emlen Roosevelt, "Early Recollections: Bankers." Typescript copy at the Theodore Roosevelt Association, Oyster Bay, N.Y., 4.

64. Robinson, Corinne Roosevelt, *My Brother Theodore Roosevelt* (New York: Scribner's Sons, 1921), 118.

65. Jacob Riis, *Theodore Roosevelt the Citizen* (New York: Outlook Company, 1904), 48.

66. Harbaugh, *Power and Responsibility,* 11.

67. Elting E. Morison, ed., *The Letters of Theodore Roosevelt,* 2 vols. (Cambridge, Mass.: Harvard University Press, 1951).

68. Ibid.

CHAPTER 3: ASSEMBLY

1. Bayrd Still, *Mirror for Gotham: New York as Seen by Contemporaries from Dutch Days to the Present* (New York: Fordham University Press, 1994), 239.

2. Joseph Bucklin Bishop, *Theodore Roosevelt and His Time Shown in His Letters,* vol. 1 (New York: Charles Scribner's Sons, 1920), 10.

3. Will M. Clemens, *Theodore Roosevelt: The American* (New York: F. Tennyson Neely, 1899), 35.

4. Howland, 12.

5. Nicholas Roosevelt, *Theodore Roosevelt: The Man as I Knew Him* (New York: Dodd, Mead, 1967), 14.

6. Edmund Morris, *The Rise of Theodore Roosevelt* (New York: Coward, McCann & Geoghegan, 1979), 227.

7. Robinson, 119.

8. Carleton Putnam, *Theodore Roosevelt: The Formative Years, vol. 1, 1858–1886* (New York: Charles Scribner's Sons, 1958).

9. Busch, 41.

10. Miller, 122.

11. Huybertie Pruyn Hamlin, ed. Alice Kenney, *An Albany Girlhood* (Albany: Washington Park Press, 1990), 55.

12. Miller, 126.

13. Morison, *Letters,* 1471.

14. William Draper Lewis, *The Life of Theodore Roosevelt* (New York: United Publishers, 1919), 62.

15. Roosevelt, *An Autobigraphy,* 43.

16. Alvin F. Harlow, *Theodore Roosevelt: Strenuous American* (New York: Julian Messner, 1943), 84.

17. Miller, 125.

18. Ibid., 123.

19. Ibid., 10.

20. Clemens, 65.

21. Roosevelt, *An Autobiography,* 76.

22. Miller, 124.

23. Edmund Morris, *The Rise of Theodore Roosevelt,* 170.

24. Roosevelt, *An Autobiography,* 82.

25. Hermann Hagedorn, *The Boys' Life of Theodore Roosevelt* (New York: Harper & Brothers, 1918), 73.

26. Harlow, 69.

27. Miller, 132.

28. Ibid., 133.

29. Riis, 55.

30. Edmund Morris, *The Rise of Theodore Roosevelt,* 176.

31. Ibid., 178.

32. Ibid., 177.

33. Miller, 136.

34. Ibid., 137.

35. George Pierson Troyer, *Adventurous Life and Heroic Deeds of Theodore Roosevelt* (New York: United, 1905), 57.

36. Robinson, 123.

CHAPTER 4: TRAGEDY

1. Morison, *Letters.*

2. Ibid.

3. Putnam.

4. David McCullough, *Mornings on Horseback* (New York: Simon & Schuster, 1981), 266.

5. Harlow, 84.

6. Harbaugh, *Power and Responsibility,* 5.

7. Putnam, 282.

8. Hagedorn, *The Boys' Life,* 81.

9. Riis, 58.

10. Putnam, 288.

11. Ibid., 292.

12. Bishop, *Theodore Roosevelt and His Time,* 22.

13. Harlow, 82.

14. Ibid., 84.

15. Putnam, 293.

16. Roosevelt, *An Autobiography,* 81.

17. Ibid., 82.

18. Ibid., 83.

19. Riis.

20. Putnam, 305.

21. Harlow, 78.

22. *New York Times,* April 10, 1883.

23. TR letter to Jonas S. Van Duzer, November 20, 1883, in Morison, *Letters.*

24. From the President Franklin D. Roosevelt Library archives, Hyde Park, N.Y.

25. Ibid.

26. Hermann Hagedorn, *Roosevelt in the Bad Lands* (New York: Houghton Mifflin, 1921), 37.

27. Theodore Roosevelt, *Works,* vol. 1, "The Lordly Buffalo" (New York: Scribner's, 1923), 205.

28. Hagedorn, *Roosevelt in the Bad Lands,* 45.

29. Putnam, 372.

30. Roosevelt, *An Autobiography,* 87.

31. Ibid.

32. Ibid.

33. *New York Herald,* February 6, 1884.

34. Bishop, *Theodore Roosevelt and His Time,* 28.

35. *New York World,* February 3, 1884.

36. Bishop, *Theodore Roosevelt and His Time,* 29.

37. Miller, 154.

38. Harbaugh, *Power and Responsibility,* 45.

39. Miller, 155.

40. Miller, 155.

41. Arthur Cutler, TR's former tutor, told Maine guide Bill Sewall of TR's state of mind: "He does not know what he says or does." Miller, 156.

42. Letter from Arthur Cutler to Bill Cutler, in Harbaugh, *Power and Responsibility,* 47.

43. Morris, *The Rise of Theodore Roosevelt,* 242.

44. Putnam, 389.

45. Harbaugh, *Power and Responsibility,* 47.

46. Morris, *The Rise of Theodore Roosevelt,* 249.

47. Putnam, 391.

48. Ibid., 410.

49. Ibid., 397.

50. Morris, *The Rise of Theodore Roosevelt,* 251.

51. Putnam, 399.

52. Pringle, 48.

53. Brands, *Selected Letters,* 168.

54. Morris, *The Rise of Theodore Roosevelt,* 256.

CHAPTER 5: BADLANDS

1. Lincoln A. Lang, *Ranching with Roosevelt* (Philadelphia: J. B. Lippincott, 1926), 13.

2. National Park Service brochure, Theodore Roosevelt National Park, N.D.

3. Olaf T. Hagen and Ray H. Mattison, "Pyramid Park: Where Roosevelt Came to Hunt," *The State Historical Society of North Dakota* 19, no. 4, October 1952, 19.

4. TR letter to Bamie, from Little Missouri, June 17, 1884.

5. Roosevelt, *An Autobiography,* 94–95.

6. Ibid., 96.

7. TR letter to Bamie, from Chimney Butte Ranch, August 12, 1884.

8. TR letter to Bamie, from Little Missouri, June 17, 1884.

9. Hagen and Mattison, 20.

10. "The Badlands Really Were Bad," *Sports Afield,* September 1994.

11. TR letter to Bamie, from Chimney Butte Ranch, August 12, 1884.

12. *Literary Digest,* January 25, 1919, 62.

13. TR letter to Bamie, from Sagamore Hill, July 4, 1916.

14. "Glimpses from the Life of Theodore Roosevelt," *Literary Digest,* January 25, 1919, 55. This anecdote has been told and retold in slightly different forms in a variety of books and other publications.

15. Ibid., 56.

16. TR letter to Bamie, from the Badlands, June 7, 1886.

17. Roosevelt, *An Autobiography,* 108.

18. Otto Wolfgang, "Theodore Roosevelt, Cattleman," *Real West,* March 1969, 54.

19. TR letter to Bamie, from Elkhorn Ranch, March 20, 1886.

20. TR letter to Bamie, from Chimney Butte Ranch, December 14, 1884.

21. Ibid.

22. Wolfgang, 55.

23. TR letter to Bamie, from Elkhorn Ranch, March 28, 1886.

24. Lilian Rixey, *Bamie: Theodore Roosevelt's Remarkable Sister,* reviewed by William Harbaugh in *Book Week,* December 8, 1963.

25. TR letter to Bamie, from New York, March 19, 1885.

26. TR letter to Bamie, from Elkhorn Ranch, April 29, 1886.

27. TR letter to Bamie, from Medora, May 15, 1886.

28. Ibid.

29. Roosevelt, *An Autobiography,* 98.

30. William Wingate Sewall, *Bill Sewall's Story of T.R.* (New York: Harper and Brothers, 1919), 41.

31. Dee Brown, *Trail Driving Days* (New York: Charles Scribner's Sons, 1952), 219.

32. Ibid.

33. Wolfgang, 66.

34. De Mores letter to TR from Bismarck, Dakota Territory, September 3, 1885, and Roosevelt's reply in an undated draft, in Wolfgang, 66.

35. Roosevelt, *An Autobiography,* 102.

36. Harbaugh, *Power and Responsibility,* 62.

37. TR to Bamie, from Medora, May 15, 1886.

38. Rudolph Lehmicke, a cowboy who later became a compositor at the *Tribune,* recalled an 1887 spring roundup with Roosevelt, story from *Chicago Tribune,* in *Literary Digest,* January 25, 1919, 57–58.

39. Bill Sewall letter to his brother, from Elkhorn Ranch, on April 21, 1886, in Ray H. Mattison, *Life at Roosevelt's Elkhorn Ranch: The Letters of William W. and Mary Sewall,* reprinted from *North Dakota Historical Society Quarterly* 27: 3 and 4, 1960.

40. TR letter to Bamie, from Dickemon, Dakota Territory, April 12, 1886.

41. McCullough, *Mornings on Horseback.*

42. Report in *New York Herald,* February 13, 1886.

43. Wolfgang, 66.

44. National Park Service brochure, Theodore Roosevelt National Park, N.D.

45. Wolfgang, 66.

46. Ibid., 55.

47. Ibid., 66.

48. TR letter to Bamie, from Elkhorn Ranch, September 20, 1886.

49. TR letter to Cabot Lodge, from Oyster Bay, October 17, 1886.

50. *New York Times,* February 21, 1886.

51. *New York Sun,* October 26, 1886.

52. Ormonde de Kay, *From the Age That Is Past: Harvard Club of New York City, a History* (New York: Harvard Club of New York City, 1994), 42.

53. TR letter to Cabot Lodge, from New York, November 1, 1886.

54. Pringle, *Theodore Roosevelt: A Biography,* 81.

55. Sylvia Jukes Morris, 101.

56. TR letter to Bamie, from Elkhorn Ranch, September 20, 1886.

57. TR letter to Bamie, from Rome, January 10, 1887.

58. Report in *New York Herald,* March 28, 1887.

59. Lilian Rixey, *Bamie: Theodore Roosevelt's Remarkable Sister,* William Harbaugh's review in *Book Week,* December 8, 1963.

60. TR letter to Bamie, from Florence, January 3, 1887.

61. TR letter to Bamie, from Florence, January 6, 1887.

62. TR letter to Bamie, from Naples, January 17, 1887.

63. TR letter to Bamie, from Sagamore Hill, September 9, 1887.

64. TR letter to Bamie, from Sagamore Hill, September 13, 1887.

65. TR letter to Bamie, from Sagamore Hill, September 18, 1887.

66. Lately Thomas, *The Astor Orphans: A Pride of Lions* (Albany, N.Y.: Washington Park Press, 1999), 67.

67. Ibid.

68. Roosevelt, *An Autobiography,* 122.

69. Harbaugh, *Power and Responsibility,* 62.

CHAPTER 6: WASHINGTON

1. TR letter to Bamie, from Sagamore Hill, June 24, 1888.

2. TR letter to Bamie, from Sagamore Hill, May 14, 1888.

3. TR letter to Bamie, from Sagamore Hill, May 27, 1888.

4. TR letter to Bamie, from Sagamore Hill, June 10, 1888.

5. TR letter to Bamie, from Sagamore Hill, August 8, 1888.

6. TR letter to Bamie, from the Union League Club, July 1, 1888.

7. TR letter to Francis Parkman, from Oyster Bay, April 23, 1888.

8. TR letter to Bamie, from Sagamore Hill, August 20, 1888.

9. TR letter to Bamie, from Kootenas Lake, September 18, 1888.

10. Ibid.

11. TR letter to Bamie, from Sagamore Hill, October 5, 1888.

12. Ibid.

13. TR letter to Cecil Spring-Rice, from Oyster Bay, November 18, 1888.

14. TR letter to Bamie, from New York City, February 6, 1889.

15. TR letter to Henry Cabot Lodge, from New York, March 25, 1889, in Brands, *Selected Letters,* 57.

16. TR letter to Bamie, from the Union League Club, June 2, 1889.

17. TR letter to Henry Cabot Lodge, from New York, April [precise day unknown], 1889, in Brands, *Selected Letters,* 58.

18. William Dudley Foulke, *Roosevelt and the Spoilsmen* (New York: National Civil Service Reform League, 1925), 12.

19. Matthew F. Halloran, *Theodore Roosevelt—Civil Service Commissioner,* 60.

20. Ibid.

21. Roosevelt, *An Autobiography,* 132–33.

22. Foulke, 6.

23. Harbaugh, *Power and Responsibility,* 76.

24. Donald H. Harvey, *The Civil Service Commission* (New York: Praeger, 1970), 9.

25. TR letter to Bamie, from the Union League Club, June 2, 1889.

26. Harbaugh, *Power and Responsibility,* 78.

27. Roosevelt, *An Autobiography,* 134–35.

28. Halloran, 63.

29. TR letter to Anna and Henry Cabot Lodge, from Washington, D.C., June 12, 1889.

30. TR letter to Bamie, from Sagamore Hill, October 13, 1889.

31. Hermann Hagedorn, *The Roosevelt Family of Sagamore Hill* (New York: Macmillan, 1954), 39.

32. TR letter to Henry Cabot Lodge, from Washington, D.C., August 23, 1890, in Brands, *Selected Letters,* 73.

33. TR letter to Bamie, from Washington, D.C., February 1, 1891.

34. TR letter to Henry Cabot Lodge, from Washington, D.C., June 24, 1889, in Brands, *Selected Letters,* 63–64.

35. TR letter to Henry Cabot Lodge, from Washington, D.C., July 22, 1891, in Brands, *Selected Letters,* 79.

36. TR letter to Henry Cabot Lodge, from Washington, D.C., June 29, 1889, in Brands, *Selected Letters,* 64.

37. TR letter to James Brander Matthews, July 31, 1889, in Brands, *Selected Letters,* 69.

38. TR letter to Bamie, from Washington, D.C., March 15, 1891.

39. TR letter to Bamie, from Washington, D.C., March 21, 1891.

40. TR letter to Francis Parkman, from Washington, D.C., July 13, 1889, in Brands, *Selected Letters,* 68.

41. TR letter to Corinne, from Washington, D.C., July 28, 1889.

42. TR letter to Bamie, from Washington, D.C., May 15, 1891.

43. TR letter to Bamie, from Medora, N.D., September 1, 1891.

44. TR letter to Bamie, from Deadwood, S.D., August 26, 1892.

45. TR letter to Bamie, from Sioux City, Iowa, September 2, 1892.

46. Edmund Morris, *The Rise of Theodore Roosevelt,* 457.

47. TR letter to James S. Clarkson, from Washington, D.C., April 22, 1893, in Brands, *Selected Letters,* 84.

48. TR letter to Bamie, from Elkhorn Ranch, September 16, 1893.

49. TR letter to Bamie, from Washington, D.C., December 17, 1893.

50. TR letter to Bamie, from Washington, D.C., January 7, 1894.

51. TR letter to Bamie, from Washington, D.C., February 25, 1894.

52. Edmund Morris, *The Rise of Theodore Roosevelt,* 472.

53. TR letter to Bamie, from Sagamore Hill, June 10, 1894.

54. Edmund Morris, *The Rise of Theodore Roosevelt,* 474.

55. TR letter to Bamie, from Sagamore Hill, August 18, 1894.

56. TR letter to Bamie, from Washington, D.C., October 13, 1894.

57. TR letter to Henry Cabot Lodge, from Washington, D.C., October 24, 1894, in Brands, *Selected Letters,* 96.

58. Sylvia Jukes Morris, *153.*

59. TR letter to Bamie, from Washington, D.C., October 22, 1894.

60. TR letter to Bamie, from Washington, D.C., December 26, 1894.

61. TR letter to Henry Cabot Lodge, from Washington, D.C., December 9, 1894, Brands, *Selected Letters,* 97.

62. TR letter as commissioner to Miss Carrie Harrison of Wellesley College on January 7, 1895, in Harvey, 118.

63. TR letter to Bamie, from Washington, D.C., March 16, 1895.

64. TR letter to Bamie, from Washington, D.C., April 14, 1895.

65. TR letter to Bamie, from Washington, D.C., April 21, 1895.

66. TR letter to Bamie, from Washington, D.C., April 27, 1895.

67. Roosevelt, *An Autobiography,* 137.

68. Halloran, 61.

CHAPTER 7: POLICE COMMISSIONER

1. Avery Delano Andrews, *Citizen in Action: The Story of Theodore Roosevelt as Police Commissioner,* unpublished ms. from a member of the Police Board, 1955, Library of Theodore Roosevelt Birthplace, NYC, 9.

2. Roosevelt, *An Autobiography,* 172.

3. Ibid.

4. de Kay, 326.

5. Harbaugh, *Power and Responsibility,* 83.

6. *New York World,* May 17, 1895.

7. Andrews, 36.

8. TR letter to Lodge, from New York, May 18, 1895.

9. TR letter to Bamie, from New York, May 19, 1895.

10. TR letter to Lodge, from New York City, May 18, 1895.

11. TR letter to Bamie, from Sagamore Hill, June 23, 1895.

12. TR to Lodge, from New York, July 20, 1895.

13. Jay S. Berman, "Theodore Roosevelt as Police Commissioner of New York: The Birth of Modern American Police Administration," in *Theodore Roosevelt: Many-Sided American* (Hempstead, N.Y.: Hofstra University, 1992), 171–83.

14. de Kay, 65.

15. TR letter to Bamie, from Sagamore Hill, June 30, 1895.

16. Roosevelt, *An Autobiography,* 196.

17. TR letter to Bamie, from Sagamore Hill, September 29, 1895.

18. Harbaugh, *Power and Responsibility,* 84.

19. Ibid., 85.

20. *New York World,* August 8, 1895.

21. TR letter to Bamie, from Sagamore Hill, October 27, 1895.

22. TR letter to Lodge, from New York, September 15, 1895.

23. *New York Times,* July 12, 1895.

24. TR letter to Bamie, from Sagamore Hill, June 8, 1895.

25. Avery Delano Andrews, "Theodore Roosevelt as Police Commissioner," *New York Historical Society Quarterly,* April 1958, an excerpt from Andrews's unpublished memoirs, TR Birthplace, NYC, 119.

26. Ibid., 120.

27. TR letter to Bamie, from Sagamore Hill, October 6, 1895.

28. TR letter to Bamie, from New York, April 19, 1896.

29. Sylvia Jukes Morris, 162.

30. TR letter to Bamie, from Washington, D.C., February 3, 1895.

31. TR letter to Bamie, from Sagamore Hill, December 26, 1896.

32. TR letter to Bamie, from New York, February 28, 1897.

33. TR letter to Bamie, from Sagamore Hill, December 13, 1896.

34. Andrews, "Theodore Roosevelt as Police Commissioner," 134.

35. Hagedorn, *The Roosevelt Family,* 38.

36. Roosevelt, *An Autobiography,* 181.

37. TR letter to Bamie, from Sagamore Hill, December 22, 1895.

38. TR letter to Bamie, from New York City, February 2, 1896.

39. TR letter to Bamie, from Sagamore Hill, August 15, 1896.

40. Ibid.

41. TR letter to Bamie, from Sagamore Hill, September 13, 1896.

42. TR letter to Bamie, from Sagamore Hill, November 8, 1896.

43. Roosevelt, *An Autobiography,* 184.

44. TR letter to Bamie, from Sagamore Hill, November 13, 1896.

45. TR letter to Bamie, from New York City, March 14, 1897.

46. Harbaugh, *Power and Responsibility,* 92.

47. TR letter to Bamie, from New York City, April 11, 1897.

48. Harbaugh, *Power and Responsibility,* 91.

49. Andrews, "Theodore Roosevelt as Police Commissioner," 141.

50. Lincoln Steffens, *Autobiography* (New York: Harcourt Brace, 1936), 258–60.

51. TR letter to Bamie, from New York City, March 30, 1896.

CHAPTER 8: ROUGH RIDER
1. Sylvia Jukes Morris, 168.
2. Frank Uhlig Jr., "The Best of *American Heritage.*" *American Heritage*, June 7, 1964.
3. Thomas, 114.
4. Hagedorn, *The Roosevelt Family,* 50.
5. Ibid.
6. Harbaugh, *Power and Responsibility,* 98.
7. Sylvia Jukes Morris, 173.
8. TR letter to brother-in-law Douglas Robinson, April 2, 1898, TR Collection, Harvard.
9. Sylvia Jukes Morris, 172.
10. Thomas, 123.
11. Ibid., 124.
12. Leonard Wood reminiscence at dinner of the Theodore Roosevelt Association, March 24, 1919, two months after TR's death. TR Collection, Harvard.
13. Kenneth Robinson letter to his cousin Douglas Robinson, TR's brother-in-law, from training camp at San Antonio, Texas, May 17, 1898.
14. Leonard Wood reminiscence.
15. Royal A. Prentice, *The Rough Riders and the Cuban Campaign,* typescript, 1949. Prentice was quartermaster sergeant of E Troop at San Antonio.
16. TR letter to Corinne, June 7, 1898, TR Collection, Harvard.
17. Roosevelt letter to his children, June 6, 1898, from Tampa, Fla.
18. Black, Frank S. (editor), *New York and the War with Spain: The History of the Empire State Regiments* (Albany: Argus Company, 1903), 259.
19. Letter of Winthrop Chanler to his wife, from Tampa, Fla., June 14, 1898.
20. H. Paul Jeffers, *Colonel Roosevelt: Theodore Roosevelt Goes to War, 1897–1898* (New York: John Wiley & Sons, 1996), 189.
21. Ibid.
22. TR letter to Corinne, June 7, 1898, TR Collection, Harvard.

23. John D. Miley Papers, Lyall Squair Collection, NYS Library, Albany, N.Y.

24. Black, 68.

25. TR letter to Lodge, June 10, 1898, from Port Tampa.

26. TR letter to Lodge, June 12, 1898, from Port Tampa.

27. TR letter to Corinne, June 15, 1898, from Gulf of Mexico.

28. Morris, *The Rise of Theodore Roosevelt,* 636.

29. TR letter to Corinne, from troopship near Santiago. June 20, 1898.

30. Jeffers, *Colonel Roosevelt,* 213.

31. TR letter to Corinne, from Las Guasimas. June 25, 1898.

32. TR letter to Lodge, from outside Santiago. July 3, 1898.

33. TR letter to Corinne, from camp five miles from Santiago, June 27, 1898.

34. Sylvia Jukes Morris, 181.

35. TR quoted after reunion of the Rough Riders Association in 1917, in David M. Gosoroski, *VFW,* August 1997, 29.

36. TR letter to Lodge, from outside Santiago, July 3, 1898.

37. Black, 86.

38. Thomas, 130.

39. William Chapin Deming, *Roosevelt in the Bunk House and Other Sketches: Visits of the Great Rough Rider to Wyoming in 1900, 1903, and 1910* (Laramie, Wyo.: Laramie Printing Company, 1927), 7. Deming was publisher of the *Wyoming Tribune-Leader,* a friend of Roosevelt's, and a U.S. Civil Service commissioner from 1923 to 1930.

40. TR letter to Leonard Wood, from outside Santiago, July 4, 1898.

41. Ibid.

42. TR letter to Lodge, from outside Santiago, July 3, 1898.

43. Maj. Gen. J. Ford Kent letter to Gen. William Shafter, July 1, 1898, Lyall Squair Collection, NYS Library, Albany, N.Y.

44. TR letter to Corinne, from Gulf of Mexico, June 15, 1898.

45. Keith Douglas, "The Man Who Walked up San Juan Hill While Teddy Roosevelt Rode a Mule," *Yankee,* January 1980, 162.

46. Theodore Roosevelt, "The Rough Riders," in Mario R. DiNunzio, ed., *Theodore Roosevelt: An American Mind* (New York: Penguin, 1995), 28.

47. TR diary entry, July 1, 1898, TR Collection, Harvard.

48. Deming, 7.

49. Jeffers, *Colonel Roosevelt,* 235.

50. Black, 118.

51. Theodore Roosevelt, "The Rough Riders," 30.

52. Ibid.

53. Associated Press interview from Las Vegas, N.M., for a reunion of four surviving Rough Riders on June 16, 1964. Lyall D. Squair Collection, NYS Library, Albany, N.Y. The AP interview quotes Jesse D. Langdon, 84, of East Rockaway, N.Y., chairman of the Association of Rough Riders at the time. The other survivors attending were Frank C. Brito, 86, Las Cruces, N.M.; Charles Hopping, 91, Long Beach, Calif.; and Arthur Tuttle, 84, Salinas, Calif.

54. Theodore Roosevelt, "The Rough Riders," 32.

55. Jeffers, *Colonel Roosevelt,* 240.

56. Theodore Roosevelt, "The Rough Riders," 35.

57. Ibid., 34.

58. Ibid., 33.

59. Jeffers, *Colonel Roosevelt,* 242.

60. Harbaugh, *Power and Responsibility,* 105.

61. Sylvia Jukes Morris, page 183. Morris attributes the quote to R. W. Stallman's biography of Crane, published by Braziller in 1968.

62. Ibid., 187.

63. Edith letter to her husband, July 18, 1898, TR Collection, Harvard.

64. TR letter to Lodge, from outside Santiago, July 7, 1898.

65. Hagedorn, *The Roosevelt Family,* 56.

66. TR letter to Lodge, from outside Santiago, July 7, 1898.

67. Garcia letter to Shafter, from Cuba, July 5, 1898, Squair Collection, NYS Library, Albany, N.Y.

68. Garcia letter to Shafter, from Cuba, July 19, 1898, Squair Collection, NYS Library, Albany, N.Y.

69. Edmund Morris, *The Rise of Theodore Roosevelt,* 658.

70. TR letter to Alice Roosevelt, from Santiago, July 18, 1898, in Brands, *Selected Letters,* 197.

71. Deming, 9.

72. Nasaw, 145.

73. Hagedorn, *The Roosevelt Family,* 57.

74. *New York Sun,* September 13, 1898.

75. Ibid.

76. Ibid.

77. Hagedorn, *The Roosevelt Family,* 59.

CHAPTER 9: GOVERNOR

1. Joseph Bucklin Bishop, *Theodore Roosevelt and His Time Shown in His Letters,* vol. 1, 110.

2. Roosevelt, *An Autobiography,* 281.

3. Ibid.

4. Thomas, 137.

5. TR letter to Lodge, from Oyster Bay, September 19, 1898, TR Collection, Harvard.

6. Harbaugh, *Power and Responsibility,* 108.

7. Robinson, 183.

8. Ibid.

9. Ibid.

10. Ibid.

11. Louis J. Lang, ed., *The Autobiography of Thomas Collier Platt* (New York: B. W. Dodge, 1910), 16.

12. Louis J. Lang, 371.

13. Clemens, 182.

14. Louis J. Lang, 373.

15. Clemens, 184.

16. Ibid., 185.

17. Oliver E. Allen, *The Tiger: The Rise and Fall of Tammany Hall* (Reading, Mass.: Addison-Wesley, 1993), 195.

18. Nasaw, 148.

19. Oliver E. Allen, 195.

20. Ibid.

21. Riis, 204.

22. *New York Sun,* October 10, 1898.

23. Louis J. Lang, 373.

24. TR letter to William Dudley Foulke, November 25, 1898, in Morison.

25. Louis J. Lang, 374.

26. Harlow, 187.

27. TR letter to William T. Ferguson, January 4, 1899, in Morison.

28. TR letter to Spring-Rice, from Oyster Bay, November 25, 1898.

29. Bishop, *Theodore Roosevelt and His Time Shown in His Letters,* vol. 1, 112.

30. Thomas, 136.

31. Albert Loren Cheney, *Personal Memoirs of the Home Life of the Late Theodore Roosevelt* (Washington, D.C.: Cheney Publishing Company, 1919), 32. Anecdotes from Roosevelt family friend and editor of the Oyster Bay *Pilot.*

32. Riis, 207.

33. Mrs. James Russell Parsons, *Perchance Some Day* (privately printed, 1951), 123. Collection of Peter Scanlan, Albany, N.Y.

34. *Public Papers of Theodore Roosevelt, Governor, 1899, State of New York,* 10. Legislative Library, Albany, N.Y.

35. Ibid., 20.

36. Ibid., 21.

37. Ibid., 24.

38. Ibid., 25.

39. Ibid.

40. Clemens, 190.

41. Roosevelt, *An Autobiography,* 289.

42. Lothrop Stoddard, *Master of Manhattan: The Life of Richard Croker* (New York: Longmans, Green, 1931), 125.

43. Roosevelt, *An Autobiography,* 289.

44. Harlow, 197.

45. Roosevelt, *An Autobiography,* 297.

46. Ibid.

47. Louis J. Lang, 375.

48. Harlow, 192.

49. Roosevelt, *An Autobiography,* 294.

50. TR letter to Thomas Roberts Slicer, April 6, 1900, TR Collection, Harvard.

51. Isabelle K. Savell, *The Governor's Mansion in Albany* (Albany, N.Y.: New York State Executive Chamber, 1962), 18.

52. Alice Roosevelt, *Crowded Hours* (New York: Scribner's, 1932), 26.

53. TR letter to Wintie Chanler, March 23, 1899, TR Collection, Harvard.

54. Miller, 325.

55. Sylvia Jukes Morris, 195.

56. Cheney, 29.

57. Ibid., 30.

58. Harlow, 196.

59. G. Wallace Chessman, *Governor Theodore Roosevelt: The Albany Apprenticeship, 1898–1900* (Cambridge, Mass.: Harvard University Press, 1965), 230.

60. Harlow, 196.

61. Chessman, *Governor Theodore Roosevelt,* 230.

62. Sylvia Jukes Morris, 196.

63. Miller, 325.

64. Robinson, 187.

65. Ibid., 188.

66. Miller, 326.

67. TR secretary Amy Cheney recollection in interview files, TR Collection, Harvard.

68. TR letter to Thomas Collier Platt, January 12, 1899, in Morison.

69. TR letter to General Johnston, February 8, 1899, TR Collection, Harvard.

70. Robinson, 190.

71. *Public Papers,* 51.

72. Harlow, 194.

73. Ted Conover, *Newjack: Guarding Sing Sing* (New York: Random House, 2000), 185–86.

74. *Public Papers,* 52.

75. Ibid., 54.

76. Ibid., 58.

77. Riis, 218.

78. Ibid., 220.

79. Ibid., 223.

80. Robinson, 194.

81. TR letter to Winthrop Chanler, from Executive Chamber, Albany, March 23, 1899.

82. Louis J. Lang, 375.

83. TR letter to Elihu Root, from Executive Chamber, Albany, March 14, 1899.

84. Roosevelt, *An Autobiography,* 308.

85. Harlow, 193.

86. TR letter to Seth Low, August 3, 1900, TR Collection, Harvard.

87. Louis J. Lang, 375.

88. Harlow, 194.

89. Roosevelt, *An Autobiography,* 299.

90. *Public Papers,* 293.

91. Sylvia Jukes Morris, page 201.

CHAPTER 10: VICE PRESIDENT

1. TR letter to Bellamy Storer, from Oyster Bay, July 1, 1899.

2. George E. Mowry, *The Era of Theodore Roosevelt and the Birth of Modern America (1900–1912)* (New York: Harper & Row, 1958), 48.

3. TR letter to Caspar Whitney, from Oyster Bay, August 3, 1899.

4. Hagedorn, *The Boys' Life,* 222.

5. Miller, 331.

6. TR letter to Lodge, from Albany, January 30, 1900.

7. *Public Papers,* 204.

8. Walter F. McCaleb, *Theodore Roosevelt* (New York: Albert & Charles Boni, 1931), 94.

9. TR letter to Bamie, December 17, 1899.

10. TR letter to John Hay, from Albany, February 7, 1899.

11. Miller, 331.

12. Ibid.

13. *Public Papers,* 60.

14. TR to Cecil Spring-Rice, August 11, 1899.

15. *Public Papers,* 32.

16. *Public Papers,* 60.

17. TR letter to Mack, January 5, 1900, Squair Collection, NYS Library, Albany, N.Y.

18. Two letters, TR to John Huston Finley, from Albany, November 13, 1899.

19. Ferdinand C. Iglehart, *Theodore Roosevelt: The Man as I Knew Him* (New York: Christian Herald, 1919), 140.

20. Edmund Morris, *The Rise of Theodore Roosevelt,* 712.

21. Miller, 336.

22. Louis J. Lang, 375.

23. TR letter to William Sheffield Cowles, from Albany, January 22, 1900.

24. Henry F. Pringle, *Theodore Roosevelt: A Biography* (New York: Harcourt Brace, 1931), 149.

25. TR letter to Cecil Spring-Rice, from Albany, January 27, 1900.

26. Miller, 335.

27. Louis J. Lang, 383.

28. TR letter to Lodge, from Albany, February 3, 1900.

29. Robinson, 195.

30. TR letter to Maria Longworth Storer from Albany, December 2, 1899.

31. TR letter to Joel Chandler Harris, from the White House, June 9, 1902.

32. TR letter to Kermit Roosevelt from the White House, November 24, 1902.

33. Sylvia Jukes Morris, epigraph, 1.

34. TR letter to Hugh F. Leonard, from Albany, December 7, 1899.

35. TR letter to Douglas Robinson, from Albany, January 22, 1900.

36. Riis, 234.

37. Miller, 338.

38. Hagedorn, *The Boys' Life,* 225.

39. Miller, 339.

40. Padover, 287.

41. TR letter to James Coolidge Carter, from Newburgh, February 28, 1900.

42. TR letter to Seth Low, from Albany, March 7, 1900.

43. Chessman, *Governor Theodore Roosevelt,* 246.

44. Ibid., 247.

45. TR letter to Lucius Nathan Littauer, from Albany, March 24, 1900.

46. Riis, 229.

47. Chessman, *Governor Theodore Roosevelt,* 339.

48. Sylvia Jukes Morris, 205.

49. Robinson, 196.

50. Miller, 340.

51. Morison, 1337.

52. Miller, 342.

53. Morison, 1341.

54. TR letter to Lodge, from Oyster Bay, June 25, 1900.

55. Miller, 342.

56. Busch, 147.

57. Anonymous reporter quoted in Harvard oral histories interview files, TR Collection, Harvard.

58. Deming, 47.

59. "Roosevelt's Campaign for Vice-President," by Hon. Josiah A. Van Orsel, chair of the Republican State Committee in Wyoming during Roosevelt's 1900 visit, in Deming, 55.

60. Busch, 276.

61. Unpublished Sturdevant ms., from March, 1910, in Squair TR Collection, NYS Library, Albany.

62. Busch, 276.

63. Sylvia Jukes Morris, 205.

64. Arthur Wallace Dunn, *From Harrison to Harding* (New York: Reprint Services Corp., 1922). The author recalled overhearing Hanna raging about Roosevelt; repeated in other Harvard interviews, TR Collection, Harvard.

65. Edith Kermit Roosevelt diary entry, March 4, 1901, TR Collection, Harvard.

66. Edith Kermit Roosevelt letter to Emily Tyler Carow, March 5, 1901, TR Collection, Harvard.

67. G. Wallace Chessman, *Theodore Roosevelt and the Politics of Power* (Boston: Little, Brown, 1969), 107.

CHAPTER 11: RIDE TO THE PRESIDENCY

1. Sylvia Jukes Morris, 206.

2. Ibid., 209.

3. Ibid.

4. Ibid.

5. TR letter to William H. H. Llewellyn, July 13, 1901, TR Collection, Harvard.

6. Thomas, 157.

7. TR letter to Endicott Peabody, May 7, 1901, TR Collection, Harvard.

8. Sylvia Jukes Morris, 210.

9. Author interview with Ann Marie Linnabery, education director, Theodore Roosevelt Inaugural Site, Buffalo, N.Y., based on her lecture, "North Creek to Buffalo: Journey to the Presidency."

10. Charles S. Olcott, *The Life of William McKinley,* vol. 2 (New York: Houghton Mifflin, 1916), 309.

11. Olcott, 315.

12. *New York Herald,* September 15, 1901.

13. Exhibit at Roosevelt Inaugural Site, Buffalo, N.Y.

14. Miller, 348–49.

15. Olcott, 316.

16. *New York Herald,* September 15, 1901.

17. Olcott, 317–20.

18. Richard B. Williams, "TR Receives His Summons to the Presidency," *Bell Telephone Magazine,* Autumn 1951, 197–99.

19. Ibid., 199–201.

20. TR letter to Lodge, from Buffalo, September 9, 1901, TR Collection, Harvard.

21. Ibid.

22. Nasaw, 156.

23. Ibid.

24. Ibid., 157; *New-Yorker,* September 26, 1901.

25. TR letter to John St. Loe Strachey, an English editor, in response to Strachey's request for background on Hearst, October 25, 1906, in Nasaw, 210.

26. Olcott, 320–22.

27. *New York World,* September 15, 1901.

28. TR letter to Lodge, September 9, 1901.

29. Miller, 349.

30. Tahawus Club private history, published privately, Adirondack Museum Archives, Blue Mountain Lake, N.Y., 54.

31. Edward A. Harmes, "T.R.'s Ride from Tahawus to North Creek," in Adirondack Mountain Club's *Adirondac* magazine, November-December 1963, 89.

32. Tahawus Club private history, 55.

33. Harmes, 89.

34. Alfred Lee Donaldson, *A History of the Adirondacks,* vol. 1 (Harrison, N.Y.: Harbor Hill Books, 1977), 155.

35. Watson B. Berry, "Late Noah LaCasse, Mountain Guide, Cherished T.R.'s Gift," *Watertown Daily Times,* July 5, 1958.

36. Olcott, 322–23.

37. Ibid., 324.

38. Williams, 201.

39. Harmes, 89–90.

40. Williams, 202–203.

41. Harmes, 90.

42. Olcott, 326.

43. Eloise Cronin Murphy, *Theodore Roosevelt's Night Ride to the Presidency* (Blue Mountain Lake, N.Y.: Adirondack Museum, 1977), 20.

44. Tahawus Club private history, 55.

45. Murphy, 21.

46. Tahawus Club register, Adirondack Museum Archives.

47. *New York Herald,* September 22, 1901.

48. Murphy, 21.

49. Williams, 204.

50. Murphy, 23–24.

51. *New York Herald,* September 22, 1901.

52. Murphy, 25.

53. *New York Times,* September 14, 1981.

54. *Albany Evening Journal,* September 14, 1901.

55. Ibid.

56. TR letter to Wintie Chanler, from Buffalo, N.Y., September 14, 1901, in Thomas, 247.

57. *New York Herald,* September 15, 1901.

58. *Albany Times-Union,* September 15, 1901.

59. *New York World,* September 15, 1901.

SELECTED
BIBLIOGRAPHY
AND SOURCES

BOOKS

Abbott, Lawrence F. *Impressions of Theodore Roosevelt.* New York: Doubleday, Page, 1919.

Allen, Gay Wilson. *William James: A Biography.* New York: Viking Press, 1967.

Allen, Oliver E. *The Tiger: The Rise and Fall of Tammany Hall.* Reading, Mass.: Addison-Wesley, 1993.

Bishop, Joseph Bucklin. *Theodore Roosevelt and His Time Shown in His Letters.* 2 vols. New York: Charles Scribner's Sons, 1920.

———, ed. *Theodore Roosevelt's Letters to His Children.* New York: Charles Scribner's Sons, 1919.

Black, Frank S., ed. *New York and the War with Spain: The History of the Empire State Regiments.* Albany: Argus Company, 1903.

Brands, H. W. *T.R.: The Last Romantic.* New York: Basic Books, 1997.

———, *The Selected Letters of Theodore Roosevelt.* New York: Cooper Square Press, 2001.

Brant Jr., Donald Birtley. "Theodore Roosevelt as New York City Police Commissioner." Senior thesis, Princeton University, 1964.

Brown, Eleanor. *The Forest Preserve of New York State.* Glens Falls, N.Y.: Adirondack Mountain Club, 1985.

Burgess, John W. *Reminiscences of an American Scholar.* New York: Columbia University Press, 1934.

Burroughs, John. *Camping & Tramping with Roosevelt.* Boston: Houghton, Mifflin, 1907.

Burt, Silas W. *My Memoirs of the Military History of the State of New York during the War for the Union, 1861–65.* Albany: Argus Company, 1870.

Burton, David H. *Theodore Roosevelt: Confident Imperialist.* Philadelphia: University of Pennsylvania Press, 1968.

Busch, Noel F. *TR: The Story of Theodore Roosevelt and His Influence on Our Times.* New York: Reynal, 1963.

Carr, Joseph B. *Manual for the Use of the Legislature of the State of New York.* Albany, N.Y.: Weed, Parsons, 1883.

Carter, Robert A. *Buffalo Bill Cody: The Man behind the Legend.* New York: John Wiley & Sons, 2000.

Cheney, Albert Loren. *Personal Memoirs of the Home Life of the Late Theodore Roosevelt.* Washington, D.C.: Cheney Publishing, 1919.

Chessman, G. Wallace. *Governor Theodore Roosevelt: The Albany Apprenticeship, 1898–1900.* Cambridge, Mass.: Harvard University Press, 1965.

———. *Theodore Roosevelt and the Politics of Power.* Boston: Little, Brown, 1969.

Clemens, Will M. *Theodore Roosevelt: The American.* New York: F. Tennyson Nely, 1899.

Conover, Ted. *Newjack: Guarding Sing Sing.* New York: Random House, 2000.

Corry, John A. *A Rough Ride to Albany: Teddy Runs for Governor.* New York: Fordham University Press, 2001.

Cutright, Paul Russell. *Theodore Roosevelt: The Making of a Conservationist.* Chicago: University of Illinois Press, 1985.

———. *Theodore Roosevelt the Naturalist.* New York: Harper & Brothers, 1956.

Dalton, Kathleen. *Theodore Roosevelt: A Strenuous Life.* New York: Alfred A. Knopf, 2002.

de Kay, Ormonde. *From the Age That Is Past: Harvard Club of New York City, A History.* New York: Harvard Club of New York City, 1994.

Deming, William Chapin. *Roosevelt in the Bunk House and Other Sketches: Visits of the Great Rough Rider to Wyoming in 1900, 1903 and 1910.* Laramie, Wyo.: Laramie Printing Company, 1927.

DenDooven, Gweneth, ed. *Theodore Roosevelt: The Story Behind the Scenery.* Las Vegas, Nev.: KC Publications, 1974.

DiNunzio, Mario R., ed. *Theodore Roosevelt: An American Mind.* New York: Penguin Books, 1995.

Donaldson, Alfred Lee. *A History of the Adirondacks* Vol. 1. Harrison, N.Y.: Harbor Hill Books, 1977.

Einstein, Lewis. *Roosevelt: His Mind in Action.* Boston: Houghton Mifflin, 1930.

Ellis, Edward S. *From the Ranch to the White House: A Life of Theodore Roosevelt.* New York: Hurst & Company, 1906.

Essig, Mark. *Edison & the Electric Chair.* New York: Walker & Company, 2003.

Farb, Nathan. *The Adirondacks.* New York: Rizzoli International Publications, 1985.

Felsenthal, Carol. *Alice Roosevelt Longworth.* New York: G. P. Putnam's Sons, 1988.

Foulke, William Dudley. *Roosevelt and the Spoilsmen.* New York: National Civil Service Reform League, 1925.

Gilborn, Craig. *Durant: The Fortunes and Woodland Camps of a Family in the Adirondacks.* Sylvan Beach, N.Y.: North Country Books, 1981.

Gilman, Bradley. *Roosevelt the Happy Warrior.* Boston: Little, Brown, 1921.

Graff, Henry F., ed. *The Presidents: A Reference History.* 2nd ed. New York: Macmillan, 1997.

Graham, Frank Jr. *The Adirondack Park: A Political History.* New York: Alfred A. Knopf, 1978.

Hagedorn, Hermann. *The Boys' Life of Theodore Roosevelt.* New York: Harper & Brothers, 1918.

————. *The Roosevelt Family of Sagamore Hill.* New York: Macmillan, 1954.

Hamlin, Huybertie Pruyn. *An Albany Girlhood.* Ed. Alice P. Kenney. Albany, N.Y.: Washington Park Press, 1990.

Harbaugh, William Henry. *Power and Responsibility: The Life and Times of Theodore Roosevelt.* New York: Farrar, Straus and Cudahy, 1961.

Harlow, Alvin F. *Theodore Roosevelt: Strenuous American.* New York: Julian Messner, 1943.

Howland, Harold. *Theodore Roosevelt and His Times.* New Haven: Yale University Press, 1921.

Iglehart, Ferdinand C. *Theodore Roosevelt: The Man as I Knew Him.* New York: The Christian Herald, 1919.

Jamieson, Paul, ed. *The Adirondack Reader.* Glens Falls, N.Y.: Adirondack Mountain Club, 1982.

Jeffers, H. Paul. *Colonel Roosevelt: Theodore Roosevelt Goes to War, 1897–1898.* New York: John Wiley & Sons, 1996.

————. *Commissioner Roosevelt: The Story of Theodore Roosevelt and the New York City Police, 1895–1897.* New York: John Wiley & Sons, 1994.

Jordan, David M. *Roscoe Conkling of New York: Voice in the Senate.* Ithaca, N.Y.: Cornell University Press, 1971.

Keller, Morton, ed. *Theodore Roosevelt: A Profile.* New York: Hill and Wang, 1967.

Kennedy, William. *O Albany!* New York: Washington Park Press/Viking, 1984.

Kerr, Joan Paterson. *A Bully Father: Theodore Roosevelt's Letters to His Children.* New York: Random House, 1995.

Lang, Lincoln A. *Ranching with Roosevelt.* Philadelphia: J. B. Lippincott, 1926.

Lardner, James, and Thomas Reppetto. *NYPD: A City and Its Police.* New York: Henry Holt, 2000.

Lewis, R. W. B. *The Jameses: A Family Narrative.* New York: Farrar, Straus and Giroux, 1991.

Lewis, William Draper. *The Life of Theodore Roosevelt.* New York: United Publishers, 1919.

Longworth, Alice Roosevelt. *Crowded Hours.* New York: Scribner's, 1932.

Lutts, Ralph H. *The Nature Fakers.* Golden, Colo.: Fulcrum, 1990.

Lyon, James B. *New York in the Spanish-American War.* 3 vols. Albany: State Printers, 1900.

McCaleb, Walter F. *Theodore Roosevelt.* New York: Albert & Charles Boni, 1931.

McCullough, David. *Mornings on Horseback.* New York: Simon & Schuster, 1981.

Meltzer, Milton. *Theodore Roosevelt and His America.* New York: Franklin Watts, 1994.

Miller, Nathan. *Theodore Roosevelt: A Life*. New York: William Morrow, 1992.

Morison, Elting E., ed. *The Letters of Theodore Roosevelt*. 2 vols. Cambridge, Mass.: Harvard University Press, 1951.

Morris, Edmund. *The Rise of Theoodore Roosevelt*. New York: Coward, McCann & Geoghegan, 1979.

————. *Theodore Rex*. New York: Random House, 2001.

Morris, Sylvia Jukes. *Edith Kermit Roosevelt: Portrait of a First Lady*. New York: Coward, McCann & Geoghegan, 1980.

Mowry, George E. *The Era of Theodore Roosevelt and the Birth of Modern America (1900–1912)*. New York: Harper & Row, 1958.

Murlin, Edgar L. *The New York Red Book 1900: An Illustrated Legislative Manual of the State*. Albany, N.Y.: James B. Lyon, 1900.

Murphy, Eloise Cronin. *Theodore Roosevelt's Night Ride to the Presidency*. Blue Mountain Lake, N.Y.: Adirondack Museum, 1977.

Nasaw, David. *The Chief: The Life of William Randolph Hearst*. Boston: Houghton Mifflin Company, 2000.

Naylor, Natalie A., Douglas Brinkley and John Allen Gable, eds. *Theodore Roosevelt: Many-Sided American*. Interlaken, N.Y.: Heart of the Lakes Publishing, 1992.

O'Brien, Kathryn E. *The Great and the Gracious on Millionaires' Row*. Sylvan Beach, N.Y.: North Country Books, 1978.

O'Connor, Stephen. *Orphan Trains: The Story of Charles Loring Brace and the Children He Saved and Failed*. Boston: Houghton Mifflin, 2001.

Padover, Saul K. *The Genius of America: Men Whose Ideas Shaped Our Civilization*. New York: McGraw-Hill, 1960.

Perry, Ralph Barton. *The Thought and Character of William James*. New York: George Braziller, 1954.

Pringle, Henry F. *Theodore Roosevelt: A Biography*. New York: Harcourt Brace & Company, 1931.

Putnam, Carleton. *Theodore Roosevelt: The Formative Years. Vol. 1, 1858–1886*. New York: Charles Scribner's Sons, 1958.

Rauchway, Eric. *Murdering McKinley: The Making of Theodore Roosevelt's America*. New York: Hill and Wang, 2003.

Renehan, Edward J., Jr. *John Burroughs: An American Naturalist*. Hensonville, N.Y.: Black Dome Press, 1998.

————. *The Lion's Pride: Theodore Roosevelt and His Family in Peace and War.* New York: Oxford University Press, 1998.

Reynolds, Cuyler. *Albany Chronicles: A History of the City Arranged Chronologically.* Albany: J. B. Lyon Company, 1906.

Riis, Jacob. *Theodore Roosevelt the Citizen.* New York: The Outlook Company, 1904.

Robinson, Corinne Roosevelt. *My Brother Theodore Roosevelt.* New York: Charles Scribner's Sons, 1921.

Roosevelt, Nicholas. *Theodore Roosevelt: The Man as I Knew Him.* New York: Dodd, Mead, 1967.

Roosevelt, Theodore. *An Autobiography.* New York: Da Capo Press, 1985.

————. *Diaries of Boyhood and Youth.* New York: Scribner's, 1928.

————. *Letters of Theodore Roosevelt to His Children.* New York: Scribner's, 1919.

————. *Letters to Kermit from Theodore Roosevelt.* New York: Scribner's, 1946.

————. *Outdoor Pastimes of an American Hunter.* New York: Scribner's, 1905.

————. *The Winning of the West.* vol. 1. New York: G. P. Putnam's Sons, 1889.

Roosevelt, Mrs. Theodore, Jr. *Day before Yesterday.* Garden City, N.Y.: Doubleday & Company, 1959.

Ross, D. Michael. *The Albany Academy.* Albany, N.Y.: Albany Academy, 2000.

Savell, Isabelle K. *The Governor's Mansion in Albany.* Albany, N.Y.: New York State Executive Chamber, 1962.

Sewall, William Wingate. *Bill Sewall's Story of T.R.* New York: Harper and Brothers, 1919.

Shaw, Albert. *A Cartoon History of Roosevelt's Career.* New York: The Review of Reviews Company, 1910.

Simon, Linda. *Genuine Reality: A Life of William James.* New York: Harcourt Brace, 1998.

Still, Bayrd. *Mirror for Gotham: New York as Seen by Contemporaries from Dutch Days to the Present.* New York: Fordham University Press, 1994.

Stoddard, Lothrop. *Master of Manhattan: The Life of Richard Croker.* New York: Longmans, Green, 1931.

Sullivan, Mark. *Our Times: The United States. The Turn of the Century.* New York: Charles Scribner's Sons, 1926.

Thayer, William Roscoe. *Theodore Roosevelt: An Intimate Biography.* Boston: Houghton Mifflin, 1919.

Thomas, Lately. *The Astor Orphans: A Pride of Lions.* Albany, N.Y.: Washington Park Press, 1999.

Troyer, George Pierson. *The Adventurous Life and Heroic Deeds of Theodore Roosevelt.* New York: United, 1905.

NEWSPAPERS

Adirondack Daily Enterprise
Albany Argus
Albany Evening Journal
Albany Times Union
New York Herald
New York Journal
New York Sun
New York Times
New York World
Springfield (Ohio) Union
Syracuse Herald-American
Washington Post

PERIODICALS

Adams, Charles C. "The New York State Wild Life Memorial to Theodore Roosevelt." *Natural History* 19 no. 6 (1919).

Andrews, Avery Delano. "Theodore Roosevelt as Police Commissioner." *New York Historical Society Quarterly* (April 1958).

Blankman, Edward J. "Hail to the Chief." *Adirondack Life* (Winter 1976).

Dalton, Kathleen. "Why America Loved Teddy Roosevelt." *The Psychohistory Review,* no. 3 (Winter 1979).

Douglas, Keith. "The Man Who Walked up San Juan Hill While Teddy Roosevelt Rode a Mule." *Yankee* (January 1980).

Forest and Stream. "New York Fish and Game Interests: From Governor Roosevelt's Messages." January 13, 1900.

Harbaugh, William. "Bamie: Theodore Roosevelt's Remarkable Sister." *Book Week,* December 8, 1963.

Harmes, Edward A. "TR's Ride from Tahawus to North Creek." *The Adirondac,* November-December 1963.

The Literary Digest. "Glimpses from the Life of Theodore Roosevelt." January 25, 1919.

Marvinney, Sandy. "Theodore Roosevelt, Conservationist." *New York State Conservationist,* June 1996.

McDowell, Bart. "Theodore Roosevelt." *National Geographic,* October 1958.

Natural History. "Theodore Roosevelt. In Memoriam." January 1919.

Naval Historical Foundation. "Brief History of the Navy Department until 1945." May 1980.

New York Masonic Outlook. "Theodore Roosevelt's Initiation." March 1938.

The Outlook 105 (September–December 1913). New York: The Outlook Company.

Personality 2, no. 1 (May 1928). "Theodore Roosevelt's Diaries."

Roosevelt, George Emlen. "Theodore Roosevelt." *The Christian Endeavor World,* October 24, 1912.

Sports Afield. "The Badlands Really Were Bad." September 1994.

Tahawus Club Register, May 12, 1878. Adirondack Museum, Blue Mountain Lake, N.Y.

Uhlig, Frank Jr. "Theodore Roosevelt and the Navy." *American Heritage,* June 7, 1964.

Welling, Richard. "Theodore Roosevelt at Harvard: Some Personal Reminiscences." *The Outlook,* October 27, 1919.

Williams, Richmond B. "TR Receives His Summons to the Presidency." *Bell Telephone Magazine,* Autumn 1951.

Wolfgang, Otto. "Theodore Roosevelt, Cattleman." *Real West,* March 1969.

ARCHIVES, LIBRARIES, AND COLLECTIONS

Adirondack Museum at Blue Mountain Lake, N.Y.

Adirondack Park Agency

Adirondack Park Visitor Interpretive Center. Paul Smiths, N.Y.

Albany Institute of History & Art

Albany Public Library (Rare Books Room)

Executive Mansion. Archives. Albany, N.Y.

Harvard Club of New York City

Houghton Library. Harvard University (Theodore Roosevelt Collection)

New York State Archives. Albany, N.Y.

New York State Capitol. Archives. Albany, N.Y.

New York State Department of Environmental Conservation. Albany, N.Y.

New York State Legislative Library. Archives. Albany, N.Y.

New York State Library. Special Collections and Manuscripts (Lyall D. Squair Collection). Albany, N.Y.

New York State Museum. Albany, N.Y.

Paul Smith's College (Cubley Library Archives)

President Franklin D. Roosevelt Library. Archives. Hyde Park, N.Y.

Sagamore Hill. Theodore Roosevelt Historic Site. Oyster Bay, N.Y.

Scanlan, Peter, Private collection of Theodore Roosevelt material. Albany, N.Y.

Smithsonian Institution (National Portrait Gallery)

State University of New York College of Environment and Forestry (Theodore Roosevelt Wildlife Collection). Syracuse, N.Y.

Theodore Roosevelt Birthplace, New York City

State University of New York at Albany Library

ACKNOWLEDGMENTS

I've been colliding with the outsized historical figure of Theodore Roosevelt during the twenty years that I've spent as a staff writer at the Albany *Times Union*. I might have been writing a political story at the Capitol and all of a sudden, in an oil painting outside the Senate chamber or in a faded photograph in the Legislative Correspondents' Association press room, there was TR. Or, while taking my kids on a summer trout fishing expedition in the Adirondacks, we'd run into historical markers describing TR's famous midnight ride from Mount Marcy to assume the presidency. It didn't seem to matter where I ventured in and around the capital city—Executive Mansion, Kenmore Hotel, Pine Bush Preserve, First Church of Albany, Fort Orange Club—I discovered that TR had been there and typically had done something noteworthy in each place.

Eventually, I summoned the courage to take on this prolific and protean political presence as a biographical subject. Even with a narrow focus—TR's political education prior to his presidency—this book pushed me to my limits and challenged me to develop new skills as a biographer. In the end, the writing journey was a pleasurable one, especially because of a community of family, friends, colleagues, and accomplices in the act of archival research who made the lifting on my part much lighter.

Starting closest to home, I would like to acknowledge the assistance of the staffs at the New York State Library and the New York State Archives in Albany. Jim Corsaro, who retired four years ago after thirty-four years as associate librarian of the State Library's manuscripts and special collections, was a catalyst for this project. He helped the State Library acquire the 300,000-item Lyall D. Squair Collection of Theodore Roosevelt Memorabilia shortly before his retirement, urged me to dig into TR's political career in Albany, and helped me navigate the vast trove of material amassed by Squair, a retired librarian from Syracuse, New York, who had filled his house with TR memorabilia after a lifetime spent collecting it. Also, Paul Mercer, Fred Bassett, Melinda Yates, and Vicki Weiss of the State Library staff were helpful, as were James Folts, Robert Arnold, and Judy Hohmann of the State Archives staff.

I'd also like to thank Peter Scanlan of Albany, a noted collector of TR material who graciously opened up his impressive private collection of TR books, letters, photographs, and ephemera for my research. I'm appreciative of David Brown of Albany, an antiquarian book collector who loaned me from his formidable library anything I asked for regarding TR. I thank Paul Huey, a New York State historian and archaeologist, for sharing his research on the list of places TR visited in the Albany region; Craig Carlson, an archivist at the Albany County Hall of Records; Jennifer Benedetto, librarian at the Albany Institute of History and Art; Ellen Breslin, legislative librarian at the New York State Legislative Library; Jim Flaherty, manager of the Fort Orange Club; and a quartet of remarkable repositories of Albany history for their encouragement and generous support: William Kennedy, Jack McEneny, Virginia Bowers, and Norman Rice.

At the Theodore Roosevelt Birthplace in Manhattan, several staff members were friendly and helpful during my research, including Charles Marcus and Katherine Hansen. I'm grateful to the staff at the Houghton Library at Harvard University, where the Theodore Roosevelt Collection is housed, for their assistance in my research. In particular, I owe a large debt to Wallace Dailey, curator of the TR Collection, who was exceptionally helpful in pointing me toward fruitful archival material and who graciously shared his deep reservoir of information about TR and his family. John Gable, executive director of the Theodore Roosevelt Association and a TR expert nonpareil, was generous with his time, pointed me in the right direction on several occasions, and was encouraging when we met in Albany and Buffalo at the TR centennial symposium. At the Buffalo event I also had the opportunity to gather helpful advice from historians and TR biographers I greatly admire, including Edmund Morris, H. W. Brands, Kathleen Dalton, and Douglas Brinkley. In particular, Ed Renehan, author of the delightful *The Lion's Pride,* has been particularly supportive throughout the research and writing phase and kindly offered suggestions as an early reader of the manuscript.

I am grateful to the staff at Sagamore Hill, TR's home and historical site in Oyster Bay, New York; archivists Alycia Vivona and Raymond Teichman of the Franklin D. Roosevelt Library; Janice Kuzan, assistant director at the Theodore Roosevelt Inaugural Site in Buffalo; James Barber, historian at the National Portrait Gallery in Washington, D.C.; Martin Sullivan, former director of the New York State Museum; Bruce Kaye, chief of interpretation at the Theodore Roosevelt National Park in Medora, North Dakota; the staff at the library and archives of the Harvard Club of New York City; curator Jane Mackintosh and the library staff at the Adirondack Museum in Blue Mountain Lake; the staff at the Tahawus Club in the Adirondacks; and Bob Morrison, owner of Aiden Lair. For joining me as we retraced TR's Mount Marcy climb on a wet and miserable September weekend, I thank two good men and skilled backcountry hikers: my brother-in-law, Tim O'Donnell, and Drew Cullen, a friend who put us up in rustic splendor at his Adirondack cabin during our Marcy adventure.

After two decades, the *Times Union* has become a sort of second home and continues to be a supportive and satisfying place to work as a newspaper reporter. What makes it so are the fine people, whom I can't thank adequately for their collegial spirit as we labor to put out the first rough draft of history each day. I must single out some colleagues at the paper for their friendship, encouragement, and help: Doug Blackburn, Rob Brill, Phil Wajda, Harry Haggerty, Mike Huber, Teresa Buckley, Carol DeMare, Fred LeBrun, Mike Goodwin, John Carl D'Annibale, Steve Jacobs, Michael P. Farrell, Skip Dickstein, Lori Kane, Rex Smith, Jim Wright, Bill Dowd, Mike Spain, and Larry VanAlstyne. I also thank several fellow writers and friends who have fortified me with encouragement along the way: Bob Whitaker, Joe

Layden, Chris Mercogliano, Cliff Lee, Scott Landry, Mark Sharer, Joe Persico, George Madison, and Jim Greenfield.

I'm deeply grateful to my agent, Dan Mandel, who spurred me to take on this subject, helped shape the book proposal, and found a perfect fit with Free Press. I've never before had the good fortune to work with an editor as skillful and good-natured as Bruce Nichols. Bruce brought to the manuscript not only a rich knowledge of political history and a personal affinity for TR, but a remarkable dexterity as a line editor whose surgical cuts and suggestions for additions made the book immeasurably better. Bruce's assistant, Hui Xie, kept the editing process flowing smoothly. I thank copyeditor Peg Haller, whose extraordinary skill and precision made an important contribution page after page.

First and foremost, it was my family who provided me with the support and encouragement that sustained me throughout the research and writing of this book. I thank my parents, Bonnie and Ken Grondahl, and my brothers, Gary and Dave, for their unwavering love. I'm grateful to my wife's parents, Jack and Charlotte O'Donnell, and my wife's brothers and sisters for their kindness and friendship.

Finally, I must offer a deep and heartfelt thank-you to my wife, Mary, to whom I dedicate this book. I am forever grateful for her deep understanding, limitless patience, steadfast love, and generous nature. I am doubly blessed with two terrific children, Sam and Caroline, who continually remind me what TR clearly understood, that nothing revives one's spirits like a few hours of play with your kids.

INDEX

About the Author

Paul Grondahl is a staff writer at the Albany *Times Union,* where his articles have received numerous awards. He received a master's degree in English from the University at Albany and a bachelor's degree from the University of Puget Sound in Tacoma, Washington. He is the author of *Mayor Corning: Albany Icon, Albany Enigma.* He lives in Guilderland, New York, with his wife and two children.